Lesbian, Gay, Bisexual, and Transgender Aging

# Lesbian, Gay, Bisexual, and Transgender Aging

## Research and Clinical Perspectives

Douglas Kimmel, Tara Rose, and
Steven David, Editors

COLUMBIA UNIVERSITY PRESS  NEW YORK

COLUMBIA UNIVERSITY PRESS
*Publishers Since 1893*
New York    Chichester, West Sussex

Copyright © 2006  Columbia University Press

Library of Congress Cataloging-in-Publication Data
Lesbian, gay, bisexual, and transgender aging : research and clinical
perspectives / Douglas Kimmel, Tara Rose, and Steven David, editors.
p.      cm.
Includes bibliographical references and index.
ISBN 0–231–13618–8 (cloth : alk. paper) — ISBN 0–231–50985–5   (e-book)
1. Older sexual minorities—United States.  2. Older gays—United States.
3. Aging—United States.    I. Kimmel, Douglas C.  II. Rose, Tara.  III. David, Steven.
HQ76.25.L494 2006
306.76'60846—dc22

2005035782

Columbia University Press books are printed on
permanent and durable acid-free paper.

Printed in the United States of America

c 10 9 8 7 6 5 4 3 2 1

# CONTENTS

# PREFACE

Today's lesbian, gay, bisexual, and transgender (LGBT) elders grew up in the early days of radio, telephone, and audio recordings. By contrast, most readers of this book probably grew up with television sets in their living rooms, and possibly with personal computers on their desks. Today there are many means of communicating with others who are LGBT, including use of the Internet to connect with people in different parts of the country or the world; previously LGBT newsletters and social groups, when they did exist, were difficult to find. In order to bridge this generational chasm, for readers who are younger, imagine growing up when unmarried adult women were "spinsters" or "old maids" and unmarried adult men were "lifelong bachelors." Homosexuality was a sickness, a sin, and a disgrace; it was not discussed and, if mentioned at all, was described as a sexual perversion. Media reports were exclusively about arrests, scandals, and public figures being exposed as "perverts." Not only were there no open role models in the family, there were very few in the community or even in the world of arts and literature; most were not considered positive role models for young people. In those days, it was best to keep one's homosexual desires secret, and it was unusual to find a same-sex mate for a long-term relationship.

The key to unlocking this prison of secret shame and concealed identity was empirical research. In 1948 and 1953, the Kinsey studies demonstrated that there was a continuum of sexual behavior from heterosexual to homosexual, with bisexuality in the middle; as many as 10% of men were thought to have had more than incidental homosexual experience after adolescence. Word of these data spread in the underground press among the fledgling "homophile" organizations. In 1957, Hooker's study demonstrated that homosexuality could not be diagnosed by psychological tests widely used at that time; in fact, she found that matched pairs of homosexual and heterosexual men could not be identified by the experts on those tests. These empirical data were bolstered by LGBT mental health professionals, who began to articulate their clinical expertise and knowledge, bolstering the empirical data findings. They argued that basing the psychological model of homosexuality on mental hospital residents or psychiatric patients was inherently biased and that the disorders of mental health patients did not result from their sexual orientation but from the same causes for homosexual and heterosexual patients. Eventually, in 1973 and 1974, the American Psychiatric Association and the American Psychological Association (respectively) removed the stigma of mental illness from homosexuality. This change of definition may have resulted in the largest reduction of the number of people thought to be mentally ill in the history of modern psychiatry.

Empirical research then began to focus on understanding the diversity of the LGBT population, their coping styles, and ways in which the stigma of homosexuality affects their well-being. These studies involved primarily young adults as research participants; few focused on middle-aged or older respondents. Likewise, clinical writing focused on LGBT identity development, self-esteem, and establishing a gay-affirmative life. Little emphasis was placed on issues of aging or the concerns of middle-aged people planning to grow old.

In the 1980s the AIDS epidemic struck, and much of the clinical and research focus shifted to the multiple issues related to preventing infection, maintaining a healthy life, and coping with death. The research on LGBT people and AIDS has continued, although the articles published still rarely focus on older adults.

The 1990s and the new century have brought an almost exponential increase in the study of LGBT midlife and older adults. Indeed, a third of these studies were published in 2000 or later. Across multiple disciplines—including psychology, social work, sociology, anthropology, nursing, law, and medicine—researchers and clinicians are now actively concerned with the needs of and services for this population. Academic and clinical training programs also appear more ready to address the LGBT population, incorporating the research and clinical findings regarding sexual minorities into broader discussions within and across disciplines involved in the study of aging.

This book grew out of a symposium on LGBT aging at the annual meeting of the American Psychological Association (APA) in 2002. Steven David organized the event in his role as co-chair of the Aging Taskforce of the Society for the Psychological Study of Lesbian, Gay, and Bisexual Issues, Division 44 of the APA. The task force decided the next step would be to publish an edited book on the topic and issued a call for papers. Douglas Kimmel, Tara Rose, and Steven David agreed to be co-editors and reviewed proposals for inclusion in the book.

The editors sought to be comprehensive and integrative. We wanted chapters to include information on bisexuals and transgender people to the extent possible. We also wanted ethnic minority aging issues to be integrated throughout the book, although empirical research data are sparse. Historically, research findings often have been limited to white, socioeconomically secure, educated people; however, there are a few studies in which participants with less social privilege have taken risks and shared their experiences with interviewers or on questionnaires. Recently, it has become easier for researchers to find older LGBTs as society has extended basic human rights and reversed discriminatory policies.

This book incorporates key multidisciplinary issues in the field, with each chapter presenting a topic critical for providing services or conducting research with LGBT midlife and older adults. It begins with an introduction to the historical context of LGBT aging research and clinical practice, followed by chapters focusing on the issues of transgender aging and bisexual aging. Physical and mental health is the topic of the fourth chapter. The next chapters focus on sexuality for lesbians, bisexuals, and gay men. The following chapters deal with victimization, alcohol and drugs, retirement plans, grandparenthood, legal concerns, and end-of-life issues for LGBT elders. The final three chapters examine community needs, housing needs, and the SAGE model of services. The book concludes with an extensive bibliography of all identified published reports on LGBT elders; it will be updated periodically on the APA Division 44 Aging Taskforce Web page (www.apa.org/divisions/div44/).

This book has three goals. First, we hope to provide clinicians and professionals who provide services to midlife and older adults with information and tools to help them serve their LGBT clients and patients. Second, we hope that the reader observes not only the many differences but also the many commonalities that LGBT people in midlife and their later years share with their heterosexual counterparts. Third, we hope that the book inspires researchers and clinicians to work together, to ask new questions and suggest new answers that will contribute to this burgeoning field.

We have great appreciation for LGBT older adults, who have lived bravely, sometimes quietly for survival and at other times openly and active politically. This book is dedicated to them. As they have lived their lives, they have created a foundation for LGBT pioneers of all ages. Wherever they have lived in the world, LGBT midlife and older adults have faced discrimination and homophobia, but many lead fulfilling lives. We owe them our gratitude. As a token of our appreciation, a significant portion of the royalties from this book will go to the Malyon–Smith Fund of APA's Division 44 for doctoral dissertation research on LGBT issues.

Every published book involves many helpful hands and minds. We are grateful to the chapter authors for their work in synthesizing the literature to create this one-volume reference. We especially thank John Michel (who passed away during the writing of this book), Shelley Reinhardt, Roy Thomas, and the editorial staff at Columbia University Press; and copyeditor Carol Anne Peschke. We are grateful to each other and to our partners and children, who shared our time so we could complete this project.

*Douglas Kimmel*
*Tara Rose*
*Steven David*

Lesbian, Gay, Bisexual, and Transgender Aging

# Historical Context for Research on Lesbian, Gay, Bisexual, and Transgender Aging

*Douglas Kimmel, Tara Rose, Nancy Orel, and Beverly Greene*

In the 1970s, often considered the early days of the modern gay movement in the United States, there was little awareness of aging lesbians, gay men, bisexuals, and transgender people. Donald Vining had retired and was working on the first volume of *A Gay Diary* (Vining, 1979). Del Martin and Phyllis Lyon had been together for many years (Martin & Lyon, 1972) and wrote a chapter on "The Older Lesbian" (1979). Other leaders of the earlier gay movement were also middle-aged activists: Franklin Kameny in Washington, D.C., Barbara Gittings in Philadelphia, and Harry Hay in California (Katz, 1976); each became a personal pioneer in lesbian, gay, bisexual, and transgender (LGBT) aging.

Most of the images of older gay people were not very positive at the time, however. Gustave Aschenbach in Mann's (1913/1925) *Death in Venice* and Karen and Martha in Hellman's (1934/1961) *The Children's Hour* were well-known fictional but negative portrayals of an aging gay man and two lesbians, respectively. Gay and lesbian bars yielded negative images of old alcoholics mourning their lost youth. Perhaps most insidious was the belief that the gay life was for young people, who should enjoy it while they were still attractive. The stereotype used to disparage homosexuality was, "It may be fun when you're young, but wait until you are old, unwanted, and alone." Naturally, it was assumed that old lesbians and gays would have no spouses or children to care for them in their old age. Likewise, there was little incentive for young gay people to avoid tobacco, alcohol, or other drugs because they had little hope of living into a healthy old age; indeed, suicide was always considered to be a possible solution. Moreover, the gay movement was seen as primarily limited to the young white community, with little relevance to older lesbians and gay men of color.

## Early Research

The first empirical challenge to this nearly universal negative portrait of aging sexual minorities was in the doctoral research of Jim Kelly, a social work student at the University of Southern California. Kelly presented his work at the 1972 meeting of the Gerontological Society of America and won the student award for the year's best dissertation. Ironically, when the society's president announced the award at the opening reception, he said the paper was on "an unmentionable topic"; this drew immediate attention.

Other early studies, in addition to Kelly's (1977) published study of older gay men, included Williams and Weinberg (1971), Kimmel (1977), and Berger (1980) on older gay men; Minnegerode and Adelman (1978) on older lesbians and gay men; and Raphael and Robinson (1980) on older lesbians. These empirical studies, although based on nonrandom samples, presented a very different picture than the previous negative stereotypes. Older lesbians and gay men were seen as functioning well in their middle age and aging years. Many were in long-term relationships. Nearly all had some supportive friendship network that served as a buffer against social oppression. Levels of depression and other indices of adjustment seemed no different from similar samples of the general population (Berger, 1982a). Sexual life was continuing for most of the gay men, and several reported it was better than earlier in life because they paid more attention to their partner's desires and were more accepting of their own (Kimmel, 1979). There was evidence that these older men were more adjusted to their sexual and erotic attractions than were younger gay men (Weinberg & Williams, 1974). Later research has supplemented these early findings by examining the complexity of aging patterns among LGBT people and has generally found negative outcomes to be the result of factors other than sexual orientation (see chapter 4, this volume).

At the time these early studies were conducted, the findings conflicted with the assumptions arising from the sociological perspective that older sexual minorities, from the population cohort that had lived through a highly repressive period of U.S. history, would be poorly adjusted. The Great Depression, World War II, and the purge of presumed communists and homosexuals by Senator Joseph McCarthy and the U.S. House Committee on Un-American Activities created excessive stress in their lives (Loughery, 1998; Katz, 1976; Miller, 1995). The possibility that this population of LGBT elders could be healthy and productive seemed incongruous with the societal challenges they had faced throughout their histories.

Historical factors, including the urban migration from rural farms beginning in the 1930s and, later, World War II, brought gay men and lesbians together, and they found somewhat open "secret societies." Gay bars emerged, and popular areas for meeting other gay men developed and led to a robust gay environment in New York City (Chauncey, 1994). San Francisco became a gay urban center also as a result of the military, shipping, and international port facilities (D'Emilio, 1981/1989/1993). Additionally, World War II brought gay men and lesbians together in the armed forces, at least until the antihomosexual purge began midway through the war (Shilts, 1993, pp. 107–108; Williams & Weinberg, 1971). Similar "secret societies" were found in African American communities, where lesbians and gay men might be more apt to gather in one another's private homes. Although they were sometimes present in public clubs, they were often targets of racial discrimination within the LGBT community and were not always welcome in these venues; therefore many socialized primarily with other African Americans. Racism certainly influenced the degree to which many lesbians and gay men of color interacted with the broader lesbian and gay community, shrinking their potential pool of allies and their social circle as they grew older.

In the 1950s, other than government employees, whose jobs were at particularly high risk if they were discovered to be homosexual, some lesbians and gay men began to live their private lives with some level of comfort, albeit with great discretion (Miller, 1995). Those in public life maintained long-term relationships but obscured them through the use of adjacent homes with secret connecting passages (Brown, 1976) or lived separate lives, meeting only on weekends. Nonetheless, many gay men and lesbians did maintain fairly open, long-term relationships (cf. Adelman, 1986; Harwood, 1997; Vacha, 1985; Vining, 1981). Social groups, especially those meeting in private homes, provided important contacts and mutual support in many communities, including the African American community (Adams & Kimmel, 1997).

In the 1960s, the threat of police harassment, entrapment, and prison was ever present, heightened during political campaigns and when elections drew near. Arrests in popular gay male venues by undercover police officers and raids on gay bars ruined lives because the names of those arrested were routinely published in newspapers, causing disgrace, loss of employment, family disruption, excommunication from church, or worse. Often the bars were organized so that gay men and lesbians had separate dance areas but could readily come together and switch dance partners to appear to be heterosexual couples when police raided the bar (McGarry & Wasserman, 1998, p. 79). Many gay men spent some time in jail, and some of the most vital contacts in the gay community were with friendly bail bond agencies and supportive lawyers. In this historical context, the rebellion by the gay male and transgender patrons of the Stonewall Inn was monumental, eliciting broader support in New York City and causing demonstrations, which lasted several days in June 1969 (Loughery, 1998; Miller, 1995). At that time there was a kind of paradigm shift; as Harry Hay (1990, p. 5) phrased it, "I became we": One's individual sexual or erotic experiences and feelings changed from being an individual condition to a group membership.

## Developing Consciousness of LGBT Aging

Simultaneous interest in issues pertinent to older lesbians and gay men began emerging in the mid-1970s on both U.S. coasts. In California, an organization of professionals and students interested in the characteristics and concerns of aging (i.e., gerontology) emerged with the name National Association for Lesbian and Gay Gerontology (NALGG). It published a newsletter from 1978 to 1994, held a national conference in 1981, and published a bibliography in 1989. Many NALGG members were involved with the American Society on Aging, based in San Francisco. In 1992, the society formed an interest group that has become the primary professional link for LGBT gerontologists: the Lesbian and Gay Aging Interest Network (www.asa.org/lgain).

In 1977, Jim Dorff, a younger gay man in New York whose lover was older, brought together a small group of people interested in the needs of homebound elderly lesbians and gay men, including an author (D.K.). By the third meeting, the group had expanded to include several professionals, older gay men, and a reporter for a gay newspaper; it was the reporter who suggested the acronym SAGE, and the name was coined: Senior Action in a Gay Environment (now Services and Advocacy for GLBT Elders). The mission evolved to focus on social and educational activities under the leadership of cofounder Chris Almvig; initially, there was little demand for homebound services. Since its beginning, SAGE has been closely involved with building a sense of gay and lesbian community, as one of the organization's core tenets was that *community* implies caring for its vulnerable members (Grenwald, 1984). In this spirit of community building, an early leader of SAGE went on to found a program for LGBT youth in New York City (Hetrick-Martin Institute), and others went on to work on AIDS issues in the 1980s. SAGE now has a wide range of activities and services (see chapter 15, this volume).

Mainstream gerontologists often were surprised when presented with NALGG or SAGE information at conferences. They had never thought sexual orientation was relevant to their work. This probably reflected the belief, based on media presentations of parades and demonstrations, that all gay people were young. Additionally, the persistent stereotype that sexual orientation was all about sex, coupled with the assumption that older people were asexual, celibate, or just disinterested in sex, led many to segregate sexuality and sexual orientation from gerontological issues and research. The interactions between sexual orientation, erotic orientation, love, and relationships were not well recognized. The professionals' reactions were not necessarily negative; it had just never occurred to many that it made a difference that not all clients were heterosexual (Berger & Kelly, 1986). The professional community of gerontologists meeting older lesbian and gay peers was also helpful in changing these underlying but erroneous assumptions. The impact of these LGBT aging organizations was educational and helped to build links with mainstream gerontology professions.

With its activities and extensive services for LGBT elders, SAGE is featured in a widely distributed documentary about lesbian and gay aging, shown in many college classrooms and frequently on public television: *Silent Pioneers* (Snyder & Winer, 1985). Another film that gives a positive educational view of aging includes an open lesbian living in a nursing home: *Golden Threads* (Winer & Eaton, 1999). A third film, *Living with Pride: Ruth Ellis at 100* (Welbon, 1999) portrays an African American lesbian. Another film, *Tiny & Ruby: Hell Divin' Women* (Schiller & Weiss, 1986), profiles African American 1940s jazz trumpeter Tiny Davis and her partner, Ruby Lucas. These documentaries also present aspects of 20th-century gay life in the United States. Other nonfiction films and books on lesbian and gay history likewise provide portraits of people growing older and the ways in which they coped with living conditions in the earlier years of their adulthood (Katz, 1976; Marcus, 1992).

Autobiographical reports of growing older also shed some light on the aging process for gay men and lesbians. The cautiously open life of Howard Brown (1976), a commissioner of health for New York City in the 1970s, contrasts sharply with the closeted struggle of Martin Duberman (1991), a professor of history during the same period, and with the life of Roger Brown (1996), a closeted professor of psychology in a long-term gay relationship. Gertrude Stein and Alice Toklas were together from 1907 until Stein's death in 1946 (Souhami, 1991). Donald Vining's diary, beginning in 1933 with his youth as the son of a lesbian and continuing through the beginning of his long-term relationship after World War II and the emergence of the gay community in the 1970s, provides a contemporaneous record of events and feelings that avoids the historical problems of retrospective reports (Vining, 1979/1996, 1980, 1981, 1983, 1993). The journals of May Sarton (1984, 1988) likewise provide a unique first-person account of a lesbian growing old in a rural area and the effects of a physical health crisis.

An inclusive review of all the published literature in LGBT gerontology is of only historical curiosity because most of the samples are small and idiosyncratic. A list of published articles is included as the final chapter in this volume. Three themes have emerged that reflect significant findings from the classic research projects:

- There is wide diversity among the older LGBT population, as great as in the general aging population, including homeless HIV-infected gay men (Meris, 2001), lesbian grandmothers (chapter 10, this volume), and every combination of class, ethnicity, and living situation. The classic qualitative interview studies have revealed some of this diversity but have been limited primarily to fairly open, urban samples of generally well-educated men and women. Ethnic and racial minorities and rural samples are seldom included; if they are, they also tend to be open about their sexuality, well educated, and otherwise atypical.
- Sexual orientation—defined by reference to the gender of persons one loves in an erotic or sexual way, a matter of the heart, not of one's sexual behavior—interacts with each unique life in both predictable and unpredictable ways. For example, some people lead lives that reflect both same-gender and other-gender relationships while maintaining a gay, lesbian, bisexual, or transgender orientation in their personal outlook. Others may shift from heterosexual to homosexual or bisexual self-images or change gender entirely. The presence of a spouse, children, and grandchildren does not indicate either sexual orientation or gender identity.
- The intersection of social change and historical cohort is profound, such that earlier generations of LGBT elders may differ sharply from those currently entering their retirement years in the United States. Therefore it may be important to read the LGBT research literature of earlier periods to grasp the lives of today's elders. It should also be noted that aging itself is changing dramati-

cally in industrialized nations so that, for many, there is a prolonged period of healthy life after the traditional retirement age. Therefore, the aging of the post-Stonewall LGBT generation will differ from the pattern of today's elders in many ways.

Growing awareness of people in same-sex relationships and recognition of their claim to legal protection and civil rights is a social change with major impact on LGBT people who are growing older in coupled relationships in the United States, Canada, Australia, and several European countries. Although same-sex couples receive no federal benefits in the United States (e.g., Social Security), state laws concerning hospital visitation, inheritance, funeral arrangements, and disposition of the remains are beginning to recognize domestic partners as equivalent to spouses (see chapter 11, this volume). Dozens of cities recognize domestic partners, and several states are extending statewide legal benefits to domestic partners. Vermont and Massachusetts offer civil unions and legal marriage, respectively, at present. Thus insurance coverage, health care decision-making powers, and survivor benefits sometimes are available to same-sex partners. In time, full marital benefits may be available to same-sex couples, including federal Social Security and the right for an immigrant to live with one's partner in the United States permanently.

## Relations with Families

Each chapter in this book places some emphasis on family relationships, including the family of origin and the family of support one creates. LGBTs have a variety of family life cycle patterns and may be in different places in their cycle than their heterosexual peers. Examples of writings for gay and lesbians about life span issues and family life cycle include Kimmel (1990, 1992) and Slater (1995). Relations with family often become more important as they age and become more dependent on others. This can be particularly true for those with physical or mental limitations who need to rely on others for most basic needs. If one can afford it, it is possible to meet one's health and physical care needs without family help and support, of course. Because family and friends tend to be very mobile, some LGBT elders maintain connections over greater distance through electronic communication. For some LGBT elders who have not been accepted by family in the past, maintaining distant communication may feel like the only option. In fact, many LGBT elder couples must work to create legal arrangements to help clarify their own relationship and limit the legal power of other family members (see chapter 11, this volume).

## Bisexual Aging

Issues and concerns of older bisexual men and women have rarely been explored but may differ in important ways from those of lesbians and gay men (Keppel, 1991; Weinberg, Williams, & Pryor, 2001). For example, bisexuals in the United States may be more likely than gay men or lesbians to have been married and perhaps to maintain a relationship with the spouse and with their children. They may therefore have more complicated legal and financial obligations as they move into late adulthood than do people who have never been legally married. Bisexuals may also be more likely than lesbians or gay men to consider forming a long-term relationship with a partner of the other gender in late life and inherit heterosexual family support. However, bisexual men and women may find themselves excluded from heterosexual family relationships after they come out as bisexual. Furthermore, bisexuals sometimes are distrusted by lesbians or gay men who believe that they can pass or switch to heterosexuality if necessary. They are also perceived as unreliable, undependable, or likely to bring someone of the other gender into an exclusively lesbian or gay social group. Similarly, bisexuals are viewed negatively by heterosexuals who stereotype them as promiscuous, secretive, and likely to bring HIV and other infections into a heterosexual relationship.

Bisexuals may have family ties and involvements that, at times, set them apart from gay and lesbian elders. One bisexual man described his gay friends' discomfort when his daughter called him on his cell phone to ask that he pick up his granddaughter after school (Kristiansen, 2004). The gay friends seemed to resent the disruption of their group activities and to envy the bisexual man's commitment to a valuable family role they did not have. Although younger lesbian and gay couples have children today, in previous generations it was unusual to have children unless one was once married.

Bisexuals probably are more likely than lesbians or gay men to be comfortable in mixed-gender groups in late life and perhaps also to be willing to accept others' assumptions of their heterosexuality. Conversely, they may be more motivated to come out as bisexual because most people stereotype individuals as monosexual: either heterosexual or homosexual. These issues are discussed in detail in chapter 3.

## Multicultural Issues

Most descriptions of lesbians and gay men are devoid of images of lesbians, bisexuals, and gay men of color. The lesbian and gay community is pictured as primarily young, able bodied, financially well off, educated, and white (Greene, 2002). As a rule, the wide spectrum of diversity that characterizes the community as a whole has not been represented in public images of lesbians and gay men or in the psychological literature. This absence has important implications for the assumptions we make about the lesbian and gay experience. Like sexuality and sexual orientation, aging is embedded in cultural contexts, and its meaning is composed of a range of cultural determinants. Every culture has its own expectations about the roles that members occupy and the status accorded them during different developmental periods. Therefore any discussion about the experience of aging for lesbians and gay men must first delineate *which* lesbians and gay men.

For example, the absence of the financial benefits of marriage may have disproportionate effects on African American lesbians, whose incomes tend to be lower than those of their white counterparts. G. Croom (personal communication, July 14, 2004) reports that in an informal sample of aged African American lesbians, many respondents had concerns about who would provide care for them if they were in ill health. Compared with their white counterparts, more African American lesbians have children. For those who do, there may be less concern about who will take care of them as their age advances; however, this always depends on the quality of their relationships with children and family members.

The interaction between the lesbian and gay civil rights movement and other civil rights movements is another important contextual variable in the experience of aging for lesbians and gay men of color. Older ethnic minority lesbians and gay men may have experienced more overt and pernicious forms of racism than the current generation. Those experiences include racism within the broader lesbian and gay community. This racism, combined with heterosexism within their ethnic community, influences decisions about coming out, long-term relationships, and relationships with family members. The need for buffers against racism, the importance of family ties, and cultural values often outweigh the need to identify with the LGBT community throughout their lives (Adams & Kimmel, 1997). This conflict between different sources of community support may leave some ethnic minority elders disproportionately vulnerable to loneliness and with a paucity of LGBT peers later in life. They may feel the need to be more closeted in order to have their emotional, social, spiritual, and physical needs met by friends, family, professional service providers, and the community. Unfortunately, there has been very little empirical research on aging among older LGBT people of color.

## Ageism and Heterosexism

It is interesting to note similarities between the social construction of sexual orientation as a sexual minority status and the social construction of aging. Both social categories are evaluated negatively and have flagrant acts of discrimination associated with them. It is likely that older LGBT people are therefore at risk for double or triple minority status, based on age, sexual orientation, and gender.

In reality, however, each social category cuts across all demographic groups. Knowing a person's age or LGBT orientation gives no clue about any of his or her other social statuses. If someone reveals that she is 75, we know only the approximate year of her birth, not her state of health, wealth, or well-being. If we are told that the person is bisexual, we know only that the person has experienced attraction and perhaps love toward people of both sexes. If we are introduced to a 60-year-old lesbian, we know neither her ethnic background nor her social class, nor whether she has children, a partner, or living parents. In truth, these other social facts often reveal more than sexual orientation or age. In the United States and many other cultures, a person's age is more significant than many other social characteristics. This effect is known as a master status (Becker, 1963). It applies also to LGBT people, who often find that the knowledge of their minority sexual orientation is perceived to be more significant than any other aspect of their background, behavior, or performance.

This perspective raises the question of multiple minority status. What is often called the LGBT community is, in fact, many smaller populations that have in common only their minority sexual orientation. Issues such as age, race, ethnicity, religion, class, and gender often are more relevant to a person's sense of self and sense of community than is sexual orientation.

The assumption that everyone is, or should be, heterosexual is called heterosexism (Garnets & Kimmel, 1991/1993). Heterosexism is "An ideological system that denies, denigrates, and stigmatizes any non heterosexual form of behavior, identity, relationship, or community" (Herek, 1990, p. 90). Related terms are *homophobia,* the irrational fear of homosexuals, and *heterocentrism,* the assumption that everyone is heterosexual.

Negative stereotypes about older people are regarded as ageism, a term coined by Butler (1980, p. 8):

There are three distinguishable yet interrelated aspects to the problem of ageism: 1) prejudicial attitudes toward the aged, toward old age, and toward the aging process, including attitudes held by the elderly themselves; 2) discriminatory practices against the elderly, particularly in employment, but in other social roles as well; and 3) institutional practices and policies which, often without malice, perpetuate stereotypic beliefs about the elderly, reduce their opportunities for a satisfactory life, and undermine their personal dignity.

Because it is possible to conceal sexual orientation and, perhaps to a lesser degree, age, the two characteristics have some similar social constructions. For example, in some social circles, both old age and minority sexual orientation are perceived as being best to avoid if possible; they are both dealt with by "Don't ask, don't tell" policies. In extreme cases, both old age and minority sexual orientation evoke irrational fear and avoidance in some people, who tend to fear close contact and physical touching with both groups.

Additional social constructions perceive both old age and minority sexual orientation to be abnormal. For example, both old age and minority sexual orientation have been the focus of an active search for their biological origins and possible prevention or cure. Moreover, both old age and sexual orientation are confused by naive people with associated conditions: aging with senility, sexual orientation with gender role.

In modern Western societies, both old age and minority sexual orientation are characterized primarily through reference to their perceived disadvantages, as opposed to their advantages. Losses are thought to exceed gains; strengths are seen only as compensations for weakness. Likewise, both old age and minority sexual orientation evoke discriminatory views that emphasize the importance of fertility and propagation as normative. In contrast, both old age and minority sexual orientation are conferred special status in some cultures, in which the individuals may be seen as having special powers resulting from their minority status (Kimmel, 2002).

Despite these similar social constructions, there are several clear differences between ageism and heterosexism. First, most people hope to become old one day; few hope to become a sexual minority. Second, no one attributes aging to one's individual choice or upbringing. Third, families openly acknowledge and celebrate becoming older, but few families celebrate their children coming out as lesbian, gay, bisexual, or transgender. Fourth, organized religious institutions and moral guardians do not urge older people to avoid acting old but often urge sexual minorities to avoid acting on their erotic or romantic attractions. Fifth, businesses offer senior discounts to attract elder consumers, but few places of business advertise that they are "gay friendly." Finally, politicians solicit contributions and votes by proposing "elder affirming" policies while at the same time soliciting contributions and votes by proposing discriminatory policies targeting sexual minorities.

In many ways our society is becoming age irrelevant. Mandatory retirement age has been all but eliminated. People are marrying and starting families in midlife: One is never too old to join a gym, fall in love, or begin to lift weights. Likewise, our society is becoming more of a gender-irrelevant culture in which clothing, tattoos, jewelry, and athletics are similar for males and females. Gender discrimination has been reduced and is usually illegal. Unisex bathrooms are widely available, thanks to the Americans with Disabilities Act that requires wheelchair accessible toilets, much to the relief of transgendered people who cannot use either female or male facilities with complete comfort.

## The Impact of Heterosexism on Programs and Services for LGBT Elders

Although the aging network is required by the Older Americans Act of 1965 to provide programs and services for *all* older adults, most of these programs and services assume a heterosexual older population. In fact, research has indicated that the aging network is more intolerant of LGBT elders and more heterosexist than the general health care system because the attitudes and beliefs within the aging network have gone unchallenged (Brotman, Ryan, & Cormier, 2003). Heterosexism on the part of some aging service providers further marginalizes lesbian and gay elders with discriminatory policies (Berkman & Zinberg, 1997; Cahill, South, & Spade, 2000; Peterson & Bricker-Jenkins, 1996). A 1994 study of Area Agencies on Aging revealed that 96% of these agencies did not offer any programs or services specifically designed for LGBT elders; additionally, nearly 50% of the Area Agencies on Aging surveyed reported that gays and lesbians would not be welcomed at senior centers if their sexual orientation were known (Cahill, South, & Spade, 2001). As a result, many LGBT elders have been discouraged from using these agencies and organizations (McFarland & Sanders,

2003). Nonetheless, the results of the focus groups and the preliminary analysis of comments from survey respondents in a study by Orel (chapter 10, this volume) indicate that LGBT elders would benefit from programs and services that specifically address their unique needs and concerns.

## The Impact of Ageism in the LGBT Community

LGBT elders experience numerous challenges because of their sexual orientation and gender identity. Many now face additional challenges and stigma due to ageism. Like their heterosexual counterparts, LGBT elders face many obstacles in our youth-oriented society. However, the obstacles for LGBT elders are intensified by society's continuing stigmatization of homosexuality.

Research indicates that the LGBT community is more ageist than the general public (Cahill, South, & Spade, 2000; Ehrenberg, 1996). Like the heterosexist attitudes that go widely unchallenged in the aging network, ageist attitudes within the LGBT community often go uncontested. Recent research exploring LGBT elders' perceptions of the gay and lesbian community indicates that LGBT elders do not feel welcome in the youth-focused LGBT community (Brotman, Ryan, & Cormier, 2003). LGBT elders sometimes believe that the gay and lesbian community focuses all of its attention and resources on the needs of its younger members but ignores the needs of its senior members. According to Brotman, Ryan, and Cormier (2003, p. 198), "Ageism, beauty, and youthfulness are values that reign supreme within most gay and lesbian communities, making it difficult for older members to feel like they belong."

## Addressing the Marginalization of LGBT Elders Through a Continuum of Affirming Services

In order to work with LGBT elders, it is important to acknowledge and address our own internalized heterosexism, sexism, and ageism. Service providers need to develop a heightened sensitivity to the unique issues facing LGBT elders. Equally crucial are advocacy efforts to eradicate prejudice and discrimination not only against LGBT elders but also against LGBT people of any age.

Although numerous federal, state, and local agencies offer a wide variety of physical and psychosocial programs and services for older adults, because of heterosexist cultural attitudes very few of these programs explicitly recognize or support the issues confronting LGBT elders (National Gay and Lesbian Task Force Policy Institute, 1999). Most regrettably, numerous federal, state, and local policies specifically exclude LGBT elders and their same-gender partners. For example, although Social Security survivor benefits often are an essential part of a heterosexual widow's or widower's income, same-gender partners are denied this benefit (chapter 11, this volume).

LGBT elders need services as extensive as those available to the general older adult population. However, these programs and services must be tailored to meet the specific needs and concerns of the LGBT population. They should be supportive of the LGBT experience and offered in an environment where LGBT elders can connect with others similarly situated. "This connectedness to others who are like oneself offers an environment that does not need to be defended, explained, or justified and helps ease the transitional stresses associated with the aging process" (Nystrom & Jones, 2003, p. 294).

Services for LGBT elders must be available on multiple levels, from individuals to organizations, communities, and the larger society. Ideally, the services currently available to the general older adult population would be expanded to meet the unique needs and concerns of LGBT elders (see chapter 13, this volume). This modification of existing services will not be possible until the providers of these services and programs recognize and acknowledge the unique needs of LGBT elders and address existing heterosexist attitudes and beliefs that have discouraged or prevented LGBT elders from using these services. Finally, providers and researchers should collaborate to ensure that the services provided meet the documented needs of LGBT elders. An example of this collaboration is in the housing projects being developed in different areas of the United States. Some of these developments are publicly funded projects or private endeavors based on extensive need assessments of the LGBT community (see chapter 14, this volume.)

The American Psychological Association (APA) has developed *Guidelines for Psychotherapy with Lesbian, Gay & Bisexual Clients* (www.apa.org/pi/lgbc/guidelines.html), which contains a section on older people, and *Guidelines for Psychological Practice with Older Adults* (www.apa.org/practice/Guidelines_for_Psychological_Practice_with_Older_Adults.pdf), which mentions LGBT clients. Other useful publications on aging are also available from the APA (www.apa.org/pi/aging/publications.html). The Gay and Lesbian Medical Association (www.glma.org) also developed a helpful set of guidelines that assists professionals in creating a welcoming environment by, for example, displaying brochures and visible nondiscrimination statements including specific reference not only to age, race, ethnicity, physical ability or attributes, and religion, but also to sexual and gender identity. These guidelines offer LGBT patients and clients clues as they scan an office environment and standardized forms to determine how much they feel comfortable sharing with their service providers.

# Conclusion

In three decades, the multidisciplinary field of LGBT gerontology has moved from the hidden recesses of secret support groups into the full range of activities and services. Many pioneers of the movement, and of the larger gay rights movement, are now entering their senior years. It will be important to collect oral histories of these pioneers so that their valuable contributions will be remembered and honored. In addition, a variety of housing alternatives, appropriate services, and opportunities for continued interaction with the emerging field of LGBT gerontology will be a fitting tribute to the courageous leadership and mentorship of these pioneers.

This field offers all the opportunity one could imagine to provide innovative services and conduct research. As recently as 10 years ago, a participant's sexual orientation was not identified unless the research specifically focused on LGBT topics. The medical field and social sciences can realize important advantages by routinely inquiring as to a participant's sexual orientation and studying whether the subset of LGBT respondents differ from or are similar to the broader heterosexual population, in much the same way that early research moved beyond an exclusive focus on male participants and began to explore differences between men and women. Within the field of LGBT gerontology, today's clinical work and research will become the historical context of the next generation of elders. Here, in the present, we have an opportunity to ensure that LGBT elders representing the full spectrum of diversity are included in all types of research studies and that there is room for them in all services provided. Clinicians and scientists should collaborate and include these groups in their research sample or as part of a reasonable subsample. From such studies we can determine both the unique needs of LGBT elders and their similarities with the needs of heterosexual older adults. If this book stimulates such research and the resulting practical applications, it will have achieved one of its most important goals.

## REFERENCES

Adams, C. A. Jr., & Kimmel, D. C. (1997). Exploring the lives of older African American gay men. In. B. Greene (Ed.), *Ethnic and cultural diversity among lesbians and gay men* (pp. 132–151). Thousand Oaks, CA: SAGE.

Adelman, M. (1986). *Long time passing: Lives of older lesbians.* Boston: Alyson.

Becker, H. S. (1963). *Outsiders: Studies in the sociology of deviance.* New York: Free Press.

Berger, R. M. (1980). Psychological adaptation of the older homosexual male. *Journal of Homosexuality, 5*(3), 161–174.

Berger, R. M. (1982a). *Gay and gray: The older homosexual man.* Urbana: University of Illinois Press.

Berger, R. M. (1982b). The unseen minority: Older gays and lesbians. *Social Work, 27,* 236–242.

Berger, R. M., & Kelly, J. J. (1986). Working with homosexuals of the older population. *Social Casework, 67,* 203–210.

Berkman, C., & Zinberg, G. (1997). Homophobia and heterosexism in social workers. *Social Work, 42,* 319–332.

Brotman, S., Ryan, B., & Cormier, R. (2003). The health and social service needs of gay and lesbian elders and their families in Canada. *The Gerontologist, 43,* 192–202.

Brown, H. (1976). *Familiar faces, hidden lives: The story of homosexual men in America today.* New York: Harcourt.

Brown, R. (1996). *Against my better judgment: An intimate memoir of an eminent gay psychologist.* New York: Harrington Park Press.

Butler, R. N. (1980). Ageism: A foreword. *Journal of Social Issues, 36*(2), 8–11.

Cahill, S., South, K., & Spade, J. (2000). *Outing age: Public policy issues affecting gay, lesbian, bisexual, and transgender elders.* Washington, DC: National Gay and Lesbian Task Force Policy Institute.

Chauncey, G. (1994). *Gay New York.* New York: Basic Books.

D'Emilio, J. (1981, January/1989/1993). Gay politics and community in San Francisco since World War II. *Socialist Review, 55,* 77–104. [Revised and reprinted in Vicinus, M. M., & Chauncey, G. Jr. (Eds.). (1989). *Hidden from history: Reclaiming the gay and lesbian past* (pp. 456–473). New York: New American Library. Reprinted in Garnets, L. D., & Kimmel, D. C. (1993). *Psychological perspectives on lesbian and gay male experiences* (pp. 59–79). New York: Columbia University Press.]

Duberman, M. (1991). *Cures: A gay man's odyssey.* New York: Dutton.

Ehrenberg, M. (1996). Aging and mental health: Issues in the gay and lesbian community. In C. J. Alexander (Ed.), *Gay and lesbian mental health: A sourcebook for practitioners* (pp. 189–209). New York: Harrington Park Press.

Garnets, L. D., & Kimmel, D. C. (1991/1993). Lesbian and gay male dimensions in the psychological study of human diversity. In L. D. Garnets & D. C. Kimmel (Eds.),

*Psychological perspectives on lesbian and gay male experiences* (pp. 1–51). New York: Columbia University Press.

Greene, B. (2002). Older lesbians' concerns in psychotherapy: Beyond a footnote to the footnote. In F. Trotman & C. Brody (Eds.), *Psychotherapy and counseling with older women: Cross cultural, family, and end of life issues* (pp. 161–174). New York: Springer.

Grenwald, M. (1984). The SAGE model for serving older lesbians and gay men. *Homosexuality and Social Work, 2*(2–3), 53–61.

Harwood, G. (1997). *The oldest gay couple in America: A 70-year journey through same-sex America.* Secaucus, NJ: Birch Lane.

Hay, H. (1990, April 22–28). Identifying as gay: There's the key. *Gay Community News, 5.*

Hellman, L. (1934). *The children's hour.* New York: Knopf. [W. Wyler (Producer & Director). (1961). *The children's hour* (Motion picture). Released by United Artists Corp.]

Herek, G. (1990). The context of antigay violence: Notes on cultural and psychological heterosexism. *Journal of Interpersonal Violence, 5,* 316–333.

Katz, J. (1976). *Gay American history.* New York: Thomas Y. Crowell.

Kelly, J. J. (1977). The aging male homosexual: Myth and reality. *The Gerontologist, 17,* 328–332.

Keppel, B. (1991). Gray-haired and above suspicion. In L. H. Hutchins & L. Kaahumanu (Eds.), *Bi any other name: Bisexual people speak out* (pp. 154–158). Boston: Alyson.

Kimmel, D. C. (1977). Psychotherapy and the older gay man. *Psychotherapy: Theory, Research, and Practice, 14,* 386–393.

Kimmel, D. C. (1979). Life-history interviews of aging gay men. *International Journal of Aging and Human Development, 10,* 239–248.

Kimmel, D. C. (1990). *Adulthood and aging: An interdisciplinary, developmental view.* New York: Wiley.

Kimmel, D. C. (1992). The families of older gay men and lesbians. *Generations, 17*(3), 37–38.

Kimmel, D. C. (2002). Aging and sexual orientation. In B. E. Jones & M. J. Hill (Eds.), *Mental health issues in lesbian, gay, bisexual, and transgender communities* (pp. 17–36). Washington, DC: American Psychiatric Publishing.

Kristiansen, H. W. (2004). Narrating past lives and present concerns: Older gay men in Norway. In G. Herdt & B. de Vries (Eds.), *Gay and lesbian aging: Research and future directions* (pp. 235–261). New York: Springer.

Loughery, J. (1998). *The other side of silence.* New York: Holt.

Mann, T. (1913/1925). Death in Venice. In *Death in Venice and other stories* (Translated by K. Burke). New York: Knopf.

Marcus, E. (1992). *Making history.* New York: HarperCollins.

Martin, D., & Lyon, P. (1972). *Lesbian/woman.* New York: Bantam.

Martin, D., & Lyon, P. (1979). The older lesbian. In B. Berzon & R. Leighton (Eds.), *Positively gay* (pp. 134–145). Milbrae, CA: Celestial Arts.

McFarland, P., & Sanders, S. (2003). A pilot study about the needs of older gays and lesbians: What social workers need to know. *Journal of Gerontological Social Work, 40*(3), 67–80.

McGarry, M., & Wasserman, F. (1998). *Becoming visible: An illustrated history of lesbian and gay life in twentieth-century America.* New York: Penguin.

Meris, D. (2001). Responding to the mental health and grief concerns of homeless HIV-infected gay men. *Journal of Gay and Lesbian Social Services, 13*(4), 103–111.

Miller, N. (1995). *Out of the past: Gay and lesbian lives from 1869 to the present.* New York: Vintage.

Minnigerode, F. A., & Adelman, M. (1978). Elderly homosexual women and men: Report on pilot study. *Family Coordinator, 27,* 451–456.

National Gay and Lesbian Task Force Policy Institute. (1999). *Aging initiative.* Washington, DC: Author.

Nystrom, N., & Jones, T. (2003). Community building with aging and old lesbians. *American Journal of Community Psychology, 31,* 293–300.

Peterson, J. K., & Bricker-Jenkins, M. (1996). Lesbians and the health care system. *Journal of Gay and Lesbian Social Services, 5*(1), 33–47.

Raphael, S., & Robinson, M. (1980). The older lesbian: Love relationships and friendship patterns. *Alternative Lifestyle, 3,* 207–229.

Sarton, M. (1984). *At seventy.* New York: Norton.

Sarton, M. (1988). *After the stroke.* New York: Norton.

Schiller, G., & Weiss, A. (Producer & Director). (1986). *Tiny & Ruby: Hell divin' women* [Motion picture]. (Available from Jezebel Productions, P.O. Box 1348, New York, NY 10011.)

Shilts, R. (1993). *Conduct unbecoming: Gays and lesbians in the U.S. military.* New York: St. Martin's Press.

Slater, S. (1995). *The lesbian family life cycle.* New York: Free Press.

Snyder, P. (Producer), & Winer, L. (Director). (1985). *Silent pioneers* [Motion picture]. (Available from Filmmakers Library, 124 East 40th Street, New York, NY 10016.)

Souhami, D. (1991). *Gertrude and Alice.* San Francisco: Pandora.

Vacha, K. (1985). *Quiet fire: Memories of older gay men.* Trumansburg, NY: Crossing Press.

Vining, D. (1979/1996). *A gay diary* (Vol. 1, 1933–1946). New York: Masquerade.

Vining, D. (1980). *A gay diary: 1946–1954* (Vol. 2). New York: Pepys Press.

Vining, D. (1981). *A gay diary: 1954–1967* (Vol. 3). New York: Pepys Press.

Vining, D. (1983). *A gay diary: 1967–1975* (Vol. 4). New York: Pepys Press.

Vining, D. (1993). *A gay diary: 1975–1982* (Vol. 5). New York: Pepys Press.

Weinberg, M. S. (1970). The male homosexual: Age-related variations in social and psychological characteristics. *Social Problems, 17,* 527–537.

Weinberg, M. S., & Williams, C. J. (1974). *Male homosexuals: Their problems and adaptations.* New York: Oxford.

Weinberg, M., Williams, C., & Pryor, D. (2001). Bisexuals at midlife: Commitment, salience, and identify. *Journal of Contemporary Ethnography, 30*(2), 180–208.

Welbon, D. (Producer & Director). (1999). *Living with pride: Ruth Ellis at 100* [Motion picture]. (Available from www.sistersinthelife.com or www.sistersincinema.com/filmmakers/ywelbon/ruth_ellis.html.)

Williams, C. J., & Weinberg, M. S. (1971). *Homosexuals and the military*. New York: Harper & Row.

Winer, L. (Producer, Writer, & Director), & Eaton, K. (Producer). (1999). *Golden threads* [Motion picture]. (Available from Women Make Movies, Inc., 462 Broadway, Suite 500WS, New York, NY 10013.)

# 2

# Trans Aging

*Loree Cook-Daniels*

Andrew adored Mr. Adams. Not only was he lucid—some days it seemed as if nearly all of the nursing home residents weren't—but he was charming. And so interesting! He had traveled so many places in the world and had so many wonderful stories he was willing to share.

So he was very concerned when Mr. Adams came to his office one day and asked whether he could close the door. Something was clearly wrong. While Mr. Adams wheeled into place, Andrew came from behind his desk to draw a chair close to him. For a while, Mr. Adams wouldn't say anything, just hanging his head down. Then, to Andrew's horror, he saw a tear drip down Mr. Adams's face and into his lap. Andrew took his hand and very gently said, "Tell me, please."

Slowly, haltingly, his face always turned away from Andrew, Mr. Adams did. Two of the nurse aides had begun making fun of his penis whenever they caught him alone during dressing or toileting. "They've noticed my...um, urine...doesn't come out the end of my penis like, uh, most men's," he said. Plus they made fun of his penis's small size. Gradually they had begun escalating their behavior, trying to make him get an erection through various means and taunting him when nothing happened. Eventually, two days ago, they had anally raped him with something; he didn't know what.

Andrew was appalled. He discussed Mr. Adams's options with him, but he said "no" to everything: no reporting to authorities, no seeing a doctor, and no, he didn't particularly want the nursing home to fire the aides, because they might come back and "hurt me." And most emphatically, no telling his nephew, who had been appointed his guardian and was his only relative. "What do you want me to do?" Andrew asked. "I don't know," Mr.

Adams answered. "I just felt I had to tell someone, and you are the only person I ever talk to."

*P*oor Andrew. He's the nursing home's social worker, in charge of the emotional and psychological well-being of the residents. Where does he begin to untangle the complex knot Mr. Adams has just handed him?

One place too many people begin, when presented with anything involving a transgender or intersex person, is genital configuration. We humans like to think there are clear boundaries between the categories we automatically put people into: This one is a gay man, that one is a cross-dresser, and the one over there is a transsexual. For most of us, the baseline on which many of these categories are built is the genitals: If someone has a penis, he's male; a vagina, and she's female.

Transgender and intersex people challenge these baseline assumptions, which is one of the reasons they are subject to so much hostility, not only from the heterosexual, gender-normative majority but also from gay and lesbian people. Constantly navigating that hostility is one of the primary tasks of transgender and intersex elders. But it is by no means the only one.

## Transition

As in the lesbian and gay community, *coming out* is a term used in the transgender community to refer to telling others of one's own or one's loved one's gender identity instead of (or in addition to) one's sexual orientation. However, *transition* is a more important concept for the trans community. *Transition* usually refers to a process during which a person is perceived as changing (or having changed) hir[1] gender identity from either female to male (FTM) or male to female (MTF) (Bockting & Coleman, 1992; Brown & Rounsley, 1996; Devor, 1997; Ettner, 1999; Israel & Tarver, 1997; Meyerowitz, 2002). Although not all trans people transition (because many trans people do not want to be seen as definitely male or female, or they are female in some places, male in others, or they identify as trans but do nothing to modify their appearance), it is an extremely significant process for many trans people and their significant others, friends, family, and allies (SOFFAs).

Like coming out among lesbians and gay men, transition usually begins with an internal process of questioning or exploration that may be shared, if at all, with only one or a few others (Brown & Rounsley, 1996; Devor, 1997; Ettner, 1999). These days—depending, of course, on the person's socioeconomic status— the search is then likely to move to the World Wide Web, where the transgender person seeks information about gender identity and, possibly, a Listserv through which sie can speak with other transgender people. People in larger communities may also find in-person support groups to attend. In contrast to gay people's coming out, however, transgender people's transition must go public fairly quickly.

One reason it must go public is that trans people who want to modify their bodies through hormones or surgery (unless they choose to use over-the-counter herbal supplements or black market sources) must enlist the assistance of at least one physician (Brown & Rounsley, 1996; Ettner, 1999; Israel & Tarver, 1997; Kirk, 1996). These physicians often require a trans person to be "certified" as sane and suffering from the *Diagnostic and Statistical Manual of Mental Disorders, Fourth Edition (DSM–IV)* diagnosis of Gender Identity Disorder by at least one mental health professional (American Psychiatric Association, 2000; Meyer et al., 2001).

The second reason many transgender people must go public is that the changes they make to live out their transgender identity are, by definition, obvious to everyone who is able to recognize the person by sight, sound, or name. At least eventually, those around someone using cross-gender hormones will begin seeing physical changes such as breasts developing on an MTF or a beard developing on an FTM. Listeners will hear the voice changes wrought by testosterone in an FTM and may notice an MTF's attempts to change her pitch, intonation, or speech pattern. Intimates may notice the individual's personal smell changing (Boenke, 2003; Tucker, in press).

More obviously, most MTFs and many FTMs change their wardrobes dramatically, beginning to publicly wear clothes that are widely identified with the target gender rather than their birth gender. Most transsexuals change at least their first names to something the general public identifies as belonging to their target gender. Many also seek to change their name or gender designation on documents such as driver's licenses, school records, birth certificates, and many others, requiring explicit conversations or correspondence with multiple bureaucrats (Brown & Rounsley, 1996; Denny, 1994; Israel & Traver, 1997; Sullivan, 1990).

## Transitioning in Later Life

A substantial proportion of transgender people do not transition until late middle age or later (Cook-Daniels, 2002b). To some still-unknown degree, this is a cohort phenomenon caused by publicly available information about transgender people reaching a critical mass. People who have struggled with gender questions all their lives may not have realized until now, with the availability of the World Wide Web and more literature on gender variance, that there was a name for their feelings and courses of action they could take (Meyerowitz, 2002).

Other elders decide to transition in later life because of life course milestones such as retirement (eliminating the need to transition on the job), children moving out of the house (reducing the need to present a particular family image), or the death of parents (freeing the transgender person or SOFFA from the prospect of coping with their reactions). A health crisis may precipitate transition if it prompts the elder to decide that the time to live the way sie wants to is running out. Similarly, an elder may simply reach a point of exhaustion in hir efforts to present hirself as a manly man or feminine woman and decide that the charade is no longer worth upholding. Sometimes older transitioning people simply declare, "I've done everything everyone wanted me to do. It's my turn now" (Cook-Daniels, 2002b, p. 5).

Many aspects of transitioning are the same whether one is 20 or 70. However, there are some differences for people who transition at older ages.

- **Health concerns.** Statistically, older people are more likely than young people to have chronic conditions such as heart disease and high blood pressure. These conditions may make gender-related surgeries and cross-gender hormone therapy more risky or even impossible (Israel & Tarver, 1997; Kirk, 1996).
- **More entrenched social roles.** Many people believe it's harder to make significant changes in an interpersonal relationship that has been in a specific pattern for 30 years than it is in a relationship that is, say, only 3 years old. Similarly, it may be more difficult to change speech patterns and physical mannerisms that have been reinforced for 50 years than it is to change 20-year-old patterns (Cook-Daniels, 2002b).
- **Dating difficulties.** Particularly for heterosexual MTFs, being single in old age sharply reduces one's dating pool because of the low ratio of older men to older women. However, lesbian MTFs may also face a constrained dating pool because many older lesbians will not consider dating an MTF; several older lesbian dating e-mail lists the author has contacted refuse to accept MTF members. FTMs may experience difficulties finding someone willing to accept a sexual partner who does

not have a functioning penis (Devor, 1997). Certainly, beginning to date again after 30 or 40 years of marriage (in the cases where a trans person's partnership dissolves during transition) is a daunting prospect for many people.

- **Legal concerns.** Although marriage is an important benefit for adults of all ages, it becomes more critical as disabilities accumulate and retirement and death near (Cook-Daniels, 2004). One elder MTF known to the author is currently negotiating with the Social Security Administration over whether they will grant her spouse of many decades spousal benefits, given that the couple now appears to have an (illegal) same-sex marriage. Courts have decreed that transgender people could not claim a spouse's inheritance or sue for malpractice on behalf of a late spouse because their marriages were ruled invalid (Minter, 2001). Other legal concerns that may be more pressing for older than younger transitioning people include changing Social Security and Veterans Administration records to protect earnings records and benefits (Cook-Daniels, 2002b).

- **Employment issues.** Employment is of great concern to many people who transition later in life but before full retirement. Many such people are in traditionally gender-segregated professions (often chosen decades earlier as a way of hiding or trying to change one's transness) and find the prospect or reality of being the minority gender in that profession untenable. Others lose their jobs through blatant employment discrimination (which is still legal in most jurisdictions) or end up moving as a way of managing the stress of transitioning. As is well known, subtle (albeit illegal) age discrimination in hiring is rampant. Some older transgender job seekers face not only that barrier but also additional hurdles, either because they are visibly trans or because they have chosen to closet their transgender history and consequently cannot declare or must somehow alter their past employment history to avoid revealing their previous name or gender (Cook-Daniels, 2002b).

## Transition and Mental and Physical Health Professionals

As noted, many transgender people depend on medical professionals for the hormones or surgeries they need or want. In turn, these physicians usually require written certifications (often just called "the letter" in the transgender community) from mental health professionals attesting to the sanity and Gender Identity Disorder diagnosis of the person in question (Ettner, 1999; Israel & Tarver, 1997; Kirk, 1996; Meyer et al., 2001). These letters help reassure physicians that the client is unlikely to later change hir mind and sue for malpractice.

The Harry Benjamin Standards of Care (HBSOC), designed to promote the health and welfare of people with gender identity disorders, probably are far more influential in this matter than are malpractice fears, however. The HBSOC are maintained by the Harry Benjamin International Gender Dysphoria Association, Inc. (HBIGDA). Although HBIGDA has only about 350 members worldwide, the HBSOC influence the actions of thousands of physicians and therapists and guide the life course of tens (if not hundreds) of thousands of transgender people and SOFFAs. The HBSOC require one letter from a qualified mental health professional before a person can start hormones or (for FTMs) have chest reconstruction and letters from two such professionals before one can undergo genital surgery (Meyer et al., 2001).

To obtain the letter authorizing hormones, the HBSOC generally require the transgender person to live, publicly and full-time, as their target gender for at least 3 months or have at least 3 months of psychotherapy. Surgery permission letters generally require, among other things, "12 months of successful continuous full time real-life experience" in the target gender, and, at the mental health professional's discretion, "regular responsible participation in psychotherapy throughout the real-life experience" (Meyer et al., 2001).

Not surprisingly, requiring transgender people to jump through a mental health hoop to obtain medications and plastic surgeries that are freely available to nontransgender individuals often creates anxiety, anger, fear, and resentment among transgender people and SOFFAs. They often perceive that the process labels them mentally ill until proven otherwise, and they are fearful and angry that—to a degree that is rivaled perhaps only by prisoners and the severely domestically abused—their life choices are under someone else's control. Many are incensed that a truth they have understood about themselves for decades must be explained to the satisfaction of a relative stranger who, in most cases, has no personal experience with (and may have little professional training about) the phenomenon (Israel & Tarver, 1997). These stressful emotions often are exacerbated for transgender people who have a mental illness, are old or in poor health, or have some other characteristic that they fear will be used by the mental health professional to deny them access to transgender-related health care services (Munson & Cook-Daniels, 2003).

Older people may be particularly concerned about interacting with mental health professionals if they will be perceived as gay or lesbian after transition because many early gender specialists (i.e., those whom older people may have consulted in their 20s, 30s, and 40s) believed that a sex change was a "cure" for homosexuality. Therefore, a biological man who was attracted to women and wanted to be a woman (and who therefore probably would be a lesbian after transition) was, by definition, not a candidate for a sex change (Meyerowitz, 2002). Similarly, people who had borne or sired children sometimes were viewed as not "real" transsexuals because they had functioned sexually in their birth gender. These beliefs, though now officially repudiated by the HBSOC, are still adhered to by some practitioners. For instance, in 1994 the office staff of one surgeon frequently used by transsexuals refused to continue a discussion with the author about the possibility of sex change surgery once it was revealed that the potential client had borne a child.

Cost is a related issue. Almost no public or private health insurance system will pay for gender-related surgery (which can cost anywhere from $6,000 to more than $100,000, depending on what procedures are done), and many will not pay for cross-gender hormones. Because insurance coverage of mental health care is still universally inadequate, adding a mental health gatekeeper to the mix only heightens what many perceive to be an already insurmountable financial barrier (Israel & Tarver, 1997).

## Early Transitioners and Nontransitioners in Later Years

Of course, not every older transgender person transitioned late in life; many have been living in their gender of choice for decades and no longer face the challenges just enumerated. Others never went through transition. However, these people still face challenges unique to older transgender people.

Some of these challenges relate to what was required by the gatekeepers when the then-young person transitioned. For many years, psychiatrists and other professionals required transsexuals to divorce their spouses (which is still occasionally mandated by surgeons and even governments before a sex change can be completed). They often encouraged transsexuals to move to a new place and construct a personal history consistent with their target gender (Meyerowitz, 2002). These practices resulted in trans people losing even more of their social and interpersonal support systems than might otherwise have been the case. The isolation in turn made transsexuals even more dependent on the professionals for help in shaping their emerging self-images. Unfortunately, sometimes these professionals held quite negative opinions. Meyerowitz (2002, p. 107) says of the gender specialists in the United States, "In the mid-twentieth century the more vocal psychologists and psychiatrists were less inclined to sympathy. As they saw it, transsexuals were not only mentally ill but also willfully annoying" (for other examples, see de Savitsch, 1958; Lothstein, 1983; Money & Ehrhardt, 1972). We can only speculate on the long-term impact these provider practices and attitudes may have had on people who decades ago went "stealth" (that is, did not disclose their gender change) and have since had little to no contact with other trans people; Claudine Griggs's *S/he: Changing Sex and Changing Clothes* (1998) illuminates some of the possible consequences.

## Health Care Issues in Later Life

A transgender person's involvement with the health care profession does not end once transition is completed because most transgender people who use hormones to alter their bodies continue to use those hormones—and therefore regularly consult a physician for new prescriptions—for life (Israel & Tarver, 1997; Kirk, 1996). Very often, these physicians have little or no training in cross-gender hormone therapy or other transgender-related medical issues, so the transgender person bears the burden of doing medical research and educating hir own physician or accepting care that not only is not ideal but also may be harmful. This risk may be greater for older people.

Transgender elders also experience fear and difficulties seeking treatment for non–trans-related medical problems. Although some MTFs are financially and physiologically able to sculpt bodies that even health care professionals perceive as biologically female, most naked transgender bodies bear body parts, scars, or other physical evidence that may contradict or cause questioning of the patient's apparent gender when sie was clothed (i.e., "noncongruent" bodies). In other words, many transgender people do not have the option of keeping their gender history a secret from health care professionals. This opens transgender people to everything from casual questions to blatant discrimination or abuse by those professionals. For instance, the documentary *Southern Comfort* details the death of Robert Eads, an FTM, from ovarian cancer; many physicians refused to treat Eads because of their discomfort with his transgender body (Davis, 2001). Transgender people's "noncongruent" bodies may also lead to embarrassing, disrespectful, and perhaps even hostile treatment in sex-segregated health care settings such as hospitals. Even SOFFAs have reported problems accessing high-quality, respectful health care because of providers' transphobia (Munson & Cook-Daniels, 2001).

These problems intensify as the transgender person ages and begins to experience more acute and chronic conditions and disabilities, resulting in increased contact with health care professionals and institutions. Particularly worrisome to many transgender elders is the prospect of needing intimate personal assistance from paid aides or, even worse, needing to reside in a nursing home (Cook-Daniels, 2002b). Although many elders dread the indignity they perceive to be associated with these services, the services represent actual danger for transgender elders such as Mr. Adams, who often fear encountering insensitive or prejudiced aides when they are most physically and emotionally vulnerable. Transgender elders who use hormones also worry that if they are confined to a health care institution, that facility may deny them their hormones. Consequently, transgender elders may resist accepting health care in even life-threatening circumstances (Middlebrook, 1998); Kay (1998) presents a fictional exploration of the psychological and social implications of the death of a previously undisclosed transsexual.

Transgender elders who have not transitioned physiologically also may dread contact with health care professionals and institutions. For example, a butch woman may worry that a nursing home will require her to throw out her wardrobe and instead acquire and dress in "female" attire. A male cross-dresser may resist seeing a physician for a medical problem, fearing that the doctor or nurse will notice and remark on his shaved underarms and legs.

## Legal and Financial Issues in Later Life

Those who serve elders know how crucial legal documents (e.g., powers of attorney, living wills, marriage and divorce papers, pension documents, birth certificates, and wills) can become in accessing services and benefits elders need and in carrying out elders' wishes (see chapter 11, this volume). Like all other elders, transgender people and SOFFAs may need assistance or support in getting these documents in order. However, there are issues unique to transgender people and their families of which service providers and advocates should be aware.

One area critical to transgender people and their partners is legal marriage and all its accompanying benefits, such as access to Social Security and other pension systems, survivor benefits, inheritance rights, the right to make emergency medical decisions, and the right to hospital visitation and same-room nursing home placement (Cook-Daniels, 2004; Minter, 2001).

One type of legal marriage involving a transgender person occurs when a couple was married before transition, when they were "heterosexual." Although one partner's transition turns the couple into a "same-sex" pair, it is widely believed that the marriage remains valid, under the presumption that only the parties to a marriage can dissolve it. In another variation, some apparently same-sex couples have obtained legal marriages because they used birth certificates showing that legally the couple consists of a female and a male. In still other cases, a seemingly heterosexual couple has married even though both members of the couple were born the same sex (a fact they may not disclose to those issuing the marriage certificate). However, few of these types of marriages have been tested in the courts or through application to Social Security or other programs, and the results of those that have been tested are mixed; in some cases the marriages were upheld and consequent rights were granted, whereas in other cases the couple's marriage was ruled invalid and benefits were denied (Minter, 2001).

Another area in which transgender elders and SOFFAs may need assistance is ensuring that all Social Security, Veterans Administration, pension, life insurance, and similar records reflect the transgender person's current name and gender designation to ensure that services and benefits are not held up when they are needed because of confusion over who is applying. However, the full implications of these changes must be considered carefully; as mentioned earlier, the Social Security Administration contacted one transgender elder concerning her "same-sex marriage" when her wife applied for benefits. Apparently they noticed that the elder had previously changed her name and gender designation on Social Security records. Although other couples have sailed through these bureaucratic waters, the importance of Social Security benefits to most elders' financial well-being suggests that this is an area where much more thinking and advocacy are needed.

Unless Medicare begins to provide full prescription drug coverage, the cost of hormones will continue to be an issue for low-income transgender elders. Many transgender people also have their blood tested regularly to monitor hormone levels and related health issues; this lab work may represent a significant portion of a low-income elder's budget (Israel & Tarver, 1997).

## Social Concerns

Many transgender people find that once their transition is complete, the only people who know of their transgender history are their sexual partners, their children, and one or two physicians. (However, sometimes even these key people do not know; for stories of three such families see Cook-Daniels, 2002a; Kay, 1998; Middlebrook, 1998.) Even for such nondisclosing or "stealth" transsexuals, however, this comfortable status quo can change in an instant with the onset of an acute medical problem or the death of a partner. The implications of a health care crisis include the possibility of health professionals' refusal to treat a transgender person, having to fight to be placed in the appropriate sex-segregated room or ward, and having to explain to multiple health care providers why one has a "noncongruent" body.

The death of a transgender mate can present serious challenges to the widow or widower, who may be called on to explain hir partner's body to multiple professionals whose job it is to attend to a death and possibly to those from whom sie will later seek benefits (Cook-Daniels, 2002a; Kay, 1998). Fortunately, the death of a transgender person's nontrans mate does not require the transgender person to immediately out hirself, although that may become necessary in the course of handling postdeath business. However, a mate's death does mean that the older transgender person is more vulnerable to the possibility of needing personal care assistants (given that sie has lost the usual caregiver, hir spouse) and, with time, may face the prospect of dating and having to come out to potential sexual partners.

It is at the time of such crises that a transgender elder or SOFFA may suddenly seek services or support after many years of avoiding services advertised as catering to transgender people.

## Implications

Let's return to Mr. Adams and Andrew. Are Mr. Adams's genitals of concern? It is conceivable that a constellation of medical conditions could lead to a "normal" man having the genital conditions we see here. A simple question along the lines of, "Has the size or function of your penis changed in the last few months or years?" should quickly determine whether a new medical condition has developed.

If there has been no recent change in his genital status, chances are good that Mr. Adams is a normal FTM or intersex person. FTMs of all ages are still very unlikely to have a phalloplasty (the surgical construction of a penis) because of exorbitant cost, dissatisfaction with current surgical procedures, or a belief that one can be male without having a penis. FTMs are more likely to have a small organ, previously known as a clitoris, that has been stimulated into growth by testosterone. In some cases, FTMs undergo a procedure called a metoidioplasty, in which the clitoris is released from its hood, thereby gaining additional length. FTMs may also undergo a surgery that creates a scrotum out of the labia majora. In most of these cases (and, indeed, in some cases of phalloplasty), the urethral opening is not moved, creating a scenario similar to what Mr. Adams has described (Sullivan, 1990).

Alternatively, Mr. Adams could be intersex. Although there are many different intersex conditions, one of the most common ones (estimated at one in 2,000 births) is hypospadias, in which the urethral opening is in the perineum or along the penile shaft (*Frequency*, 2004).

If genitals aren't a concern, many people's next question will be about Mr. Adams's identity: Is he FTM or intersex? Like the question about genitals, the identity question serves the questioner's curiosity and desire to put everyone into neat boxes far more than it serves the person being asked. Worse, trans people's identity labels tell the observer nothing. Terminology in the transgender community is hotly contested: any given "transsexual" may have had or not had surgery; a "cross-dresser" may identify as female, male, bigendered, transgendered, or something else entirely; a "genderqueer" may be the most masculine-looking person you know; and many people with a "trans history" refuse to identify as anything other than female or male. In addition, many transgender people call themselves "intersex" to reflect their belief that they were born with a biological condition affecting their gender, and many "intersex" people have never heard the term, both because it is a new one (such people used to be called hermaphrodites) and because many intersex people have never had a discussion about intersex issues with a health care provider or anyone else because their parents kept their status (and, often, the fact that they had genital surgery as infants) a secret, out of shame and the advice of health care professionals (Intersex Society of North America, n.d.).

The labels a person uses for hirself are critical in one way: Knowing and consistently using the label, pronoun, and name a person prefers is crucial to conveying respect and support for the right of self-determination. And self-determination and respect are exactly where we should be when we deal with trans elders and SOFFAs (and everyone else): What do *they* believe they need help with? What issues do *they* identify as problematic and not problematic? What outcomes would *they* like to see?

Further questioning of Mr. Adams could lead us in many directions. Exploring his fears of reporting the aides or the assault might reveal previous traumas that need treatment. Further exploration of why Mr. Adams doesn't want to tell his guardian what has happened might lead to a discovery of more abuse or exploitation or could indicate a long-standing history of shame or family secrets. A discussion about Mr. Adams's feelings of isolation and his interests could lead to hooking him up with the local "armchair travelers" group or arranging for nearby schoolchildren to come by and listen to his magnificent stories.

If it turns out that Mr. Adams is at a point in his life where he wants to connect with other people who are like him in regard to being transgender or intersex (particularly if he wants age peers), we have some options. Many urban areas have a transgender support group, and they might welcome Mr. Adams, particularly if transportation for him can be arranged (note, however, that FTMs often are scarce in such groups, but a few areas have FTM-specific groups). Only one local area, high in the Pacific Northwest, is known to have a group of older trans people who meet, and theirs is an informal network of friends who get together whenever someone has a party. There is also an online support group, ElderTG, for trans and intersex people and SOFFAs age 50 and older (for further information, see www.forge-forward.org/tan/index.php). An excellent way for individuals and organizations to support trans elders is to teach them how to use e-mail and provide them with computer access so that they can connect with others, even if only by e-mail. Finally, some SAGE-like organizations include aging trans individuals and make an effort to be trans-sensitive (Milwaukee's SAGE is one of those).

Professionals such as Andrew who discover that they're working with trans elders also have an e-mail–based resource: the Transgender Aging Network, which sponsors a Listserv focusing on announcements, new resources, ongoing research, and peer-to-peer advice. This can be accessed through the Transgender Aging Network Web site, which also contains other educational resources (www.forge-forward.org/tan/index.php).

## Conclusion

Ultimately, what Mr. Adams most needs is what we all most need: someone to hold our hand, listen to us carefully and respectfully, trust and honor our self-assessments, and help us exactly as we say we need to be helped. Given most professionals' lack of personal contact with transgender people and their subsequent reliance on stereotypes and outdated theories, however, professionals serving transgender, intersex, and SOFFA elders need to be especially careful not to fall into the all-too-common trap of substituting their own agenda for this simple, client-driven one.

While you are determining the individual transgender elder's needs, nevertheless, it can help to keep in mind some of the unique issues transgender elders and SOFFAS face that are not shared by other elders under the larger LGBT umbrella. To recap, these issues include the following:

- The public nature of a gender transition precludes the typical LGB coming out pattern of controlled disclosure and exposes the elder and hir SOFFAs to the comments and reactions of even strangers.
- "Noncongruent" bodies mean that accepting any health care or personal assistance services delivered when the client is partially or fully naked exposes the elder to caregivers' reactions and stereotypes, which may cause trauma or result in the elder refusing to accept care.
- Legal identity and related paperwork issues may need to be addressed to ensure that the elder and hir SOFFAs have access to earned benefits and support.
- Because almost all trans elders are forced into mental health care whether they needed it or not in order to effect their gender transition, they may carry animosity toward the idea of seeking mental health care.
- Because of hormone, surgery, and related medical costs and because of loss of family-based and job-based financial support through transphobia, older trans people and their SOFFAs may have greater financial hardship than other elders, including LGBs.

## NOTE

1. *Hir* and *sie* belong to one of several gender-neutral pronoun systems; they will be used throughout this chapter to encompass not only males and females but also people who claim a gender identity beyond male and female.

## REFERENCES

American Psychiatric Association. (2000). *Diagnostic and statistical manual of mental disorders* (4th ed.). Washington, DC: Author.

Bockting, W. O., & E. Coleman (Eds.). (1992). *Gender dysphoria: Interdisciplinary approaches in clinical management.* Binghamton, NY: Haworth.

Boenke, M. (Ed.). (2003). *Trans forming families: Real stories about transgendered loved ones* (2nd ed.). Hardy, VA: Oak Knoll Press.

Brown, M. L., & Rounsley, C. A. (1996). *True selves: Understanding transsexualism; for families, friends, coworkers, and helping professionals.* San Francisco: Jossey-Bass.

Cook-Daniels, L. (2002a). FTM post mortem. *Connectivity, 7*(1), 15–16. Retrieved August 30, 2004, from www.forge-forward.org/newsletters/v07i01/postmortem.htm.

Cook-Daniels, L. (2002b). *Transgender elders and SOFFAs: A primer.* Milwaukee, WI: Forge. Retrieved August 30, 2004, from www.forge-forward.org/handouts/TransEldersSOFFAs-web.pdf.

Cook-Daniels, L. (2004). Why gay marriage is an issue for abuse professionals. *Victimization of the Elderly and Disabled, 7*(2), 20, 27.

Davis, K. (Director & Producer). (2001). *Southern comfort* [Motion picture]. (Available from New Video Group, 126 Fifth Ave, 15th Floor, New York, NY 10011.)

Denny, D. (1994). *Identity management in transsexualism: A practical guide to managing identity on paper.* King of Prussia, PA: Creative Design Services.

de Savitsch, E. (1958). *Homosexuality, transvestism and change of sex.* Springfield, IL: Charles C Thomas.

Devor, H. (1997). *FTM: Female-to-male transsexuals in society.* Bloomington: Indiana University Press.

Ettner, R. (1999). *Gender loving care: A guide to counseling gender-variant clients.* New York: W.W. Norton.

*Frequency: How common are intersex conditions?* (2004, January 1). Retrieved August 7, 2004, from www.isna.org/drupal/node/view/91.

Griggs, C. (1998). *S/he: Changing sex and changing clothes.* New York: Oxford.

Intersex Society of North America. (n.d.). www.isna.org/drupal/index.php.

Israel, G. E., & Tarver, D. E. (1997). *Transgender care: Recommended guidelines, practical information, and personal accounts.* Philadelphia: Temple University Press.

Kay, J. (1998). *Trumpet: A novel.* New York: Pantheon.

Kirk, S. (1996). *Physician's guide to transgendered medicine.* Blawnox, PA: Together Lifeworks.

Lothstein, L. M. (1983). *Female-to-male transsexualism: Historical, clinical and theoretical issues.* Boston: Routledge & Kegan Paul.

Meyer, W. III, Bockting, W., Cohen-Kettenis, P., Coleman, E., DiCeglie, D., Devor, H., et al. (2001). The standards of care for gender identity disorders: Sixth version. *International Journal of Transgenderism, 5*(1). Retrieved August 30, 2004, from www.symposion.com/ijt/soc_2001/index.htm.

Meyerowitz, J. (2002). *How sex changed: A history of transsexuality in the United States.* Cambridge, MA: Harvard University Press.

Middlebrook, D. W. (1998). *Suits me: The double life of Billy Tipton.* Boston: Houghton Mifflin.

Minter, S. (2001). *Transgender elders and marriage: The importance of legal planning.* Milwaukee, WI: Transgender Aging Network. Retrieved August 30, 2004, from www.forge-forward.org/handouts/TGElders-Marriage-ShannonMinter.pdf.

Money, J., & Ehrhardt, A. (1972). *Man & woman, boy & girl: The differentiation and dimorphism of gender identity from conception to maturity.* Baltimore: John Hopkins University Press.

Munson, M., & Cook-Daniels, L. (2001). *SOFFAs interfacing with healthcare professionals.* Milwaukee, WI: Forge. Retrieved August 30, 2004, from www.forge-forward.org/handouts/SOFFA-Healthcare.pdf.

Munson, M., & Cook-Daniels, L. (2003). Trans+/SOFFAs and mental health: Survey results. *Connectivity, 7*(2–3). Retrieved August 30, 2004, from www.forge-forward.org/newsletters/vo7io2/MHsurveyresults.html.

Sullivan, L. (1990). *Information for the female to male cross dresser and transsexual.* Seattle: Ingersoll Gender Center.

Tucker, N. P. (Ed.). (in press). *Desire in transition: An anthology by, for, and about partners and potential partners of transgender, intersex, and gender queer people.*

# 3

# The Aging Bisexual
## *The Invisible of the Invisible Minority*
### *Sari H. Dworkin*

*I*n today's youth-oriented culture the aged are invisible. Even more invisible
are elders who identify as bisexual. This chapter reviews what we know about
bisexuality (covering types of bisexuals, development of a bisexual identity),
gender differences, relationships (covering couples, marriages, and families),
and common concerns of the aging bisexual. It ends with implications for service providers and researchers.

Today in the United States it is difficult to continue to call the gay and lesbian
population invisible. Television portrays gay and lesbian characters more positively than ever before. Political leaders come out and run for office as openly
gay or lesbian. Numerous states have passed or are attempting to pass domestic
partnership, civil union, and same-sex marriage laws. Many businesses offer
medical and other benefits to unmarried couples, including same-sex domestic
partners. There are gay and lesbian books, magazines and travel guides, and
the Internet has a plethora of lesbian, gay, and bisexual (LGB) sites. This is not
meant to imply that discrimination against the LGB population is over, but
there is greater visibility of this population. That said, the visibility is of a young
adult population. As in society as a whole, older adults are much more likely
to be invisible.

Even less visible than lesbian and gay elders are bisexual elders (Kingston,
2002; Smith, 2002). "There is no room for bisexuality within the older generation" (Kingston, 2002, p. 4). When a bisexual person falls in love he or she
sometimes begins to identify (publicly or privately) as lesbian, gay, or heterosexual and thus becomes invisible as a bisexual aging person.

Despite the politically correct addition of B for bisexuality to most LG writing, there are few articles, books, or affirmative representations of bisexual

elders. The automatic addition of B for bisexual to almost everything written on the lesbian and gay population makes it even harder to know what really describes bisexual people of any age. Most scholarly research either does not address bisexuals at all (Smith, 2002) or collapses the bisexual subjects into the lesbian and gay subjects' pool because of its small sample size. Therefore this chapter is based on the limited available research, on anecdotal literature, and on the author's conceptualizations about what bisexual elders need from service providers.

## Types of Bisexual People

Masters and Johnson (1979) studied a group of "ambisexuals" whom they defined as people who are sexually attracted to both genders, who have shown no interest in a committed relationship, who are sexually mature, and college educated. They were only able to find twelve persons matching this description in a nationwide search of the United States lasting several months in 1968 (pp. 145–147). In contrast, Kinsey, Pomeroy, and Martin (1948, p. 656) reported that "nearly half (46%) of the [male] population engages in both heterosexual and homosexual activities, or reacts to persons of both sexes, in the course of their adult lives."

Zinik (1985) describes three types of bisexuals: simultaneous bisexuals, who have sexual activity with both genders at the same time; concurrent bisexuals, who have parallel sexual experiences with men and with women during the same period; and serial bisexuals, who alternate sexual activity with male partners and female partners during their lifetime. Klein (1993) theorizes four types of bisexuals: transitional bisexuals, who are really moving from a heterosexual identity to a lesbian or gay identity; historical bisexuals, who live their lives as either homosexual or heterosexual but whose history shows bisexual experiences or fantasies; and sequential bisexuals and concurrent bisexuals, who are similar to Zinik's serial and concurrent bisexuals.

Fourteen years earlier, Ross (1979) suggested eight types: defensive bisexuals, who are hiding their nonheterosexual identity, exploring a new identity, or transitioning from heterosexual to gay or lesbian; married bisexuals, who are heterosexually married but engage in or fantasize about same-gender sexual relations or who self-identify as bisexual; ritual bisexuals, who adopt some or all of a group's culture; equal bisexuals, for whom gender is truly unimportant; Latin bisexuals, who consider the person who is on top during the sexual act heterosexual (this is found in African American culture as well); experimental bisexuals, who want to see what same- or other-gender sex is like; secondary bisexuals, who are heterosexual but have no heterosexual outlets; and technical bisexuals, who are prostitutes having sex with any gender for pay. Weinberg, Williams, and Pryor (2001) suggest four types of bisexuals based on an assessment of sexual feelings, behaviors, and romantic feelings using the Kinsey sexual continuum in their large 1994 study of bisexuals in San Francisco. Their types are pure bisexuals, who are equally attracted to men and women (few people in their subject pool qualified); midtype bisexuals (in the middle of at least one dimension of sexual behaviors or romantic feelings and in the middle range of the other two dimensions); heterosexual-leaning types (more heterosexual than homosexual on all dimensions); and homosexual-leaning types (who are more homosexual than heterosexual on all dimensions).

Most recently, Weinrich and Klein (2002) did a cluster analysis of sexual orientation using the Klein Sexual Orientation Grid (KSOG) with 1,803 women and men. KSOG uses the Kinsey continuum for seven different variables, and subjects rate these seven variables for the past, present, and ideal. Their results clustered people into the following orientations: heterosexual, bi-heterosexual, bisexual–bisexual, bisexual lesbian or gay, and lesbian or gay. Therefore these authors include bisexuals leaning more toward the heterosexual or homosexual ends of the Kinsey continuum in addition to those in the middle of the continuum. Obviously bisexual identity is complex and varied, so discovering how people develop a bisexual identity is going to prove difficult.

## Bisexual Identity Development

Immediately after "Ego Dystonic" homosexuality was removed from the *Diagnostic and Statistical Manual* (*DSM*), studies centered on the process by which one develops a nonheterosexual sexual identity through a series of stages. These stage models did not include the development of a bisexual sexual identity. In fact, they foreclosed the possibility of a bisexual identity by having the final, healthy stage be a stage of commitment to a gay or lesbian identity. Early models based on the dichotomy of either lesbian or gay identity or heterosexual identity precluded the possibilities of fluidity and flexibility of sexual identity (Bradford, 2004). The process of developing a bisexual identity is still largely unexplored despite the Weinberg, Williams, and Pryor (1994) seminal study, in which bisexual identity development was seen to follow four stages: initial confusion, finding and applying the label, settling into the identity, and continued uncertainty. Recent researchers have questioned this final stage of continued uncertainty. Even Weinberg, Williams, and Pryor (2001) in their follow-up to their original study recognize that bisexual identity can be and usually is stable and certain.

The most recent research on bisexual identity development recognizes that a bisexual sexual identity may be even more complex than the development of a gay or lesbian sexual identity (Bradford, 2004; Weinrich & Klein, 2002). Brown (2002) proposes a theoretical stage model for bisexual identity development that incorporates gender differences. For both men and women, however, Brown theorizes that a bisexual identity is a stable identity. Bisexuals appear to have an open gender schema in which sexual attraction is independent of one's gender. Brown's first three stages follow Weinberg, Williams, and Pryor's (1994) stage model but ends with the final stage as one of identity maintenance. For a positive bisexual identity Brown asserts that one needs a supportive community, friends, or partner.

Bradford's (2004, p. 5) qualitative study of 24 self-identified bisexual men and women "sought to discover how bisexual people experience their identities, [and] once their identities are established how they cope with stigma, form communities, and see themselves." From the results of the study she develops the following stage model for bisexual sexual identity:

- Stage one: Questioning reality, a stage of doubt that successfully ends with the belief in one's own experience.
- Stage two: Inventing identity, a stage of searching for meaning that successfully ends with the creation of one's own definition of bisexual sexual identity.
- Stage three: Maintaining identity, a stage in which bisexuals encounter a sense of isolation and invisibility that successfully ends with a sense of forming needed community and increased self-reliance.
- Stage four: Transforming adversity, a stage in which many bisexuals become social activists that successfully ends with personal satisfaction with acknowledgment of a bisexual identity.

## Midlife and Aging Bisexuals

Weinberg, Williams, and Pryor (1994, 2001) have been following a group of bisexually identified men and women from the San Francisco area since 1983. In their 1994 book, *Dual Attraction,* they developed a bisexual identity stage model whose final stage, as previously mentioned, was uncertainty stemming from the amorphous nature of the bisexual identity. Whereas lesbians and gays seemed to come to closure around their sexual identity, bisexuals did not. The myths and stereotypes about bisexuality fueled this uncertainty, seen in the early interviews done in 1983. Weinberg, Williams, and Pryor interviewed these people again in 1988 and in 1994. This follow-up study is particularly relevant to this chapter because the subjects were of middle age and older. In addition, their follow-up study contradicted the findings of their earlier research.

In 1994 Weinberg, Williams, and Pryor interviewed 37 of the original group and added 19 new people for a total of 56 interviewees. Subjects consisted of 23 men, 28 women, and 5 transsexuals (2 postoperative male to female, 1 postoperative female to male, and 2 transgendered men with no surgery, living as women). All were white, lived in the San Francisco area, had high levels of education, and were middle class. They ranged in age from 35 to 67, with an average of 49.8 years of age. All subjects had identified as bisexual for more than 20 years.

The researchers were attempting to find out how salient a bisexual identity is at middle age and older. Each subject was interviewed for an hour to an hour and a half. Subjects were asked about "sexual feelings, attitudes toward monogamy, types of current relationships, self definition as bisexual, sexual lifestyle and partners, the bisexual community, the personal impact of AIDS, the social climate with other sexual groups, and personal regrets about the past" (Weinberg, Williams, & Pryor, 2001, p. 185). Some additional questions focused on whether they perceived themselves to have changed over the years and the number of their sexual partners over the past 12 months who were men, women, or transgendered. The Kinsey sexual continuum was used for subjects to rate their sexual identity. The researchers compared the answers with those given in the previous studies, looking for patterns.

The results are as follows. Sexual activity had decreased. This was attributed to less desire, less libido, less energy, and increased responsibilities (new occupations, grandchildren). Women also added menopause and not feeling sexually attractive as reasons for the decline in sexual activity. Men added fear of AIDS. More men than women were seeking sexual partners. About a half of the sample were sexually active with only one gender. A third were exclusively heterosexual in their behavior, and often there was a move toward monogamy in these relationships. Monogamy was attributed to being too busy for more than one partner or having moved to an area that had a small or nonexistent LGBT community. Some of those interviewed relented to intense pressure to move toward heterosexuality. More than one-fifth became exclusively homosexual in later life. Women stated this was because they tired of heterosexual men, and men said that gay sexual partners were easier to find. A number of those interviewed moved toward socializing and dating only one gender because the Bisexual Center in San Francisco closed, making it more difficult to find an eligible social community where both genders were present and might be open to sexual partnering or friendship.

The closing of the Bisexual Center, though making community more difficult, made it more important for these middle-aged men and women to assert their bisexual identity. Many who had been uncertain about their bisexual identity at a younger age were now certain they were bisexual. Weinberg, Williams, and Pryor (2001) take this finding to mean that a bisexual identity is stable. The bisexual feelings of the participants in this study did not go away even though their bisexual identity played a less salient role in their lives. Perhaps these older bisexuals came to the same conclusion as Keppel (1991, p. 158): "I can't think of a better way to spend my retirement than living and loving bisexually."

In contrast to the findings of Weinberg, Williams, and Pryor that older bisexuals felt positive about their sexual identity, Grossman, D'Augelli, and Hershberger (2000) found that the bisexual subjects had more internalized homonegativity, which the authors interpreted to mean that bisexuals feel less positive about their sexual identity than gays or lesbians. This interpretation is based on a very small bisexual sample, however: 25 men and 9 women out of their sample of 416 older lesbians, gays, and bisexuals. Other current research calls this finding into question (Bradford, 2004; Brown, 2002; Weinberg, Williams, & Pryor, 2001). Nonetheless, they point out that the results of their study suggest that more LGB individuals are coming out at later ages, and therefore it is crucial that psychologists understand these populations.

It appears that bisexual identity development may be complicated by the lack of understanding about this population and the still prevalent belief that sexual orientation is dichotomous. Nevertheless, bisexual identity appears to remain stable into middle and older age for those who have fully acknowledged this self-identification. However, all of the studies recognize gender differences.

## Gender Differences

In the Grossman et al. (2000) study of 416 older LGB people (8% of whom identified as bisexual), some gender differences were noted. The report did not separate bisexual men and women from the other groups, so it is not possible to say with any certainty that these gender differences were noted within the bisexual population. Nevertheless, these differences are important to examine. Men had more discomfort related to their sexual identity. They also showed more suicidal ideation related to their sexual identity and had more alcohol abuse. Women were more out in terms of their sexual identity and spent more time with LGB others. Social support mitigates against stigma, and this was more evident for women than for men. This supports findings that women are better able than men to meet their affiliative needs (Smith, 2002; Yoakan, 2002).

For women, midlife and older ages sometimes are a time of restlessness, reassessment, and regeneration (Kovacs, 1992; Mercer, Nichols, & Doyle, 1989). Caregiving responsibilities decrease, and many women can focus on creativity and other activities (Mercer, Nichols, & Doyle, 1989). In a study of older lesbians, Sang (1992) found that they reprioritize their lives, and some focus more on intimacy. Gabby and Wahler (2002) reviewed 68 articles about older lesbians. Although it is dangerous to generalize the findings to bisexual women, some trends may be similar. These studies portrayed a positive picture of older lesbians. They were sexually active, some in monogamous and some in non-monogamous relationships. Serial monogamy was preferred over casual sex. Fifty percent felt sexually and physically attractive. These lesbians believed their sexual identity would affect their adaptation to aging in the following ways: "kinship relationships, friendships, love relationships, support systems, sexuality, organizations joined, places frequented, professionals whose service are used, attitudes toward aging, plans for old age and participation in senior citizens' groups and activities" (Gabby & Wahler 2002, p. 6). There is no reason to believe that this would not be true for bisexual women as well. Another finding in this review of articles was that older lesbians were more liberal, political, and feminist. In interviews with 27 bisexual women, Dworkin (2002) notes that feminism and liberal politics gave older bisexual women the freedom to identify as bisexual and to break free of societal limits. Brown (2002) also notes that feminism helps women in their identity process but that if the feminist community is not supportive, it can also hinder this identification.

For older women, moving out of the heterosexual box may be easier because "we consider ourselves above suspicion when we are demonstrative in public. Gray hair carries a certain immunity we intend to enjoy" (Keppel, 1991, p. 157). Gender roles affect men's and women's ability to add same-gender sex to their repertoire and to identify as bisexual. Men often feel threatened by the possibility of gay relationships, whereas women are validated by the possibility of lesbian relationships (Brown, 2002). Men are afraid of the stigma and anxious about their sense of masculinity. Keppel (1991) believes that bisexual women observing other women's relationships with one another makes the prospect of a woman lover attractive. Bisexual women in heterosexual relationships may have an easier time considering the possibility. In Weinrich and Klein's (2002) cluster analysis, both male and female bi-heterosexuals seemed more erotically adventuresome than the other categories. They wanted more same-gender activity in their lives. Gender differences show up in more areas than seeking out potential partners.

Health is a major issue. Both bisexual men and bisexual women have health concerns; certainly health becomes even more of an issue as people age. Heterosexism affects access to care because nonheterosexuals are wary of disclosing their sexual identity to health care providers for fear of rejection or substandard health care (Mathieson, Bailey, & Gurevich, 2002; Powers, Bowen, & White, 2001). HIV and AIDS usually are thought of as only a men's issue, and yet both lesbian and bisexual women are unsure of what constitutes risky behavior for women and want this information from health providers (Mathieson, Bailey, & Gurevich, 2002). Bisexual men see HIV and AIDS as an issue that they need to discuss (Bradford, 2004). Lesbians and bisexual women seem to have fewer breast exams and Pap smears than heterosexual women, which is a concern especially as this population ages. There is a myth that women who have sex with women are not at risk for cervical cancer (Powers, Bowen, & White, 2001). Because many bisexual women are having sex with men, the risk of cervical cancer must be addressed with these women.

## Relationships: Couples, Marriages, and Families

Elder bisexual men and women have many different types of relationships, from monogamous heterosexual relationships to monogamous same-gender relationships to polyamorous relationships (Coleman, 1985a, 1985b; Dworkin, 2001; Edser & Shea, 2002; Edwards, 2002; Gochros, 1985; Jones & Jones, 1991; Martin, 1998; Rust, 1996; Wolf, 1985). Nonmonogamous relationships are devalued in our society. Polyamorous is the sex-positive term for nonmonogamous relationships. Also, families come in many different arrangements, including stepfamilies, same-gendered parents, and single-parent families (Martin, 1998).

According to Yoakan (2002), bisexual men in heterosexual marriages struggle to balance their commitment to their wives with their commitment to the gay community. Likewise, an unpublished study by Dworkin (1996) found that many bisexual women in heterosexual marriages were negotiating with their husbands for the acceptance of a female partner. This has been supported by Weinrich and Klein's work (2002) that showed that both male and female bisexual heterosexuals appear to be more adventurous in their erotic desires.

One of the myths about bisexuals is that they can never be monogamous. Edser and Shea (2002) studied bisexual men in committed, long-term marriages (25% of the couples had been married for 30 years, and another 20% had been married for 20–29 years) to see how their bisexuality affected their Global Rating of Marriage (GRM). Most of the men were still attracted to men but had stopped same-gender sex either before they got married or shortly after. They were out to their spouses about their bisexual identity. Forty percent were age 46 and older, so this study has implications for middle-aged and older bisexual men in heterosexual marriages. Those with the highest GRM scores (most satisfied) had good communication in their marriage and had frequent and satisfying sexual relationships. These authors conceptualize bisexuality as either dualistic bisexuality (a need to have sexual relations with men and women), or volitional bisexuality (an ability to choose sex either with both genders or with only one gender). The couples with the highest GRM scores in this study were volitional bisexuals. The husbands attributed their successful marriages to their spouses' acceptance and understanding of their bisexual identity and to good communication about bisexuality and other marital issues. Communication was found to be the key in a study by Wolf (1985) as well. Wolf also found that whereas younger couples in which the husband is bisexual tend to socialize more with other lesbian or gay couples, older couples socialize more with heterosexual couples. This finding may have reflected cohort effects whereby the older couples knew fewer gay and lesbian couples.

Coming out to one's spouse as bisexual is not always positive, nor is this disclosure a simple one-time incident (Gochros, 1985). Reactions differ depending on the context of the entire marriage. Most disclosures of a spouse's bisexuality in a heterosexual marriage cause a crisis (Coleman, 1985a, 1985b; Gochros, 1985). A greater acceptance of and openness to bisexuality often enable couples to weather this crisis. In contrast, if one person is lesbian or gay, the marriage is less likely to survive.

Sometimes the disclosure of bisexuality is part of a midlife crisis (Coleman, 1985b; Edwards, 2002). For men it may be a sudden regret over the path they took (heterosexual marriage) and weariness about men's traditional roles (Coleman, 1985b). For women it may be a sudden attraction to a particular woman or recognition that they got married because of societal pressure, and now that they are older this is not satisfying (Edwards, 2002).

Coming out as a bisexual in a heterosexual marriage does not involve only the spouse. For those with children and grandchildren, the decision to disclose their bisexuality can be difficult. Most LGB seniors with children consider their children the most important part of their lives (Herdt, Beeler, & Rawles, 1997). Children create a unique set of additional problems surrounding disclosure of sexual identity, such as legal problems (custody battles), the need to explain same-gendered partners, and the presence of LGB-themed literature in their homes. Many LGB seniors find it demeaning to consider hiding their sexuality at this age (Herdt, Beeler, & Rawles, 1997). Wolf (1985) found that in 50% of couples with school-age children, the children already had an awareness of their father's homosexuality (or bisexuality). In Coleman's study (1985b) only a third were out to their children, and disclosures did not happen until the children were 18 years old. None of the studies looked at relationships with grandchildren. Certainly couples dealing with these issues, as well as single bisexual people, need a supportive community.

## Community Support

Community is important for everyone no matter what their sexual identity is. Social support lessens stress. The aging sometimes are isolated (Grossman, D'Augelli, & Hershberger, 2000), and LGB elders may be more isolated. This isolation can be attributed to many factors. As previously mentioned, the culture (both LGB and heterosexual) focuses on youth. In addition, the elderly often have more health problems and less energy and have lost friends and family to deaths and therefore may find it difficult to reach out (Grossman, D'Augelli, & Hershberger, 2000). Bisexuals have the added problems of being stigmatized by both heterosexuals and lesbians and gays (Grossman, D'Augelli, & Hershberger, 2000; Kingston, 2002). They also have fewer community organizations than lesbians, gays, or heterosexuals to link up with that will affirm their bisexuality (Smith, 2002). Having fewer bisexual organizations or centers can lead bisexual elders to choose a safer label such as heterosexual, gay, or lesbian (Keppel, 2002).

One study on LGB support networks found that bisexuals have more heterosexuals in their support network than lesbian and gay men (Grossman, D'Augelli, & Hershberger, 2000). This study also found that the more people in an elder's support network and the more out the person was to his or her support network, the more satisfied he or she was with that support. Another small study of LGB subjects of various ages (age and sexual identity were collapsed when no differences were found) noted that involvement in LGB culture, visibility as an LGB person, and social support from heterosexuals at work and school signified well-being (Luhtanen, 2003).

Stearns and Sabini (1997) looked at the dyadic adjustment of LGB couples associated with level of community involvement. They found that involvement with community changed over the life span. For women the community became less important as they aged. The authors hypothesize that older women don't structure their sexual identity around community or political involvement. These women may be less invested in autonomy and therefore find their relationship more important to structuring their sexual identity than participation in community and political events as they age. In addition, the ageist assumptions of LGB communities are offensive to them and become another barrier to participation in community and political events. The authors also found that men attended LGB bars more than the women did and found their sense of community support in that venue.

Boxer (1997) found that LGB people who are middle aged and older tend to be the ones staffing LGB community centers. Often retired, they have more time than younger people to take on volunteer roles. This may make it easier for the upcoming generation of bisexual older people in urban areas to find the supportive LGB community they desire.

## Common Concerns with a Bisexual Twist

All elders address issues concerning retirement, retirement communities, possibility of needing a nursing home, financial arrangements, health provisions, illness, estate planning, wills, powers of attorney, and death arrangements (Ritter & Terndrup, 2002). They face ageism, discrimination against the disabled (for those with physical disabilities), racism, and sexism. The bisexual aged also face heterosexism, homophobia, and biphobia (Baron & Cramer, 2000). Biphobia is a fear of people who don't identify or behave as either gay or lesbian or heterosexual.

Financial planning is especially burdensome for the older bisexual in a same-gender relationship (Noyes, 2004). Compared with heterosexual couples, these couples lose money in taxes, Social Security survivor benefits, pension survivor benefits, and long-term care plans (each must have one) and are heavily taxed on inherited retirement plans. They must pay estate taxes on inherited residences even if jointly owned. Finally, they need extra legal protections in living wills, powers of attorney, titles, and deeds (see chapter 11, this volume). In a study examining women and men in same-gender relationships and men and women in heterosexual cohabiting and married couples, heterosexual married couples had the highest level of postretirement planning, and female same-gender couples had the worst financial planning (Mock, 2001). For bisexuals this suggests that bisexual women in same-sex couples probably do the least amount of financial planning, and bisexual men and women partnered with the other gender probably have the best financial planning (see chapter 9, this volume).

Nonheterosexual older people, especially those of advanced age, often worry more about housing than financial needs. The middle aged are also beginning to worry about housing needs as they age. There is an increased desire for retirement communities and assisted living facilities that are specifically for the LGB aged or where sexual identity is irrelevant (Baron & Cramer, 2000; Gabby & Wahler, 2002; Hamburger, 1997). As Hamburger (1997, p. 24) states, "By the time we inhabit our last home, most of us don't want to come out anymore."

All bisexual elders' concerns have implications for service providers. The current situation will not change unless service providers such as mental health professionals, medical professionals, lawyers, financial planners, and administrators and staff of retirement communities, assisted living facilities, and nursing homes become advocates for the aging bisexual population.

## Implications for Service Providers

Mental health professionals must assume that they will see bisexual elders as well as lesbian or gay elders. Along with the concerns of all sexual minority elders (e.g., affirmative housing, sensitive health care, and legal rights), bisexual elders need mental health services that affirm bisexuality (Keppel, 2002). Therapists should be concerned with some specific areas, such as coming out as bisexual at an older age. Smith (2002, p. 2) highlights questions therapists should ask their older bisexual clients:

- Are there relationship problems around the issue of the client's bisexual orientation?
- Is the client confused or frightened by the same-sex or dual-sex attractions he or she is experiencing?

- Can the client discuss these feelings with a significant other, if he or she has one?
- Does the client have any type of support network available to help with his or her concerns?

It is important to remember that older bisexual clients may want to access heterosexual as well as or instead of lesbian or gay community support. Service providers need to be sensitive to the difficulties of finding a supportive community where bisexuality is accepted.

Another area for attention involves bisexuals' interest in or current involvement with nontraditional relationship patterns such as polyamory (or nonmonogamy); service providers must guard against judgments based on their biases (Dworkin, 2001; Rust, 1996). They also may be called on to help a family deal with the crisis around the disclosure of a bisexual identity.

Health care providers must understand the different health needs of the bisexual aging population. Part of this understanding is an awareness of the realities of life for this oppressed population (Mathieson, Bailey, & Gurevich, 2002; Powers, Bowen, & White, 2001). It is crucial that health providers emphasize the need for breast exams and Pap smears for bisexual women and provide information on STD, HIV, and AIDS to bisexual men and women.

Service providers need to understand that older bisexuals are not likely to talk about sexuality at all, much less about a bisexual orientation (Ritter & Terndrup, 2002). It may be up to the service provider to broach the issue. In their review of the literature about lesbian and gay aging, Ritter and Terndrup (2002) also warn against service providers buying into the stereotypes of the isolated, invisible, sad LGBT elder or the well-adjusted, happy LGBT elder who has weathered oppression so well and become so strong that life does not present any more problems. It is always important to listen to the particular person's story.

A person's story is likely to include financial and health concerns. Financial planners, lawyers, and government officials all must work to reform Social Security regulations, federal tax and property laws, Medicare, and Medicaid to meet the needs of the bisexual aging population (Noyes, 2004). Current laws and regulations are biased in favor of heterosexual aging people and bisexuals in recognized heterosexually married couples. There will not be full equality until all of these laws and regulations geared to assist the aged meet the needs of an aging population who identify as gay, lesbian, bisexual, or transgender.

In addition, short-term goals for service providers include focusing on the immediate needs of bisexual seniors with crisis phone lines and outreach services

(Hamburger, 1997). These immediate needs include assistance with current and future housing and help with social service agencies that do not cater to or even recognize nonheterosexual seniors. There are outreach programs such as Gay and Lesbian Outreach to Elders in San Francisco and San Francisco Homeshare for shared housing (Hamburger, 1997). Programs such as these are likely to be found in larger cities. Bisexual seniors living in rural areas often need to rely on the sensitivity of local service providers.

Probably the most important need is for service providers to become educated about this population (Hamburger, 1997). A recent addition to the Joint Commission on the Accreditation of Healthcare Organizations will help ensure that this education happens. The commission has agreed to "add sexual orientation as one aspect of the rights of patients in long term care to receive support and respect from institutional staff" (Carlson & David, 2004, p. 23). Information from research will also help with this education.

More research specifically addressing bisexuality and the needs of bisexual seniors must be done. Although many issues for aging bisexuals are common to all aging people, and some are similar to lesbian and gay issues or to heterosexual aging issues, others are specific to the bisexual aging population. As discussed in this chapter, the development, acceptance, and disclosure of bisexual sexual identity, health, HIV and AIDS, relationship constellations, families, children, retirement, retirement communities, nursing homes, and legal problems all affect the bisexual aged. More needs to be known about all of these factors. Such research might be conducted through the National Institute of Health, where large population studies often occur (Boxer, 1997).

One glaring omission in the limited body of research is research on ethnically and racially diverse bisexual people; likewise, social class usually is not considered. In fact, all the studies reviewed in this chapter were done with primarily white, highly educated subject pools. Race and class are additional factors that people working with the bisexual elderly should consider. Also, as is often true in research, men are studied more than women. Aging bisexual women must figure more prominently in future research. There are more issues to be researched. For example, how satisfied are bisexual men and women in monogamous relationships and in polyamorous relationships as the partners age? How does health affect the life satisfaction of bisexual people in couples and of single bisexual people? How does a bisexual identity affect life satisfaction as aging occurs? How do aging bisexuals fare in retirement homes when these retirement facilities are geared to heterosexuals or, more recently, to gay and lesbian populations?

# Conclusion

Bisexual elders are complex people. Tomorrow's bisexual seniors will have different needs than those of today. For example, today's bisexual elders grew up in a more oppressive climate than tomorrow's bisexual elders are likely to face (Ritter & Terndrup, 2002). The new visibility of LGB people is helping many older adults to come out (Herdt & Beeler, 1998). The greater health and vitality of the aged opens new possibilities for older people who are discovering or rediscovering their sexual identity. All these changes have implications for the needs of bisexual elders. Despite, or perhaps because of, this population's greater visibility, discrimination still exists (Boxer, 1997). As the baby boom generation ages and the social climate becomes more receptive, the amount of research specific to bisexual seniors probably will increase. The picture will become clearer, and the needs of aging bisexuals will be more appropriately met.

## REFERENCES

Baron, A., & Cramer, D. W. (2000). Potential counseling concerns of aging lesbian, gay, and bisexual clients. In R. M. Perez, K. A. DeBord, & K. J. Bieschke (Eds.), *Handbook of counseling and psychotherapy with lesbian, gay, and bisexual clients* (pp. 207–223). Washington, DC: American Psychological Association.

Boxer, A. M. (1997). Gay, lesbian, bisexual aging into the 21st century. *Journal of Gay, Lesbian, and Bisexual Identity, 2*(3–4), 187–197.

Bradford, M. (2004). The bisexual experience: Living in a dichotomous culture. *Journal of Bisexuality, 4*(1–2), 7–23.

Brown, T. (2002). A proposed model of bisexual identity development that elaborates on experiential differences of women and men. *Journal of Bisexuality, 2*(4), 67–91.

Carlson, H. M., & David, S. (2004, Spring). Task force on aging. *Division 44 Newsletter, 20*, 23.

Coleman, E. (1985a). Bisexual women in marriages. In F. Klein & T. J. Wolf (Eds.), *Bisexualities, theory and research* (pp. 87–99). New York: Haworth.

Coleman, E.(1985b). Integration of male bisexuality and marriage. In F. Klein & T. J. Wolf (Eds.), *Bisexualities, theory and research* (pp. 189–207). New York: Haworth.

D'Augelli, A. R., Grossman, A. H., & O'Connell, T. S. (2001). Aspects of mental health among older lesbian, gay, and bisexual adults. *Aging and Mental Health, 5*(2), 149–158.

Dworkin, S. D. (1996, August). *Bisexual women, understanding sexual identity: Research in progress.* Paper presented at the annual meeting of the American Psychological Association Convention, Toronto, Canada.

Dworkin, S. H. (2001). Treating the bisexual client. *Journal of Clinical Psychology; In Session: Psychotherapy in Practice, 57*, 671–680.

Dworkin, S. H. (2002). Biracial, bicultural, bisexual: Bisexuality and multiple identities. *Journal of Bisexuality, 2*(4), 93–107.

Edser, S. J., & Shea, J. D. (2002). An exploratory investigation of bisexual men in monogamous, heterosexual marriages. *Journal of Bisexuality, 2*(4), 5–43.

Edwards, N. (2002, Spring). Bisexuals, "real" lesbians, "political" lesbians: Sexual orientation across the lifecourse. *Outword, 8*, 3, 7.

Gabby, S. G., & Wahler, J. J. (2002). Lesbian aging: Review of a growing literature. *Journal of Gay and Lesbian Social Services, 14*(3), 1–21.

Gochros, J. S. (1985). Wives' reactions to learning that their husbands are bisexual. In F. Klein & T. J. Wolf (Eds.), *Bisexualities, theory and research* (pp. 101–111). New York: Haworth.

Grossman, A. H., D'Augelli, A. R., & Hershberger, S. L. (2000). Social support networks of lesbian, gay, and bisexual adults 60 years of age and older. *Journal of Gerontology: Series B: Psychological Sciences and Social Sciences, 55B*, P171–P179.

Hamburger, L. (1997). The wisdom of non–heterosexually based senior housing services. *Journal of Gay and Lesbian Social Services, 6*(1), 11–25.

Herdt, G., & Beeler, J. (1998). Older gay men and lesbians in families. In C. J. Patterson & A. R. D'Augelli (Eds.), *Lesbian, gay, and bisexual identities in families* (pp. 177–196). New York: Oxford University Press.

Herdt, G., Beeler, J. & Rawles, T. W. (1997). Life course diversity among older lesbians and gay men: A study in Chicago. *Journal of Gay, Lesbian, and Bisexual Identity, 2*(3–4), 231–246.

Jones, B., & Jones, P. (1991). Growing up with a bisexual dad. In L. H. Hutchins & L. Kaahumanu (Eds.), *Bi any other name: Bisexual people speak out* (pp. 159–166). Boston: Alyson.

Keppel, B. (1991). Gray-haired and above suspicion. In L. H. Hutchins & L. Kaahumanu (Eds.), *Bi any other name: Bisexual people speak out* (pp. 154–158). Boston: Alyson.

Keppel, B. (2002, Spring). The challenges and rewards of life as an outspoken bisexual elder. *Outword, 8*, 1, 6.

Kingston, T. (2002, Spring). "You have to speak up all the time": Bisexual elders address issues, concerns of aging. *Outword, 8*, 4–5.

Kinsey, A. C., Pomeroy, W. B., & Martin, C. E. (1948). *Sexual behavior in the human male*. Philadelphia: W. B. Saunders.

Klein, F. (1993). *The bisexual option* (2nd ed.). New York: Harrington Park Press.

Kovacs, A. L. (1992). Introduction: Gender issues at midlife. In B. R. Wainrib (Ed.), *Gender issues across the life cycle* (pp. 105–106). New York: Springer.

Luhtanen, R. K. (2003). Identity, stigma management and well-being: A comparison of lesbian/bisexual women and gay/bisexual men. *Journal of Lesbian Studies, 7*(1), 85–100.

Martin, A. (1998). Clinical issues in psychotherapy with lesbian, gay, and bisexual-parented families. In C. J. Patterson & A. R. D'Augelli (Eds.), *Lesbian, gay, and bisexual identities in families* (pp. 270–291). New York: Oxford University Press.

Masters, W. H., & Johnson, V. E. (1979). *Homosexuality in perspective.* Boston: Little, Brown.

Mathieson, C. M., Bailey, N., & Gurevich, M. (2002). Health care services for lesbians and bisexual women: Some Canadian data. *Healthcare for Women International,* 23(2), 185–196.

Mercer, R. T., Nichols, E. G., & Doyle, G. C. (1989). *Transitions in a woman's life.* New York: Springer.

Mock, S. E. (2001). Retirement intentions of same-sex couples. *Journal of Gay and Lesbian Social Services,* 13(4), 81–86.

Noyes, A. (2004). *Study: Aging gay couples face fiscal burden.* Retrieved February 3, 2004, from storynews.yahoo.com/news?tmpl=story;=/p020040131/copo/studyaginggaycouplesfacefiscalburden.

Powers, D., Bowen, D. J., & White, J. (2001). The influence of sexual orientation on health behaviors in women. *Journal of Prevention and Intervention in the Community,* 22(2), 43–60.

Ritter, K. Y., & Terndrup, A. I. (2002). *Handbook of affirmative psychotherapy with lesbians and gay men.* New York: Guilford.

Ross, M. (1979). Bisexuality: Fact or fallacy. *British Journal of Sexual Medicine,* 6, 49–50.

Rust, P. C. (1996). Monogamy and polyamory: Relationship issues for bisexuals. In B. A. Firestein (Ed.), *Bisexuality: The psychology and politics of an invisible minority* (pp. 127–148). Thousand Oaks, CA: SAGE.

Sang, B. (1992). Counseling and psychotherapy with midlife and older lesbians. In S. H. Dworkin & F. J. Gutierrez (Eds.), *Counseling gay men and lesbians: Journey to the end of the rainbow* (pp. 35–48). Alexandria, VA: AACD Press.

Smith, P. R. (2002, Spring). Bisexuality: Reviewing the basics, debunking the stereotypes for professionals in aging. *Outword,* 8, 2, 8.

Stearns, D. C., & Sabini, J. (1997). Dyadic adjustment and community involvement in same-sex couples. *Journal of Gay, Lesbian, and Bisexual Identity,* 2(3–4), 265–283.

Weinberg, M. S., Williams, C. J., & Pryor, D. W. (1994). *Dual attraction: Understanding bisexuality.* Oxford: Oxford University Press.

Weinberg, M. S., Williams, C. J., & Pryor, D. W. (2001). Bisexuals at midlife: Commitment, salience, and identity. *Journal of Contemporary Ethnography,* 30(2), 180–208.

Weinrich, J. D., & Klein, F. (2002). Bi–gay, bi–straight, and bi–bi: Three bisexual subgroups identified using cluster analysis of the Klein Sexual Orientation Grid. *Journal of Bisexuality,* 2(4), 109–139.

Wolf, T. J. (1985). Marriages of bisexual men. In F. Klein & T. J. Wolf (Eds.), *Bisexualities, theory and research* (pp. 135–148). New York: Haworth.

Yoakan, J. R. (2002, Spring). Network news. *Outword,* 8, 1, 7.

Zinik, G. (1985). Identity conflict or adaptive flexibility? Bisexuality reconsidered. In F. Klein & T. J. Wolf (Eds.), *Bisexualities, theory and research* (pp. 7–19). New York: Haworth.

# 4

# Physical and Mental Health of Older Lesbian, Gay, and Bisexual Adults

*Arnold H. Grossman*

———————

*I*t has been increasingly recognized that a psychology of health that neglects the environmental and social context fails to address variables that influence choices and well-being (Lee & Owens, 2003). Nothing could be truer when one examines aspects of physical and mental health of older lesbian, gay, and bisexual (LGB) adults because they came of age in a psychosocial environment in which heterosexism, homophobia, and stigmatization were more powerful and less challenged than they are today. Although it is important to recognize the diversity of LGB experiences with regard to ethnicity, race, religion, and socioeconomic status, it is also vital to understand the developmental experiences shared by members of minority groups based on sexual orientation, sexual identity, and gender expression.

Being a member of a minority group that is not recognized as a legitimate minority deserving equal constitutional protection leads to marginalization, discrimination, and violence that directly affect physical and mental health (DiPlacido, 1998). Additionally, this unrecognized minority group status communicates to LGB people that they do not fit in their environment, and it underscores the point that they are oppressed and disempowered, which threatens their mental health and social well-being. Furthermore, this minority status imposes enormous adaptive demands on them (Mallon, 1999). Because the developmental imperative is heteronormativity, with an either male or female construction concurrent with a sexual attraction to the opposite birth sex, the stigma becomes the focus of attention. Everything about them is understood in terms of the master status stigma of homosexuality; it overshadows all their other social identities (e.g., as professionals, parents, family members, and friends) (Grossman, 2000).

This stigmatization had a great impact on the lives of today's generation of older LGB adults (i.e., currently 60 or older) because they lived their early developmental years (40 or less), when homosexuality was classified as a mental illness in the *Diagnostic and Statistical Manual of Mental Disorders* (it was not removed from that list until 1973). Additionally, they grew up with strong admonishments that being homosexual was not only pathological but also sinful and immoral. These views remained largely unchallenged until the 1969 Stonewall Inn riots in Greenwich Village, New York City, that marked the beginning of the modern lesbian, gay, bisexual, and transgender (LGBT) civil rights movement, which happened when today's older LGB adults were approximately 35 years of age or older. The incongruence between their needs and experiences and societal and cultural structures resulted in minority stress (DiPlacido, 1998; Meyer, 1995). Some studies have linked this stress to greater mental health problems, emotional distress, depressive mood, and high-risk sexual behaviors among gay and bisexual men and with excessive cigarette smoking, heavy alcohol consumption, and excessive weight among lesbian and bisexual women. However, there is evidence that many LGB people deal successfully with minority stress, so that it does not lead to negative health outcomes. Social support and certain personality characteristics, such as hardiness and high self-esteem, have been found to moderate the negative effects of stress (DiPlacido, 1998; Grossman, D'Augelli, & Hershberger, 2000).

## A Study of LGB Adults 60 and Over

Grossman, D'Augelli, and O'Connell (2001) examined the physical and mental health, as well as other related variables such as support networks, internalized homophobia, and loneliness, of 416 LGB adults aged 60 to 91. A survey research design with a self-administered questionnaire was used. In order to obtain a national sample for the study, agencies and groups providing social, recreation, and support services to older LGB adults were identified through agency networks and community leaders. A contact person for the study at each of the 19 sites (18 in the United States and 1 in Canada) agreed to recruit participants. Each participant completed the questionnaire anonymously and returned it in a sealed envelope. Data collection occurred from 1997 to 1998. A response rate could not be calculated because the number of adults available at each site could not be ascertained. (For complete descriptions of the assessment instruments and additional procedures see D'Augelli et al., 2001; Grossman & D'Augelli,

2001; and Grossman, D'Augelli, & Hershberger, 2000.) Characteristics of the participants, the names or main characteristics of the assessment indices, and pertinent findings are reported in this chapter, and implications for further research and services are discussed.

## *Participants*

Of the 416 participants, 297 (71%) were men and 119 (29%) women. The average age was 68.5 (*SD* = 5.8), with a range from 60 to 91 years. Ninety-two percent identified as lesbian or gay and 8% as bisexual (25 men and 9 women). More than three-fourths (*n* = 327, or 79%) were members of LGB-identified agencies or groups, with the remaining 89 (21%) being social contacts but not lovers or roommates. Approximately one-third (32%) of the participants were parents, with 111 of the 382 lesbian and gay and 22 of the 34 bisexual older adults having children. With regard to gender, two-thirds of the women were parents, compared with 41% of the men.

A large percentage of the participants described themselves as European, Caucasian, or white (95%); 3% indicated that they were African American or black, and 2% were Hispanic or Latino or Latina. One-third (34%) reported living in a major metropolitan area, and approximately another third (36%) said they lived in a small city. The remaining participants indicated that they lived in a suburb (10%), a small town or rural area (13%), or another type of community (7%), such as a senior residence. Sixty-five percent had received a bachelor's or higher degree, 14% reported associate degrees or various certificates as their highest degrees, and 21% said they were high school graduates.

About one-half of the participants (47% of the men and 50% women) reported having a current same-sex partner (no other-sex partners were reported), with relationships averaging 15.5 years (with no significant differences between male and female relationships with respect to longevity). However, not all of those with partners resided with them. Almost two-thirds (63%) of the participants reported living alone, and only 29% said they lived with a partner. Of the others, 2% lived with friends, 2% lived with relatives, and 4% were homeless. Most of the participants (74%) were retired, 18% were working, 3% were receiving disability payments, and 5% were continuing to work despite being retired from other work. Regarding personal yearly income, 15% reported earning less than $15,000, 44% between $15,000 and $35,000, and 41% more than $35,000.

# Findings

## Physical Health

### Physical Health and Physical Activity Indicators

Three-quarters of the participants described their physical health as good to excellent, 21% described it as fair, and only 4% reported their physical health status to be poor or very poor. There was no apparent difference in physical health between men and women or between gay men, lesbians, and bisexuals. However, people living with a partner ($M = 4.11$, $SD = .70$) reported significantly better physical health than those living alone ($M = 3.88$, $SD = .82$), $F(1, 406) = 7.21$, $p < .01$. Not surprisingly, physical health was related to household income, with those reporting better physical health having higher incomes, $r = .24$, $p < .001$. Additionally, people who experienced less lifetime victimization were found to report better physical health, $r = -.14$, $p < .01$, and people who identified more people in their support networks also reported better physical health.

Although 60% of the older adults stated that their physical health never or seldom stood in the way of doing the things they wanted to do, the remaining 40% indicated that it sometimes, often, or very often did. More than half of the participants (57%) indicated that they regularly participated in exercise activities (e.g., walking, hiking, jogging, biking, or swimming), 27% did sometimes, and 16% never or seldom exercised. Regarding their ability to perform physical activities (e.g., walking, shopping, and working around the house), a little more than half of the participants (55%) indicated that their ability had not changed in the past 5 years. However, 37% said it was somewhat or much worse; only 8% indicated that it was somewhat or much better. Thirty-six percent of the participants reported having a physical disability or handicap, and 16% of those indicated that they needed an assistive device (e.g., cane or walker).

### HIV and AIDS

Although most participants (93%) knew people diagnosed as HIV positive or with AIDS, an equally large percentage (90%) said they were "very unlikely" or "unlikely" to be infected with HIV. However, only 48% said they had ever been tested for HIV, and 40% indicated that they did not expect to be tested.

## Mental Health

More than four-fifths (84%) of the older LGB adults indicated that their ability to think clearly and concentrate was good or excellent, and approximately two-thirds (68%) said their cognitive functioning had not changed in the past 5 years. However, 20% indicated that their cognitive functioning had become worse, whereas 12% thought their ability to think clearly had improved. Concurrent with their ability to think clearly and concentrate, almost three-fourths (73%) reported that their memory was good or excellent, but 29% indicated that their memory had become worse in the past 5 years. At the same time, 65% said their memory had stayed the same in the previous 5-year period (D'Augelli et al., 2001).

## Mental Health Indicators

Most of the participants (84%) reported that their mental health was good or excellent, 14% said it was fair, and 2% poor. Analyses of variance were used to examine differences in reported mental health between men and women, between gay men or lesbians and bisexuals, and between those who did or did not live with a partner. No differences were found between men and women, $F(1, 406) = .52$, *ns,* or between gay men or lesbians and bisexuals, $F(1, 405) = .001$, *ns.* However, older adults living with a partner rated their mental health significantly more positively than those who lived alone, $F(1, 405) = 9.13, p < .01$. But no relationships were found between reported mental health and either the amount of time spent with other LGB people or the number of LGB organizations to which the participants belonged.

## Mental Health and Sexual Orientation

More than three-quarters of the participants (80%) said they were "glad to be lesbian, gay or bisexual"; only 8% reported being depressed about their sexual orientation, and 9% said they had received counseling to stop their same-sex feelings. Seventeen percent did say they wished they were heterosexual.

## Suicidal Thoughts and Attempts

Ten percent of the sample said they had sometimes or often considered suicide, and 4% said they had considered committing suicide in the last year. No differences were found in suicidal thoughts between those who currently lived alone and those who currently lived with a partner or between gay men or lesbians and bisexual people; and there were no significant relationships between suicidal thoughts and age, household income, support network size, or extent of involvement in LGB organizations. Of those who ever had thought of suicide, 29% said those thoughts were related to their sexual orientation, with men reporting significantly more suicidality related to their sexual orientation than women, $F(1, 406) = 6.77, p < .01$. Fifty-two people

(13%) reported a suicide attempt at some point in their lives, with most doing so between the ages of 22 and 59.

## Current Mental Health Status

Regarding changes in their mental health status over the past 5 years, 33% reported that their mental health was better currently than it was 5 years ago, 54% said it had stayed the same, and 13% indicated that it had become worse. However, 11% of the older adults described themselves as having a mental disability or illness. As with physical health, current mental health was significantly positively related to household income, $r = 22, p < .001$, indicating that the older adults reporting higher income had better mental health. However, a significant negative relationship was found between victimization and mental health, $r = -14, p < .01$, indicating that the older adults reporting more victimization had lower levels of mental health.

The older LGB adults who indicated that they had a mental disability or illness were compared with those who did not. As reported by D'Augelli and his colleagues (2001, p. 153), many significant differences were found.

> Participants acknowledging a mental disorder rated their emotional and mental health lower, reported more lifetime suicidal ideation, more lifetime suicidal ideation related to their sexual orientation, and more suicidal ideation in the last year. These participants were lower in self-esteem, and had more negative views of their own sexual orientation. They said they were lonelier, and had less control over their loneliness compared to those without a mental disability. Finally, those with a mental disorder had more alcohol and drug use.

## Loneliness

Loneliness (measured by the University of California at Los Angeles Loneliness Scale; Hays & DiMatteo, 1987) was experienced by a number of the LGB older adults. Feelings of isolation were reported by 13% of the participants, and 27% reported that they felt a lack of companionship. There was no relationship between age and loneliness, $r = .05$, *ns*, and there was no relationship between loneliness and the amount of time spent with other LGB adults or involvement in LGB organizations. As with the number of previously reported relationships related to household income, those reporting higher incomes were less lonely, $r = -.18, p < .001$; predictably, the older LGB adults who reported more people in their support network were less lonely, $r = -.23, p < .001$. No significant differences in loneliness were found either between men and women or between gay men or lesbians and bisexuals; however, as expected, those living with partners reported significantly less loneliness than those living alone, $F(1, 410) = 19.19$, $p < .001$.

## Self-Esteem

Most of the older LGB adults reported fairly high levels of self-esteem ($M = 34.85$, $SD = 4.5$), as measured by the Rosenberg Self-Esteem Scale (Rosenberg, 1965). Most participants also reported low levels of internalized homophobia (measured by the Revised Homosexuality Attitude Inventory; Shidlo, 1994), with men reporting significantly more negative attitudes toward homosexuality than women. And as would be expected, those living alone reported more internalized homophobia than those living with a partner, $F(1, 409) = 10.44$, $p < .01$. There was no difference in internalized homophobia between gay men or lesbians and bisexuals; however, participants with more household income reported less internalized homophobia, $r = -.11$, $p < .05$. And as would be expected, those who had greater involvement in LGB organizations and those who had more people in their support networks reported less internalized homophobia.

## Alcohol and Substance Use

Current substance use was measured by two standard measurements. Alcohol use was measured by the Alcohol Use Disorders Identification Test (AUDIT; Bohn, Babor, & Kranzler, 1995), designed to identify people whose alcohol consumption could jeopardize their health. We found that only 38 people (9%) of the sample could be classified as problem drinkers. Men reported significantly more alcohol use than women, and significantly more men could be classified as problem drinkers. Eleven participants added the comment that they were recovering alcoholics. In this sample, no difference in alcohol use was found between those living alone and those living with a partner, and there was no variance in alcohol use based on the number of people in their support networks or their involvement with LGB organizations. Furthermore, alcohol use was not related to age, household income, or past victimization experiences.

Drug use over the past 12 months was measured by the Drug Abuse Screening Test (DAST-10; Skinner, 1982). No significant involvement with drugs (not including alcoholic beverages) in the past year was reported by any of the participants, with 83% of the older adults reporting no evidence of drug use at all. Some people wrote unsolicited comments on their questionnaires, such as, "I don't do drugs," and "No drugs ever!"

## Correlates of Mental Health

To examine the factors that correlated with mental health indicators, analyses using the major mental health variables and the demographic variables of age, personal income, health, and cognitive function were conducted. As reported by D'Augelli et al. (2001, p. 154):

> Better current mental health was significantly associated with higher current income, better health and cognitive function, higher self-esteem, more positive views of one's sexual orientation, feeling less suicidal because of one's sexual orientation, being less lonely, and having more control over loneliness. In addition, those who reported diminished mental health in the past five years were older, reported worse health and cognitive functioning, had lower self-esteem, and were lonelier.

Being a parent was also related to the mental health of this sample of older LGB adults. Those who reported having no children were significantly lonelier ($M = 14.45$, $SD = 4.3$) than those who were parents. Also, those who were parents reported more positive change in their mental health in the past 5 years than nonparents ($M = 3.60$, $SD = 0.9$ vs. $M = 3.27$, $SD = 0.9$, $t(401) = 4.07$, $p < .05$). However, parents had more often thought about suicide over their lifetimes than who were not parents ($M = 1.64$, $SD = 0.7$ vs. $M = 1.45$, $SD = 0.7$; $t(403) = 2.42$, $p < .05$), and more parents also reported suicide attempts: 19% of the parents reported a past suicide attempt, compared with 11% of the nonparents (D'Augelli et al., 2001).

## Support Networks

Social support has been found to be important to well-being because of its ability to moderate the effects of stress (Alloway & Bobbington, 1987; Cohen & Willis, 1985) and as a buffer against stressful life events on health outcomes among elderly people (Silliman, 1986). Also, it was thought that social support would be especially powerful among older LGB adults in light of their past and current experiences of stigmatization and minority stress.

The support networks of the 416 older adults consisted of 2,612 individuals, with an average network consisting of 6.3 people. Close friends were the most common members of these networks, with 90% of the participants listing at least one. Other substantial categories of people listed by the older adults as members of their support networks were partners (listed by 44%), other relatives (listed by 39%), siblings (listed by 33%), and social acquaintances (listed by 32%). Only 15% of the older LGB adults listed co-workers, 4% parents, and 3% husbands or wives (just 10 of the 382 gay and lesbian and 3 of the 34 bisexual older adults listed husbands or wives as members of their support networks).

The network members' ages ranged from 15 to 94 (average age = 58); half (49%) were under 60 years, and half were 60 or older. However, the participants were significantly older than their network members, $t(387) = 23.56$, $p < .001$, by an average of 10 years, which was true for men as well as women.

As expected, men's networks contained more gay and bisexual men (54%) than women's networks (10%), and women's networks had more women (75%), both lesbian and heterosexual, than men (26%). Bisexual women and men had significantly more heterosexual people in their networks than did lesbian and gay participants, $F(2, 390) = 6.07$, $p < .01$. Finally, women (lesbian and bisexual) listed significantly more people in their networks than did men, $t(414) = 2.94$, $p < .01$.

Most of the people in the participants' networks were aware of their sexual orientation, a finding that may be inflated because of the source of the sample. Specifically, an average of six people in the networks "definitely knew" of the participants' sexual orientation, an average of two people "definitely or probably suspected," and an average of 2.5 people "did not know or suspect." The older LGB adults were more satisfied with the support they received from those who definitely knew of their sexual orientation than from those who suspected or were unaware of it. Not surprisingly, they were most satisfied with the support given by their lovers or partners, and they were very satisfied with the support from close friends or co-workers. Surprisingly, they were not significantly more satisfied with the support they received from people who were of the same sexual orientation or from people who were close to them in age. As would be expected, the more satisfied the older LGB adults felt with the support they received, the less lonely they felt, $r = -.32$, $p < .01$. Examining the types of support the older LGB adults received revealed that almost three-fourths (72%) reported general social support, almost two-thirds (62%) emotional support, and more than half (54%) practical support. Other types of support received were advice and guidance (41%) and financial support (13%) (Grossman, D'Augelli, & Hershberger, 2000).

## Living Alone or with a Partner

Analyses were conducted to compare the 260 older LGBT adults who lived alone (63% of the sample) with the 122 (29%) who lived with a partner on major study variables. Not surprising, those who lived with partners fared much better. They reported that they were significantly less lonely and were in significantly better physical and mental health. These older LGB adults also reported more people in their support networks and proportionately more people in those networks who were aware of their sexual orientation, and they were more satisfied with the support their networks provided (Grossman, D'Augelli, & Hershberger, 2000). Those living with partners also reported less suicidal thinking in the last year (D'Augelli et al., 2001).

## *Discussion*

Before discussing the implications of the findings, it is important to note the study's limitations and, consequently, the limits of the findings' generalizability. Although this is the largest study of older LGB adults to date and has a more heterogeneous sample than other studies of this population, it is based on a convenience sample because obtaining a random sample of this size is not economically feasible. Although there is more variability in income and educational level in this study than in previous studies, most of the participants were well educated and white, and they were of middle-income status. Furthermore, self-identification was used to determine sexual orientation; therefore, the study has a fundamental selection bias in that only those willing to self-identify as LGB became research participants, and sexual minority adults who did not so identify were not included in the study. Also, the findings are biased in favor of older LGB adults who participate in LGB-identified social groups or agencies, and they may not be typical of older LGB people who do not. Consequently, the participants are likely to be more representative of those who are open enough about their sexual orientation to join groups and be less isolated.

Although older LGB adults constitute a diverse group (and only some of them are included in the study described in this chapter), they are a cohort of people who lived their developmental years when support for their lives and many stress-buffering factors did not exist. Some directly participated in the sociopolitical events that influenced their lives, and others were empowered by these events and were able to disclose their sexual orientation for the first time (Herdt & Beeler, 1998). As American society has continued to change its perceptions of LGB people, other older LGB people have been encouraged to attend support and social groups and to construct positive identities (Friend, 1989, 1990). This overall mastery of the minority stress associated with their developmental years is apparent in many of the findings from the older LGB participants in this study, and it is consistent with the findings of Berger (1996) and Kehoe (1989). Most of the older LGB adults in the study reported low levels of internalized homophobia, high levels of self-esteem, and excellent or good mental health. Although these findings reflect the positive mental health of these older LGB adults today, this may not have been true throughout their lives. Much has been written on internalized homophobia, but there is a dearth of empirical data regarding its prevalence. Shidlo (1994) reported that, in sum, the extant studies suggest that 25–33% of lesbians and gay men may have negative attitudes or feelings about their homosexuality at some point in their lives. However, it is important to recognize the impact of this factor on psychological adjustment, including identity information, self-esteem, psychological integrity, and patterns of cognition. Internalized homophobia has also been thought to be one important determinant of psychopathological conditions. (Shidlo, 1994).

There is a misperception that rates of mental illness are generally high among older people, but that may be a function of the small sample sizes taken from nursing home populations. In fact, older adults have rates of affective disorders lower than those of younger adults, and their rates of anxiety disorders approximate those of the general population (Sue & Sue, 1999). The older LGB adults in the current study reported no evidence of drug use in the past year, and only a small percentage (9%) appeared to have problems with alcohol. These findings are different for the general aging population. It is estimated that 17% of adults aged 60 and older abuse alcohol or prescription drugs.

Although most older adults turn to a spouse or a member of their families of origin for assistance and support in coping with aging, most older LGB adults live alone: 63% in the study reported here and 65% and 75% in two previous studies (Cahill, South, & Spade, 2000). The older LGB adults in this study described support networks that consisted mainly of close friends, but almost half (44%) also listed partners. As would be expected, the participants reported being most satisfied with the support they received from their partners, and they were also very satisfied with the support provided by close friends and co-workers, apparently creating families of choice. However, the most important factor they identified in determining support satisfaction was that the support group member knew of their sexual orientation, with the sexual orientation of the support group member not being an important factor.

Despite the fact that the majority of the older LGB adults in this study appeared to have developed some resilience to the minority stress in their lives, evidence of distress remains. For example, 27% reported feeling lonely, 10% reported sometimes or often considering suicide, and 17% still wished they were heterosexual. Another distressing factor for a large number of participants (93%) was having known many people who were HIV positive or had died of AIDS. The psychosocial impact of living with, surviving, and losing many friends and acquaintances to HIV and AIDS warrants further research with LGBT elders.

One mental health indicator, support, was related to physical health: The older LGB adults who had more people in their network reported better physical health. Additional research is needed to determine the nature of this correlation between these two aspects of health among older LGB adults. Most participants (75%) reported their health to be good to excellent, with two-thirds saying it stayed the same or improved over the past 5 years. No significant difference in physical health was reported between men and women or between gay men or lesbians and bisexuals. Other intriguing findings were that 84% of the older LGB adults reported engaging in exercise, and 89% said that their physical health does not interfere with the things they want to do. Because these data are from older LGB adults who attend social, recreation, or support groups, it is evident that further research is needed concerning the physical health mental health of older LGB adults who cannot or do not attend such groups.

In sum, the findings of the study illustrate one of the dominant themes that have appeared in the gerontology literature in recent years: the concept of successful aging. As defined by Rowe and Kahn (1997, 1998), successful aging has three components: good physical health, retention of cognitive abilities, and continuing engagement in social and productive activities. These dimensions are not entirely independent. For example, good physical health makes it more likely that older adults will retain the mental functioning that enables them to remain socially active. The majority of the older LGB adults in the study reported factors that enable them to stay healthy and able, such as regular exercise and avoidance of alcohol and other substance use. Additionally, many of them were highly educated, and the degree to which older adults maintain cognitive functioning appears to be linked to education. Those who are the best educated indicate the least cognitive decline. Despite the fact that some felt loneliness, lack of companionship, and isolation, the majority of the older LGB adults maintained social connectedness and participation in their lives. Although this may be partly attributed to the selection bias of the sample, the older LGB adults in the study had substantial support networks, which provided them with opportunities to give as well as receive support, and engage in important social and productive activities.

# Meeting the Physical and Mental Health Needs of Older LGB Adults

Although there are no accurate numbers of LGB people in the United States, researchers estimate that approximately 3–8% of the population are so identified, which would be about 1–3.5 million older LGBT people (65 years and older), and it is estimated that by 2030 this number will climb to 2–7 million people (Shankle et al., 2003). Although older people have many similar physical and mental health needs as they age, there are some that are unique to older LGB adults. Many of those needs have been identified in the study reported in this chapter, but others have not. For example, a community survey of 280 older adults (94% of whom identify as LGB) by the Chicago Task Force on LGBT Aging (Wiggins, 2003) found that there was a need for access to preventive health care services, advocacy by health care professionals, a senior center for social and intellectual stimulation, and the education of health care providers about sexual orientation, gender identity, and the sexual health needs of older LGB adults. Related findings were reported by Brotman, Ryan, and Cormier (2003), resulting from their Canadian study of 32 people using focus groups with older gay men and lesbians and their families. The results emphasized the impact of discrimination on the health and access to health services of these populations, issues relating to invisibility, and historic and current barriers to health care.

While echoing some findings of the Chicago Task Force's survey, an investigation of the health and housing needs of aging lesbians in Toronto (Ross, Scott, & Wexler, 2003, p. 24), involving 257 women in either focus groups or a survey, found that there was not only a need to educate health and mental health care systems about the needs of older lesbians, but also a need for lesbian communities to respond to lesbian health needs; the illustrative comment was, "We aren't out as much as gay men; therefore, people don't really know our needs." Particular comments also focused on the need to establish communities in order to promote reciprocity and decrease isolation among younger and older lesbians, with older lesbians sharing wisdom and experience and younger lesbians taking on physical tasks.

Porter, Russell, and Sullivan (2004) bring attention to the special needs of old and poor gay men. Using a case study of two older gay men in inner city Sydney, Australia, they communicate the dire situation of single older gay men growing old in poverty and unconnected to the gay community. They point out the importance of educating mainstream service providers to be sensitive to the fact that single older gay men access and rely on the services of a system that does not recognize nonheterosexuals. As others have communicated, Porter et al. indicated that although these gay men face problems similar to those of older adults in general, such as loneliness, poor health, and low income, they may be at greater risk for additional problems such as poor mental health caused by stigmatization and hostility toward homosexuals. This may be especially true for older gay men accessing institutional care, particularly in areas where religious organizations dominate in nonprofit care. Porter et al. conclude that the stories of both men make clear that the presence (or absence) of caring relationships is a primary factor in the construction of identity and that such caring is a significant contributor to their well-being. Consequently, addressing social isolation becomes an important issue that requires the attention not only of the mainstream aged care and support services but also of the gay community. The authors call on the gay community to reach out to its most disadvantaged members, especially those with chronic health and social disadvantages, such as the older, poor gay men who participated in their study. They also point out the potentially significant role for social researchers with an interest in gay and lesbian studies to sensitize their colleagues in designing research projects that include gay and lesbian people.

As indicated earlier, many older lesbian and gay older adults live alone (63–75%); some of these people experience isolation when they are separated from their partners by institutional barriers or death. Some also experience affective problems, such as depression, when they lose friends through death. Others may need medical referrals, financial consultation, or supportive counseling to cope with day-to-day problems or distressing thoughts. And as they get older they may need additional counseling or affirmative psychotherapy not only to help them face issues that come with aging (i.e., by developing pride and a sense of integrity associated with their life's accomplishments) but also to help them navigate end-of-life decisions (Chernin & Johnson, 2003).

## Conclusion

Like older people in general, older LGB adults want safe and understanding environments in which their physical and mental health needs are met. They seek health care providers and staff who understand and are open about LGB health risks, senior sexuality, and recognition of partners and families of choice. They want access to preventive health care and opportunities for intellectual stimulation and meaningful volunteerism. They are also asking for informal (nonbar) settings in which to meet others and establish communities to minimize isolation and loneliness, because most live alone (Ross, Scott, & Wexler, 2003; Wiggins, 2003), and to develop support networks consisting mostly of people who know about their sexual orientation (Grossman, D'Augelli, & Hershberger, 2000).

More knowledge is needed to identify other physical and mental health needs of older LGB adults. Academic and government research should take the lead in obtaining this knowledge by routinely incorporating questions about sexual orientation, sexual behavior, and gender identity into survey research. Research is particularly needed on experiences and issues facing older LGB adults in minority populations as well as those living in rural, suburban, and urban areas, immigrants, and those who are sexually active with members of the same sex but do not identify as LGB and do not have contact with LGB communities. Research is also needed on the concerns of older LGB adults (see chapter 13, this volume) and on the evaluation of existing services they receive related to their physical and mental health needs (Cahill, South, & Spade, 2000; Porter, Russell, & Sullivan, 2004).

## ACKNOWLEDGMENTS

The author acknowledges the co-investigator of the major study reported in this chapter, Dr. Anthony R. D'Augelli, of the Department of Human Development & Family Studies at Pennsylvania State University, for his significant contributions to the study. The author also acknowledges the Research Challenge Fund of the Steinhardt School of Education of New York University, which awarded a grant so that the major study reported in this chapter could be conducted.

## REFERENCES

Alloway, R., & Bobbington, R. (1987). The buffer theory of social support: A review of literature. *Psychological Medicine, 98,* 91–108.

Berger, R. M. (1996). *Gay and gray: The older homosexual man* (2nd ed.). New York: Harrington Park Press.

Bohn, M. J., Babor, T. F., & Kranzler, H. R. (1995). The Alcohol Use Disorders Identification Test (AUDIT): Validation of a screening instrument for use in medical settings. *Journal of Studies in Alcohol, 56,* 423–432.

Brotman, S., Ryan, B., & Cormier, R. (2003). The health and social service needs of gay and lesbian elders and their families in Canada. *The Gerontologist, 43,* 192–202.

Cahill, S., South, K., & Spade, J. (2000). *Outing age: Public policy issues affecting gay, lesbian, bisexual and transgender elders.* New York: The Policy Institute of NGLTF.

Chernin, J. N., & Johnson, M. R. (2003). *Affirmative psychotherapy and counseling for lesbians and gay men.* Thousand Oaks, CA: SAGE.

Cohen, S., & Willis, T. A. (1985). Stress, social support and the buffering hypothesis. *Psychological Bulletin, 98,* 310–357.

D'Augelli, A. R., Grossman, A. H., Hershberger, S. L., & O'Connell, T. S. (2001). Aspects of mental health among older lesbian, gay, and bisexual adults. *Aging & Mental Health, 5*(2), 149–158.

DiPlacido, J. (1998). Minority stress among lesbians, gay men, and bisexuals: A consequence of heterosexism, homophobia, and stigmatization. In G. M. Herek (Ed.), *Stigma and sexual orientation: Understanding prejudice against lesbians, gay men, and bisexuals* (pp. 138–159). Thousand Oaks, CA: SAGE.

Friend, R. A. (1989). Gay aging: Adjustment and the older gay male. *Alternative Lifestyles, 3,* 231–248.

Friend, R. A. (1990). Older lesbian and gay people: A theory of successful aging. *Journal of Homosexuality, 20*(3–4), 99–118.

Grossman, A. H. (2000). Homophobia and its effects on the inequitable provisions of health and leisure services for older gay men and lesbians. In C. Brackenridge, D. Howe, & F. Jordan (Eds.), *JUST leisure: Equity, social exclusions and identity* (pp. 105–118). Eastbourne, UK: Leisure Studies Association.

Grossman, A. H., D'Augelli, A. R., & Hershberger, S. L. (2000). Social support networks of lesbian, gay, and bisexual adults 60 years of age and older. *Journal of Gerontology: Psychological Sciences, 55B,* P171–P179.

Grossman, A. H., D'Augelli, A. R., & O'Connell, T. S. (2001). Being lesbian, gay, bisexual, and 60 or older in North America. *Journal of Gay and Lesbian Social Services, 13*(4), 23–40.

Hays, R. D., & DiMatteo, M. R. (1987). A short-form measure of loneliness. *Journal of Personality Assessment, 51,* 69–81.

Herdt, G., & Beeler, J, (1998). Older gay men and lesbians in families. In C. J. Patterson & A. R. D'Augelli (Eds.), *Lesbians, gay, and bisexual identities in families; Psychological perspectives* (pp. 177–196). New York: Oxford University Press.

Kehoe, M. (1989). *Lesbians over sixty speak for themselves.* New York: Haworth.

Lee, C., & Owens, R. G. (2003). *The psychology of men's health.* Buckingham, UK: Open University Press.

Mallon, G. P. (1999). Knowledge for practice with transgendered persons. In G. P. Mallon (Ed.), *Social services with transgendered youth* (pp. 1–18). New York: Haworth.

Meyer, I. H. (1995). Minority stress and mental health in gay men. *Journal of Health and Social Behavior, 36,* 38–56.

Porter, M., Russell, C., & Sullivan, G. (2004). Gay, old, and poor: Service delivery to aging gay men in inner city Sydney, Australia. *Journal of Gay & Lesbian Social Services, 16*(2), 43–57.

Rosenberg, M. (1965). *Society and the adolescent self-image.* Princeton, NJ: Princeton University Press.

Ross, E., Scott, M., & Wexler, E. (2003). *Environmental scan on the health and housing needs of aging lesbians.* Toronto: OLIVE and Sherbourne Health Centre.

Rowe, J., & Kahn, R. (1997). Successful aging. *Gerontologist. 37,* 433–440.

Rowe, J., & Kahn, R. (1998). *Successful aging.* New York: Pantheon.

Shankle, M. D., Maxwell, C. A., Katzman, E. S., & Landers, S. (2003). An invisible population: Older lesbian, gay, bisexual, and transgender individuals. *Clinical Research and Regulatory Affairs, 20*(2), 159–182.

Shidlo, A. (1994). Internalized homophobia: Conceptual and empirical issues in measurement. In B. Greene & G. Herek (Eds.), *Lesbian and gay psychology: Theory, research, and clinical applications.* Thousand Oaks, CA: SAGE.

Silliman, R. A. (1986). Social stress and social support. *Generations, 10*(3), 18–20.

Skinner, H. (1982). *The Drug Abuse Screening Test (DAST): Guidelines for administration and scoring.* Toronto: Addiction Research Foundation.

Sue, D. R., & Sue, D. (1999). *Counseling the culturally different: Theory and practice* (3rd ed.). New York: Wiley.

Wiggins, P. (Ed.). (2003). *LGBT persons in Chicago: Growing older—A survey of needs and perceptions.* Chicago: Chicago Task Force on LGBT Aging.

# 5

# Sexuality in the Lives of Aging Lesbian and Bisexual Women

## Linda Garnets and Letitia Anne Peplau

*T*his chapter considers sexuality in the lives of aging lesbian and bisexual women. Current scientific knowledge about sexuality in aging lesbian and bisexual women is very limited. Middle-aged and older lesbians are not included in general studies of aging, which focus on heterosexuals, nor are they typically included in studies of lesbian issues, which focus on younger sexual minority women (Peplau, Fingerhut, & Beals, 2004). Available studies on lesbian aging are descriptive, cross-sectional surveys (e.g., Almvig, 1982; Bradford & Ryan, 1991; Deevey, 1990; Kehoe, 1988; Raphael & Robinson, 1980; Sang, 1991). Convenience samples are the norm and underrepresent many segments of the lesbian and bisexual population. Existing studies tend to sample middle- and upper-middle-class, well-educated white women from urban areas. Women who are not open about their sexual orientation or connected to lesbian organizations are largely absent from available research.

Two perspectives provide a useful background for understanding lesbian sexuality. The first is a gender perspective that emphasizes commonalities in the experiences of women regardless of sexual orientation and differences between the sexualities of women and men. There is growing evidence that human sexuality takes somewhat different forms in women and men (Peplau, 2003). Increasingly, researchers with diverse theoretical orientations have shown that women's sexuality tends to be relationship-focused, with love and intimacy typically playing a more prominent role in sexuality for women than for men (Golden, 1996). Consider, for example, how two participants in Sears's (1989, p. 425) study defined a homosexual. A lesbian explained that this is a person who "has intimate love for a person of the same sex." A gay man, in contrast, defined a homosexual as "someone who has sex with the same sex." What these comments illustrate is that men are more likely to sexualize and women to romanticize their sexual orientation. Analyses that consider men and women together run the risk of taking men's experience as the standard and missing important aspects of women's sexuality. Consequently, we have proposed a new paradigm for understanding women's sexualities and sexual orientation that acknowledges women's distinctive life experiences (Peplau & Garnets, 2000). One implication is that older lesbian and bisexual women's sexuality may more closely resemble the pattern of adult development of women in general rather than the pattern of gay or heterosexual men (Kertzner & Sved, 1996).

A second perspective relevant to understanding women's sexual lives concerns historical and cultural change. Lesbians from different generations have grown, developed, lived, and worked in differing social environments. Each generation of lesbians is influenced by different political and historical forces and a distinctive set of social attitudes and opportunities (Parks, 1999). Older lesbians today reached adulthood prior to the 1960s, before the gay rights movement. World War II brought many lesbians together for the first time in the armed forces. In urban centers, gay and lesbian bars provided a place to meet others and socialize, but they were raided repeatedly, and patrons were arrested. In sharp contrast, the generation of women entering midlife today has lived in a world of greater tolerance for homosexuality. Political and social efforts by gay rights groups have increased public awareness of lesbian and bisexual communities, expanded civil rights protection, and lessened social constraints on the lives of lesbian, gay men, and bisexuals (Boxer, 1997). Lesbians are openly becoming mothers, positive models of lesbians exist in the media, there are many well-developed lesbian communities, and same-sex marriage has become a reality in some parts of the country. Unfortunately, we know little about how these major social shifts have affected the sexual lives of lesbian and bisexual women.

This chapter reviews available research on the sexuality of aging lesbian and bisexual women. We begin by considering how sexuality is conceptualized and presenting research on general characteristics of lesbian sexuality. Next we review empirical studies on sexuality, first in lesbian relationships and then for single lesbians. Available scientific information about life span issues and about the sexuality of bisexual women is presented. We conclude with a discussion of sexual health and problems among lesbians.

## Conceptualizations of Sexuality

How should lesbian and bisexual sexuality be conceptualized? Many have argued that conventional definitions of sex, based largely on the experiences of heterosexual men, are problematic (McCormick, 1994). In Western cultural traditions, sex is what you do with your genitals, and real sex means hetero-sexual intercourse. Some sexual acts are labeled foreplay, suggesting that they don't count as real sex. Critics argue that using a male norm of penile penetra-tion as the standard for sex creates problems for understanding women's sexu-ality, particularly for women who are intimate with other women. In addition, a focus on genital sex carries an age bias because it is more likely to apply to younger than to midlife or older people, who engage in more varied nongenital sexual behavior (Robinson, 1983).

How might researchers more fruitfully conceptualize women's sexuality? A study that allowed lesbian participants to define sexual activity as they wanted suggests that a broader conceptualization might be useful (Loulan, 1987). More than 90% of lesbians in this sample included hugging, cuddling, and kissing as sexual activities. More than 80% listed touching and kissing breasts and holding body to body. Similarly, in a survey of 2,525 lesbian and bisexual readers of the *Advocate* (Lever, 1995), many women were enthusiastic about nongenital activi-ties. On a five-point scale from "I love it" to "I don't like it and won't do it," 91% of lesbians said they love hugging, caressing, and cuddling, 82% love French kissing, and 74% love just holding hands. Reflecting on this issue, Rothblum (1994b, p. 634) asked whether lesbians "can reclaim erotic, non-genital experi-ences as real sex." Future research should examine more closely what lesbian women consider sex and then, using women's own definitions, determine the frequency of sexual behavior over the course of lesbian lives.

## Lesbian Sexuality

What are some of the general characteristics of lesbian sexuality identified in empirical studies? The majority of lesbians have had sex with fewer than 10 female partners during their lifetime (Bell & Weinberg, 1978; Lever, 1995). The frequency of sexual activity for lesbians diminishes with increasing age, as it does for heterosexual women (Herbert, 1996; Loulan, 1987). Nonetheless, many lesbians are sexually active in midlife, and sex continues to be an important part in the lives of older women (Deevey, 1990; Raphael & Robinson, 1980). The majority of midlife lesbians reported being sexually active with a partner (71% in the Cole & Rothblum 1991 study and 74% in the Sang 1993 study). Bell and Weinberg (1978) found that although older lesbians were less sexually ac-tive than younger lesbians, the majority were still sexually active, primarily with age-peer partners.

Lesbian sex can include a range of activities (Bell & Weinberg, 1978). More than 50% of lesbians in Loulan's (1987) study reported giving and receiving the following activities with their partner: touch breasts, kiss breasts, lick breasts, put fingers in vagina, have oral sex, put tongue in vagina, and masturbate partner. The most commonly reported sexual activities are manual–genital contact and oral–genital stimulation (Hurlbert & Apt, 1993; Lever, 1995). In a few older studies approximately one-third of lesbian women used tribadism, or body contact, as a means of achieving orgasm (Jay & Young, 1977; Saghir & Robins, 1973). In the survey of *Advocate* readers (Lever, 1995), women in their teens and 20s and some in their 30s were more experimental with adventurous sex practices (e.g., group sex, strap-on dildos, or bondage) than older women.

Lesbian sexual expression typically is partner focused. Research suggests that, compared with heterosexuals, lesbian partners share more equally in the initiation of sex (Blumstein & Schwartz, 1983; Lever, 1995). Leigh (1989) found that the most important predictor of sexual frequency for coupled lesbians was a desire to please the partner. This is consistent with Lever's (1995) finding that lesbians enjoy caressing a partner's breasts and sucking her nipples more than receiving such attention themselves. In a study of lesbians who had had sex with both men and women (Schaefer, 1977), lesbians reported that sex with women was more tender, considerate, partner related, and excitingly diversified and less aggressive.

Many lesbians have had substantial heterosexual arousal and experience. More than three-quarters of lesbians report having had heterosexual intercourse at some point in their lives (Herbert, 1996). Almost half the older lesbians who have been studied have been married sometime during their lives (Beeler et al., 1999; Bradford & Ryan, 1991; Deevey, 1990).

There appear to be some differences between the sexual experiences of lesbian and heterosexual women. Masturbation occurs more frequently among lesbians than among heterosexual women (Hurlbert & Apt, 1993; Kinsey et al., 1953; Laumann et al., 1994). Moreover, when compared with heterosexual women, lesbians were found to be more sexually arousable (Coleman, Hoon, & Hoon, 1983) and more comfortable using erotic language with a partner (Wells, 1990). Lesbians appear to spend more time with whole-body stimulation (kissing, hugging, touching, and holding) than do heterosexuals, who may be more focused on genital contact and orgasm (Blumstein & Schwartz, 1983; Masters & Johnson, 1979).

Comparative studies also suggest that lesbians have orgasms more often during sexual interactions than do heterosexual women. Kinsey et al. (1953)

compared heterosexual women who had been married for 5 years with lesbians who had been sexually active for 5 years. Among these women, 17% of the heterosexuals compared with only 7% of the lesbians never had an orgasm. Only 40% of the heterosexual women had orgasm easily (i.e., 90–100% of the time they had sex), compared with 68% of the lesbians. As Kinsey suggested, these findings may reflect differences in the knowledge and sexual techniques of women's partners. But differences in the emotional quality of sexual experiences may be equally important. Other studies also reported high rates of orgasm among lesbians (Coleman, Hoon, & Hoon, 1983; Lever, 1995; Loulan, 1987; Matthews, Tartaro, & Hughes, 2003).

There appears to be a paradox in lesbian relationships. On one hand, lesbian relationships may increase the likelihood of orgasm. On the other hand, many lesbians emphasize their enjoyment of nongenital kissing and cuddling, activities that are not necessarily associated with orgasm. A better understanding of these issues is needed.

## Sexuality in Adult Lesbian Couples

Research indicates that personal relationships constitute an important context for sexual expression for many lesbians. A substantial proportion of lesbian women are currently in a romantic relationship (see review in Peplau & Beals, 2004). For example, in a large-scale survey of lesbians, 65% of women reported being in a same-sex primary relationship (Morris, Waldo, & Rothblum, 2001). A recent survey of more than 2,600 African American lesbians found that 41% of women were in a committed relationship (Battle et al., 2002). Most research on sexuality among lesbians has studied partner relationships. This section reviews these empirical findings about sexuality in the relationships of adult lesbians, focusing on sexual satisfaction and its correlates, sexual frequency, the controversy surrounding the meaning of *sex* for lesbians, and sexual exclusivity in lesbian relationships.

### *Sexual Satisfaction and Its Correlates*

Most lesbians report being highly satisfied with the sexual aspects of their current relationships (Eldridge & Gilbert, 1990; Peplau, Cochran, & Mays, 1997; Peplau et al., 1978). Comparative studies find much similarity between the sexual satisfaction of lesbian, gay, and heterosexual couples. Illustrative findings come from the American Couples Study, which surveyed several thousand lesbian, gay, married, and cohabiting heterosexual couples (Blumstein & Schwartz, 1983). Roughly two-thirds of lesbians, gay men, wives, and husbands were classified as satisfied with their sex life. In another comparative study, Kurdek (1991) found no differences in sexual satisfaction scores between lesbian, gay, and heterosexual couples.

Greater sexual satisfaction is associated with greater sexual frequency (Blumstein & Schwartz, 1983; Peplau et al., 1978). However, sexual satisfaction in women has been found to be more strongly associated with emotional factors, particularly the quality of the relationship, rather than with physical sexual variables, such as frequency of sexual interactions or orgasm (Hawton, Gath, & Day, 1994; Herbert, 1996; Hurlbert & Apt, 1993). Closeness appears to be an important motive for sex among lesbians. Leigh (1989) asked homosexuals and heterosexuals to rate reasons for having sex. Results indicated that women (both lesbian and heterosexual) attached greater importance to expressing emotional closeness than did men. A sample of Dutch lesbian couples responded to a list of possible reasons for cuddling and having sex (Schreurs, 1993). The motives for having sex could not be distinguished from motives for cuddling. Moreover, sexual interaction and cuddling were rated more highly when they were aimed at feeling physically and emotionally close rather than sexual arousal or the wish for an orgasm.

Finally, research has consistently demonstrated that couples who are happy with their sex life have happier relationships in general (Eldridge & Gilbert, 1990; Kurdek, 1991; Peplau, Cochran, & Mays, 1997).

## Sexual Frequency

How sexually active are lesbians, in general, and how important is sexuality in their lives? Several studies have assessed the frequency of sexual behavior among lesbian women in a current relationship (e.g., Blumstein & Schwartz, 1983; Bryant & Demian, 1994; Lever, 1995; Loulan, 1987). In an early study, Jay and Young (1977) asked lesbians how often they "have sex" in their relationship. There was wide variation in sexual frequency in this sample. One percent of women reported having sex more than once a day, 4% once a day, and the majority, 57%, had sex several times a week. Twenty-five percent of women had sex once a week and 8% less often. For 5% of women, sex was not currently a part of their relationship. A national study of 398 black lesbian women in committed relationships also asked about sexual frequency during the past month (Peplau, Cochran, &

Mays, 1997). In this sample, 11% of women indicated having sex more than three times a week, 47% indicated one to three times per week, and 41% of women reported having sex less than once a week. These data are useful in illustrating the variability in sexual frequency among lesbian couples but cannot be seen as general base rates because all studies use unrepresentative samples.

Sexual frequency declines over time in lesbian relationships (Loulan, 1987; Peplau et al., 1978). Data from the American Couples Study are illustrative. Among women who had been together 2 years or less, 76% had sex one to three times a week or more than three times a week. Among couples together for 2–10 years, the comparable figure was 37%, and among couples together more than 10 years, only 27% had sex one to three times a week or more than three times a week. Both the partners' age and the duration of the relationship contributed to this pattern, but relationship length was a stronger factor than age for lesbians. Lever's (1995) survey of *Advocate* readers also found that sexual frequency was negatively associated with the length of time that a lesbian couple had been together. In the first year of a relationship, a third of couples had sex three or more times a week, in the second year this declined to 20%, and after the second year it was 10%.

Lesbian couples report having sex less often than either heterosexual or gay male couples. (For a recent exception, see Matthews, Tartaro, & Hughes, 2003, who found no differences in sexual frequency in a demographically matched sample of lesbian and heterosexual women.) The American Couples study compared sexual frequency among lesbian, gay male, and heterosexual couples who had been together less than 2 years, 2–10 years, or more than 10 years. At each stage, lesbians reported having sex less often. More recently, Lever (1995, p. 25) compared responses from lesbians who participated in the *Advocate* survey with national data on heterosexuals. She concluded that "after only two years together, lesbians have sex less frequently than married heterosexual couples do after ten years."

## The Controversy over Lesbian Sexuality

The empirical finding that lesbian couples have sex less frequently than other couples and that sexual frequency declines rapidly in lesbian relationships is sometimes called "lesbian bed death." The interpretation of this pattern is controversial (see review by Fassinger & Morrow, 1995). A common suggestion has been that gender socialization leads women to repress and ignore sexual feelings and that the impact of this socialization is magnified in a relationship with two female partners (Nichols, 1987). Another view has been that women have difficulty being sexually assertive or taking the lead in initiating sexual activities with a partner, leading to low levels of sexual activity. Blumstein and Schwartz (1983, p. 214) suggested that "lesbians are not comfortable in the role of sexual aggressor and it is a major reason why they have sex less often than other kinds of couples." A third possibility is based on the presumption that men are generally more interested in sex than women. In this view, both lesbian and heterosexual women may experience low sexual desire because of work pressures, the demands of raising children, health issues, and so on. In heterosexual couples, the male partner's greater level of desire and willingness to take the initiative in sex encourage women to engage in sexual activity. This does not occur in lesbian couples. Efforts to test these possibilities systematically would be useful.

A further issue concerns whether low sexual frequency should be considered a problem, as is suggested by the term "lesbian bed death." Fassinger and Morrow (1995, p. 200) challenged this view: "Is lack of sexual desire or genital activity a 'problem' in a loving and romantic woman-to-woman relationship? From whose point of view?...Who determines what is sexually normative for lesbians?" Indeed, both historical analyses of 19th-century American women (e.g., Faderman, 1981) and contemporary accounts of lesbians highlight the existence of passionate and enduring relationships between women that do not involve genital sexuality. Rothblum and Brehony (1993) have reclaimed the 19th-century term "Boston marriage" to describe romantic but asexual relationships between lesbians today. Such relationships call into question the assumption that an absence of genital sex is necessarily a sign of a dysfunctional relationship.

## Sexual Exclusivity and Sexual Openness

Among contemporary lesbian couples, sexual exclusivity appears to be the norm (Blumstein & Schwartz, 1983; Peplau et al., 1978). The most common relationship pattern among lesbians is serial monogamy (Kehoe, 1988). In a survey by Bryant and Demian (1994), 91% of lesbians said their current relationship was sexually exclusive, and 90% said they had never broken their agreement about being monogamous. In a recent study of 160 lesbians from Vermont who obtained civil union status for their relationships (Campbell, 2002), 92% of women reported that their relationship (mean length of 9 years) was sexually exclusive both in principle and in practice. Only 4% indicated that they had had sex with another person since their relationship began. Kurdek (1991) found that sexual fidelity was positively related to relationship satisfaction for lesbians.

Most research on lesbian sexuality has studied white women. In an investigation of 398 black lesbians in relationships (mean length of just over 2 years), more variation was found in sexual exclusivity (Peplau, Cochran, & Mays, 1997). Most women (54%) said they had not had sex with someone else since their current relationship began, but a significant minority (46%) had had extradyadic sex, usually with only one person. Similarly, most lesbians (57%) said that they and their partner had an agreement that did not permit sex with others, but again, a sizable minority did not have an exclusivity agreement.

## Sex and the Single Lesbian

The precise percentage of midlife lesbians who are single is unknown, and estimates range from 33% to 43% (Bradford & Ryan, 1991, 40%; Fertitta, 1984, 43%; Sang, 1991, 33%). Midlife lesbians who define themselves as single may be seeing one woman, many women, or no one. Some lesbians are single by choice. Other lesbians, like many heterosexuals, change partners during their lifetime and may have periods when they are single. Available research provides little information about lesbians' reasons for being single, the myriad ways in which lesbian singles construct their lives, or how relationship status affects women's quality of life (Kimmel & Sang, 1995).

Obviously, lack of a suitable sex partner can affect how often midlife adults have sex (Levy, 1994). Compared with their heterosexual counterparts, middle-aged and older lesbians may actually have advantages in finding new romantic or sexual partners. Given women's greater longevity than men, the pool of eligible female partners is greater than the pool of male partners in midlife and beyond. Unlike midlife men, who often seek younger sex partners, adult lesbians tend to be attracted to women in their own age group (Kehoe, 1986; Raphael & Robinson, 1980). Furthermore, youth is less important as a standard of partner desirability among lesbians than among heterosexual or gay men (Blumstein & Schwartz, 1983). Consequently, we can speculate that lesbians may have a somewhat better chance of finding a new partner than do their heterosexual counterparts. Research on this point would be valuable.

In a study of midlife lesbians, Raphael and Robinson (1980) found that single lesbians had more lesbian friends than coupled lesbians of the same age. Similarly, Beeler et al. (1999) found that lesbians without partners were more likely to be highly involved with the gay community and more likely to spend social evenings with close friends. In a small sample of single midlife lesbians (Coss,

1991), women reported that having a relationship would be welcome, but only if it "fit in" and was not disruptive to the satisfying balance they had achieved in their work and social lives.

Single lesbians range from women who are sexually active to those who are celibate. The *Advocate* survey (Lever, 1995) compared lesbians who were dating with those who had a steady partner. In both groups, about a third of women rated their current sex life as "great." Lever (1995, p. 27) noted that, in comparison to women with partners, single lesbians may have a "feast-or-famine mentality" about sex. Masturbation may also be a source of sexual pleasure for single lesbians. In Loulan's (1987) study, 26% of the lesbians were single and 12% were casually involved. In both groups of women, 92% reported masturbating, and most of these women (75%) reported masturbation frequencies of 2 to 20 times per month.

Celibacy (with or without masturbation) also may be part of many lesbians' life experience. In the survey of *Advocate* readers, 4 in 10 women reported a period of 1 year or longer within the past 5 when they had gone without sex with another woman (Lever, 1995). One in 20 had gone without sex for 5 years. In Loulan's (1987) study, the majority of lesbians (78%) had been celibate at some point, with 38% celibate for periods from 1 to 5 years and 8% celibate for 6 years or more. Most lesbians (84%) described their celibacy as self-chosen to some degree.

## Life Span Issues

A comprehensive analysis of sexuality in the lives of lesbian women would consider how various developmental milestones affect women's sexuality. Each stage of development is associated with distinctive biological changes, social influences, and coping tasks. Unfortunately, researchers have yet to address life span issues among sexual minority women, and so we are able merely to sketch some of the relevant topics.

### *Coming Out in Midlife and Later Life*

There is growing evidence that women's sexual orientation can change over time. Young women who marry men and lead heterosexual lives may change course in midlife and identify as lesbians (Deevey, 1990; Herdt, Beeler, & Rawls, 1997; Kertzner & Sved, 1996; Raphael & Robinson, 1980). For example, in Sang's

(1991) study of 110 lesbians between the ages of 40 and 59, 25% of the women identified as lesbian for the first time in midlife. Of the women who came out in midlife, 39% had their first same-sex sexual experience before midlife but had not labeled themselves lesbian until midlife. Charbonneau and Lander (1991) studied 30 midlife women ranging in age from the mid-30s to the mid-50s. With few exceptions, these women had never considered the possibility that they could be lesbians and were initially very surprised to find out at midlife that they had fallen in love with a woman.

## Bisexual Women's Life Course

Almost no research has been conducted on aging among bisexual women (see chapter 3, this volume). The best available source of information is a longitudinal study by Weinberg, Williams, and Pryor (2001). Self-identified bisexual women recruited from the Bisexual Center in San Francisco were interviewed in 1983, 1988, and 1996. In 1996, women ranged in age from 35 to 67, with an average age of 50 years. Over time, women reported a decrease in involvement with sex. About three-fifths of the women described their sex lives as becoming worse—as less active, less meaningful, or less fulfilling. Sexual interests competed with life course responsibilities such as work and family roles for a constant or declining amount of energy. Some women attributed their lack of interest in sex to the onset of menopause, and women were more likely than men to attribute a perceived decrease in sexual attractiveness to aging.

When first studied in 1983, most women were engaging in sex with both men and women. By 1996, one-third of the women were having sex exclusively with men. Their reasons for this change included a move toward monogamy, a desire for a simpler life, decreased opportunities for same-sex partners, and pressure from life course expectations to fit into the heterosexual culture. In addition, by 1996, one-fifth of the women were having sex with women only, explaining this change as resulting from a move toward monogamy, past difficulties finding satisfactory same-sex partners, and concern about AIDS.

During the course of this longitudinal study, four-fifths of the women who identified as bisexual in 1988 continued to self-define as bisexual in 1996. Continuation of dual attractions and positive feelings about them resulted in increased certainty and positivity about their bisexual identity. As bisexuals aged, they relied on their history of sexual feelings and attractions to determine their sexual identity, not their current sexual behavior or relationships. So even some women who were in a monogamous relationship with a man continued to view themselves as bisexual. In contrast, some women decreased their involvement in the bisexual community over time, in some cases because they had entered a different phase of the life course in which commitment to work or a partner took most of their energy.

## Role Changes: Work and Relationships

Throughout their adult lives lesbians derive meaning, satisfaction, and identity from both work and relationships. Lesbians are more likely than traditional heterosexual women to be employed full time, and evidence suggests that work has greater salience and significance for lesbians (Kimmel & Sang, 1995; Peplau & Fingerhut, 2004). For midlife lesbians, a major challenge is finding a balance between work and relationships (Fertitta, 1984; Sang, 1991). Hall and Gregory (1991) found that lesbians between 35 and 50 years old reported that work demands contributed to a decline in their eroticism. All but one of the 18 women in this sample reported infrequent sex as a problem and linked it to demanding work schedules and a lack of time together.

An important topic for future research concerns the impact of children on sexuality in lesbian relationships. It has been estimated that as many as 25% of lesbians may be raising children (Peplau & Beals, 2004). For lesbian and heterosexual mothers alike, having young children may be associated with decreases in sexual frequency, especially when the children are young (Blumstein & Schwartz, 1983).

## Menopause and Sexuality

Among the most significant biological changes that women deal with as they age is menopause (Leiblum, 1990). Menopausal heterosexual women report concerns with sexual functioning, arousal time, and vaginal dryness. They may also worry about their decreasing sexual desire and desirability and may fear disappointing their male partner (Leiblum, 1990; Morokoff, 1988). Available research suggests that menopause may affect lesbian women somewhat differently. For example, Winterich (2003) found that some heterosexual women got complaints from their husbands about menopausal symptoms, but lesbians did not report complaints from their partners.

Two studies have examined lesbians' experience of menopause. Cole and Rothblum (1991) administered a questionnaire to 41 women, ages 43 to 68 years, recruited through local and national lesbian newspapers and conferences. Seventy-five percent of these lesbians reported that their sex lives were as good or more enjoyable after menopause. Some of the positive sexual changes in their lives since menopause included increased orgasm, increased sexual frequency, greater self-acceptance, and greater freedom. Forty-six percent stated that the frequency of sex had remained the same since the onset of menopause. Most women reported little change in the types of sexual activities they enjoyed.

Sang (1993) reported similar findings from a questionnaire study of 110 lesbians between the ages of 40 and 59. She used an open-ended questionnaire that asked about various issues concerning midlife, including sexuality and menopause. Fifty percent reported that their sex life was more open and exciting than in the past. Better sex was attributed to being able to be more open and vulnerable, to enhanced communication, to less pressure about orgasms, and to the greater importance of touching, loving, and sharing. More research is needed to shed light on lesbians' experience of sex at and after menopause.

## Sex After Age 60

Only two studies, both by Kehoe (1986, 1988), have examined sexual issues for lesbians over age 60. A total of 150 women ranging in age from 60 to 86 were recruited from lesbian and feminist publications and organizations and through personal contacts. Nearly half of the women in each study had previously been in heterosexual marriages. Most lesbians who had had sex with both men and women viewed lesbian relationships as less sexually demanding and more sexually gratifying, emotional, affectionate, and sharing than heterosexual ones (Kehoe, 1986). In both samples, a majority of women characterized sex as an important part of a lesbian relationship.

At the time of the studies, some of the older women were in lesbian couples (20% in the 1986 sample and 43% in the 1988 sample). However, a majority of the women (68% in 1986 and 53% in 1988) were celibate and had had no sexual experience with a woman in the past year. Most celibacy was caused by lack of opportunity and was not by choice. Perhaps because of the high rates of celibacy, only 33% of lesbians in the 1988 sample reported that they were somewhat to very satisfied with their sex life during the last year. When asked how their relationships with women after age 60 differed from those when they were younger, most lesbians in the 1988 sample reported that commitment and compatibility were more important than sex. What these women wanted in their relationship was companionship, affection, and enduring tenderness.

## Sexual Health

In this section we consider several aspects of sexual well-being, including physical changes of aging, body image, sexual coercion, sexually transmitted diseases, and HIV and AIDS.

### *Physical Changes of Aging*

In midlife, health problems increasingly intrude in women's lives. No research has examined the impact of bodily changes, illness, or disability on the sex lives of lesbians. Findings for heterosexual women may be relevant to lesbians. For example, arthritis and back pain are fairly common in older women and may affect physical mobility and sexual comfort (Levy, 1994). Hysterectomy, which is more common among midlife women, may lead to decreased sexual desire and reduced sexual sensations among some heterosexual women (Leiblum, 1990). Whether hysterectomies have similar consequences for lesbians is unknown. More research is needed to explore how sex is affected by the physical changes of aging for lesbians.

### *Body Image*

Lesbians may be less vulnerable than their heterosexual peers to cultural attitudes that only youthful, thin bodies are beautiful and sexually attractive (Krakauer & Rose, 2002). Because lesbians are not in sexual relationships with men, the importance of standard norms about physical appearance may be lessened (Rothblum, 1994a). Lesbians' conception of physical attractiveness tends to emphasize such functional qualities as agility, stamina, and strength rather than characteristics conventionally valued in women by heterosexual men (Cogan, 1999; Deaux & Hanna, 1984; Heffernan, 1999). Blumstein and Schwartz (1983) found that lesbians were less "looks-ist" than gay men or heterosexual women and men. In their large sample, whether a lesbian rated her partner as physically beautiful or not did not affect her own sexual fulfillment, her happiness, or her belief that the relationship will last.

Although many women are concerned about dieting and being fat, there is evidence that lesbians are less likely than heterosexual women to be preoccupied with weight and body image (Siever, 1994). Krakauer and Rose (2002) found that lesbians had fewer body weight concerns after coming out than before coming out. Compared with heterosexual women, lesbians generally report fewer worries about appearance and weight (Herzog et al., 1992), higher ideal weights for themselves (Brand, Rothblum, & Solomon, 1992), less concern with dieting (Gettleman & Thompson, 1994), less concern about a partner's appearance (Siever, 1994), and fewer negative feelings about their bodies (Bergeron & Senn, 1998).

Krakauer and Rose (2002) found that women made changes in their appearance after coming out as lesbian in the direction of becoming more butch or androgynous in appearance, or at least less feminine. For example, a majority reported cutting their hair shorter and wearing more comfortable shoes. The desire to convey group membership and to signal prospective partners were primary reasons for changes in appearance. Similarly, Cogan's (1999) study of 181 women ranging in age from 17 to 58 also found that lesbians changed their appearance after coming out. These women indicated that these changes were influenced by a desire to be identified as lesbians and to feel a sense of belonging within the lesbian and bisexual community. These results suggest that one purpose of lesbian beauty standards is functional: to allow lesbians to identify each other and to provide a group identity that is distinct from that of women in the dominant culture (Rothblum, 1994a).

## Sexual Coercion

Lesbians, like all other women, are vulnerable to sexual victimization throughout the life course. Little is known about how early experiences of sexual abuse, usually by men, affect the sexual lives of lesbians in adulthood. A few studies have addressed the sexual coercion or violence that can occur between partners in lesbian relationships. Estimates of the incidence of sexual coercion by another woman vary widely, from 2% to more than 50% (Duncan, 1990; Rose, 2003; Tjaden & Thoennes, 2000; Waldner-Haugrud & Gratch, 1997; Waterman, Dawson, & Bologna, 1989). These experiences represent a broad range, from unwanted kissing or being pressured to have sex to unwanted penetration and threats of physical violence. We need to know more about the prevalence and features of same-sex partner violence among lesbian couples.

## Sexually Transmitted Diseases

Sexually transmitted disease (STD) appears to be less common in women who identify as lesbian or who are sexually active only with women than in bisexual or heterosexual women or gay men (GLMA, 2000; Solarz, 1999). This may result, in part, from lower rates of STD transmission through vaginal, oral, or anal penile contact. STDs appear to be transmissible between women and have been reported among lesbians. These include human papillomavirus, bacterial vaginosis, candidiasis, and trichomonas vaginalis (GLMA, 2000).

## HIV and AIDS

The impact of HIV and AIDS on the lesbian community and the risks of female–female HIV transmission remain underresearched (GLMA, 2000). Woman-to-woman HIV transmission is low (Solarz, 1999). A small study among serodiscordant lesbians (i.e., pairs in which one partner is HIV positive and the other HIV negative) found significant rates of high-risk sexual activities (e.g., having sex during menses, mutually masturbating with shared sexual toys), but there was no evidence of female-to-female HIV transmission (Raiteri et al., 1994). When women who identify as lesbian or who have sex with women contract HIV, it is usually because they have had unprotected sex with men or used intravenous drugs (Solarz, 1999).

## Conclusion

A growing body of scientific evidence provides the ingredients for a new paradigm for understanding lesbian sexuality that captures the uniqueness, diversity, and complexity of lesbian experiences (Fassinger & Morrow, 1995). A woman-defined sexuality would conceptualize "a whole-body/whole person sexuality, one that encompasses the use of a variety of sensual/sexual activities, physical sensations, emotional meanings, interpersonal pleasurings, and satisfactions" (Iasenza, 2002, p. 118). As one lesbian put it, "Physicality is now a creative non-institutionalized experience. It is touching and rubbing and cuddling and fondness.... Its only goal is closeness and pleasure. It does not exist for the Big Orgasm.... Our sexuality may or may not include genital experience" (Echols, 1989, p. 218). Such an approach would rely on women's own definitions of what is pleasurable, integrate nongenital activities into definitions of sex, include the subjective dimension of sex, examine the context in which sexuality takes place and the mutuality of the interaction, examine dimensions of sexuality (e.g., behavior, cognition, emotions, sociocultural factors), and articulate the complexity of lesbian sexual and emotional experiences. This paradigm bodes well for aging lesbians and bisexual women who have intimate relationships with women because the ability to enjoy touching, cuddling, rubbing, and fondness does not decline with age. The key may be to have continued opportunities for these physical aspects of intimacy despite bereavements, mobility limitations, or chronic diseases.

REFERENCES

Almvig, C. (1982). *The invisible minority: Aging and lesbianism.* Unpublished master's dissertation, Utica College of Syracuse University, Syracuse, New York.

Battle, J., Cohen, C. J., Warren, D., Fergerson, G., & Audam, S. (2002). *Say it loud, I'm black and I'm proud: Black pride survey 2000.* New York: The Policy Institute of the National Gay and Lesbian Task Force.

Beeler, J. A., Rawls, T. W., Herdt, G., & Cohler, B. J. (1999). The needs of older lesbians and gay men in Chicago. *Journal of Gay and Lesbian Social Services, 9*(1), 31–49.

Bell, A. P., & Weinberg, M. S. (1978). *Homosexualities: A study of diversity among men and women.* New York: Simon & Schuster.

Bergeron, S. M., & Senn, C. Y. (1998). Body image and sociocultural norms: A comparison of heterosexual and lesbian women. *Psychology of Women Quarterly, 22,* 385–401.

Blumstein, P., & Schwartz, P. (1983). *American couples: Money, work, sex.* New York: Morrow.

Boxer, A. (1997). Gay, lesbian, and bisexual aging into the twenty-first century: An overview and introduction. *Journal of Gay, Lesbian, and Bisexual Identity, 2*(3–4), 187–197.

Bradford, J., & Ryan, C. (1991). Who we are: Health concerns of middle-aged lesbians. In B. Sang, J. Warshow, & A. Smith (Eds.), *Lesbians at midlife: The creative transition* (pp. 147–163). San Francisco: Spinsters.

Brand, P. A., Rothblum, E. R., & Solomon, L. J. (1992). A comparison of lesbians, gay men, and heterosexuals on weight and restrained eating. *International Journal of Eating Disorders, 11,* 253–259.

Bryant, A. S., & Demian. (1994). Relationship characteristics of American gay and lesbian couples: Findings from a national survey. *Journal of Gay and Lesbian Social Services, 1*(2), 101–117.

Campbell, S. M. (2002, July 6). *Gay marriage: A descriptive study of civil unions in Vermont.* Poster presented at the International Conference on Personal Relationships, Halifax, Nova Scotia, Canada.

Charbonneau, C., & Lander, P. (1991). Redefining sexuality: Women becoming lesbian in midlife. In B. Sang, J. Warshow, & A. Smith (Eds.), *Lesbians at midlife: The creative transition* (pp. 35–43). San Francisco: Spinsters.

Cogan, J. C. (1999). Lesbians walk the tightrope of beauty: Thin is in but femme is out. *Journal of Lesbian Studies, 3*(4), 77–89.

Cole, E., & Rothblum, E. (1991). Lesbian sex after menopause: As good or better than ever. In B. Sang, J. Warshow, & A. Smith (Eds.), *Lesbians at midlife: The creative transition* (pp. 184–193). San Francisco: Spinsters.

Coleman, E. M., Hoon, P. W., & Hoon, E. G. (1983). Arousability and sexual satisfaction in lesbian and heterosexual women. *The Journal of Sex Research, 19,* 58–73.

Coss, C. (1991). Single lesbians speak out. In B. Sang, J. Warshow, & A. Smith (Eds.), *Lesbians at midlife: The creative transition* (pp. 132–140). San Francisco: Spinsters.

Deaux, K., & Hanna, R. (1984). Courtship in the personals column: The influence of gender and sexual orientation. *Sex Roles, 11,* 363–372.

Deevey, S. (1990). Older lesbian women: An invisible minority. *Journal of Gerontological Nursing, 16*(5), 35–38.

Duncan, D. (1990). Prevalence of sexual assault victimization among heterosexual and gay/lesbian university students. *Psychological Reports, 66,* 65–66.

Echols, A. (1989). *Daring to be bad: Radical feminism in America, 1967–1975.* Minneapolis: University of Minnesota Press.

Eldridge, N. S., & Gilbert, L. A. (1990). Correlates of relationship satisfaction in lesbian couples. *Psychology of Women Quarterly, 14,* 43–62.

Faderman, L. (1981). *Surpassing the love of men.* New York: William Morrow.

Fassinger, R. E., & Morrow, S. L. (1995). Overcome: Repositioning lesbian sexualities. In L. Diamant & R. D. McAnulty (Eds.), *The psychology of sexual orientation behavior, and identity* (pp. 197–219). Westport, CT: Greenwood Press.

Fertitta, S. (1984). *Never married women in the middle years. A comparison of lesbians and heterosexuals.* Unpublished doctoral dissertation, Wright University, Los Angeles.

GLMA (Gay and Lesbian Medical Association) & Columbia University Center for LGBT Health. (2000). Lesbian, gay, bisexual, and transgender health: Findings and concerns. *Gay and Lesbian Medical Association Journal, 4*(3), 101–151.

Gettleman, T. E., & Thompson, J. K. (1994). Actual differences versus stereotypical perceptions of body image and eating disturbance: A comparison of male and female heterosexual and homosexual samples. *Sex Roles, 25,* 1–18.

Golden, C. (1996). What's in a name? Sexual self-identification among women. In R. C. Savin-Williams & K. M. Cohen (Eds.), *The lives of lesbians, gays, and bisexuals* (pp. 229–247). New York: Harcourt Brace.

Hall, M., & Gregory, A. (1991). Subtle balances: Love and work in lesbian relationships. In B. Sang, J. Warshow, & A. Smith (Eds.), *Lesbians at midlife: The creative transition* (pp. 122–133). San Francisco: Spinsters.

Hawton, K., Gath, D., & Day, A. (1994). Sexual function in a community sample of middle-aged women with partners: Effects of age, marital, socioeconomic, psychiatric, gynecological, and menopausal factors. *Archives of Sexual Behavior, 23,* 375–395.

Heffernan, K. (1999). Lesbians and the internalization of societal standards of weight and appearance. *Journal of Lesbian Studies, 3*(4), 121–127.

Herbert, S. E. (1996). Lesbian sexuality. In R. P. Cabaj & T. S. Stein (Eds.), *Textbook of homosexuality and mental health* (pp. 723–742). Washington, DC: American Psychiatric Press.

Herdt, G., Beeler, J., & Rawls, T. W. (1997). Life course diversity among older lesbians and gay men: A study in Chicago. *Journal of Gay, Lesbian, and Bisexual Identity, 2*(3–4), 231–246.

Herzog, D. B., Newman, K. L., Yeh, C. J., & Warshaw, M.(1992). Body image satisfaction in homosexual and heterosexual women. *International Journal of Eating Disorders, 1*, 391–396.

Hurlbert, D. F., & Apt, C. (1993). Female sexuality: A comparative study between women in homosexual and heterosexual relationships. *Journal of Sex & Marital Therapy, 19*, 315–327.

Jay, K., & Young, A. (1977). *The gay report: Lesbians and gay men speak about sexual experiences and life styles.* New York: Summit.

Iasenza, S. (2002). Beyond "lesbian bed death": The passion and play in lesbian relationships. *Journal of Lesbian Studies, 6*(1), 111–120.

Kehoe, M. (1986). Lesbians over 65: A triply invisible minority. *Journal of Homosexuality, 12*(3–4), 139–152.

Kehoe, M. (1988). Lesbians over sixty speak for themselves. *Journal of Homosexuality, 16*(3–4).

Kertzner, R. M., & Sved, M. (1996). Midlife gay men and lesbians: Adult development and mental health. In R. P. Cabaj & T. S. Stein (Eds.), *Textbook of homosexuality and mental health* (pp. 289–303). Washington, DC: American Psychiatric Press.

Kimmel, D. C., & Sang, B. E. (1995). Lesbians and gay men in midlife. In A. R. D'Augelli & C. J. Patterson (Eds.), *Lesbian, gay, and bisexual identities over the lifespan* (pp. 190–214). New York: Oxford University Press.

Kinsey, A. C., Pomeroy, W. B., Martin, C., & Gebhard, P. H. (1953). *Sexual behavior in the human female.* Philadelphia: Saunders.

Krakauer, I. D., & Rose, S. M. (2002). The impact of group membership on lesbians' physical appearance. *Journal of Lesbian Studies, 6*(1), 31–43.

Kurdek, L. A. (1991). Sexuality in homosexual and heterosexual couples. In K. McKinney & S. Sprecher (Eds.), *Sexuality in close relationships* (pp. 177–191). Hillsdale, NJ: Erlbaum.

Laumann, E. O., Gagnon, J. H., Michael, R. T., & Michaels, S. (1994). *The social organization of sexuality: Sexual practices in the United States.* Chicago: University of Chicago Press.

Leiblum, S. R. (1990). Sexuality and the midlife woman. *Psychology of Women Quarterly, 14*, 495–508.

Leigh, B. C. (1989). Reasons for having and avoiding sex: Gender, sexual orientation, and relationship to sexual behavior. *Journal of Sex Research, 38*, 199–209.

Lever, J. (1995, August 22). The 1995 *Advocate* survey of sexuality and relationships: The women. *Advocate,* 22–30.

Levy, J. A. (1994). Sex and sexuality in later life stages. In A. S. Rossi (Ed.), *Sexuality across the life course* (pp. 287–309). Chicago: University of Chicago Press.

Loulan, J. (1987). *Lesbian passion: Loving ourselves and each other.* San Francisco: Spinsters.

Masters, W. H., & Johnson, V. E. (1979). *Homosexuality in perspective.* Boston: Little, Brown.

Matthews, A. K., Tartaro, J., & Hughes, T. L. (2003). A comparative study of lesbian and heterosexual women in committed relationships. *Journal of Lesbian Studies,* 7(1), 101–114.

McCormick, N. B. (1994). *Sexual salvation.* Westport, CT: Praeger.

Morokoff, P. J. (1988). Sexuality in perimenopausal and postmenopausal women. *Psychology of Women Quarterly, 12,* 489–511.

Morris, J. F., Waldo, C. R., & Rothblum, E. D. (2001). A model of predictors and outcomes of outness among lesbian and bisexual women. *American Journal of Orthopsychiatry, 71,* 61–71.

Nichols, M. (1987). Lesbian sexuality: Issues and developing theory. In Boston Lesbian Psychologies Collective (Ed.), *Lesbian psychologies* (pp. 97–125). Chicago: University of Illinois Press.

Parks, C. A. (1999). Lesbian identity development: An examination of differences across generations. *American Journal of Orthopsychiatry, 69,* 347–361.

Peplau, L. A. (2003). Human sexuality: How do men and women differ? *Current Directions in Psychological Sciences, 12,* 37–40.

Peplau, L. A., & Beals, K. P. (2004). The family lives of lesbians and gay men. In A. L. Vangelisti (Ed.), *Handbook of family communications* (pp. 233–248). Mahwah, NJ: Erlbaum.

Peplau, L. A., Cochran, S. D., & Mays, V. M. (1997). A national survey of the intimate relationships of African American lesbians and gay men. In B. Greene (Ed.), *Ethnic and cultural diversity among lesbians and gay men* (pp. 11–38). Thousand Oaks, CA: SAGE.

Peplau, L. A., Cochran, S., Rook, K., & Padesky, C. (1978). Loving women: Attachment and autonomy in lesbian relationships. *Journal of Social Issues, 34*(3), 7–27.

Peplau, L. A., & Fingerhut, A. (2004). The paradox of the lesbian worker. *Journal of Social Issues, 60*(4), 719–735.

Peplau, L. A., Fingerhut, A., & Beals, K. P. (2004). Sexuality in the relationships of lesbians and gay men. In J. Harvey, A. Wenzel, & S. Sprecher (Eds.), *Handbook of sexuality in close relationships* (pp. 350–369). Mahwah, NJ: Erlbaum.

Peplau, L. A., & Garnets, L. D. (Eds.). (2002). Women's sexualities: New perspectives on sexual orientation and gender. *Journal of Social Issues, 56*(2).

Raiteri, R., Fora, R., Gopammomo, P., Russo, R., Lucchini, A., Terzi, M. G., Giacobbi, D., & Sinicco, A. (1994). Seroprevalence, risk factors and attitude to HIV-1 in a representative sample of lesbians in Turin. *Genitourinary Medicine, 70,* 200–205.

Raphael, S. M., & Robinson, M. K. (1980). The older lesbian: Love relationships and friendship patterns. *Alternative Lifestyles, 3*(2), 207–229.

Robinson, P. K. (1983). The sociological perspective. In R. B. Weg (Ed.), *Sexuality in the later years: Roles and behavior* (pp. 82–103). New York: Academic Press.

Rose, S. (2003). Community interventions concerning homophobic violence and partner violence against lesbians. *Journal of Lesbian Studies, 7*(4), 125–139.

Rothblum, E. D. (1994a). Lesbians and physical appearance: Which model applies? In B. Greene & G. M. Herek (Eds.), *Lesbian and gay psychology: Theory, research, and clinical applications* (pp. 84–97). Thousand Oaks, CA: SAGE.

Rothblum, E. D. (1994b). Transforming lesbian sexuality. *Psychology of Women Quarterly, 18,* 627–641.

Rothblum, E. D., & Brehony, K. A. (Eds.). (1993). *Boston marriages: Romantic but asexual relationships among contemporary lesbians.* Amherst: University of Massachusetts Press.

Saghir, M. T., & Robins, E. (1973). *Male and female homosexuality: A comprehensive investigation.* Baltimore: Williams & Wilkins.

Sang, B. (1991). Moving towards balance and integration. In B. Sang, J. Warshow, & A. Smith (Eds.), *Lesbians at midlife: The creative transition* (pp. 206–214). San Francisco: Spinsters.

Sang, B. (1993). Existential issues of midlife lesbians. In L. D. Garnets & D. C. Kimmel (Eds.), *Psychological perspectives on lesbian and gay male experiences* (pp. 500–516). New York: Columbia University Press.

Schaefer, S. (1977). Sociosexual behavior in male and female homosexuals. *Archives of Sexual Behavior, 6,* 355–364.

Schreurs, K. M. G. (1993). Sexuality in lesbian couples: The importance of gender. *Annual Review of Sex Research, 4,* 49–66.

Sears, J. T. (1989). The impact of gender and race on growing up lesbian and gay in the South. *National Women's Studies Association Journal, 1,* 422–457.

Solarz, A. L. (Ed.). (1999). *Lesbian health: Current assessment and directions for the future.* Washington, DC: National Academy Press.

Waldner-Haugrud, L. K., & Gratch, L. V. (1997). Sexual coercion in gay/lesbian relationships: Descriptions and gender differences. *Violence and Victims, 12*(1), 87–98.

Waterman, C. K., Dawson, L. J., & Bologna, M. J. (1989). Sexual coercion in gay male and lesbian relationships: Predictors and implications for support services. *The Journal of Sex Research, 26,* 118–124.

Weinberg, M. S., Williams, C. J., & Pryor, D. W. (2001). Bisexuals at midlife: Commitment, salience, and identity. *Journal of Contemporary Ethnography, 30,* 180–208.

Wells, J. W. (1990). The sexual vocabularies of heterosexual and homosexual males and females for communicating erotically with a sexual partner. *Archives of Sexual Behavior, 19,* 139–147.

Winterich, J. A. (2003). Sex, menopause, and culture: Sexual orientation and the meaning of menopause for women's sex lives. *Gender & Society, 17,* 627–642.

# 6

# Gay Men and Aging
## *Sex and Intimacy*

*Edward A. Wierzalis, Bob Barret, Mark Pope, and Michael Rankins*

―――――⟨∞⟩―――――

As a human condition, age parallels the distinctions of gender, race, and sexual orientation. "The beginning of old age is ambiguous and many chronologically *old* people are active sexually, physically, emotionally, and intellectually" (Kimmel, 2000, p. 66). So how does aging affect the context of people's lives, their self-esteem, intimacy, and relationships? What types of relationships will play a part in maintaining a satisfying life as they age? These universal questions present a specific set of challenges and rewards for gay men as they age.

Sexual behavior is an important issue for all boys and men in our society and is subject to a host of societal messages (Pope & Barret, 2002). One does not have to look far to see the overt sexual messages that infuse every aspect of our culture. "Male sexuality in our cultural view is shaped by the scripts boys are offered almost from birth, by the cultural lessons they learn throughout the life course, among them the belief in a sometimes overpowering male sex drive and the belief that men have immutable sexual needs that are manifested over and above individual attempts at repression" (Blumstein & Schwartz, 1990, p. 310). Desirable men appear in the media as strong, aggressive, sexually skillful, athletic, confident, and, above all, young. Regardless of sexual orientation, men have to deal with these images and undoubtedly struggle with their inability to embody all these idealized masculine traits (Pollack, 1998). Depictions of hypermasculinity are particularly visible in the gay male culture and include such images as buffed bodybuilders, men dressed in uniforms or leather, and men who have frequent casual sex. Men who do not personify "machismo" in an attempt to refute the negative stereotype about gay men risk appearing to be effeminate and not "real" men. These social images do not serve aging gay and bisexual men well.

## Gay Men and Aging: An Overview

Over the last three decades several researchers (Adelman, 1990; Berger, 1996; Friend, 1980; Isay, 1996; Kelly, 1977; Kimmel, 1978; Quam, 1993; Pope, 1997) have begun to address aging in the gay male community. Gay men face aging issues similar to those of their heterosexual counterparts, but enough difference exists that discussion of this population's challenges and issues is warranted. "Although the stresses of aging experienced by the gay male are similar to those of the heterosexual male, they are compounded by societal stigmatization of sexual orientation and the emphasis on youth within gay culture. Older gay males face issues of a stigmatized sexual orientation, invisibility related to their sexual orientation, and general negative stereotypes and discrimination regarding aging" (Brown et al., 1997, p. 6). To date, no studies have focused solely on bisexual aging men's sexuality, although several respondents in studies have been bisexual in behavior. Therefore, we cannot shed any light on the sexuality of aging bisexual men in this chapter; however, they undoubtedly share some characteristics with aging gay men as well as with aging heterosexual men.

Discussion of the sexual and intimacy needs of middle-aged and elderly gay men requires an examination of the developmental experiences and issues that shape many of their mental and emotional responses. Generations of gay men emerge into their years as older adults bearing witness to the prejudice and rejection they have known throughout their lives. Although the atmosphere in which gay men, bisexuals, and lesbians live today involves greater visibility, older gay men came out in a climate of severe oppression and stigmatization.

> Homosexuals over the age of 65 [in 1997] were born before 1932 and thus began to formulate their understanding of homosexuality when the stigmatization of homosexuality ... constituted the dominant discourse. This discourse was not significantly challenged until the late 1960s when gay liberation, a "quintessential identity movement" galvanized by the Stonewall rebellion of 1969, topicalized and condemned it, replacing it with a discourse constructing homosexuality as a positive political identity imbuing the homosexual not with stigma, but with status. (Rosenfeld, 1999, p. 122)

This new status imbues life with potential and promise for gay men as they seek intimacy and forge relationships. Now cohorts of gay men are living more openly—many in intimate relationships—offering encouragement to earlier generations of gay men entering midlife and their later adult years. The opportunity exists for a better quality of life for gay and bisexual men as they age because greater understanding of sexual behavior, intimacy, and relationships in later life continues to emerge. Nonetheless, many older gay and bisexual men struggle with the vestiges of stigma and shame that were so evident in their youth. Because of the absence of empirical information on older bisexual men, this chapter focuses on issues of gay men; however, some sexual issues and changes with aging are likely to be parallel.

## Life Span and Identity Development

Developmental issues across the life span of gay men differ from those experienced by heterosexual men in many ways, including the process of coming out. This developmental task challenges gay men on both a personal and societal level throughout their lives. The life course patterns of men exploring their sexual identities and the timing of their coming out contribute to essential differences that are reflected in the composition of their individual lives. As they enter their adult years, gay men possess the historically specific ideologies associated with the period of their coming out. "The adjustment of older gay males and lesbians probably has been shaped by the sociohistorical context in which they came of age" (Cooney & Dunne, 2001, p. 852). This cohort effect is often relevant to physicians, psychologists, counselors, and other clinicians when working with older gay men as they navigate aging and seek to maintain active sexual lives and emotionally intimate relationships.

As they age, gay men must examine the processes engaged in during their lifetime in order to make healthy, satisfying transitions through the developmental tasks associated with growing older. "Gay identity represents an interplay between internal drives and needs and interpersonal socio-systemic interaction and feedback. This varies across individuals, with historical time, culture and ecological circumstance, and within individuals as a function of development and experience" (Wahler & Gabbay, 1997, p. 2). The filters of ethnicity, socioeconomic status, and other unique aspects of individual difference converge to shape the unique experience of being gay, being sexually active, and developing intimate relationships. Research has shown that coming out to oneself is an important developmental stage to accomplish successfully and that it is an important reflection of psychological health. One study of an early cohort, by Weinberg and Williams (1975), found that well-adjusted older gay men had rejected the idea that homosexuality was an illness, had close and supportive associations with other gay men, and were not interested in changing their sexuality.

Because the coming out process can begin at any age, not just adolescence, the energy needed and the stress associated with that process can have different impacts depending on when it occurs. The tasks of self-concept reformation during the coming out process can be overwhelming (Pope & Barret, 2002). For example, it can be common for older gay men who came out when they were substantially past adolescence to have all the problems associated with those of teenagers who have just begun dating. Similarly, sexual or intimacy experiences earlier in life may leave lasting effects on preferences, behaviors, and attitudes toward sexual relationships throughout adulthood. Likewise, family background, parents' marital example, and cultural values often affect mature sexual and relationship beliefs and expectations.

## Cultural Considerations and Aging

Contrary to stereotypes, aging gay men in American society are not all middle-class white men in jeans; they come in many different ages, sizes, colors, and economic classes (Adams & Kimmel, 1997; Pope, 1995; Pope & Barret, 2002). The belief that the typical older gay man is alone and socially disconnected is a myth that reflects the prevailing stigmatizing discourse on aging and gay men. As cultural patterns and values influence developmental experiences, so too does culture color the diverse manner in which men experience aging and express themselves sexually. The gay community cannot be thought of as a single entity but as microcommunities, each including people with a variety of body types, ages, abilities, disabilities, and social and economic privileges (similar to that which exists within the nongay community); this diversity contributes to the decisions gay men make as they experience aging and seek physical intimacy and sex. Gay men entering middle to late life can be influenced by age-related changes both physically and socially and consequently may be accepting and open to more individuals regardless of age, color, and social and economic status. Within the larger gay male population many organizations exist that promote interaction between older gay men and minority individuals.

## Identity and Intimacy

Even though sexual experimentation is often associated with gay men, the desire in middle to late life to experience both emotional and physical intimacy
does not diminish (Pope & Schulz, 1990). Sexual activity in various forms remains an important part of gay men's lives as they move into middle to late life.
Studies by Pope and Schulz (1990), Gray and Dressel (1985), and Berger (1982)
reported that gay men between the ages of 40 and 80 remained sexually active
and were "somewhat or very satisfied" with their sex lives. Some respondents
in Kimmel's (1978) study reported that sexual pleasure was greater than when
they were younger.

Intimate relationships vary widely within the gay community. Gay men often find intimacy with a significant other elusive. The gay community plays an
important role in supporting an environment of acceptance for relationships
within a group of friends as well as between two individuals. Whether or not
a gay man has sex does not change his self-identified sexual orientation; he is
still gay. Money (1990) suggests that falling in love is the definitive criterion of
sexual orientation and thus sexual identity. A gay man experiencing a sexually
intimate relationship with another man confirms his being gay. Gay men can be
abandoned by family and friends, scorned by society, and unsure that they want
to belong in gay society. Therefore, the importance of intimacy through sexual
activity becomes a validating experience, especially when one feels rejected on
many other social dimensions. Thus sexual intimacy, love, and personal identity may merge for gay men in ways that differ from the experiences of bisexual
or heterosexual men. "Sexuality is more than what we do; it is who we are"
(Driggs & Finn, 1991, p. 79), and many gay men clarify their homosexual status
within the boundaries of sexual expression.

Finding a partner with whom to share intimacy on a physical, emotional,
and spiritual level often can be a significant developmental experience that both
encourages and reflects greater self-acceptance. "How to have a satisfying long-
term relationship and what the role of sex is in that relationship is the primary
sexuality issue that adult gay men must address" (Pope & Barret, 2002, p. 163).
Partnership and sexual intimacy play a vital role in making aging transitions less
isolating and burdensome to help gay men through this aspect of their developmental journey. The types and forms of long-term relationships in the lives
of older gay men are not limited to domestic partners who share a home and a
bank account. Bonds of intimacy and sexuality may stretch across continents,

long periods of separation, and seemingly independent living arrangements. These bonds may be maintained with several intimate friends. They may or may not involve physical sexual activities currently or in the past.

## Dyadic Long-Term Relationships

Rankins and Pope (2000) reported that many lesbians and gay men are in committed, long-term relationships, often taking on many responsibilities associated with civil marriage. Unlike legally married people, however, lesbian and gay men cannot share in the economic and legal benefits of civil marriage. Rights that married people take for granted, such as the ability to visit a sick or injured spouse in the hospital, can be denied to same-sex spouses (see chapter 11, this volume). It can be difficult for gay men when their committed relationships are not recognized, or not fully recognized, under the law. "Our culture does not take gay relationships seriously—when they're considered at all" (Kaufman & Raphael, 1996, p. 187).

Recently there has been a determined effort to validate same-sex relationships as more gay men and lesbians seek to solidify and legitimatize a significant relationship for life. Participation in public commitment ceremonies and recognized unions and, for some, access to same-sex partner benefits are experiences unavailable to earlier cohorts that may ultimately affect late life well-being (Hostetler & Cohler, 1997). The availability of same-sex marriage in Canada and some other countries, civil unions, domestic partnerships in the United States, and an emerging marriage rights movement may allow many gay men to find themselves in a legal relationship for the first time in their lives. There is not adequate information yet to detail how the legalization of same-sex relationships might affect later life. As society continues to negotiate the legalization of same-sex relationships, gay men and lesbians will continue to partner for life, maintaining loving and intimate relationships and possibly divorcing as well.

Several surveys (Bell & Weinberg, 1978; Harry, 1984; Kurdek & Schmitt, 1986) found that 40–60% of gay men are involved in a steady romantic relationship. And, contrary to popular reports, both lesbians and gay men form long-lasting cohabiting relationships (Herek, 1991; Peplau, 1991). Men in long-term relationships are part of an increasing number of lesbians and gay men creating families through foster care, surrogacy, insemination, and adoption. Despite the social stigma and lack of social support, gay men establish close relationships without the consensual norms provided to heterosexual couples through the course of their development and socialization. The challenges for gay men in long-term relationships can be formidable within a mainstream society that does not acknowledge their experiences and needs. Gay men in long-term relationships "begin not only with a mutual understanding of their own gender but also with a shared knowledge of their own often similar struggle to come to terms with their difference" (Sullivan, 1998, p. 152). Thus there is opportunity within this shared experience for gay men at any age to forge the bonds of healthy, long-term relationships.

## Aging, Sexuality, and Physical Attractiveness

Gay men have to struggle in a unique way with the physical changes of aging. The "majority of negatives around aging involve the body.... . Gay men are deeply invested in their bodies, and many feel that their body is their best asset—not only for sex, but for feelings of attractiveness, power, and success" (Kooden & Flowers, 2000, p. 28). As an oppressed group, gay men seek means by which they can feel acceptance and pride. Physical attractiveness and sexual activity become the means by which "gay men tend to commodify their bodies like so many packages of meat" (p. 28). Upon entering their middle to late adult years, gay men can be confronted by a loss of social valuation as physical and sexual changes affect what has been a source of self-esteem. "By assigning so much value to the one thing that is most negatively affected by aging, many gay men are setting themselves up for a horrible experience ... when their bodies begin to change" (p. 29). Gay men experience many of the same changes that occur for nongay men as age influences their sexual functioning. "For example, slower and less firm erections result from a variety of factors, both psychosocial and physical; the sense of impending ejaculation tends to disappear; and the need for ejaculation at each sexual occasion is reduced" (Kimmel & Sang, 1995, p. 206). These changes in no way eliminate the need and desire for physical intimacy with another man. Recent pharmaceutical products can even provide erectile functioning seldom seen in young men.

## Intimacy Versus Loneliness

The dialectic between being attached to one or more intimate partners and feeling isolated and alone is all too often a developmental issue. Psychologists, counselors, and other clinicians see gay male clients who are confronting issues of aging across the life span. The following are some short clinical examples. (The names of the men have been changed in this section and the sections that follow.)

- Jeff, 30 and prematurely balding, experiences anxiety attacks related to his fear of dying alone. "If I don't find a partner in the next 3 years, I will be single for the rest of my life! No one will want me when I am totally bald!"
- Mike talks about being trapped in a relationship that has run its course. "I would leave in a second if I were 35, but at 48, I would just be alone and miserable. Who wants a 48-year-old man today?"
- John, 80, reminisces about his life with a partner of 40 years. "We had great years together, and I miss him terribly. His death was awful, and the loneliness that followed was not easy. But today I still have a great life. Recently I moved into a progressive care facility. Most of the people there are straight and I have not come out to them, but they are becoming good friends and I hope one day I can tell them about my life. Actually for the first time in my life I have a girl friend. We hug and sometimes kiss but that's about it. Her attention helps me not feel so lonely."

Certainly some gay men find a partner for life or a group they embrace as "chosen family," lessening isolation and separateness. The experiences associated with rejection by family, peers, and society may foster a long-established behavior and attitude of withdrawal, causing some gay men to be alone in their late adult years. Single and coupled older gay men may find themselves caught in a tension between their need for sex and their need for other kinds of intimacy. "Some gay men seek intimacy in different relationships from those in which they seek sex, whereas other gay men look for both sex and intimacy in the same relationship" (Kaufman & Raphael, 1996, p. 93). The need for support and insight during these years in their adult life is paramount in helping gay men form healthy and sexual fulfilling relationships with other men. Caregivers and clinicians will have an important role to play in this matter, as the following clinical perspectives demonstrate.

Intimacy and loneliness are common themes that underlie many of the issues brought by clients. Older gay men engage these issues with a poignancy that is often touching. Rueben, who came out in his 40s, initially presented as a lonely and discouraged 55-year-old. Since he had come out, he had had only two relationships that lasted for any length of time, and he had been alone for the past 3 years. "I don't know what to do. Most of my friends are in relationships, and I get tired of hanging out with them. The few gay men I know my own age either want to hang out in bars and clubs or just sit at home alone. Neither of those options interests me." Encouraged to find gay organizations where his volunteer time would be valued, he began to change his life. "When I first went to the community center, I felt like a useless old man with a body that would not interest anyone. But you know what? All of a sudden these young guys were coming around, and I began to realize they were hitting on me! When one got bold enough to ask me to go to lunch with him, I began to find out about a whole new culture, one that I did not know existed. These bars that cater to older men and young men who are interested in them are new to me. There are organizations and even cruises geared to increasing the interaction between older men and those who are attracted to them. I even have been asked to pose naked in a magazine that features older gay men! What a life I have discovered! Every now and then I stop and ask myself if this is a good thing for someone like me to be doing, but I can't see the harm in it and I am having a great time. Right now I am dating a 35-year-old, and we are talking about moving in together. And I see the same thing going on with men in their 60s and even 70s. I am beginning to see that I have some fine years ahead of me; my life is not over, not by a long shot."

The idea of joining the "Daddy" culture may not appeal to all older gay men, but there are many venues within gay subcultures where the wisdom and experience of older gay men is honored. Local Bear and Leather clubs often provide groups that can meet some of the belonging needs of all gay men, but particularly older gay men who may need the availability of planned social events and outings to encourage then to get out and avoid isolation. Other organizations such as Primetimers and Services and Advocacy for GLBT Elders (SAGE) also create activities that allow older gay men to find more relationships. Helping clients find these subcultures may require the psychologist to do some of the investigatory work and even to advocate with gay organizations to set up services and activities for seniors.

The advent of Internet chat rooms enables all gay men, but particularly older gay men, to make contact with other men around the world. Although some fear the real danger of the addictive potential of Internet chat, others are finding men they never would have met and creating unique kinds of relationships that, though limited, offer companionship and intimacy. There are dangers of exploitation in these relationships, and clinicians may need to explore the extent of involvement and caution the client about being alert for signals that they are being used. Naturally, the same potential exists in local, face-to-face relationships, but the danger is greater in a medium that allows people to present themselves in whatever package they choose.

Many older gay clients, including those in relationships, find themselves more focused on emotional intimacy and less concerned with sexual performance. Miguel, whose partner died after a 25-year relationship, made this comment about dating and sexual activity: "I have been dating a few men, some of them younger than me. And I have discovered that simply lying with them and kissing and touching each other is so much more important than getting off. I love the unhurried way we just hold each other." Clients speak of their appreciation of others and their growing awareness of what each person brings to their relationship. One client spoke of his growing awareness of the richness of his life. "I have come to value friendship above all else. Even my partner is most precious to me because of the friendship we share. We still get in bed naked, hold each other, and talk about our lives together. He means so much more to me now than he did when we were younger. I guess we have learned to overlook each others' faults and to really value each other in what seems so very wonderful."

Sexual activity may increase or decrease as men age. Although sexual performance may subside, the range of erotic fantasy can extend and enliven. For older gay men, the availability of sex continues to be a source of pleasure for many. For those who want and can afford them, prescription drugs can promote erections and prolonged sexual activity. Some older gay men find themselves more sexually active and engaged in their 50s and 60s than when they were younger because they have more free time, less stressful lives, and more self-acceptance. Although age may limit the number of men attracted to them, older men can continue to be successful in finding sex partners if they seek them out. Henry, at 83, was surprised when he was "hit on" in a gay bar. "That has not happened to me in a long time, and we had a great time together. Part of what really turned him on was my body! I would never have believed that was possible, but it happened. And I have yet another memory for reflection and a cause for hope that this might happen again sometime."

## Sexual Activity and the Older Gay Man

There is much research on the sexuality of older adults (Brecher, 1984; Bulcroft & O'Connor, 1986; Cooney & Dunne, 2001; Kimmel, 1990; Thompson, 1994).

Middle-aged and older gay men are represented in this discourse to identify their specific characteristics and concerns about aging, sex, and intimacy issues (Adelman, 1990; Dorfman et al., 1995; Kimmel & Sang, 1995; Pope, 1997; Pope & Schulz, 1990).

Studies that have been conducted by Kimmel (1977) and Pope and Schulz (1990) confirm the presence of sexual activity and even the increase in that activity among gay men as they enter middle to late adult years. In the Pope and Schulz sample, respondents indicated both the desire for and the ability to function in sexual situations. Kimmel's subjects pointed out some of the advantages in aging for the gay man, such as more focus on the other person and less on orgasm itself, more relaxed and satisfying sexual interactions, and less frequent but more satisfying activities. Driggs and Finn (1991, p. 79) recommend the view that "sexuality is a lifelong process involving feelings, fantasies, and behaviors that promotes an adaptive, pleasurable, and competent use of your body to experience affection and intimacy and to build personal identity." Thus an active sex life for the older gay man supports their continual development of healthy sexual identities and more satisfying relationships in later life. Gay men share an interest in making sure each partner is sexually pleasured in an intimate relationship and have a greater degree of verbal and nonverbal communication during lovemaking. This characteristic helps define the unique nature of gay relationships, leading to greater satisfaction for gay men as they develop supportive relationships in later life.

Having satisfying long-term relationships and determining what role sex will play in those relationships are issues to be dealt with by gay men at all ages. Gay men seek to satisfy their need to feel some connection, even if through casual sex (Wierzalis, 2001). Maintaining the health and sexual vitality of a primary relationship is a challenge especially for gay men in long-term relationships. Gay men who have no single formal and committed relationship may exercise options such as short- or long-term sexual friendships, seeking partners in social activities or bars, paying other man for sex, and using the Internet to find intimacy. Almost all men also masturbate to exercise or relieve their sexual needs.

Older gay men who hold to the idea that the physical changes in their body lessen physical attractiveness and desirability will be distressed by the aging experience. Clinicians and other mental health professionals working with such men can encourage them to seek new ways, possibly erotic massage, to continue to experience their body's sexual potential. Creative clinicians can encourage older gay men who seek both sexual and relationship outlets by learning about the community resources, becoming advocates for older gay men, and embracing their own aging with excitement and vigor. Knowing that relationship potential exists everywhere and living one's own life in that belief empower the clinician in offering the older gay man a perspective that can be a springboard to a fuller life. This perspective can even be important in the face of chronic illness or significant losses that can make aging appear to be years of decline and despair.

Assessing gay identity development and determining the stage a client is in can be important in sensitively and effectively addressing client issues. This is especially true for older gay men who may have delayed or avoided the developmental tasks associated with adopting a positive identity. Confusion or lack of self-acceptance compounds the intimacy, relationship, sexual activity, and aging concerns an older gay man will want to address. For example, the client may be expecting more tolerance for ambiguity in his social presentation of self, whereas the clinician is expecting more integration of identity into all aspects of the client's life, especially at this life stage. Lower levels of self-esteem are associated with the first stages of identity formation and higher levels with acceptance of self at the later stages. Berger (1996) found that those who were less satisfied with their gay identity had more psychosomatic complaints than those who were more satisfied. Older gay men can present with physical complaints that can impede their sexual functioning, and these complaints can stem from an unresolved and complicated sexual identity.

## Sexually Transmitted Diseases and Older Gay Men

Any discussion on sexual activity and intimacy needs must include a discussion of the impact of sexually transmitted disease (STD) and HIV. Life has changed dramatically for all gay men since the beginning of the AIDS pandemic (Pope & Barret, 2002). The spread of AIDS may have led to different lifestyle choices and approaches to partnering and may even have affected social support (Cooney & Dunne, 2001, p. 852). Many gay men have lost life partners, lovers, friends, extended family members, mentors, and role models. The gay community has been devastated by these losses. Older gay men are as vulnerable today to STD and HIV infection as any in the cohort of gay men. Those who seek intimacy through unprotected sex face the potential for infection. "Wanting to be intimate and wanting to be loved are powerful forces driving some gay men to relate at any cost" (Wierzalis, 2001, p. 202). Gay men who deny the risk of HIV can choose to engage in unsafe sex with multiple and sometimes anonymous partners. If they react with fear to HIV, they may be obsessed with the risk involved in sex and opt for total abstinence. The practice of "total safe sex" or "safer sex" may include a condom for oral sex, rubber gloves during mutual masturbation, and no deep kissing. This practice may prove less satisfying, leaving the man distressed and unfulfilled but unlikely to contract HIV or another STD. There are also other ways to interpret the practice of safer sex that can provide for creative and satisfying sexual activity. At this time in the United States, safer gay male sex typically means use of a condom for anal sex unless both partners have tested negative for HIV and have both used condoms for anal or vaginal sex (if practiced) for at least the past 6 months. If one partner is HIV positive, however, more protection may be desired and is appropriate.

Older gay men may have experienced the loss of many friends in their peer group to AIDS, possibly resulting in complicated bereavement, anger, depression, and survivor's guilt as they continue to explore issues of intimacy and sexual activity. They juggle aging, sexuality, loss, intimacy, and relationship issues, all from their perspective of being gay. Clinicians and other caregivers can play an important role in helping older gay men maintain vibrant and satisfying sexual lives by overcoming such irrational denial or fear of HIV. Those who come out late in life and many others seeking sexual intimacy need support and accurate information about the presence of STD and HIV. "Sex is an integral part of most clients' lives. Our task is to enable them not only to have safer sex but also to have great sex" (Kain, 1996, p. 61). Support groups and friendship networks can provide creative and alternative ways for clients to explore sexual experiences in a responsible and safe yet satisfying manner.

Other health issues may affect sexual interest or performance, and it is best to discuss the details openly with a supportive health care provider who has a positive attitude about sexuality and about gay male relationships. Depression can affect libido, which can also be one sign of this common mental health problem; usually depression can be treated satisfactorily. Chronic pulmonary diseases can affect the ability to engage in many activities, including sexuality; adjustments in sexual behavior, the support of a partner, and available oxygen nearby may relieve anxiety and allow sexual satisfaction. Diabetes, surgery for prostate problems, and other conditions can affect erections and may require creative sexual solutions that can provide satisfaction without erections or even without an orgasm. Finally, erectile difficulty may reflect cardiovascular health and should be discussed with a physician because it could be an early warning sign of more serious health problems, which may be manageable with exercise or medication.

Medications to correct mental health and physical health problems can also affect sexual interest and performance. Some (but not all) antidepressant medications suppress sexual function, which typically is not a positive side effect for sexually active men (excepting those who experience premature ejaculation). Increases in sexual activity or the precursors to such activity can be seen as a positive behavioral response to improvements in the man's emotional and physical health.

The choice of appropriate sexual behavior for each client may be different. Autoerotic behavior (masturbation) may be fulfilling for many men, but others want physical intimacy or sex with a partner. Some men prefer the use of sexual toys, multiple partners, bondage activities, erotic role playing, or various sadomasochistic scenarios.

Encouraging physical exercise, social activities, and artistic outlets might also be useful for those who are less inclined to overtly meet their sexual needs. In this case, the goal is to channel sexual energy into creative activities (similar to the psychodynamic defense mechanism of sublimation). Such activities might include painting, sculpting, writing, gardening, walking, weight lifting, and other pursuits.

Many of the problems associated with aging affect gay and nongay people equally. Depending on the client's illness (e.g., arthritis, cardiovascular disease, pulmonary disease) and the type of sexual behaviors in which he engages (e.g., oral sex, anal sex, masturbation), the clinician may want to recommend ways in which the client could increase flexibility, muscle tone, and strength or modify his sexual behaviors in order to maintain an active sex life. As they age, gay men need to know that an erotic life is part of human life and is not limited to the young and fit.

## Recommendations

In this chapter, issues of sex and intimacy that aging gay men confront in their daily lives were discussed. The issues we have looked at span a broad range of years in a man's life including those in which he is healthy and independent as well as those in which he may be frail and live in a health care facility. The recommendations presented here attempt to address the full range of such issues.

### *Nonjudgmental Approach*

Clinicians are encouraged to address the problems facing aging gay men in a matter-of-fact, nonjudgmental manner. When addressing any sexual issue with gay men, clinicians are encouraged to be comfortable themselves in talking about sexual behavior and sexual orientation. It is important to be straightforward and nonjudgmental in tone and behavior. Gay clients will be particularly attuned to the nuances of how such issues are presented. They will be sensitive to signs of discomfort, hesitancy, or disapproval in voice or manner. This is particularly true for older gay men because almost all have experienced some form of discomfort and even hostility around their sexual orientation. Likewise, the clinician may be uncomfortable speaking about sex with a man of advanced years, who may be stereotyped as too old for sex.

Even a simple statement such as "Are you married?" indicates an assumption that all people are heterosexual because marriage is limited in almost all U.S. jurisdictions to opposite-sex couples. A better phrasing is, "Do you have a companion or sexual partner?" It is important not to assume that all clients are heterosexual because that assumption can be reflected in communication, both verbal and nonverbal, to the client. Such communication can cause gay male clients not to trust the clinician as readily, which sets up a dynamic that is difficult to correct later.

Another important communication issue is the use of the current phrases. For example, there is a difference between the terms "sexual orientation" and "sexual preference." "Sexual orientation" is generally seen as a less negative term. "Sexual preference" implies choice, and many LGBT clients don't see their identity as a choice, whereas the term "sexual orientation" often is seen as referencing an innate identity.

## Assessment of Identity Stage

Clinicians are encouraged to assess clients for their gay identity development stage. The assessment of the identity stage is important in addressing the client's issues more sensitively and effectively. This is especially true for older gay men, who may have delayed or avoided the developmental tasks associated with adopting a positive identity.

## Awareness of Culture and Resources

Clinicians are encouraged to be aware of the gay male culture and the local and national institutions that can help gay clients. Clinicians demonstrating an awareness of the gay culture are more easily trusted and accepted. It is important to be aware of the sociopolitical issues, specific knowledge related to aging within the culture, necessary information to help the client make informed choices about care and retirement, institutional barriers that confront older gay men, and ways to meet intimacy and relational needs within the gay community. Clinicians need to appreciate the history, culture, ethics, and sense of community that define the older gay male client (Pope, 1995).

## Awareness of Heterosexism and Discrimination

Clinicians are encouraged to be aware of the heterosexism and discrimination that aging gay men face. The special needs of this cultural minority arise partly from the oppression and discrimination that have helped define the gay community. Issues include the lack of civil rights, secret or semisecret lives, rejection or ostracism by families of origin, societal censure, lowered self-esteem caused by internalized homophobia, the fear and reality of physical violence, and campaigns of hatred and vilification by right-wing political groups and fundamentalist religious groups (Cooper, 1989). Sensitivity to this discrimination and the concomitant special needs will be rewarded with higher levels of trust and openness from the client.

## Positive Attitude Toward Sexuality

Clinicians are encouraged to see sexual activity for the aging gay man as positive. Sexual activity should be seen as facilitative, an aid to better emotional and physical health, not as something bad and negative. Gay men are sexual throughout their lives (Berger, 1996; Kelly, 1977; Pope & Schulz, 1990; Vacha, 1985), which may be a direct result of their socialization into the dominant male sex role in the United States. It may also be a result of the particular institutions in the gay male subculture, such as bars and other gay-related social venues, which foster these attitudes and provide a testing ground for their concomitant behavior. Even older gay men who are hospitalized or institutionalized may want some level of sexual activity with other men or with themselves. If clinicians think of an aging gay man as asexual, they may not discuss sexual behaviors and healthy relationships with the client and thus fail to provide appropriate care and information on infectious diseases and other conditions that might affect his sexual response, function, or relationships.

## Flexibility

Clinicians are encouraged to be flexible in understanding the types of sexual behaviors gay male clients choose for themselves. The choice of appropriate sexual behavior for each client may be different, and the clinician's role is to be flexible in regard to helping older gay men express themselves sexually.

## *Awareness of Emotional Health*

Clinicians are encouraged to recognize that depression and other health issues may affect sexual interest or performance and to offer to discuss the details with their clients or patients. More satisfying sexual activity or interest often can be noted as a positive behavioral response to improvements in the client's emotional and physical health.

# Conclusion

Many of the problems associated with aging affect all older men, regardless of sexual orientation. For a gay man, depending on the presenting problem and the sexual behaviors in which he engages, there are many clinical recommendations that can help him maintain an active sex life. Intimacy, sex, and significant relationships are long-term goals that start earlier in one's life and continue into old age.

REFERENCES

Adams, C. L. Jr., & Kimmel, D. C. (1997). Exploring the lives of older African American gay men. In B. Greene (Ed.), *Ethnic and cultural diversity among lesbians and gay men* (pp. 132–151). Thousand Oaks, CA: SAGE.

Adelman, M. (1990). Stigma, gay lifestyles, and adjustment to aging. A study of later-life gay men and lesbians. *Journal of Homosexuality, 20*(3–4), 7–32.

Bell, A. P., & Weinberg, M. S. (1978). *Homosexualities: A study of diversity among men and women.* New York: Simon & Schuster.

Berger, R. M. (1982). Psychological adaptation of the older homosexual male. *Journal of Homosexuality, 5*(3), 161–175.

Berger, R. M. (1996). *Gay and gray: The older homosexual man* (2nd ed.). Boston: Alyson.

Blumstein, P., & Schwartz, P. (1990). Intimate relationships and the creation of sexuality. In D. P. McWhirter & S. A. Sanders (Eds.), *Homosexuality/heterosexuality: Concepts of sexual orientation* (pp. 307–320). New York: Oxford University Press.

Brecher, E. M. (1984). *Love, sex, and aging.* Boston: Little, Brown.

Brown, L. B., Sarosy, S. G., Cook, T. C., & Quarto, J. G. (1997). *Gay men and aging.* New York: Garland.

Bulcroft, K., & O'Connor, M. (1986). The importance of dating relationships on quality of life for older persons. *Family Relationships, 35,* 397–401.

Cooney, T. M., & Dunne, K. (2001). Intimate relationships in later life: Current realities, future prospects. *Journal of Family Issues, 22,* 838–858.

Cooper, C. (1989, April). Social oppressions experienced by gays and lesbians. In P. Griffin & J. Genasce (Eds.), *Strategies for addressing homophobia in physical education, sports, and dance*. Workshop presented at the annual convention of the American Alliance for Health, Physical Education, Recreation, and Dance, Boston.

Dorfman, R., Walters, K., Burke, P., Hardin, L., Karanik, T., & Sliverstein, E. (1995). Old, sad, and alone: The myth of the aging homosexual. *Journal of Gerontological Social Work, 24*(1–2), 29–44.

Driggs, J. H., & Finn, S. E. (1991). *Intimacy between men*. New York: Plume/Penguin.

Friend, R. A. (1980). GAYging: Adjustment and the older gay male. *Alternative Lifestyles, 3*, 231–248.

Gray, H., & Dressel, P. (1985). Alternative interpretations of aging among gay males. *The Gerontologist, 25*, 83–87.

Harry, J. (1984). *Gay couples*. New York: Praeger.

Herek, G. M. (1991). Myths about sexual orientation: A lawyer's guide to social science research. *Law and Sexuality, 1*, 133–172.

Hostetler, A. J., & Cohler, B. J. (1997). Partnership, singlehood, and the lesbian and gay life course: A study in Chicago. *Journal of Gay, Lesbian, and Bisexual Identity, 2*, 199–230.

Isay, R. A. (1996). *Becoming gay: The journey to self-acceptance*. New York: Pantheon.

Kain, C. D. (1996). *Positive HIV affirmative counseling*. Alexandria, VA: American Counseling Association.

Kaufman, G., & Raphael, L. (1996). *Coming out of shame: Transforming gay and lesbian lives*. New York: Doubleday.

Kelly, J. (1977). The aging male homosexual: Myth and reality. *Gerontologist, 17*, 328–332.

Kimmel, D. C. (1977, November). Patterns of aging among gay men. *Christopher Street*, 28–31.

Kimmel, D. C. (1978). Adult development and aging: A gay perspective. *Journal of Social Issues, 34*(3), 113–130.

Kimmel, D. C. (1990). *Adulthood and aging*. New York: Wiley.

Kimmel, D. C. (2000). Including sexual orientation in life span developmental psychology. In B. Greene & G. L. Croom (Eds.), *Education, research, and practice in lesbian, gay, bisexual, and transgendered psychology: A research manual* (pp. 59–73). Thousand Oaks, CA: SAGE.

Kimmel, D. C., & Sang, B. E. (1995). Lesbians and gay men in midlife. In A. R. D'Augelli & C. A. Patterson (Eds.), *Lesbian, gay, and bisexual identities over the lifespan: Psychological perspectives* (pp. 190–224). New York: Oxford University Press.

Kooden, H., & Flowers, C. (2000). *Golden men: The power of gay midlife*. New York: HarperCollins.

Kurdek, L. A., & Schmitt, J. P. (1986). Relationship quality of gay men in closed or open relationships. *Journal of Homosexuality, 12*(2), 85–99.

Money, J. (1990). Agenda and credenda of the Kinsey scale. In D. P. McWhirter, S. A. Sanders, & J. M. Reinisch (Eds.), *Homosexuality/heterosexuality: Concepts of sexual orientation* (pp. 41–60). New York: Oxford University Press.

Peplau, L. A. (1991). Lesbian and gay relationships. In J. C. Gonsiorek & J. D. Weinrich (Eds.), *Homosexuality: Research implications for public policy* (pp. 177–196). Newbury Park, CA: SAGE.

Pollack, W. (1998). *Real boys: Rescuing our sons from the myths of boyhood.* New York: Random House.

Pope, M. (1995). The "salad bowl" is big enough for us all: An argument for inclusion of lesbians and gays in any definition of multiculturalism. *Journal of Counseling & Development, 73,* 301–304.

Pope, M. (1997). Sexual issues for elderly lesbians and gays. *Topics in Geriatric Rehabilitation, 12*(4), 53–60.

Pope, M., & Barret, B. (2002). Counseling gay men toward an integrated sexuality. In L. D. Burlew & D. Capuzzi (Eds.), *Sexuality counseling* (pp. 149–176). Hauppauge, NY: Nova Science Publishers.

Pope, M., & Schulz, R. (1990). Sexual behavior and attitudes in midlife and aging homosexual males. *Journal of Homosexuality, 20*(3–4), 169–178.

Quam, J. K. (1993, June/July). Gay and lesbian aging. *SEICUS Report,* 14–22.

Rankins, M., & Pope, M. (2000, August). *Gay and lesbian marriage: The coming dawn.* Poster presentation at the annual convention of the American Psychological Association, Washington, DC.

Rosenfeld, D. (1999). Identity work among lesbian and gay elderly. *Journal of Aging Studies, 13*(2), 121–144.

Sullivan, A. (1998). *Love undetectable: Notes on friendship, sex, and survival.* New York: Knopf.

Thompson, E. H. Jr. (1994). Older men as invisible men in contemporary society. In E. H. Thompson (Ed.), *Older men's lives* (pp. 1–21). Thousand Oaks, CA: SAGE.

Vacha, K. (1985). *Quiet fire: Memoirs of older gay men.* Trumansburg, NY: Crossing Press.

Wahler, J., & Gabbay, S. (1997). Gay male aging: A review of the literature. *Journal of Gay and Lesbian Social Services, 6*(3), 1–20.

Weinberg, M. S., & Williams, C. S. (1975). *Male homosexuals: Their problems and adaptations.* London: Oxford University Press.

Wierzalis, E. A. (2001). *Gay men and experiences with aging.* Unpublished doctoral dissertation, University of Virginia, Charlottesville.

# 7

# The Victimization of Older LGBT Adults
## Patterns, Impact, and Implications for Intervention
### Kimberly F. Balsam and Anthony R. D'Augelli

*T*his chapter focuses on the prevalence, impact, and treatment implications of victimization in the lives of older lesbian, gay, bisexual, and transgender (LGBT) people. Very little empirical research has been conducted specifically on this topic. Therefore we review the research literature on victimization of LGBT adults and discuss how it applies to older LGBT adults. Integrating research findings with theoretical and clinical perspectives, we conclude with suggestions for health and mental health care providers who work with older LGBT adults.

## Trauma and Victimization

Throughout history, traumatic events have been an inevitable part of the human experience. Only recently have the mental health fields acknowledged the impact of traumatic events on psychological well-being. The inclusion of the diagnosis Post-Traumatic Stress Disorder (PTSD) in the *Diagnostic and Statistical Manual of Mental Disorders, Third Edition* (*DSM–III*; American Psychiatric Association, 1980) provided an official diagnostic label for the psychological sequelae of serious trauma. The diagnosis of PTSD reflects the understanding that exogenous factors can have a highly detrimental impact on individual functioning. In addition, the impact of trauma can result in symptomatic or presyndromal reactions that can be assessed not only in diagnostic, dichotomous terms but also on a continuum of traumatic symptoms (Saunders, Arata, & Kilpatrick, 1990). Recent literature has made the distinction between traumatic events in general and victimization as a specific subtype. Finkelhor and Kendall-Tackett (1997, p. 2) define victimization as "harms that occur to individuals because of other human actors behaving in ways that violate social norms." When another person is the precipitant of the trauma, the victim's psychological response has interpersonal meaning. For example, if a frail older man is physically beaten by his son, his perception of his closeness to family and his vulnerability are likely to change more than if he were hurt by an accidental fall. If an elderly woman is sexually assaulted by someone in her neighborhood, her trust in others living nearby, and her feelings of safety in her neighborhood might be more seriously diminished than if the same event occurred elsewhere.

These examples underscore the importance of considering the impact of victimization on older adults, a topic given increasing attention in the gerontological literature. Victimization of older people, often called elder abuse, can include physical abuse, sexual abuse, emotional or psychological abuse, financial or material exploitation, abandonment, neglect, and self-neglect (in which a mentally competent older adult behaves in ways that jeopardize his or her health) (Wilber & McNeilly, 2001). Although elder abuse typically is thought to be a widespread phenomenon in the United States, there is little consensus among researchers and policymakers on the scope of the problem. This lack of clarity is caused by a number of factors, ranging from the lack of a standard definition of elder abuse to the methodological difficulties inherent in studying a largely hidden phenomenon (Hafemeister, 2003). Indeed, the National Center on Elder Abuse (1998) estimated that for every reported incident of elder abuse or neglect, approximately five incidents were not reported. A 1991 report by the House Select Committee on Aging concluded that between 1 and 2 million older adults are the victims of elder abuse annually (U.S. Congress, 1991). Using 1996 data, the National Elder Abuse Study estimated that approximately 500,000 older adults in domestic settings alone were abused or neglected during that year (National Center on Elder Abuse, 1998). Other researchers have estimated that about 3–4% of the older adult population has been abused or neglected (Fulmer et al., 1999; Pillemer & Finkelhor, 1988). Many of these incidents were perpetrated by spouses or domestic partners or by adult children with whom the victims lived (Pillemer & Finkelhor, 1988). Elder abuse in nursing homes and other institutional settings has also been documented (Pillemer & Moore, 1989).

Although there have been many studies of risk factors associated with victimization of older adults, traditional gerontological research on elder abuse and victimization has never focused on the sexual orientation of the victim. Indeed, victimization based on sexual orientation is an additional form of elder abuse than can occur simultaneously with other types of elder abuse. For instance, an older lesbian can be maltreated by her adult children because of her sexual orientation and can also be mugged by someone unaware of her sexual orientation. This "add-on" quality of victimization of older adults because of their sexual orientation parallels similar phenomena experienced by other LGBT populations, such as adolescents (D'Augelli et al., 1998).

A robust body of empirical research has examined the prevalence and impact of interpersonal victimization in the general U.S. population (Kaniasty & Norris, 1992). Victimization has been linked to a wide range of mental health problems such as PTSD, depression, anxiety, substance abuse, anger problems, and eating disorders (e.g., Simon et al., 2002). In addition, victimization experiences can influence self-image, leaving a person feeling powerless or worthless. Because of the interpersonal nature of victimization, people who have experienced victimization may experience difficulties in relationships with others. These people may also be at greater risk for future victimization (Arata, 2002; Banyard, Arnold, & Smith, 2000). Repeated or multiple simultaneous victimization experiences have been associated with more psychological symptoms than single experiences (Follette et al., 1996; Messman-Moore, Long, & Siegfried, 2000).

## Victimization of LGBT People

Research on victimization historically has focused largely on violence perpetrated against females by males without consideration of the sexual orientations of victims and assailants. More recently, researchers have turned their attention to violence against lesbians, gay men, and bisexuals, both adults (Herek, 1995) and youth (Rivers & D'Augelli, 2001). A few studies have also examined victimization among transgendered adults (Lombardi et al. 2001) and transgendered youth (Grossman & D'Augelli, in press-b). LGBT people have been found to be at greater risk for victimization over the life span than heterosexual women and men (Balsam, Rothblum, & Beauchaine, 2005; Corliss, Cochran, & Mays, 2002; Tjaden, Thoeness, & Allison, 1999). This difference has also been found in retrospective reports of childhood physical and verbal abuse by parents or caretakers (Corliss, Cochran, & Mays, 2002). Higher rates of childhood sexual abuse have also been found among LGBT people than among heterosexual people (Balsam, Rothblum, & Beauchaine, 2005; Tomeo et al., 2001). The risk of sexual victimization of LGBT youth continues into adulthood, and LGBT adults, particularly men, report higher rates of sexual assault or rape than heterosexual men (Balsam, Rothblum, & Beauchaine, 2005; Hughes, Johnson, & Wilsnak, 2001). LGBT people are also victims of violence perpetrated by other LGBT people. Research on same-sex couples suggests that intimate partner violence occurs in these relationships with at least the same frequency as in heterosexual relationships (Burke & Follingstad, 1999; Greenwood et al., 2002; Ristock, 2003).

The higher risk for victimization among LGBT people may result from a number of factors. As with heterosexual people, victimization of LGBT people can occur at home and outside the home, by familiar people and by strangers, and during childhood, adolescence, and adulthood. Both LGBT and heterosexual people can experience bias-related victimization based on gender, age, socioeconomic status, nationality, race or ethnicity, religion, and disability status. However, LGBT people experience unique risks for victimization based on their sexual orientation alone. Such attacks are common. Indeed, the first federal report on bias crime commissioned by the U.S. Department of Justice (Finn & McNeil, 1987, cited in Klinger & Stein, 1994) concludes that lesbians and gay men may be the most often victimized group in the United States. In addition, hate crimes (victimization that can lead to criminal prosecution) based on sexual orientation may differ in important ways from other crimes. Dunbar (1998) reports that physical assault, sexual assault, sexual harassment, and stalking are more common in sexual orientation hate crimes than in other hate crimes. Furthermore, attacks based on sexual orientation may be more underreported than other kinds of hate crimes (Herek, 2000).

Victimization based on actual or perceived sexual orientation can begin in childhood, often as a result of visibility due to gender atypicality or coming out to family members (D'Augelli, Hershberger, & Pilkington, 1998; Harry, 1989). Pilkington and D'Augelli (1995) report that more than one-third (36%) of LGB youth have been verbally abused by an immediate family member for being LGB, and 10% have been physically assaulted by a family member. A study by D'Augelli, Hershberger, and Pilkington (1998) finds that youth living at home who disclose their sexual orientation to their families are more victimized that youth who remain silent. Likewise, LGBT youth are vulnerable to victimization by their peers at school, especially those who disclose their orientation at earlier ages and are gender atypical (D'Augelli, Pilkington, & Hershberger, 2002). LGBT people are targeted for violence based on their sexual orientation in adulthood, by strangers and by known perpetrators (Herek et al., 1997). As in childhood, more openness about sexual orientation has been associated with more bias-related victimization (Herek, Gillis, & Cogan, 1999). Additionally, the stress of living with homophobia[1] may lead some LGBT people to engage in behaviors that increase their risk of victimization, such as abusing drugs and alcohol (Perry, 1996) or running away from home as a teenager (Kruks, 1991; Noell & Ochs, 2001). Gay and bisexual men's greater risk for sexual assault may result in part from having more intimate relationships with men in adulthood. The association of HIV and AIDS with gay and bisexual men has led to increased bias-related victimization rates (Paul, Hays, & Coates, 1995).

Victimization affects LGBT people in many of the same ways that it affects heterosexuals. However, the experience of victimization is different for LGBT people. Unlike heterosexuals, LGBT people live in a society that routinely and systematically denies and denigrates their feelings, relationships, and identities. Neisen (1993), who coined the term *cultural victimization* to refer to the impact of living in a heterosexist culture, likens the experience to the trauma of physical and sexual abuse, explaining how both can lead to shame, negative self-concept, self-destructive behaviors, and a victim mentality. Root (1992) refers to the experiences of all oppressed groups as insidious trauma, the ongoing, daily stress of living with oppression that can erode well-being over time. Meyer (1995) conceptualizes minority stress as internalized homophobia, stigma (expectations of rejection and discrimination), and actual experiences of discrimination and violence. Waldo (1999) proposes a model of workplace minority stress, which includes both direct stressors (e.g., overt discrimination) and indirect stressors (e.g., the presumption of heterosexuality). Similarly, DiPlacido (1998) includes under the rubric of minority stress a broad range of stressors, such as hate crimes, discrimination, the stress of coming out, the stress of concealment, and internalized homophobia. All of these models emphasize the importance of understanding the role of the homophobic and heterosexist context in understanding the life experiences of LGBT people. Moreover, for LGBT people of color, this effect is magnified because they may experience dual cultural victimizations of both racism and heterosexism (Greene, 1994). Likewise, ageism may add to the stigma for older LGBT people. Any victimization of LGBT people therefore must be understood in the context of ongoing coping with difficulties related to diverse forms of heterosexism.

Bias-related victimization has particularly harmful psychological effects (Herek et al., 1999; Hershberger & D'Augelli, 1995) and has been linked to PTSD, depression, anxiety, and anger problems. Herek, Gillis, and Cogan (1999) also found that bias-related victimization experiences led to a sense that the world is unsafe, that people are malevolent, and that one has little control over one's environment. Bias-related victimization contributes to internalized homophobia as well as reluctance to disclose sexual orientation in the future (Garnets, Herek, & Levy, 1990). Moreover, LGBT victims may perceive any victimization experience to be related to their sexual orientation, whether or not this is the motivation of the attacker. For some, victimization may become linked with their sexual orientation, with victims of sexual victimization questioning whether the experience caused them to become LGBT (Balsam, 2002).

Vicarious victimization is the psychological impact of a traumatic event on the friends, family, and acquaintances of a victim (McCann & Pearlman, 1990). Higher prevalence of victimization experiences in the LGBT community means that an LGBT person is likely to learn of, witness, or play a supportive role in the life of a victim. For LGBT people who have never been victimized, such events may lead to their first feelings of personal vulnerability. Many LGB youth report knowledge of the victimization of open LGB youth in high schools (D'Augelli, Pilkington, & Hershberger, 2002). For LGBT people with a history of victimization, such events may increase fears and symptoms and may create a greater sense of fatality. Bias-related incidents may have a ripple effect on the LGBT community (Noelle, 2002). Herek and Berrill (1992, p. 3) describe bias-related victimization incidents as "sending a message" to the victim and the LGBT community: "Each anti-gay attack is, in effect, a punishment for stepping outside culturally accepted norms and a warning to all gay and lesbian people to stay in 'their place,' the invisibility and self-hatred of the closet." For example, the widespread publicity surrounding the 1998 murder of Matthew Shepard has implications for perceived safety, assumptions about the benevolence of people, and personal feelings about sexual orientation in LGBT people who had never met this particular victim (Noelle, 2002). Such incidents lead many LGBT people to live in fear; this fear may have an impact on their mental health and well-being (D'Augelli, 2003).

The heterosexist and homophobic cultural context not only affects the well-being of LGBT people, but it also shapes access to services for victims of violence. For certain types of victimization of LGBT adults, services might not be available. This is particularly evident in the area of domestic violence services. For example, a gay man trying to leave his abusive partner typically would not have access to a domestic violence shelter because these services generally are limited to use by women. Even if services are available, they may not be sensitive to the needs of LGBT victims. For example, a lesbian staying in a domestic violence shelter might experience homophobic responses from other shelter residents or from staff. It is not uncommon for abusive male partners to accuse their female partners of lesbianism; thus, battered heterosexual women may have developed emotionally laden negative beliefs about lesbians. These responses might be particularly strong when the shelter is for women and children; heterosexual shelter residents might have been exposed to stereotypical beliefs about homosexuality and child molestation and might feel that they have to "protect their children" from lesbian residents. Furthermore, a lesbian or bisexual woman who is leaving an abusive female partner might fear that her partner could follow her into the shelter. For transgender men or women, the issue of domestic violence shelters is particularly complex, given the gender-specific nature of domestic violence services. For example, a male-to-female transgender person may not be welcome in a women's shelter.

For LGBT survivors of other types of violence, services may also lack sensitivity to their unique challenges. For example, therapy groups for adult women molested as children might overlook specific relationship and sexual issues relevant to lesbian and bisexual women. Because many LGBT people keep their sexual orientation completely or partially hidden, LGBT victims may avoid using services, fearing being outed. For example, a married bisexual man raped by another man may avoid seeking medical or psychological care, fearing that his wife or co-workers might learn of his sexual orientation. LGBT people might also avoid seeking help or be less than honest with service providers because they are afraid of discrimination or blame. For example, a transgender woman attacked by a stranger might conceal the nature of the incident from emergency-room personnel, fearing insensitive treatment by staff. In some cases, abusive same-sex partners may threaten their partner with disclosure of sexual orientation if the victim seeks assistance. Laws in some states define domestic violence as occurring between a man and a woman; thus, some LGBT people are not afforded the legal protections available to heterosexuals who are battered by a partner. Men who are victims of physical or sexual violence might have particular difficulty seeking help because of societal stereotypes about masculinity (Merrill & Wolfe, 2000). Geographic context may play a role as well. For instance, LGBT people living in rural communities would hesitate to seek assistance from local helping resources, fearing lack of confidentiality in the local area's "grapevine" (D'Augelli & Hart, 1987; Preston et al., 2002). Thus, not only are LGBT people more often victimized than their heterosexual counterparts, but their efforts to obtain help after attacks involve many complex dilemmas not faced by heterosexual victims.

Although LGBT people experience unique risks for victimization and its mental health consequences, they also have unique competence and resilience that can protect them against or moderate the deleterious effects of victimization. Unlike heterosexuals, LGBT people routinely cope with cultural victimization. The need to deal with a stigmatizing society leads to the development of coping skills that may be used in coping with and recovering from the effects of trauma. For example, Balsam and Rothblum (2003) report that lifetime victimization is less highly correlated with psychological distress for lesbians and gay men than for heterosexual individuals. There is also evidence that LGBT people, and lesbians in particular, use psychotherapy and counseling at higher rates than heterosexuals, perhaps because of cultural norms in the LGBT community (Cochran, Sullivan, & Mays, 2003; Rothblum & Factor, 2001). LGBT individuals often create families of choice or strong support systems to combat the stress of living in an unaccepting society (Weston, 1991). These support systems can buffer against the effects of victimization. Some LGBT people also live in highly LGBT-concentrated areas with ready access to similar others. The use of professional and informal helping and support systems provides more resources to address the impact of victimization. Furthermore, the process of coming out and building an identity as an LGBT person often involves significant personal growth and self-awareness, which may increase the internal resources available to cope with the impact of trauma.

It is important to note that most research on victimization in the LGBT population has focused on lesbians and gay men. Bisexual women and men generally have been excluded from such research or grouped together with lesbians and gay men. The results of recent studies suggest that bisexual women and men may experience an even greater lifetime risk for childhood abuse and adulthood sexual assault when compared with lesbians and gay men (Russell & Seif, 2002; Udry & Chantala, 2002). More research is needed on the unique aspects of victimization in the lives of bisexual people. For example, greater invisibility may lead to more risk behaviors (substance abuse, involvement with risky sexual partners), and others' negative attitudes about bisexuality may lead to victimization. Similarly, little empirical research has focused specifically on victimization of transgender individuals, although anecdotal and clinical information suggests that they are a population at particularly high risk (Clements-Nolle et al., 2001). Although there is little research on LGBT people of color, a few large-scale studies of lesbians have demonstrated higher rates of victimization among lesbians of color than European American lesbians (Descamps, 1998; Morris & Balsam, 2003). Although little is known about whether this finding would extend to men or would be replicated in a probability sample, the findings suggest that multiple minority statuses (Greene, 1994) may lead to more risk for victimization.

## Victimization of Older People in the General Population

Compared with research on younger adults, the literature on victimization among older adults is sparse. Many studies of victimization fail to recruit older adults or do not disaggregate results by age group. An exception is Norris's (1992) epidemiological study of traumatic experiences in an ethnically diverse sample of 1,000 adults that finds that older adults (age 60 and older) reported less lifetime physical and sexual assault than their middle-aged counterparts. These differences may result from a number of factors. Older adults may be less likely to recall negative life events (Norris, 1992). Older adults may be even less likely to report criminal victimization to authorities, including recent events (U.S. Department of Justice, 1981, as cited in Falk, Hasselt, & Hersen, 1997). Differences might also result from a cohort effect. Increases in violence in society over the past century may mean that older adults were exposed to less violence in their lifetimes than younger adults. Age cohort might also have an impact on perceptions of victimization experiences. For example, changes in societal norms with regard to physical punishment may mean that older adults are less likely to view physically aggressive experiences in childhood as abuse. The relative secrecy surrounding sexual victimization before the 1970s may make some older adults unlikely to disclose such experiences. Despite lower overall rates of victimization, however, older adults are more likely to sustain injuries and need medical attention as a result of an attack (Bachman, Dillaway, & Lachs, 1998).

When the impact of victimization is considered, older adults also appear to fare better than their younger adult counterparts. In population-based studies, older people report lower rates of PTSD, but similar rates of PTSD from recent traumatic experiences, when compared with younger and middle-aged adults (Norris, 1992). However, for some people with victimization histories, symptoms may emerge or reemerge as they reach old age. Floyd, Rice, and Black (2002) suggest that intrusive thoughts and memories of traumatic events may increase as the ability to control attention decreases with age. Preferential recall for early life events means that childhood victimization experiences may also become more salient in the memories of older adults (Floyd, Rice, & Black, 2002). Additionally, the stressors associated with aging may interfere with the coping strategies previously used by older victims. For example, Allers, Benjack, and Allers (1992) suggest that unresolved sexual abuse may resurface as older adults become less independent and more physically frail. Gray and Acierno (2002) suggest that retirement, death of family members, and deterioration of health can all trigger memories and symptoms associated with previous traumas. Because older people grew up in a time in which counseling, psychother-apy, and psychological terminology were less common, these people may be more likely to have physical complaints, and trauma and its sequelae may be missed or misdiagnosed.

## Victimization of Older LGBT People

Many of the issues noted in this chapter about the impact of victimization on LGBT people and on older adults in general are relevant to the victimization of older LGBT adults. As was noted earlier, however, victimization may have distinct consequences for LGBT older adults. It is not possible to disentangle the impact of victimization in general, victimization of an older person, and victimization of an older LGBT person, but each type of victimization adds spe-cific problems. There is little research on the topic, but it is possible to speculate about the likely impact of this victimization.

We found only one study that focused directly on the victimization of old-er LGB adults. D'Augelli and Grossman (2001) surveyed 416 LGB people aged 60 and older. Two-thirds had experienced verbal abuse based on their sexual orientations in their lifetimes, 29% had been threatened with violence, 16% had been assaulted, and nearly one-third (29%) had been threatened with the disclosure of their sexual orientation. Men had been physically attacked three times more often than women (44% vs. 15%), and physical attacks of men were more serious, with 15% of the men reporting attacks with weapons, compared with 4% of the women. The more open participants had been about their sexual orientation, the more victimization they reported, a pattern also seen among LGB youth (D'Augelli, Pilkington, & Hershberger, 2002). More frequent physi-cal attacks were associated with lower self-esteem, more loneliness, and more self-reported mental health problems. In addition, 7% reported discrimination or harassment based on their sexual orientation in housing, and 19% had ex-perienced discrimination or harassment at work. Of course, it is not known whether the victimization experience was more or less prevalent and severe than for other cohorts of LGBT adults because older respondents also tended to be much less visible and open about their sexual orientations and thereby may have avoided overt victimization.

Additional relevant work on sexual orientation–motivated victimization of LGB adults ranging in age from 18 to 82 by Herek, Gillis, and Cogan (1999) found that about one-quarter of the men and one-fifth of the women had been victimized (this included robberies and property crimes). Although differential impact of victimization based on sexual orientation and other types of victimization was not studied by D'Augelli and Grossman (2001), an extrapolation of Herek, Gillis, and Cogan's (1999) findings would suggest that sexual orientation victimization of older adults would have a greater influence on their health and mental health than other forms of victimization, controlling for the nature of the attack (e.g., being mugged vs. being mugged while being called homophobic epithets).

Although older adults in general may be reluctant to discuss victimization and its impact, this may be particularly true for older LGBT people, who grew up in a time in which homophobia exerted an even more powerful influence than is currently the case. This may be especially relevant for older men, for whom acknowledging victimization can be stigmatizing because it runs counter to gender stereotypes. Older LGBT adults may not recognize victimization because of stereotypes and myths. For example, an older woman beaten by female partner may not label it domestic violence because of the stereotype that women cannot be perpetrators (Ristock, 2003). An older man beaten by a male partner might view this simply as a fight or disagreement rather than abuse. Furthermore, older LGBT adults may be reluctant to disclose partner violence because they may fear that doing so will confirm negative societal stereotypes about LGBT people (Balsam, 2001). An older victim of same-sex domestic violence may also be concerned that disclosure of the abuse may lead to rejection by others in the local LGBT community. Some LGBT communities are quite small, and some older victims of domestic violence may feel that they cannot risk making waves in their social network by reporting domestic abuse.

The normal processes of aging may leave older LGBT adults increasingly vulnerable to the effects of homophobia. As physical health declines, people may need to rely on caretakers and may be subject to homophobic responses from family members, professional caregivers, or nursing home staff (Brotman, Ryan, & Cormier, 2003). LGBT people may feel that because of homophobia, they have limited choices of caregivers and facilities. They may be reluctant to report a verbally abusive staff member in a residential care facility, for example, if they simultaneously experience some support of their sexual orientation in the facility. Financial issues resulting from homophobia, such as the lack of protections afforded to married couples, may increase an abusive partner's ability to control his or her victim. For example, if the LGBT abusive partner has been the primary wage earner, the victimized partner may be threatened with loss of pension and other assets if he or she leaves.

The cultural value placed on youth among gay men may also increase vulnerability to victimization among older gay men. For example, older gay men's concerns about self-worth may lead them to choose partners who are negligent or abusive. Older gay and bisexual men may also be subject to exploitation and victimization by young male sex workers if they pay for sex (Visano, 1991). Older lesbian and bisexual women may face less cultural pressure regarding youthfulness but may face more societal discrimination as older women. Older LGBT people in general may fear that leaving an abusive partner will mean being alone at a point in their lives at which their opportunities for finding another partner are decreasing.

As noted earlier, however, older LGBT people may have developed greater coping skills and resilience than their heterosexual peers, such as "crisis competence" (Kimmel, 1978, p. 117; Morrow, 2001) gained through learning to deal with the impact of heterosexism over the course of their lives. Greater gender role flexibility and freedom from some social norms may also increase the range of coping options for LGBT people. LGBT people who have successfully overcome the impact of victimization experiences may be better prepared to face the challenges and losses that often accompany aging. Moreover, if victimization experiences occur late in life, some LGBT people may be better prepared to cope with them thanks to their LGBT social networks (Grossman, D'Augelli, & Hershberger, 2000). Only additional research can determine how the balance of vulnerabilities and resources of older LGBT people who experience victimization influences the outcomes of the experiences.

## Conclusion

Several suggestions might help clinicians address issues of past and current victimization of older LGBT adults. First, it is important to obtain a history of a client's victimization experiences. Clinicians should conduct such a history with all LGBT clients and avoid making assumptions about victim status based on stereotypes about gender, race or ethnicity, social class, or age (e.g., that only women are victims of violence, that LGBT victims of domestic violence usually are young men, that only poor LGBT people are victimized). When assessing victimization among older LGBT people, it is important to ask questions using clear, objective terms. For example, an older gay man may be less likely to identify himself as a victim of "domestic abuse" but may more accurately answer the question, "Does your partner ever harm or hit you?" Similarly, an older lesbian may not consider herself a victim of childhood sexual abuse, but if asked whether "an adult ever touched you in an unwanted sexual way while you were growing up," she may reveal that she is still troubled by nightmares about when a relative fondled her. In addition to using behavior-specific terminology, it is important for the interviewer to convey empathy and to be nonjudgmental when discussing victimization. For older adults with cognitive or verbal impairments, physical indicators such as unexplained bruises, welts, cuts, or burns may be clues to recent or ongoing victimization (Fulmer et al., 1999). A number of screening tools exist that are useful in identifying elder abuse (see Anetzberger, 2001; Bonnie & Wallace, 2003; Fulmer, 2003).

When current or recent victimization is disclosed or suspected, it is important to follow up with an assessment of current safety. These questions may be directed to the older LGBT person or others in his or her support network. If the victimization is ongoing, the nature of the person's relationship to the perpetrator and degree of dependence on the perpetrator should be explored. It is important for the clinician to take steps to ensure the person's safety. This may prove to be a complex matter when emotional, practical, and financial barriers make the person reluctant or unwilling to consider changing their relationship with the perpetrator or even ending the relationship. This issue should be addressed carefully, helping the victim to voice all of his or her feelings, both positive and negative, toward the perpetrator and the current situation. Additionally, the possibility that the perpetrator may have threatened even greater harm if the abuse was reported should be considered. Clinicians should familiarize themselves with relevant laws regarding mandatory reporting of elder abuse; when possible, the victim should be informed and included in any steps to report the abuse. If the person lives with or is dependent on the perpetrator, alternatives for housing and care should be explored. Clinicians should familiarize themselves with resources in their area, including battered women's shelters, antiviolence projects, advocates for the aging, legal systems, and other social service systems that might be of assistance to the LGBT victim of violence. Clinicians should also work with older LGBT people to develop strategies to reduce the risk of future victimization. Additionally, clinicians should be familiar with specific state laws regarding reporting child abuse. If an older adult reports past childhood victimization and the perpetrator still has access to children, then reporting may be required.

If advanced residential care is needed, it is important to assess the nature of the caregiving the LGBT older adult is receiving or will receive in the future. Kosberg (1988) identified several characteristics that increase the probability that caregivers will abuse older people in their care. These characteristics include substance abuse, mental or emotional difficulties, inexperience with caregiving, inadequate finances, history of childhood victimization, lack of social support, unrealistic expectations about caregiving, and lack of empathy and understanding of the elderly person's condition. These issues should be considered before placement and monitored periodically during placement.

Because they may be alienated from their biological families, some LGBT older adults turn to members of the LGBT community for caregiving (Grossman & D'Augelli, in press-a). LGBT older people and their LGBT caregivers may experience high levels of social isolation, which can increase the risk of elder abuse. LGBT caregivers should be encouraged to make use of LGBT-affirmative social supports. If local supports are not available, other options may be explored. Moore (2002) describes a telephone support group for lesbian and gay caregivers living in a rural community who experienced distress when attending local, heterosexually focused support groups, particularly when they needed to hide their sexual orientation. The study found that these caregivers reported less isolation and a renewed commitment to the caregiver role when given the opportunity to discuss their concerns with other gay and lesbian caregivers. The Internet may similarly provide opportunities for connection to LGBT caregivers who are geographically isolated or homebound.

Once an older person's current safety is established, it is important to talk with the person about how he or she perceives past victimization experiences because victimization that is perceived to be related to sexual orientation may have serious implications for mental health. The person should be given the message that the victimization was not his or her fault. This concept may be particularly important to discuss with people with histories of multiple victimizations or those who have experienced prolonged abuse by a partner or family member. It is important to assess how a person's victimization history influences his or her current emotional and interpersonal functioning in order to identify symptoms and problems that may be the target of therapeutic intervention. In discussing victimization with an older LGBT adult, it may be helpful to explore the sociocultural context in which this victimization occurred. For some people, identifying links between their own individual experiences and the broader social realities of homophobia may help to reduce shame, self-blame, and a sense of isolation. The issue of vicarious victimization may also be addressed by exploring the psychological impact of violence against LGBT people in a person's social network and in his or her LGBT community.

Finally, it is important to focus on resilience when addressing issues of victimization with this population. One important way to do this is to encourage connection to the LGBT community. Clinicians should work with clients to think creatively about levels and types of involvement that match the client's needs and limitations. For example, participating in support groups, joining e-mail discussion lists, making phone calls to friends, getting connected to LGBT social service agencies, volunteering as a mentor or tutor for LGBT youth, and writing about one's life experiences for LGBT publications are all ways in which an older LGBT person might increase his or her involvement with the community. Engaging in social activism is another coping strategy that regulates painful emotions while increasing a sense of meaning in an older LGBT person's life. As older LGBT adults reflect on their lives and their past experiences, clinicians can assist them in highlighting the ways in which they successfully coped with trauma, showed strength in the face of adversity, and experienced personal growth as a result of this adversity. In these ways, the legacy of victimization can produce a future in which such events are increasingly rare. Through active involvement with local LGBT communities, older LGBT adults can make important contributions not only to their own well-being but also to the mental health of future generations.

## NOTE

1. The terms *homophobia* and *heterosexism* are used interchangeably in this chapter to refer to the social and cultural oppression of LGBT people.

## REFERENCES

Allers, C. T., Benjack, K. J., & Allers, N. T. (1992). Unresolved childhood sexual abuse: Are older adults affected? *Journal of Counseling & Development, 71,* 14–17.

American Psychiatric Association. (1980). *Diagnostic and statistical manual of mental disorders* (3rd ed.). Washington, DC: Author.

Anetzberger, G. J. (2001). Elder abuse identification and referral: The importance of screening tools and referral protocols. *Journal of Elder Abuse & Neglect, 13,* 3–22.

Arata, C. M. (2002). Child sexual abuse and sexual revictimization. *Clinical Psychology: Science and Practice, 9,* 135–164.

Bachman, R., Dillaway, H., & Lachs, M. (1998). Violence against the elderly: A comparative analysis of robbery and assault across age and gender groups. *Research on Aging, 20*, 183–198.

Balsam, K. F. (2001). Nowhere to hide: Lesbian battering, homophobia, and minority stress. *Women and Therapy, 23*(3), 25–38.

Balsam, K. F. (2002). *Traumatic victimization: A comparison of lesbian, gay, and bisexual adults and their heterosexual siblings.* Unpublished doctoral dissertation, University of Vermont, Burlington.

Balsam, K. F., & Rothblum, E. D. (2003, August). *Sexual orientation, victimization, and mental health.* Poster session presented at the annual meetings of the American Psychological Association, Toronto.

Balsam, K. F., Rothblum, E. D., & Beauchaine, T. P. (2005). Victimization over the lifespan: A comparison of lesbian, gay, bisexual, and heterosexual siblings. *Journal of Consulting and Clinical Psychology, 73*, 477–487.

Banyard, V. L., Arnold, S., & Smith, J. (2000). Childhood sexual abuse and dating experiences of undergraduate women. *Child Maltreatment, 5*, 39–48.

Bonnie, R. J., & Wallace, R. B. (2003). *Elder mistreatment: Abuse, neglect, and exploitation in an aging America.* Washington, DC: The National Academies Press.

Brotman, S., Ryan, B., & Cormier, R. (2003). The health and social service needs of gay and lesbian elders and their families in Canada. *The Gerontologist, 43*, 192–202.

Burke, L. K., & Follingstad, D. R. (1999). Violence in lesbian and gay relationships: Theory, prevalence, and correlational factors. *Clinical Psychology Review, 19*, 487–512.

Clements-Nolle, K., Marx, R., Guzman, R., & Katz, M. (2001). HIV prevalence, risk behaviors, health care use, and mental health status of transgender persons: Implications for public health intervention. *American Journal of Public Health, 91*, 915–921.

Cochran, S. D., Sullivan, J. G., & Mays, V. M. (2003). Prevalence of mental disorders, psychological distress, and mental health services use among lesbian, gay, and bisexual adults in the United States. *Journal of Consulting and Clinical Psychology, 71*, 53–61.

Corliss, H. L., Cochran, S. D., & Mays, V. M. (2002). Reports of parental maltreatment during childhood in a United States population-based survey of homosexual, bisexual, and heterosexual adults. *Child Abuse & Neglect, 26*, 1165–1178.

D'Augelli, A. R. (2003). Lesbian and bisexual female youths aged 14 to 21: Developmental challenges and victimization experiences. *Journal of Lesbian Studies, 7*(4), 9–29.

D'Augelli, A. R., & Grossman, A. H. (2001). Disclosure of sexual orientation, victimization, and mental health among lesbian, gay, and bisexual older adults. *Journal of Interpersonal Violence, 16*, 1008–1027.

D'Augelli, A. R., & Hart, M. M. (1987). Gay women, men, and families in rural settings: Toward the development of helping communities. *American Journal of Community Psychology, 15*, 79–93.

D'Augelli, A. R., Hershberger, S. L., & Pilkington, N. W. (1998). Lesbian, gay, and bisexual youths and their families: Disclosure of sexual orientation and its consequences. *American Journal of Orthopsychiatry, 68*, 361–371.

D'Augelli, A. R., Pilkington, N. W., & Hershberger, S. L. (2002). Incidence and mental health impact of sexual orientation victimization of lesbian, gay, and bisexual youths in high school. *School Psychology Quarterly, 17*, 148–167.

Descamps, M. J. (1998). *Mental health impact of child sexual abuse, rape, intimate partner violence, and hate crimes in a national sample of lesbians.* Unpublished doctoral dissertation, University of Vermont, Burlington.

DiPlacido, J. (1998). Minority stress among lesbians, gay men, and bisexuals: A consequence of heterosexism, homophobia, and stigmatization. In G. M. Herek (Ed.), *Stigma and sexual orientation: Understanding prejudice against lesbians, gay men, and bisexuals* (pp. 138–159). Thousand Oaks, CA: SAGE.

Dunbar, E. D. (1998). *Hate crime reportage: A comparison of demographic and behavioral characteristics.* Paper presented at the meetings of the American Psychological Association, San Francisco.

Falk, B., Van Hasselt, V. B., & Hersen, M. (1997). Assessment of posttraumatic stress disorder in older victims of rape. *Journal of Clinical Gerontology, 3*, 157–171.

Finkelhor, D., & Kendall-Tackett, K. (1997). A developmental perspective on the childhood impact of crime, abuse, and violent victimization. In D. Cicchetti & S. L. Toth (Eds.), *Developmental perspectives on trauma: Theory, research, and intervention. Rochester Symposium on Developmental Psychology,* Vol. 8 (pp. 1–32). Rochester, NY: University of Rochester Press.

Floyd, M., Rice, J, & Black, S. R. (2002). Recurrence of posttraumatic stress disorder in late life: A cognitive aging perspective. *Journal of Clinical Geropsychology, 8*, 303–311.

Follette, V. M., Polusny, M. A., Bechtle, A. E., & Naugle, A. E. (1996). Cumulative trauma: The impact of child sexual abuse, adult sexual assault, and spouse abuse. *Journal of Traumatic Stress, 9*, 25–35.

Fulmer, T. (2003). Elder abuse and neglect assessment. *Journal of Gerontological Nursing, 29*(6), 4–5.

Fulmer, T., Ramirez, M., Fairchild, S., Holmes, D., Koren, M. J., & Teresi, J. (1999). Prevalence of elder mistreatment as reported by social workers in a probability sample of adult day health care clients. *Journal of Elder Abuse & Neglect, 11*(3), 25–36.

Garnets, L., Herek, G. M., & Levy, B. (1990). Violence and victimization of lesbians and gay men: Mental health consequences. *Journal of Interpersonal Violence, 5*, 366–383.

Gray, M. J., & Acierno, R. (2002). Symptom presentations of older adult crime victims: Description of a clinical sample. *Journal of Anxiety Disorders, 16*, 299–309.

Greene, B. (1994). Ethnic minority lesbians and gay men: Mental health and treatment issues. *Journal of Consulting & Clinical Psychology, 62,* 243–251.

Greenwood, G. L., Relf, M. V., Huang, B., Pollack, L. M., Canchola, J. A., & Catania, J. A. (2002). Battering victimization among a probability-based sample of men who have sex with men. *American Journal of Public Health, 92,* 1964–1969.

Grossman, A. H., & D'Augelli, A. R. (in press-a). Giving help: Caregiving for older lesbian, gay, and bisexual adults. *Journal of Gay & Lesbian Social Services.*

Grossman, A. H., & D'Augelli, A. R. (in press-b). Transgender youth: Invisible and vulnerable. *Journal of Homosexuality.*

Grossman, A. H., D'Augelli, A. R., & Hershberger, S. L. (2000). Social support networks of lesbian, gay, and bisexual adults 60 years of age or older. *Journal of Gerontology: Psychological Sciences, 55,* 171–179.

Hafemeister, T. L. (2003). Financial abuse of the elderly in domestic settings. In R. J. Bonnie & R. B. Wallace (Eds.), *Elder mistreatment: Abuse, neglect, and exploitation in aging America* (pp. 382–445). Washington, DC: The National Academies Press.

Harry, J. (1989). Parental physical abuse and sexual orientation in males. *Archives of Sexual Behavior, 18,* 251–261.

Herek, G. M. (1995). Psychological heterosexism in the United States. In A. R. D'Augelli & C. J. Patterson (Eds.), *Lesbian, gay, and bisexual identities over the lifespan: Psychological perspectives* (pp. 321–346). New York: Oxford University Press.

Herek, G. M. (2000). The psychology of sexual prejudice. *Current Directions in Psychological Science, 9,* 19–22.

Herek, G., M., & Berrill, K. T. (Eds.). (1992). *Hate crimes: Confronting violence against lesbians and gay men.* Newbury Park, CA: SAGE.

Herek, G. M., Gillis, J. R., & Cogan, J. C. (1999). Psychological sequelae of hate crime victimization among lesbian, gay, and bisexual adults. *Journal of Consulting and Clinical Psychology, 67,* 945–951.

Herek, G. M., Gillis, J. R., Cogan, J. C., & Glunt, E. K. (1997). Hate crime victimization among lesbian, gay, and bisexual adults: Prevalence, psychological correlates, and methodological issues. *Journal of Interpersonal Violence, 12,* 195–215.

Hershberger, S. L., & D'Augelli, A. R. (1995). The impact of victimization on the mental health and suicidality of lesbian, gay, and bisexual youths. *Developmental Psychology, 31,* 65–74.

Hughes, T. L., Johnson, T., & Wilsnack, S. C. (2001). Sexual assault and alcohol abuse: A comparison of lesbians and heterosexual women. *Journal of Substance Abuse, 13,* 515–532.

Kaniasty, K., & Norris, F. H. (1992). Social support and victims of crime: Matching event, support, and outcome. *American Journal of Community Psychology, 20,* 211–241.

Kimmel, D. C. (1978). Adult development and aging: A gay perspective. *Journal of Social Issues, 34*(3), 113–130.

Klinger, R. L., & Stein, T. S. (1994). Impact of violence, childhood sexual abuse, and domestic violence and abuse on lesbians, bisexuals, and gay men. In R. P. Cabaj & T. S. Stein (Eds.), *Textbook of homosexuality and mental health* (pp. 801–817). Washington, DC: American Psychiatric Press.

Kosberg, J. I. (1988). Preventing elder abuse: Identification of high risk factors prior to placement decisions. *The Gerontologist, 28,* 43–50.

Kruks, G. (1991). Gay and lesbian homeless/street youth: Special issues and concerns. *Journal of Adolescent Health, 12,* 515–518.

Lombardi, E. L., Wilchins, R. A., Priesing, D., & Malouf, D. (2001). Gender violence: Transgender experiences with violence and discrimination. *Journal of Homosexuality, 42*(1), 89–101.

McCann, I., & Pearlman, L. (1990). Vicarious victimization: A framework for understanding the psychological effects of working with victims. *Journal of Traumatic Stress, 3,* 131–149.

Merrill, G. S., & Wolfe, V. A. (2000). Battered gay men: An exploration of abuse, help seeking, and why they stay. *Journal of Homosexuality, 39*(2), 1–30.

Messman-Moore, T. L., Long, P. J., & Siegfried, N. J. (2000). The revictimization of child sexual abuse survivors: An examination of the adjustment of college women with child sexual abuse, adult sexual assault, and adult physical abuse. *Child Maltreatment, 5*(1), 18–27.

Meyer, I. H. (1995). Minority stress and mental health in gay men. *Journal of Health & Social Behavior, 36*(1), 38–56.

Moore, W. R. (2002). Lesbian and gay elders: Connecting care providers through a telephone support group. *Journal of Gay & Lesbian Social Services, 14*(3), 23–41.

Morris, J. F., & Balsam, K. F. (2003). Lesbian and bisexual women's experiences of victimization: Mental health, revictimization, and sexual identity development. *Journal of Lesbian Studies, 7*(4), 67–85.

Morrow, D. F. (2001). Older gays and lesbians: Surviving a generation of hate and violence. *Journal of Gay & Lesbian Social Services, 13*(1), 151–169.

National Center on Elder Abuse. (1998). *The National Elder Abuse Incidence Study: Final report.* Washington, DC: National Aging Information Center.

Neisen, J. H. (1993). Healing from cultural victimization: Recovery from shame due to heterosexism. *Journal of Gay & Lesbian Psychotherapy, 2*(1), 49–63.

Noell, J. W., & Ochs, L. M. (2001). Relationship of sexual orientation to substance use, suicidal ideation, suicide attempts, and other factors in a population of homeless adolescents. *Journal of Adolescent Health, 29,* 31–36.

Noelle, M. (2002). The ripple effect of the Matthew Shepard murder: Impact on the assumptive worlds of members of the targeted group. *American Behavioral Scientist, 46,* 27–50.

Norris, F. H. (1992). Epidemiology of trauma: Frequency and impact of different potentially traumatic events on different demographic groups. *Journal of Consulting and Clinical Psychology, 60,* 409–418.

Paul, J., Hays, R. B., & Coates, T. J. (1995). The impact of the HIV epidemic on US gay male communities. In A. R. D'Augelli & C. J. Patterson (Eds.), *Lesbian, gay, and bisexual identities over the lifespan: Psychological perspectives* (pp. 347–397). New York: Oxford University Press.

Perry, S. M. (1996). Lesbian alcohol and marijuana use: Correlates of HIV risk behaviors and abusive relationships. *Journal of Psychoactive Drugs, 27*, 413–419.

Pilkington, N. W., & D'Augelli, A. R. (1995). Victimization of lesbian, gay, and bisexual youth in community settings. *Journal of Community Psychology, 23*, 33–56.

Pillemer, K., & Finkelhor, D. (1988). The prevalence of elder abuse: A random sample survey. *The Gerontologist, 28*, 51–57.

Pillemer, K., & Moore, D. W. (1989). Abuse of patients in nursing homes: Findings from a survey of staff. *The Gerontologist, 29*, 314–319.

Preston, D. B., D'Augelli, A. R., Cain, R. E., & Schulze, F. W. (2002). Issues in the development of HIV-preventive interventions for men who have sex with men (MSM) in rural areas. *Journal of Primary Prevention, 23*, 201–216.

Ristock, J. L. (2003). Exploring dynamics of abusive lesbian relationships: Preliminary analysis of a multisite, qualitative study. *American Journal of Community Psychology, 31*, 329–341.

Rivers, I., & D'Augelli, A. R. (2001). The victimization of lesbian, gay, and bisexual youths: Implications for intervention. In A. R. D'Augelli & C. J. Patterson (Eds.), *Lesbian, gay, and bisexual identities and youth: Psychological perspectives* (pp. 199–223). New York: Oxford University Press.

Root, M. P. P. (1992). Reconstructing the impact of trauma on personality. In L. S. Brown & M. Ballou (Eds.), *Personality and psychopathology: Feminist reappraisals* (pp. 229–265). New York: Guilford.

Rothblum, E. D., & Factor, R. J. (2001). Lesbians and their sisters as a control group: Demographic and mental health factors. *Psychological Science, 12*, 63–69.

Russell, S. T., & Seif, H. (2002). Bisexual female adolescents: A critical analysis of past research and results from a national survey. *Journal of Bisexuality, 2*(2–3), 73–94.

Saunders, B. E., Arata, C. M., & Kilpatrick, D. G. (1990). Development of a crime-related post-traumatic stress disorder scale for women within the Symptom Checklist-90–Revised. *Journal of Traumatic Stress, 3*, 439–448.

Simon, T. R., Anderson, M., Thompson, M. P., Crosby, A., & Sacks, J. J. (2002). Assault victimization and suicidal ideation or behavior within a national sample of U.S. adults. *Suicide & Life-Threatening Behavior, 32*, 42–50.

Tjaden, P., Thoeness, N., & Allison, C. J. (1999). Comparing violence over the life span in samples of same-sex and opposite-sex cohabitants. *Violence and Victims, 14*, 413–425.

Tomeo, M. E., Templer, D. I., Anderson, S., & Kotler, D. (2001). Comparative data of childhood and adolescent molestation in heterosexual and homosexual persons. *Archives of Sexual Behavior, 30*, 535–541.

Udry, J. R., & Chantala, K. M. (2002). Risk assessment of adolescents with same-sex relationships. *Journal of Adolescent Health, 31,* 84–92.

U.S. Congress, House Select Committee on Aging. (1991). *Elder abuse: What can be done?* Washington, DC: U.S. Government Printing Office.

Visano, L. A. (1991). The impact of age on paid sexual encounters. In J. A. Lee (Ed.), *Gay midlife and maturity* (pp. 207–226). Binghamton, NY: Harrington Park Press.

Waldo, C. R. (1999). Working in a majority context: A structural model of heterosexism as minority stress in the workplace. *Journal of Counseling Psychology, 46,* 218–232.

Weston, K. (1991). *Families we choose: Lesbians, gays, kinship.* New York: Columbia University Press.

Wilber, K. H., & McNeilly, D. P. (2001). Elder abuse and victimization. In J. E. Birren & K. W. Schaie (Eds.), *Handbook of the psychology of aging* (pp. 569–591). New York Academic Press.

# 8

# Use and Misuse of Alcohol and Drugs

*Derek D. Satre*

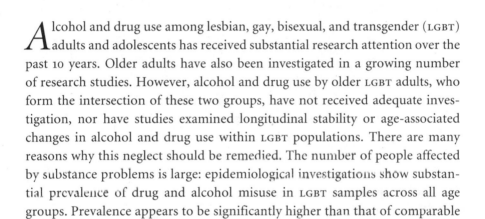

*A*lcohol and drug use among lesbian, gay, bisexual, and transgender (LGBT) adults and adolescents has received substantial research attention over the past 10 years. Older adults have also been investigated in a growing number of research studies. However, alcohol and drug use by older LGBT adults, who form the intersection of these two groups, have not received adequate investigation, nor have studies examined longitudinal stability or age-associated changes in alcohol and drug use within LGBT populations. There are many reasons why this neglect should be remedied. The number of people affected by substance problems is large: epidemiological investigations show substantial prevalence of drug and alcohol misuse in LGBT samples across all age groups. Prevalence appears to be significantly higher than that of comparable heterosexual samples. Of particular concern, cross-sectional age comparisons suggest that unlike heterosexuals, LGBT people may not sufficiently curtail substance use as they get older. The great risk to physical and mental health that substance abuse entails, especially HIV transmission risk, gives the issue a clear urgency.

This review relies on converging lines of research, including studies of older adults with drug and alcohol problems that do not specifically address LGBT issues and studies of LGBT samples, some of which examine alcohol and drug use by age. The chapter summarizes findings regarding prevalence of alcohol and drug use and misuse among LGBT and older adult samples and identifies risk factors associated with problematic use. Adaptations to treatment are described that have been recommended for older adults and LGBT people, with implications for assisting older LGBT clients with a drug or alcohol problem. Finally, this chapter identifies urban social service programs available to assist older LGBT adults with substance abuse problems, including a list of treatment resources.

## Epidemiology of Alcohol and Drug Use and Misuse

Patterns of alcohol and drug use have been described in several ways. *Substance use,* a general term for consumption, has been measured by drug type, quantity, and frequency of use. *Substance abuse,* a diagnostic term applied to both alcohol and drug use, is defined as a maladaptive pattern of use leading to clinically significant impairment or distress. In contrast, *substance dependence* is a more severe disorder potentially including tolerance, withdrawal, unsuccessful efforts to cut down, and other symptoms (American Psychiatric Association, 1994). Descriptive terms indicating excessive alcohol use include *heavy drinking* (drinking more than is recommended) and *problem drinking* (having adverse consequences). These descriptors sometimes are used to characterize maladaptive use patterns of older adults, who may not meet diagnostic criteria for substance abuse or dependence (Center for Substance Abuse Treatment, 1998).

Prevalence of substance use and misuse by LGBT people, especially older adults, is difficult to determine. Epidemiological investigations of substance use rarely include questions about sexual orientation. Studies also use varying methods to estimate prevalence, which makes it difficult to compare findings. Early studies based on community sampling conducted at bars were faulted for inflating prevalence rates. However, there is a growing consensus, based on samples drawn from a range of settings, that LGBT people use substances at higher rates than heterosexuals. Reviews have placed incidence of substance abuse in the range of 28–35% in LGBT samples and 10–12% in the general population (Cabaj, 1996). Although younger age groups have been more extensively studied, there is evidence that differences in substance use extend into middle age and later life.

Many investigators have found heavier use of alcohol, drugs, and cigarettes among gay men than among heterosexual men across the life span. In a large telephone survey conducted in four major U.S. cities by the Urban Men's Health Study (Stall et al., 2001), gay men aged 18 to 80 were asked about substances used in the previous 6 months. Reported use included 8% heavy or frequent drinking (five or more drinks at a sitting at least once a week), 42% marijuana, 20% poppers, 15% cocaine, and 12% ecstasy. In a comparison sample of heterosexual men (a national sample that included nonurban geographic areas), 9% reported heavy or frequent drinking, 11% used marijuana, 2% used cocaine, and 1% used stimulants in the previous year (Department of Health and Human Services, 2000, cited in Stall et al., 2001). Within the gay male sample, multiple drug use (using three or more illegal drugs in the previous 6 months) among gay men decreased with greater age but was still substantial (22% of men in their thirties, versus 14% of men in their forties and 7% of men aged 50 and over) (Stall et al., 2001). These findings indicate that high levels of drug use are not limited to younger gay men.

Stall and Wiley (1988) found that older gay men drank more frequently than heterosexual men of the same age. Gay men were found to experience more alcohol-related problems than heterosexual men in a Scandinavian study (Bergmark, 1999). In this survey of adults associated with a gay rights group, aged 18–91, gay men over 40 drank as much as those under 40 years of age, although detailed drinking findings by age were not reported. In another study that examined age group differences in a gay male sample (community sites including religious, social, and self-help groups such as Alcoholics Anonymous, as well as bars and university groups), Ghindia and Kola (1996) found that drug use frequency did not differ by age. In a large sample of men in Portland, Oregon and Tucson, Arizona, 31% of gay and bisexual men over 65 were smokers compared with 13% of men in the same age range, based on general population samples from Oregon and Arizona (Stall et al., 1999). This discrepancy is particularly striking, given the well-known health problems associated with smoking.

As with investigations of gay men, several studies have indicated that lesbians and bisexual women have higher rates of alcohol problems, drug use, and smoking than heterosexual women. In a community sample, McKirnan and Peterson (1989a) found that alcohol problems were reported by 23% of lesbian respondents, compared with 8% of women in a national sample. Valanis et al. (2000) found that among women over 50, 14% of lesbians and 10% of bisexual women used cigarettes, compared with 7% of heterosexual women; likewise, 19% of lesbians and 14% of bisexual women drank seven or more drinks per week, compared with 12% of heterosexual women. Gruskin et al. (2001) found high smoking rates (25% of lesbian and bisexual women compared with 13% of heterosexual women) in a managed care health plan sample, although the difference between the groups decreased with greater age. Heavy drinking, measured using stricter criteria than those used by Valanis et al. (2000), did not differ by sexual orientation and was not found in women over 50.

Transgender communities have been underinvestigated. Though not specifically examined among older adults, a high prevalence of drug problems and depression has been identified (Clements-Nolle et al., 2001). For example, this study found that 18% of male-to-female transgender people in an urban (San Francisco) sample injected street drugs in the previous 6 months and that 62% suffered from depression. Because this sample was drawn from bars and social service agencies, prevalence rates in the study probably are higher than in the general transgender population.

Epidemiological studies of older adults estimate the extent of substance use and misuse in the general population. In these studies, the prevalence of alcohol abuse and dependence in older adults varies depending on diagnostic criteria, age cutoff, and type of sample. Among community samples, current prevalence of *DSM–IV* alcohol abuse and dependence has been estimated at 1–3% for men over age 65 and 0.5–1% for women over age 65 (Bucholz, Sheline, & Helzer, 1995). Estimates of older adults drinking more than two drinks per day, a potentially harmful level, range from 6% to 9% (Bucholz, Sheline, & Helzer, 1995). Such measures may better indicate the true prevalence of problem drinking among older adults. Unfortunately, epidemiological studies of older adults generally do not include data on sexual orientation, so it is not possible to the compare LGBT prevalence with that of other adults in these samples.

One of the few studies of LGBT adults over 60 found that 9% of people in a community sample could be classified as "problem drinkers" according to the Alcohol Use Disorders Identification Test (AUDIT; D'Augelli et al., 2001). Scores on this measure were higher among people reporting the presence of a mental health problem. The investigators found that alcohol problems were significantly greater among men than women. This study was conducted among older adults involved with older LGBT social and recreation groups, who may not be representative of older LGBT adults. For example, it is possible that older adults in geographic areas without such community support are more socially isolated. Such people might have even higher rates of alcohol problems than those found in this study.

In summary, alcohol, drug, and tobacco use among older LGBT adults appears to be greater than in comparable heterosexual samples, based on epidemiological studies. Although use among older adults may be lower than the epidemic levels found in younger LGBT samples, it remains high. From a public health perspective, the increase in the proportion of older adults in the U.S. population in coming decades is expected to magnify the need for effective interventions for older adults in general (Gfroerer et al., 2003). As the prevalence estimates cited earlier indicate, future older cohorts of LGBT people may have an even greater history of drug use than older LGBT adults currently have. These lines of evidence reveal a significant problem at present that has the potential to become even larger in the near future. Therefore it is important that LGBT communities be prepared to address issues of aging and substance use.

## Consequences of Alcohol and Drug Use

Alcohol and drug abuse among older people has high personal, financial, and social costs. Adverse medical consequences are well established. For example, the physical systems negatively affected by heavy alcohol consumption include gastrointestinal, cardiovascular, endocrine, hematological, and neurological systems (Gambert & Katsoyannis, 1995; National Institute on Alcohol Abuse and Alcoholism, 2000). Illnesses involving these systems are particularly prevalent and serious among older adults. Excessive alcohol use is associated with risk of injury from falling (Stenbacka et al., 2002) and cognitive impairment (Brandt et al., 1983; Colsher & Wallace, 1990). Consequences also include social isolation, increased risk of depression, and suicide (Blow, Brockman, & Barry, 2004; Waern, 2003). Negative medical effects are also well established for use of cigarettes by older adults (Rimer et al., 1990). Smoking is also associated with higher rates of depression. Smoking and alcohol use by lesbian and bisexual women has been associated with elevated risk for cancer (Cochran et al., 2001). Based on this evidence, it is obviously desirable to limit alcohol use and to quit smoking to reduce risks to physical and mental health.

Effects of illicit drug use have not been well studied among older adults, although the health risks are clear. Use of cocaine and amphetamines causes cardiovascular disorders and other medical problems (Hong, Matsuyama, & Nur, 1991; Schindler, 1996). Amphetamine use may result in symptoms of psychosis, depression, and anxiety disorders (Williamson et al., 1997). Increased risk of unsafe sexual behavior across all age groups has been associated with drug use and heavy alcohol use (Grossman, 1995; Woody et al., 1999), perpetuating the HIV epidemic. Likewise, poor adherence to HIV medication regimens has been linked to heavy drinking (Heckman et al., 2004) and use of illegal drugs (Ingersoll, 2004). Among HIV-positive people, those with a history of alcohol abuse may be at greater risk for cognitive dysfunction than those without a history of alcohol abuse (Green, Saveanu, & Bornstein, 2004). As these studies demonstrate, clearly many major health problems are associated with alcohol and drug abuse. Unfortunately, heavy use of cigarettes, alcohol, and drugs by LGBT people means that serious medical problems will continue to be more prevalent than among heterosexuals, resulting in diminished prospects for healthy aging in a substantial percentage of the LGBT population.

## Risk Factors

Identification of factors contributing to the development of drug and alcohol abuse in older LGBT people facilitates understanding the origins of the problem and may inform effective prevention and intervention strategies. These risk factors represent the cumulative challenges associated with being LGBT and growing older. From a theoretical perspective, a life span developmental diathesis–stress model has been proposed to explain the onset of mental health problems later in life (Gatz, 1998). This model is useful in conceptually organizing the risk factors associated with late life substance abuse and dependence among LGBT adults.

Older LGBT people have vulnerabilities (diatheses) not experienced by most people in society at large, which may contribute to development of substance abuse and other disorders such as depression and anxiety. For example, older LGBT adults may be vulnerable to homophobia, leading to feelings of shame and a negative self-concept. The connection of these problems to substance abuse is well established: Heavy drinking has been associated with low levels of psychological well-being, antigay discrimination, and history of antigay harassment (McKirnan & Peterson, 1989b; Stall et al., 2001). Low self-esteem has been found to predict substance abuse among gay men (Ghindia & Kola, 1996). LGBT members of ethnic minority groups are especially vulnerable to low self-esteem, feelings of alienation, stress, and depression (Chang et al., 2003; Diaz et al., 2001). Older LGBT adults may experience isolation because they tend to be less open about their sexuality than younger adults (Kimmel, 2002). These are vulnerabilities present in the broader LGBT community but may be especially relevant to older adults, who came of age at a time when they experienced legal penalties, discrimination, and the burden of secrecy.

Older LGBT adults also face the usual stressors of aging. Stressors associated with growing older such as physical changes, retirement, and loss have been identified as potential risk factors for development of alcohol problems among older adults (Center for Substance Abuse Treatment, 1998). Chronic stress is especially harmful, especially if coping skills are not effective and social resources are inadequate (Brennan & Moos, 1990; Schutte, Brennan, & Moos, 1998; Welte & Mirand, 1995). Particularly among the current generation of older gay men it would be hard to overestimate the chronic stress associated with the AIDS epidemic, including stresses of caregiving (Irving, Bor, & Catalan, 1995). Among gay men, heavy drinking has been associated with AIDS loss (Martin et al., 1989). Current infection with HIV, which is associated with anxiety and depression, may also motivate some people to use alcohol and drugs as a coping mechanism (Dew et al., 1997).

Based on this literature, the older LGBT people most at risk for developing alcohol and drug problems appear to be those with poor self-esteem, anxiety, or depression, who experience long-term stress associated with aging or the HIV epidemic. Moreover, those who have not developed effective coping strategies and adequate social support networks, or who have lost the social networks they once relied on, are especially at risk.

## Environmental Factors

The importance of bars, private parties, and other social events at which alcohol is consumed historically has placed the use of substances at a focal point of some LGBT communities. Many older adults gained entry to the gay community at a time when bars were the only established meeting places. In addition to providing a social outlet in a bar setting, use of substances has allowed people temporarily to overcome feelings of shame or inhibition in order to meet other LGBT people (Cabaj, 1996). Not surprisingly, reliance on bars as a primary social outlet has been associated with higher rates of alcohol and drug use in correlational analyses (Stall et al., 2001). Greater tendency to socialize at bars also reduces the likelihood of stopping alcohol use after substance abuse treatment (Paul et al., 1996). These findings suggest that excessive dependence on bars as a social setting may contribute to the onset and maintenance of substance abuse or dependence.

Bars are not the only venues where substances are used. A number of high-profile events in the gay community have a significant alcohol and drug use component, as well as older participants. Circuit parties, intensive weekend-long dance events generally associated with youth, are also attended by men in their 40s and 50s (Mansergh et al., 2001; Mattison et al., 2001). A recent survey found that nearly all respondents who had attended a circuit party in the previous year used drugs during the party (75% used ecstasy, 58% used ketamine, and 36% used crystal methamphetamine), and 25% reported having unprotected anal sex (Mansergh et al., 2001). Clearly the HIV risk posed to gay men who use drugs at these parties is substantial. To a less dramatic extent, community events such as pride celebrations may be occasions for drug use. Charity fundraisers often include significant drinking.

Bars and indoor events are increasingly smoke-free, at least in major cities in the United States. However, the tobacco industry has sought to capitalize on high LGBT smoking prevalence through targeted advertising and philanthropic activities (Offen, Smith, & Malone, 2003; Smith & Malone, 2003). Because such marketing tactics are effective in recruiting new smokers and maintaining established addiction, and because rates of smoking are so high, smoking cessation and tobacco control programs are desirable.

## Identification of Alcohol and Drug Problems

The identification of alcohol and drug problems among older adults presents unique challenges, which may be compounded in LGBT communities. Substance problems of younger adults may be identified by employers, school officials, or law enforcement personnel. Older adults may be less likely than younger adults to be in contact with such potential sources of treatment referral. Older LGBT people may also be alienated from the more visible aspects of the gay community, which tends to focus on younger adults. Among people who do recognize problematic behavior, ageist biases and misinformation about aging may pose barriers to treatment referral. There may be a perception that problem behaviors reflect the effects of aging rather than alcohol and drug use or that an older person with a substance use disorder is beyond help. Heterosexual health care providers may be uninformed about LGBT issues (Center for Substance Abuse Treatment, 1998, 2001). As a result, providers may not be vigilant in screening for substance abuse in this population.

Screening in medical and social service settings is an especially important route for older adults to obtain formal treatment. For example, in a cross-sectional study of adults treated by a private health maintenance organization, older patients were more likely than younger patients to report that a physician encouraged them to enter the program (Satre, Mertens, et al., 2003). But although physicians play an important role in referral, alcohol screening of older adults in primary care is inconsistent (Reid et al., 1998). Therefore awareness of potential alcohol and drug problem indicators on the part of friends and acquaintances, as well as providers of social services to older LGBT people, is useful in facilitating treatment entry. Targeted screening of older adults in clinical settings where substance abuse prevalence is likely to be high, such as inpatient medical settings, has been the focus of some outreach programs (Satre, Knight, et al., 2003). High prevalence of alcohol and drug use among LGBT people of all ages suggests that screening for current and past alcohol and drug problems should be a standard part of any psychological screening or social service assessment.

Transgender people may be more likely than healthy LGB people to be in contact with medical providers in order to receive hormone treatments and other services. Medical appointments therefore are an important opportunity to screen for substance abuse and other mental health problems (Clements-Nolle et al., 2001). In any context, questions posed to older LGBT people regarding alcohol and drug use (quantity and frequency questions or questions about medical or other problems associated with substance use) should be respectful and nonconfrontational. Health and social service providers should avoid using terms such as *addict* and *alcoholic* to avoid the stigma that many older adults feel regarding substance abuse labels.

## Adapting Treatment for Older LGBT People

Because older LGBT people with substance abuse or dependence problems make up special populations largely neglected by both the geriatrics and the addiction fields, clinical literature and organizational resources are highly limited. The professional working with older LGBT men and women can remedy this lack of availability by becoming familiar with the needs of both older adult and LGBT populations to understand the treatment needs of those who form the intersection between these two groups.

Treatment approaches should always consider the specific needs of the individual, such as problem severity. Some older adults may drink at levels considered risky or problematic yet not meet criteria for substance abuse or dependence (Center for Substance Abuse Treatment, 1998). They are unlikely to seek out formal treatment but often come to the attention of health and social service providers. For older adults who fall into this category, brief motivational interventions (one to five short sessions) focused on health risks and other potential problems associated with drinking may be effective in reducing alcohol consumption (Blow & Barry, 2000). These treatments may be conducted in primary care and other settings, avoiding the stigma associated with addiction treatment programs.

Specific recommendations for adapting psychosocial interventions to older adults have been proposed, which also apply to individual and group treatment for substance problems. To accommodate the hearing loss and cognitive changes of some older clients, adaptations may include slower, louder speech, a slower pace of therapy, more frequent repetition of material, and simpler language (Knight & Satre, 1999). Although these modifications are not difficult, they may necessitate practice on the part of therapists not used to working with older people. Assistive listening devices, such as earphones and an amplifier, should be available for use with all hearing-impaired clients.

Further adaptation to treatment, including greater emphasis on behavioral intervention strategies, may be necessary for older clients with cognitive dysfunction (Satre, Knight, et al., 2004). HIV disease may result in problems ranging from subtle cognitive changes to dementia, which may be exacerbated by older age (Hinkin et al., 2001). Such comorbidity makes treatment more complicated. However, the presence of memory loss, executive dysfunction, or other cognitive problems is clearly no justification for denial of services. Rather, it makes treatment more urgent, in order to reduce alcohol-associated cognitive and health problems.

In a group treatment setting with older adults, it may be necessary for leaders to be more active and to provide more structure than they might with younger people. Leaders may need to make greater efforts to initiate group activities and discussion (Leszcz, 1996). It has been suggested that older adults have lower energy reserves to handle the anxiety brought on by participating in group therapy but that this anxiety may be allayed if the leader provides more group structure (Burnside, 1984). With older adults raised during the Prohibition era, in which drinking was considered evil or sinful as well as illegal, clients may have greater feelings of guilt or shame regarding drinking behavior. This sense of shame may be particularly acute among older women (Wilsnack et al., 1995). Additional cohort effects include greater perceived stigma in seeking out treatment from a mental health professional and reluctance to discuss personal problems with a stranger (Knight & Satre, 1999). Clinical issues that may need to be addressed in treatment include retirement, loss of close friends and partners to death, housing difficulties, decreased physical mobility, and health problems. Older adults in treatment are more likely to be diagnosed with alcohol dependence than drug dependence and have more medical issues than younger adults (Satre, Mertens, et al., 2003). Where possible, coordination of substance abuse treatment with medical and social services is desirable.

Older women appear to have an encouraging recovery prognosis, although empirical literature on this group is sparse. There is some evidence that older women may have better treatment retention and outcomes than other age–gender groups, based on a long-term outcome study conducted in a managed care chemical dependency program (Satre, Mertens, Areán, & Weisner, 2004). This study found that older women (age 55 and over) had higher abstinence rates than either older men or younger women 5 years after treatment. Another study examined late life gender differences more extensively in the same treatment setting. Results found that older women had a later onset of heavy drinking than older men in the same program, although drinking severity was comparable at baseline (Satre, Mertens, & Weisner, 2004). These results suggest that the chronological course of alcohol problems may differ by gender.

Older women have treatment issues such as high comorbid depression, social isolation, and guilt around substance use (Blow, 2000). Describing an outreach program targeting older low-income women, Fredrikson (1992) suggests that women-only groups may increase self-esteem and social connectedness between women in treatment. Fredrikson also observes that in this program, entry into treatment was slow and incremental for some participants and seemed to be facilitated by nonthreatening group activities with other women. However, these studies did not include data on sexual orientation. When working with older lesbian women in recovery, it has been suggested that treatment should focus on developing supportive social networks, dealing with financial difficulties, and, for some women, addressing a history of physical or sexual abuse (Finnegan & McNally, 2000). Because these topics may be more difficult to talk about in mixed groups, participation in women-only sessions may facilitate honest sharing of emotionally charged material.

Clinical topics to address in substance abuse treatment for LGBT clients also include experiences of homophobia, discrimination and violence, self-acceptance, feelings of guilt and shame, HIV and sexual risk taking, and loss of close friends and partners to AIDS (Center for Substance Abuse Treatment, 2001). Members of ethnic minority groups are likely to experience additional stressors, associated with being LGBT because of the combined effects of racism and heterosexism (Diaz et al., 2001). One study of black and Latino men over 50 who have sex with men found that most used drugs in conjunction with sex. Many were secretive about their sexual encounters, had unprotected sex, were also sexually active with women, and reported high levels of stigma about homosexuality (Jimenez, 2003). Men in these populations may be uncomfortable identifying as gay, which is likely to limit access to mainstream LGBT substance abuse treatment resources.

Transgender people may experience isolation, lack of educational and job opportunities, and poor access to health care (Clements-Nolle et al., 2001). Additional concerns include HIV, sexual identity conflict, coming out as transgender, and isolation (Bockting, Robinson, & Rosser, 1998). Providers must be aware of these issues to provide effective services.

Leaders of treatment groups that include LGBT clients should encourage an open and inclusive atmosphere and must make it clear that judgmental or homophobic attitudes will not be tolerated. The need for confidentiality must be respected, especially for older LGBT adults in treatment in mixed-orientation settings; clients must be allowed to set their own timetable for disclosure of their sexuality. Although there is risk of negative reaction in group treatment settings by disclosure, the acceptance and support offered by other group members has the potential to bring healing to the older LGBT client in treatment, even in a setting with others of very different backgrounds.

For those in recovery, establishment of sober social networks has been identified as a significant predictor of continued sobriety (Weisner et al., 2003). Likewise, not having any close family or friends who encourage drinking or drug use is associated with long-term recovery after treatment. LGBT people, especially older adults, for whom bars may have formed an integral part of social and community life, therefore face the challenge of rebuilding their social networks. LGBT Alcoholics Anonymous and other 12-step groups have experienced rapid growth as treatment resources (Paul et al., 1996). Older adults may need additional encouragement to attend these groups and possibly assistance with transportation. In major cities, older adult LGBT social groups and organized activities provide additional opportunities to build support networks.

In summary, effective treatment for older LGBT adults must take many factors into account, including the clinical issues associated with being both an older adult and LGBT. Because comorbid depression and anxiety are likely to be present and may precipitate substance abuse relapse, treatment must address these disorders as well. Counselors must also be sensitive to the ethnic and cultural heritage of their clients, bearing in mind that there are cultural differences in attitudes toward aging, sexuality and gender, and substance use. In addition to dealing with stigma regarding sexuality and gender within ethnic communities, LGBT people of color also face racism and discrimination within the LGBT community.

## Treatment Resources for Older LGBT People

Studies of mixed-age treatment settings have found that older adults generally stay in treatment longer than younger adults and have outcomes as good as or better than those of younger adults (Atkinson, Tolson, & Turner, 1993; Satre, Mertens, et al., 2003). Studies of LGBT treatment programs have found that greater age is associated with better treatment retention (Paul et al., 1996). Based on these studies, the recovery prospects of older adults should be considered good.

Several arguments have been advanced for gay-sensitive treatment contexts. These reasons include culture-specific determinants of alcohol and drug use in LGBT communities (such as HIV status, sexual behavior, and the role of gay bars) that heterosexual providers may not understand, discomfort that clients may feel in general treatment programs, and fewer opportunities to experience honest communication (Paul et al., 1996). Surveys have found that negative attitudes of health care providers toward LGBT patients are widespread (see Claes & Moore, 2000, for review). LGBT elders may be particularly concerned about discrimination by health and social service providers (Brotman, Ryan, & Cormier, 2003). For these reasons, specialized substance abuse programs that include LGBT staff offer distinct advantages.

The availability of substance abuse and dependence programs specifically designed for LGBT people varies widely but is generally better in major cities. The appendix to this chapter lists some of the largest programs nationwide and other organizations that may be useful in identifying local programs. New alcohol and drug programs are developed and old programs are closed, corresponding to fluctuations in federal, state, and local funding. The best source of up-to-date information on treatment programs is likely to be the Internet, along with social service staff at LGBT community centers in urban areas. The Internet is also the best source of information on the extensive network of LGBT 12-step organizations, which include meetings and conventions in many cities.

Some of the larger LGBT treatment programs have conducted outcome research and published descriptions of their intervention strategies. One such program in San Francisco, California is New Leaf, which was formerly known as 18th Street Services (Paul et al., 1996). This program serves a multiethnic LGBT population, including many clients dually diagnosed with both substance and mental health disorders, as well as those with polydrug use. Because the agency is also an AIDS service agency, about half the men in substance abuse treatment are HIV-positive. Services are based on a 12-step model, and regular participation in Alcoholics Anonymous or Narcotics Anonymous is expected. Clients are assigned to an individual counselor and are expected to participate in supportive groups two evenings per week for the first month of abstinence. After a month, clients are assigned to a 16-week closed treatment group that meets twice per week for 3 hours. Groups are based on cognitive social learning principles, focusing on identifying situational cues that can lead to relapse, developing coping strategies, building self-esteem, and forming healthy social networks. Although the program is not specifically geared toward older adults, the staff is trained to be sensitive to age-associated differences of patients in the program. The agency also houses a large LGBT senior outreach program, which facilitates coordinated services for older adults in recovery.

A treatment outcome study based on this program included 455 clients aged 18 to 60, with a mean age of 36 years (Paul et al., 1996). The study reported treatment outcome at 90 days, 6 months, and 1 year and examined predictors of abstinence. Results found that approximately 50% of clients reported abstinence at 90 days, which remained fairly stable up to 1 year, with some differences noted by type of substance used. Abstinence from alcohol at 1 year was associated with nonwhite ethnicity, fewer social problems, less baseline reliance on alcohol to reduce nervousness, lower self-blame, less baseline reliance on bars as a social outlet, and greater reported use of Alcoholics Anonymous after treatment.

Treatment groups and inpatient programs exclusively for older clients have been advocated because of their ability to focus on the clinical issues of older adults and to adapt treatment delivery (Blow et al., 2000). However, such programs tend to be few. Because the number of older adults in treatment is small compared with other age groups, specialized programs may not be feasible for economic and practical reasons. Even if they are available, it is possible that older LGBT people would feel isolated receiving their primary treatment in a heterosexual older adult context with clients who are unlikely to be familiar with LGBT issues. Older adult 12-step groups, which are available in some cities, are an alternative for older LGBT adults who would like to explore elder-specific recovery resources. These groups may supplement treatment received from other sources.

In summary, older LGBT adults in need of alcohol and drug treatment will rarely find specialized treatment programs specifically for them. At present, the best way for these older adults to be supported in recovery may be to use resources in the LGBT community as well as older adult 12-step groups. To build supportive social networks, participation in senior LGBT community groups (and Internet resources for adults outside urban areas) is desirable. For providers working in settings that serve either seniors of all sexual orientations or LGBT people of all ages, it is necessary to be sensitive to the particular needs of LGBT seniors and to ensure that they receive the best services possible in these more general treatment contexts.

## Need for Research

The Substance Abuse and Mental Health Service Administration has identified a number of areas in which LGBT populations warrant further research. These include the effects of age, sexual identity, discrimination, and heterosexism on substance use and abuse in LGBT people (Center for Substance Abuse Treatment, 2001). Clinical differences between gay men, lesbians, bisexuals, and transgender people also need to be clarified and effective treatments developed. Older adults should not be excluded from such studies. Likewise, epidemiological and clinical studies of substance use among older adults should collect data and report findings on sexual orientation and gender identity. Longitudinal studies should address the extent to which substance misuse continues into later life in LGBT and heterosexual populations and the social and psychological factors that may contribute to the patterns observed. Risk factors contributing to high rates of alcohol and drug use must be investigated, to develop effective prevention strategies. Future studies should examine whether older LGBT clients are well served in broader treatment contexts by investigating treatment retention and outcomes to determine which strategies will best meet the needs of this population.

## Conclusion

As researchers and service providers begin to pay more attention to the needs of older LGBT people, substance use and misuse are issues of clear importance. High levels of substance misuse put the healthy aging of LGBT people at risk. From an aging perspective, addressing substance use is a developmental as well as a clinical challenge. From a developmental perspective, a significant task for aging LGBT people is to evaluate their level of affiliation with social settings that provide a sense of community but also facilitate problematic substance use. In this sense, issues associated with aging and substance use are not relegated to age groups traditionally thought of as geriatric but are maturational hurdles for LGBT people in early and middle adulthood as well. For those who have relied heavily on bars or substance use to ease the coming-out process, to facilitate integration into the gay community, or to alleviate feelings of depression or anxiety, the challenges associated with growing older suggest a need to devise alternative strategies for building social networks.

From a clinical point of view, the growth of LGBT-focused substance abuse services and self-help groups is an encouraging sign that the need for recovery resources is being addressed. Likewise, the establishment of LGBT aging services in urban settings is an exciting development. Coordination between these two networks, with the providers in each service context mutually informed by those in the other, may be the most effective way to address the substance abuse treatment needs of older LGBT people and to promote healthy aging in LGBT communities.


APPENDIX

## LGBT Treatment Resources

National Association of Lesbian and Gay Addiction Professionals (NALGAP), 901 North Washington Street, Suite 600, Alexandria, VA 22314; phone 703-465-0539; www.nalgap.org

Addiction Recovery Services, Los Angeles Gay & Lesbian Center, McDonald/Wright Building, 1625 North Schrader Boulevard, Los Angeles, CA 90028-6213; phone 323-993-7640; www.laglc.org

New Leaf Services for Our Community, 1853 Market Street, San Francisco, CA 94103; phone 415-626-7000; www.newleafservices.org

Pride Institute (LGBT inpatient treatment centers): www.Pride-Institute.com

Nationwide Directory of LGBT Community Centers: www.glbtcentral.com/communitycenters.html

REFERENCES

American Psychiatric Association. (1994). *DSM–IV: Diagnostic and statistical manual of mental disorders* (4th ed.). Washington, DC: Author.

Atkinson, R. M., Tolson, R. L., & Turner, J. A. (1993). Factors affecting outpatient treatment compliance of older male problem drinkers. *Journal of Studies on Alcohol, 54,* 102–106.

Bergmark, K. H. (1999). Drinking in the Swedish gay and lesbian community. *Drug and Alcohol Dependence, 56,* 133–143.

Blow, F. C. (2000). Treatment of older women with alcohol problems: Meeting the challenge for a special population. *Alcoholism: Clinical and Experimental Research, 24,* 1257–1266.

Blow, F. C., & Barry, K. L. (2000). Older patients with at-risk and problem drinking patterns: New developments in brief interventions. *Journal of Geriatric Psychiatry and Neurology, 13,* 115–123.

Blow, F. C., Brockman, L. M., & Barry, K. L. (2004). Role of alcohol in late life suicide. *Alcoholism: Clinical and Experimental Research, 28*(5 Suppl), 48S–56S.

Blow, F. C., Walton, M. A., Chermack, S. T., Mudd, S. A., & Brower, K. J. (2000). Older adult treatment outcome following elder-specific inpatient alcoholism treatment. *Journal of Substance Abuse Treatment, 19,* 67–75.

Bockting, W. O., Robinson, B. E., & Rosser, B. R. (1998). Transgender HIV prevention: A qualitative needs assessment. *AIDS Care, 10,* 505–525.

Brandt, J., Butters, N., Ryan, C., & Bayog, R. (1983). Cognitive loss and recovery in long-term alcohol abusers. *Archives of General Psychiatry, 40,* 435–442.

Brennan, P. L., & Moos, R. H. (1990). Life stressors, social resources, and late-life problem drinking. *Psychology and Aging, 5,* 491–501.

Brotman, S., Ryan, B., & Cormier, R. (2003). The health and social service needs of gay and lesbian elders and their families in Canada. *Gerontologist, 43,* 192–202.

Bucholz, K. K., Sheline, Y., & Helzer, J. E. (1995). The epidemiology of alcohol use, problems, and dependence in elders: A review. In T. Beresford & E. Gomberg (Eds.), *Alcohol and aging* (pp. 19–41). New York: Oxford University Press.

Burnside, I. M. (1984). *Working with the elderly: Group process and techniques* (2nd ed.). Belmont, CA: Wadsworth.

Cabaj, R. P. (1996). Substance abuse in gay men, lesbians and bisexuals. In. R. P. Cabaj & T. S. Stein (Eds.), *Textbook of homosexuality and mental health* (pp. 783–799). Washington, DC: American Psychiatric Press.

Center for Substance Abuse Treatment. (1998). *Substance abuse among older adults.* Rockville, MD: U.S. Department of Health and Human Services.

Center for Substance Abuse Treatment. (2001). *A provider's introduction to substance abuse treatment for lesbian, gay, bisexual and transgender individuals.* Rockville, MD: U.S. Department of Health and Human Services.

Chang, C. L., Wong, F. Y., Park, R. J., Edberg, M. C., & Lai, D. S. (2003). A model for understanding sexual health among Asian American/Pacific Islander men who have sex with men (MSM) in the United States. *AIDS Education and Prevention, 15*(1 Suppl A), 21–38.

Claes, J. A., & Moore, W. (2000). Issues confronting lesbian and gay elders: The challenge for health and human service providers. *Journal of the Health and Human Services Administration, 23,* 181–202.

Clements-Nolle, K., Marx, R., Guzman, R., & Katz, M. (2001). HIV prevalence, risk behaviors, health care use, and mental health status of transgender persons: Implications for public health intervention. *American Journal of Public Health, 91,* 915–921.

Cochran, S. D., Mays, V. M., Bowen, D., Gage, S., Bybee, D., Roberts, S. J., Goldstein, R. S., Robinson, A., Rankow, E. J., & White, J. (2001). Cancer-related risk indicators and preventive screening behaviors among lesbians and bisexual women. *American Journal of Public Health, 91,* 591–597.

Colsher, P. L., & Wallace, R. B. (1990). Elderly men with histories of heavy drinking: Correlates and consequences. *Journal of Studies on Alcohol, 51,* 528–535.

D'Augelli, A. R., Grossman, A. H., Hershberger, S. L., & O'Connell, T. S. (2001). Aspects of mental health among older lesbian, gay, and bisexual adults. *Aging and Mental Health, 5,* 149–158.

Department of Health and Human Services. (2000). *National Household Survey on Drug Abuse: Summary of findings from 1999.* Rockville, MD: Department of Health and Human Services, Substance Abuse and Mental Health Services Administration, Office of Applied Studies.

Dew, M. A., Becker, J. T., Sanchez, J., Caldararo, R., Lopez, O. L., Wess, J., Dorst, S. K., & Banks, G. (1997). Prevalence and predictors of depressive, anxiety, and substance use disorders in HIV-infected and uninfected men: a longitudinal evaluation. *Psychological Medicine, 27,* 395–409.

Diaz, R. M., Ayala, G., Bein, E., Henne, J., & Marin, B. V. (2001). The impact of homophobia, poverty, and racism on the mental health of gay and bisexual Latino men: Findings from 3 US cities. *American Journal of Public Health, 91,* 927–932.

Finnegan, D. G., & McNally, E. B. (2000). Making up for lost time: Chemically dependent lesbians in later midlife. *Journal of Gay & Lesbian Social Services, 11*(2–3), 105–118.

Fredrikson, K. I. (1992). North of Market: Older women's alcohol outreach program. *The Gerontologist, 32,* 270–272.

Gambert, S. R., & Katsoyannis, K. K. (1995). Alcohol-related medical disorders of older heavy drinkers. In T. Beresford & E. Gomberg (Eds.), *Alcohol and aging* (pp. 70–81). New York: Oxford University Press.

Gatz, M. (1998). Toward a developmentally informed theory of mental disorder in older adults. In J. Lomranz (Ed.), *Handbook of aging and mental health: An integrative approach* (pp. 101–120). New York: Plenum.

Gfroerer, J., Penne, M., Pemberton, M., & Folsom, M. (2003). Substance abuse treatment need among older adults in 2020: The impact of the aging baby-boom cohort. *Drug and Alcohol Dependence, 69,* 127–135.

Ghindia, D. J., & Kola, L. A. (1996). Co-factors affecting substance abuse among homosexual men: An investigation within a midwestern gay community. *Drug and Alcohol Dependence, 41,* 167–177.

Green, J. E., Saveanu, R. V., & Bornstein, R. A. (2004). The effect of previous alcohol abuse on cognitive function in HIV infection. *American Journal of Psychiatry, 161,* 249–254.

Grossman, A. H. (1995). At risk, infected, and invisible: Older gay men with HIV/AIDS. *Journal of Association of Nurses in AIDS Care, 6,* 13–19.

Gruskin, E. P., Hart, S., Gordon, N., & Ackerson, L. (2001). Patterns of cigarette smoking and alcohol use among lesbians and bisexual women enrolled in a large health maintenance organization. *American Journal of Public Health, 91,* 976–979.

Heckman, B. D., Catz, S. L., Heckman, T. G., Miller, J. G., & Kalichman, S. C. (2004). Adherence to antiretroviral therapy in rural persons living with HIV disease in the United States. *AIDS Care, 16,* 219–230.

Hinkin, C. H., Castellon, S. A., Atkinson, J. H., & Goodkin, K. (2001). Neuropsychiatric aspects of HIV infection among older adults. *Journal of Clinical Epidemiology, 54*(Suppl 1), S44–52.

Hong, R., Matsuyama, E., & Nur, K. (1991). Cardiomyopathy associated with the smoking of crystal methamphetamine. *JAMA, 265*, 1152–1154.

Ingersoll, K. (2004). The impact of psychiatric symptoms, drug use, and medication regimen on non-adherence to HIV treatment. *AIDS Care, 16*, 199–211.

Irving, G., Bor, R., & Catalan, J. (1995). Psychological distress among gay men supporting a lover or partner with AIDS: A pilot study. *AIDS Care, 7*, 605–617.

Jimenez, A. D. (2003). Triple jeopardy: Targeting older men of color who have sex with men. *Journal of Acquired Immune Deficiency Syndrome, 33*(2 Suppl 1), S222–225.

Kimmel, D. C. (2002). Aging and sexual orientation. In B. E. Jones & M. J. Hill (Eds.), *Mental health issues in lesbian, gay, bisexual and transgender communities.* Washington, DC: American Psychiatric Publishing.

Knight, B. G., & Satre, D. D. (1999). Cognitive behavioral psychotherapy with older adults. *Clinical Psychology: Science and Practice, 6*, 188–203.

Leszcz, M. (1996). Group therapy. In J. Sadavoy, L. W. Lazarus, L. F. Jarvik, & G. T. Grossberg (Eds.), *Comprehensive review of geriatric psychiatry: II* (pp. 851–879). Washington, DC: American Psychiatric Press.

Mansergh, G., Colfax, G. N., Marks, G., Rader, M., Guzman, R., & Buchbinder, S. (2001). The Circuit Party Men's Health Survey: Findings and implications for gay and bisexual men. *American Journal of Public Health, 91*, 953–958.

Martin, J. L., Dean, L., Garcia, M., & Hall, W. (1989). The impact of AIDS on a gay community: Changes in sexual behavior, substance use, and mental health. *American Journal of Community Psychology, 17*, 269–293.

Mattison, A. M., Ross, M. W., Wolfson, T., & Franklin, D. for the San Diego HIV Neurobehavioral Research Center Group. (2001). Circuit party attendance, club drug use, and unsafe sex in gay men. *Journal of Substance Abuse, 13*, 119–126.

McKirnan, D. J., & Peterson, P. L. (1989a). Alcohol and drug use among homosexual men and women: Epidemiology and population characteristics. *Addictive Behaviors, 14*, 545–553.

McKirnan, D. J., & Peterson, P. L. (1989b). Psychosocial and cultural factors in alcohol and drug abuse: An analysis of a homosexual community. *Addictive Behaviors, 14*, 555–563.

National Institute on Alcohol Abuse and Alcoholism. (2000). *10th Special Report to the U.S. Congress on Alcohol and Health.* Washington, DC: U.S. Department of Health and Human Services.

Offen, N., Smith, E. A., & Malone, R. E. (2003). From adversary to target market: The ACT-UP boycott of Philip Morris. *Tobacco Control, 12*, 203–207.

Paul, J. P., Barrett, D. C., Crosby, G. M., & Stall, R. D. (1996). Longitudinal changes in alcohol and drug use among men seen at a gay-specific substance abuse treatment agency. *Journal of Studies on Alcohol, 57*, 475–485.

Reid, M. C., Tinetti, M. E., Brown, C. J., & Concato, J. (1998). Physician awareness of alcohol use disorders among older patients. *Journal of General Internal Medicine, 13,* 729–734.

Rimer, B. K., Orleans, C. T., Keintz, M. K., Cristinizio, S., & Fleisher, L. (1990). The older smoker: Status, challenges and opportunities for intervention. *Chest, 97,* 547–553.

Satre, D. D., Knight, B. G., Dickson-Fuhrmann, E., & Jarvik, L. F. (2003). Predictors of alcohol treatment seeking in a sample of older veterans in the GET SMART program. *Journal of the American Geriatrics Society, 51,* 380–386.

Satre, D. D., Knight, B. G., Dickson-Fuhrmann, E., & Jarvik, L. F. (2004). Substance abuse treatment initiation among older adults in the GET SMART program: Effects of depression and cognitive status. *Aging and Mental Health, 8,* 346–354.

Satre, D. D., Mertens, J., Areán, P. A., & Weisner, C. (2003). Contrasting outcomes of older versus middle-aged and younger adult chemical dependency patients in a managed care program. *Journal of Studies on Alcohol, 64,* 520–530.

Satre, D. D., Mertens, J. R., Areán, P. A, & Weisner, C. (2004). Five-year alcohol and drug treatment outcomes of older adults versus middle-aged and younger adults in a managed care program. *Addiction, 99,* 1286–1297.

Satre, D. D., Mertens, J. R., & Weisner, C. (2004). Gender differences in older adult treatment outcomes for alcohol dependence. *Journal of Studies on Alcohol, 65,* 638–642.

Schindler, C. (1996). Cocaine and cardiovascular toxicity. *Addiction Biology, 1,* 31–47.

Schutte, K. K., Brennan, P. L., & Moos, R. H. (1998). Predicting the development of late-life late-onset drinking problems: A 7-year prospective study. *Alcoholism: Clinical and Experimental Research, 22,* 1349–1358.

Smith, E. A., & Malone, R. E. (2003). The outing of Philip Morris: Advertising tobacco to gay men. *American Journal of Public Health, 93,* 988–993.

Stall, R. D., Greenwood, G. L., Acree, M., Paul, J., & Coates, T. J. (1999). Cigarette smoking among gay and bisexual men. *American Journal of Public Health, 89,* 1875–1878.

Stall, R., Paul, J. P., Greenwood, G., Pollack, L. M., Bein, E., Crosby, G. M., et al. (2001). Alcohol use, drug use and alcohol-related problems among men who have sex with men: The Urban Men's Health Study. *Addiction, 96,* 1589–1601.

Stall, R., & Wiley, J. (1988). A comparison of alcohol and drug use patterns of homosexual and heterosexual men: The San Francisco men's health study. *Drug and Alcohol Dependence, 22,* 63–73.

Stenbacka, M., Jansson, B., Leifman, A., & Romelsjo, A. (2002). Association between use of sedatives or hypnotics, alcohol consumption, or other risk factors and a single injurious fall or multiple injurious falls: A longitudinal general population study. *Alcohol, 28,* 9–16.

Valanis, B. G., Bowen, D. J., Bassford, T., Whitlock, E., Charney, P., & Carter, R. A. (2000). Sexual orientation and health: Comparisons in the women's health initiative sample. *Archives of Family Medicine, 9,* 843–853.

Waern, M. (2003). Alcohol dependence and misuse in elderly suicides. *Alcohol and Alcoholism, 38,* 249–254.

Weisner, C., Ray, T., Mertens, J. R., Satre, D. D., & Moore, C. (2003). Short-term alcohol and drug treatment outcomes predict long-term outcomes. *Drug and Alcohol Dependence, 71,* 281–294.

Welte, J. W., & Mirand, A. L. (1995). Drinking, problem drinking and life stressors in the elderly general population. *Journal of Studies on Alcohol, 56,* 67–73.

Williamson, S., Gossop, M., Powis, B., Griffiths, P., Fountain, J., & Strang, J. (1997). Adverse effects of stimulant drugs in a community sample of drug users. *Drug and Alcohol Dependence, 44,* 87–94.

Wilsnack, S. C., Vogeltanz, N. D., Diers, L. E., & Wilsnack, R. W. (1995). Drinking and problem drinking in older women. In E. Gomberg & T. Beresford (Eds.), *Alcohol and aging* (pp. 263–292). New York: Oxford University Press.

Woody, G. E., Donnell, D., Seage, G. R., Metzger, D., Marmor, M., Koblin, B. A., et al. (1999). Non-injection substance use correlates with risky sex among men having sex with men: Data from HIVNET. *Drug and Alcohol Dependence, 53,* 197–205.

# 9

## Aging Together
### The Retirement Plans of Same-Sex Couples
*Steven E. Mock, Catherine J. Taylor, and Ritch C. Savin-Williams*

D espite the increasing heterogeneity in the retirement patterns of North Americans, the retirement options older adults face often are out of step with their needs (Han & Moen, 1999; Moen, 2001). Retirement is no longer merely a male transition but also a female and a couple transition (Henkens, 1999; Smith & Moen, 1998; Szinovacz & DeViney, 2000). In addition, the nuclear family is no longer the norm (Schmitt, 2001); increasingly more households are composed of same-sex couples (Smith & Gates, 2001).[1] Acknowledging the diversity of family forms is important because policies and programs related to retirement such as Social Security are built on a template of the married couple that ignores this diversity (Cahill & South, 2002; Dolan & Stum, 1998). In this chapter we examine retirement planning of same-sex couples and how their patterns of retirement planning converge with and diverge from those of cohabiting and married heterosexual couples.

## Differential Developmental Trajectories

To focus on the normative experiences of lesbian, gay, bisexual, and transgender (LGBT) adults without ignoring their unique experiences and characteristics, a differential developmental trajectory perspective guides our examination of the retirement plans of same-sex couples (Savin-Williams, 2001a, 2001b; Savin-Williams & Diamond, 1999). The key aspects of this perspective are the developmental pathways that sexual minorities share with all adults, the unique aspects of sexual minority status that create differential experiences, and heterogeneity and diverse experiences among same sex–attracted adults. Accordingly, because retirement plans of sexual minorities are likely to be influenced by the same life course factors associated with the retirement planning of all, we expect that retirement plans of same-sex couples will be associated with the same factors that influence heterosexual couples' retirement planning. Furthermore, the amplification of gender effects within same-sex couples and the fact that in the United States same-sex couples do not receive the same level of legal recognition that married couples do implies that they are likely to adopt retirement planning strategies that differ from those of opposite-sex couples. With in-depth interview responses, in this chapter we explore heterogeneity in the retirement plans of adults in same-sex relationships.

## Couples and Retirement

To date most research on couples' retirement planning has been conducted with heterosexual couples. That literature serves as a starting point for our examination of same-sex couples' retirement planning. For couples, retirement planning is an interdependent process, involving a consideration of two retirements (Henkens, 1999; Henretta, O'Rand, & Chan, 1993; Smith & Moen, 1998). Spouses tend to aim for joint retirement (O'Rand, Henretta, & Krecker, 1992), and when retirement timing coincides for both partners there is greater satisfaction with the transition (Moen, Kim, & Hofmeister, 2001). However, heterosexual women are more likely than men to mold their retirement plans to fit their partners' planning because they are more likely to rely on their partners' retirement income (Ginn & Arbor, 1996; Han & Moen, 1999; Henkens, 1999; Moen, Sweet, & Swisher, 2001; Quick & Moen, 1998; Smith & Moen, 1998; Szinovacz, DeViney, & Davey, 2001). High marital satisfaction predicts greater planning and a desire for an earlier retirement age because satisfied couples look forward to spending more time together in retirement (Szinovacz & DeViney, 2000). An additional explanation of the link between relationship satisfaction and high levels of retirement planning is a bidirectional association between relationship satisfaction and investment in the relationship. Specifically, people with high relationship satisfaction invest resources in their relationships, and those who invest in their relationships reap the benefits of that investment with higher satisfaction (Kurdek, 1998).

## Same-Sex Couples

A growing body of research examines the lives of cohabiting and same-sex couples (Blumstein & Schwarz, 1983; Esterberg & Savin-Williams, 2000; Kurdek, 1998; Patterson, 1995; Peplau, 1991). However, little published research specifically addresses the retirement planning of cohabiting couples, and even less investigates the retirement plans of same-sex couples. Although all workers face the challenges of retirement planning with prospects of an increasingly uncertain future, same sex–attracted adults do so within an ambivalent cultural and legislative environment and without a clear normative template (Mock & Cornelius, 2003).

## Planning and Decision Making by Same-Sex Couples

Decision making by couples often is examined from the perspective of power dynamics, resource theory, and gender role socialization (Blood & Wolfe, 1960; Blumstein & Schwarz, 1983; Caldwell & Peplau, 1984; Webster & Reiss, 2001). In their study of diverse couples, Blumstein and Schwarz (1983) defined power as the ability to enforce one's way or influence important decisions. Resource theory posits that the partner with greater resources (typically income and education) loses less if the marriage dissolves and therefore has greater bargaining power within the relationship (Blood & Wolfe, 1960; Webster & Riess, 2001). However, the notion of unequal power in decision making is to some extent inconsistent with the values of nonmarried couples. For example, married couples tend to adopt a specialized division of labor (tasks are allocated to one partner or the other depending on their skills or status), but cohabitants prefer an egalitarian dynamic in which partners share all tasks (Brines & Joyner, 1999). Similarly, compared with married people, those in cohabiting relationships are more nontraditional in their gender ideology (Clarkberg, Stolzenberg, & Waite, 1995). Although a gender-based resource differential typically associated with inequality in opposite-sex couples does not exist in same-sex couples, research suggests that inequality exists within same-sex couples nonetheless (Caldwell & Peplau, 1984; Carrington, 1999).

In contrast to people in heterosexual relationships, those in same-sex relationships have a shared gender role socialization (Rutter & Schwartz, 2000). Some researchers argue that women are socialized to be more relationship oriented and egalitarian than men and that men are socialized to be more independent than women (Cross & Madson, 1997). If this is the case, then this socialized interdependence or independence ought to be reflected in same-sex couples' decision making and planning.

There is some evidence that lesbians are more egalitarian than gay male or heterosexual couples regarding division of household labor (Kurdek, 1993). For example, gay male and heterosexual couples are more likely than lesbian couples to adopt a pattern of specialization, with entire tasks allocated to one partner or the other rather than all tasks being shared by both (Kurdek, 1993). In addition, although some clinical psychological research suggests that lesbian couples are prone to becoming "fused" and gay male couples may be "disengaged" by an amplification of gender effects in same-sex couples, this stereotype may be an oversimplification (Green, Bettinger, & Zacks, 1996). Nonetheless, we expect that female couples will be more interdependent in their decision making than male couples because women are socialized to be relationship oriented. Furthermore, compared with women in same-sex relationships, men in same-sex relationships may make decisions and plans in a more unilateral fashion.

## Policy Issues Affecting LGBT Elders

Compared with their opposite-sex, married counterparts, same-sex couples have fewer policy-based protections of their well-being in old age (Cahill, South, & Spade, 2000; Dolan & Stum, 1998; chapter 11, this volume). Same-sex couples' marriages and families are not recognized by federal law (Smith & Gates, 2001) and therefore do not have access to many of the legal rights and benefits commonly received by families headed by married, heterosexual partners (Cahill, South, & Spade, 2000; Dolan & Stum, 1998). Nearly all state and federal legislation assumes those in same-sex relationships to be individuals, in contrast to heterosexual, married couples, who are considered economically interdependent (Dolan & Stum, 1998). These legal differences in both rights and responsibilities between same-sex and opposite-sex, married partners may account for some of the differential experiences of same-sex couples. For example, same-sex couples may be more likely to plan for retirement based on current satisfaction with the relationship because there are no legal ties between them.

### Social Security

Currently, when legally married people retire, they are eligible for their own Social Security benefits or an amount equal to half of the benefits owed to their partner, whichever amount is greater. Same-sex partners are not eligible for this spousal benefit, which can result in a comparative loss of retirement income for LGBT people whose partners had substantially higher incomes during their working years (Bennett, 2002; Cahill, South, & Spade, 2000).

### 401(k) Plans, Pension Plans, and Wills

In the event of a worker's death, 401(k) or pension plan benefits differ depending on whether the surviving partner was legally married. Same-sex partners are subject to taxes sometimes as high as 20% on benefits from pensions or 401(k) plans. Legally married surviving spouses are not subject to these taxes. Furthermore, federal and state inheritance taxes are written so that property left to a spouse may be exempt from taxes or taxed at a substantially lower rate than property left through other relationships, such as same-sex partnerships (Bennett, 2002; Cahill, South, & Spade, 2000; Cahill & South, 2002; Dolan & Stum, 1998).

## Housing and Care for LGBT Seniors

Research indicates widespread discrimination against sexual minorities by health care, nursing home, and social service professionals (Cahill, South, & Spade, 2000; Cahill & South, 2002; Fairchild, Carrino, & Ramirez, 1996). Expectations of discrimination may make LGBT elders less likely to seek health care in addition to making them "go back in the closet." Some retirement communities have been developed specifically for LGBT seniors, although many cannot afford these facilities and therefore are forced to rely on state, municipal, or federally subsidized housing. No federal laws and few state laws offer protection against discrimination on the basis of sexual orientation for admission into publicly funded housing (Cahill, South, & Spade, 2000).

Many employers who provide health insurance for legally married spouses do not grant health insurance for same-sex partners (Cahill & South, 2002). In addition, some LGBT elders are denied coverage under government support strategies for caregiving, including the Family and Medical Leave Act of 1993 (Bennett, 2002; Cahill, South, & Spade, 2000). Medicaid regulations also affect same-sex and married couples inequitably. Medicaid provides income and asset protections for legally married spouses of beneficiaries. That is, the spouse of the Medicaid beneficiary retains income and assets (such as the house of residence) while the spouse maintains eligibility for Medicaid. This regulation, meant as a protection against impoverishment of spouses, does not apply to same-sex partners (Cahill, South, & Spade, 2000).

## *Hypotheses and Research Questions*

### Quantitative Analyses

In keeping with the first tenet of a differential developmental trajectory perspective, individuals in same-sex relationships are expected to follow established trajectories of retirement planning. Specifically, as is typically found in research of heterosexual couples' retirement planning, age, income, and being male are expected to be associated with greater retirement planning in same-sex couples. Furthermore, like heterosexual couples, same-sex couples who support children should be engaged in less retirement planning than those with no children in the home because resources needed for child rearing are not available for retirement planning.

The second tenet of a differential developmental trajectory perspective predicts that people in same-sex relationships will forge unique paths. Although higher relationship satisfaction is expected to be associated with greater retirement planning for all couple types, for married couples and heterosexual cohabitants who have the option of marriage, other social and legal barriers to relationship dissolution may guide their judgment of relationship longevity and need for long-term planning. However, for same-sex couples who do not have those barriers to relationship dissolution, relationship satisfaction may be one of the few indicators of relationship prospects they have and therefore will be a particularly strong predictor of retirement planning.

## Qualitative Analyses

We predict that as a reflection of the amplification of gender effects, women in same-sex relationships will plan interdependently with their partners; in contrast, a unilateral (each partner plans on his own) or specialization (one partner plans for both) approach to retirement planning will be typical among men in same-sex relationships. Furthermore, we explore interview responses for potential heterogeneity in the retirement plans of same-sex couples.

# Method

Data were drawn from the Cornell Ecology of Careers (EOC) study of 4,637 men and women (1,914 couples). A combination of three central New York State samples collected from 1998 through 2000, the EOC survey was administered via telephone and was designed to examine the work and family lives of two-earner couples. Participants in two of the three samples were contacted through targeted workplace organizations. For the remaining sample, participants were drawn from census tracts that matched the other two samples.[2]

## *Participants*

The EOC participants included those who were originally contacted to participate in the study and their partners or spouses. In both the descriptive and correlational analyses for this chapter, only the person originally contacted to participate in the study is represented in order to maintain statistical assumptions of independence. Of those originally contacted to participate in the EOC study, 22 women and 7 men indicated that they were in same-sex relationships. Compared with other research on same-sex couples, a benefit of these data is that participants were not drawn from a convenience sample, snowball sample, or clinical population. Furthermore, the percentage of same-sex couples in this study is consistent with rates found in recent U.S. Census results (Smith & Gates, 2001).

Although we focus primarily on same-sex relationships in this study, we also present analyses conducted with 29 people in heterosexual cohabiting relationships and 29 people in married relationships for the purposes of comparison. These comparison groups were chosen by narrowing the entire sample of EOC participants in opposite-sex relationships to those who were within the same range of age, income, and number of children as those in same-sex relationships. Twenty-nine people in cohabiting heterosexual relationships and 29 people in married opposite-sex relationships were randomly selected from the narrowed sample.

## In-Depth Interviews

In-depth interviews were conducted with a subset of the same-sex couples from the EOC study. Potential participants were contacted first by mail and then with an introductory phone call with an invitation to participate in an interview study. Of the original 53 participants (including study respondents and partners), 20 (11 men and 9 women) agreed to be interviewed, for a response rate of 38%. Of the 33 who were not interviewed, 8 couples had moved and could not be contacted, and the rest could not be reached by phone.

## Measures

### Retirement Planning

Financial Planning

On a 100-point scale, where 0 = "no planning" and 100 = "a lot of planning," respondents rated the degree to which they were learning about retirement or health insurance options, engaging in financial preparation for retirement, and planning for health care needs. The mean of these three ratings formed the financial planning score (Cronbach's $\alpha$ = .74).[3]

## Lifestyle Planning

On the same scale, respondents rated the degree to which they are considering different housing arrangements, thinking about a second or third career after retirement, thinking about volunteer work in the community after retirement, and developing hobbies or interests. The lifestyle planning score was the mean of these four ratings (Cronbach's $\alpha$ = .62). The construction of the financial planning and lifestyle planning variables is discussed in greater detail elsewhere (Mock & Cornelius, 2001; Moen, Sweet, & Townsend, 2001).

## *Demographics*

Age was calculated by subtracting the participant's year of birth from the year the survey was taken. Racial categories were collapsed into percentage of white participants. Annual salary was the participant's self-reported own primary annual income. Children under 18 in the home was a dichotomous measure in which no children = 0 and any children = 1 and included biological and non-biological offspring.

## *Relationship Variables*

Relationship satisfaction was measured on a scale of 0 to 100, where 0 = "not satisfied at all" and 100 = "absolutely satisfied," on which respondents indicated how satisfied they were with their relationship or marriage. Years in current relationship was the number of self-reported years participants have been in their current marriage or committed relationship.

## *In-Depth Interviews and Questions*

Each interview was conducted by phone, was tape recorded, and lasted approximately 45 minutes. Participants were asked about their workplace experiences as sexual minorities, career choices, couple decision making, retirement planning, and social relations with friends, neighbors, and family. For the present study, we examined responses to the following questions about retirement planning: "Have you started thinking about retirement?" "Do you believe that your financial plans for retirement are going to be sufficient to support you?" "Do you have any plans for post-retirement volunteering or work?" "Has your partner had any influence on your retirement timing or your plans for retirement?" "Are plans being made in tandem with your partner, or as an individual?"

For analyses, an a priori theoretical framework was used to classify responses. Specifically, the first two authors (S.E.M. & C.J.T.) read the responses pertaining to retirement planning and classified participants into one of the following categories: unilateral (plans are being made independently), interdependent (plans are being made together), and specialized (one partner plans for both). Interviews were classified independently, and any discrepancies in coding were resolved by discussion. In addition to this classification system, both authors noted responses that suggested heterogeneity in retirement plans and themes that emerged from the interviews.

# Results

## *Descriptive Statistics*

Among those in same-sex relationships, women rated their financial planning significantly lower than the men did, $t(27) = 3.46$, $p \leq .01$ (table 9.1). Furthermore, for those in same-sex relationships, women tended to rate their lifestyle planning lower than men did, although the difference was not statistically significant, $t(27) = 1.28$, *ns*. Because people typically plan more for retirement as they age, and the men in same-sex relationships were significantly older than the women, $t(27) = 2.57$, $p \leq .05$, we controlled for age in a partial correlation. However, even when age was controlled for, being female was still associated with lower financial planning, partial $r = -.55$, $p \leq .05$.

For those in same-sex relationships, the average income for women was $52,000 and men's average income was $56,571. Twenty-three percent of the women in same-sex relationships and none of the men in same-sex relationships had children in the home. Both women and men in same-sex relationships were highly satisfied with their relationships, with average ratings of 90 and 91 on the 100-point scale. On average, men in same-sex relationships have been with their partners for more than 17 years, and women in same-sex relationships have been with their partners for more than 8 years, although this difference in relationship length was not statistically significant, $t(27) = 2.08$, *ns*.

TABLE 9.1

Means and Percentages for Retirement Planning,
Demographic and Relationship Variables by Relationship Type

| Variables | Relationship Type | | | | | |
| --- | --- | --- | --- | --- | --- | --- |
| | Same-Sex | | Cohabiting | | Married | |
| | Female | Male | Female | Male | Female | Male |
| Financial Planning | | | | | | |
| M | 37.34 | 68.10 | 41.35 | 34.50 | 51.55 | 53.72 |
| SD | 22.13 | 13.24 | 25.21 | 14.45 | 27.24 | 33.37 |
| Lifestyle Planning | | | | | | |
| M | 47.46 | 59.46 | 37.72 | 37.13 | 36.83 | 39.98 |
| SD | 22.26 | 18.57 | 23.33 | 11.15 | 27.22 | 27.53 |
| Age | | | | | | |
| M | 40.05 | 48.57 | 36.49 | 37.17 | 36.83 | 39.25 |
| SD | 7.51 | 8.14 | 7.34 | 9.39 | 8.03 | 8.60 |
| Percent White | 91% | 100% | 90% | 100% | 88% | 92% |
| Annual Salary | | | | | | |
| M | $52,000 | $56,571 | $42,500 | $46,450 | $39,880 | $53,670 |
| SD | $20,797 | $7,020 | $15,640 | $17,810 | $12,850 | $17,730 |
| Percent with Children Under 18 in the Home | 23% | 0% | 16% | 20% | 41% | 42% |
| Satisfaction with Current Relationship | | | | | | |
| M | 90.36 | 90.71 | 86.58 | 85.30 | 85.29 | 85.42 |
| SD | 12.23 | 8.86 | 13.02 | 15.34 | 23.94 | 11.57 |
| Years in Current Relationship | | | | | | |
| M | 8.72 | 17.57 | 2.68 | 4.60 | 9.59 | 12.33 |
| SD | 8.31 | 10.23 | 3.79 | 5.38 | 8.80 | 9.42 |
| n | 22.0 | 7.0 | 19.0 | 10.0 | 17.0 | 12.0 |

## *Correlational Analyses*

Within couple analyses revealed gender (female) was associated with lower financial planning only for those in same-sex relationships (table 9.2). Furthermore, the correlation between being female and lower financial planning was significantly greater for the same-sex couples than for the married couples, $z = 2.08$, $p \leq .05$. Although older age was positively associated with both financial and lifestyle planning, only in the married group was older age significantly associated with greater financial planning. The association between annual salary and retirement planning across all relationship types was statistically nonsignificant. Having children in the home was associated with lower financial and lifestyle planning across all couple types, but only in the cohabiting group was the correlation significant. The significance of the association between relationship satisfaction and retirement planning varied across couple types. Specifically, higher relationship satisfaction was significantly associated with greater financial and lifestyle planning among same-sex couples. Similar trends were found for cohabiting couples, but not to a significant degree. Among heterosexual married couples, relationship satisfaction was not significantly associated with retirement planning. Finally, the correlation of relationship satisfaction with lifestyle planning was significantly greater for those in same-sex relationships than for those in the married group, $z = 2.79$, $p \leq .01$, but was not significantly greater for the cohabiting group.

Consistent with our differential developmental trajectory perspective, the retirement plans of adults in same-sex relationships were linked to factors found in previous research to be associated with opposite-sex couples' retirement planning. Although previous studies found that women plan less than men, in this study the association between being female and lower planning was significant only among those in same-sex relationships. Similarly, although results suggested that higher relationship satisfaction was associated with greater retirement planning, this association was significant only for the same-sex group. For those in opposite-sex relationships, having children was associated with less financial planning, but this association was significant only among cohabitants. Although the direction of this association was similar for those in same-sex relationships, it was not statistically significant.

As expected, there were some unique patterns in the retirement planning for those in same-sex relationships. First, the association between being female and lower financial planning appeared to be stronger among same-sex couples than among opposite-sex couples, suggesting a gender amplification

**TABLE 9.2**

Correlates of Financial and Lifestyle Planning for Individuals in
Same-Sex, Cohabiting, and Married Relationships

| | Relationship Type | | | | | |
|---|---|---|---|---|---|---|
| *Variables* | Same-Sex | | Cohabiting | | Married | |
| | Financial Planning | Lifestyle Planning | Financial Planning | Lifestyle Planning | Financial Planning | Lifestyle Planning |
| Gender | | | | | | |
| *r* | -.55* | -.24 | -.15 | .02 | -.04 | .08 |
| Age | | | | | | |
| *r* | .06 | .23 | .18 | .30 | .52* | .34 |
| Annual salary | | | | | | |
| *r* | .23 | -.02 | .12 | -.07 | .27 | .07 |
| Any children under 18 in the home | | | | | | |
| *r* | -.29 | -.13 | -.41* | -.27 | -.32 | -.26 |
| Satisfaction with current relationship | | | | | | |
| *r* | .38* | .56* | .23 | .25 | -.08 | -.14 |
| *n* | 29 | | 29 | | 29 | |

* p < .05

effect. Second, compared with those in opposite-sex relationships, the correlation between relationship satisfaction and retirement planning appeared to be greater for those in same-sex relationships, possibly because satisfaction is the best predictor of future stability in relationships that are not legally bound.

## *Retirement Planning of Same-Sex Couples:*
## *A Qualitative Analysis*

Drawing from in-depth interviews with same-sex couples, we examined the second and third tenets of a differential developmental trajectory perspective: unique aspects of same-sex couples' retirement planning and potential heterogeneity among same-sex couples as they plan for retirement.

One unique aspect of same-sex couples is that both partners share a common gender socialization that may amplify gender-specific behavior that would otherwise be moderated in opposite-sex relationships. In terms of retirement planning, we expected that women would make retirement plans interdependently with their partners more often and that men's financial plans would tend to be unilateral. We also predicted that men, compared with women, would be more likely to adopt a "specialized" approach to retirement planning (one partner plans for both).

In addition, we documented the heterogeneity of retirement plans that participants discussed in their interviews. Three themes emerged from the interviews: how same-sex-couples' long-term relationships influenced their retirement planning, how coming out to family was related to retirement planning, and how same-sex couples carried out lifestyle planning for retirement.

## Interdependent, Unilateral, and Specialized Styles of Planning

We identified couples that reported interdependent, unilateral, and specialized approaches to retirement planning. Four of the 9 women (44%) and 3 of the 11 men (27%) spoke of making their retirement plans interdependently with their partners. This was the most frequently discussed style for women. One woman said in response to a question about her partner's influence on her planning,

> Well, plans, certainly. It's different being in a committed long-term relationship. You know, in terms of thinking about what we want to do, where we want to live, how we want to live. That certainly has had an influence on me. Also, I just think that she's really grounded, which is helpful to me…. I'm not all that grounded in financial stuff.

Among men, the most frequently discussed planning strategy was unilateral; that is, plans were being made independently (5 of 11 men, or 45%, and 2 of 9 women, or 22%). For example, when asked whether his partner was having any influence on his retirement planning, one man replied,

> No, not really. He has a much clearer idea of when he wants to, but then he's in a more structured field. When he talks about his retirement, it in some way affects me, but not because it makes me think that I have to too. Really, all it means is like, "Oh my God, he's going to be here all the time!" That kind of thing.

For both men and women, when they reported that their retirement plans were being made unilaterally, it was most often because of an age difference. This man explained in response to a question about his partner's influence, "No, because we haven't really talked that much about my retirement. We've talked about, you know, the fact that there's an age difference, but we haven't done a lot of planning or anything for it." Similarly, a woman whose partner is 13 years older than her said, "She is doing a lot of retirement stuff, but it hasn't influenced me."

Both women and men seemed equally likely to adopt a specialized approach to retirement planning (2 of 9 women, 22%, and 2 of 11 men, 18%). However, the specialized approach sometimes was not adopted willingly. One woman explained how she is the reluctant leader in retirement planning in her home:

[My partner] is not a really great long-term money planner. And she doesn't have the means…even to toss a little away. So one of the things, I think one of the things that really kind of gets me about the retirement thing is that I feel like I've got to plan for both of us. And that just feels dreadfully overwhelming, you know.… I'm constantly pulling her back to the table and trying to get her to have opinions about certain things.… It's just not pleasant to have to play that role.

Another woman reported, "She mainly does it. I mean if I had to I could but she really finds interest in all that stuff [retirement planning] so I just let her do it and she's like, 'Look this is the best deal,' and I'm like, 'Okay, cool, let's do it!'" One man talked about how his partner takes the lead in their planning:

My partner has got me more involved with financial planning. When we got together, we decided to go to a financial advisor; one that we thought was more open to same-sex couples. Then we went to my attorney and had some discussions on our future for legal purposes.…Right now we're due for a follow-up appointment, and [my partner] has been the one saying, "We ought to make that appointment," because I could go on forever and not make the appointment.

Thus, a specialized approach to planning usually was taken because one partner was more skilled with financial matters than the other partner.

## Heterogeneity of Retirement Plans

Same-sex couples varied broadly in the extent to which they engaged in retirement planning. Some rarely thought about retirement, and others engaged in extensive planning. Often younger couples planned less. When asked about her planning, a young woman talked about how little she is doing, although she did mention her workplace pension: "No, I guess, I mean I know that it's time to do that, but I'm not doing that. It [pension contribution] is very minimal, but there is something. And it's a mandatory thing, it's not something that I have planned for." Similarly, another woman with a workplace pension plan said she had not thought a lot about retirement planning:

> Well, I let [my employer] put in what they put in for my retirement, and then when [the pension plan] sends me the little thing every month, I look at it and go, "Isn't that nice?" And I put it away. I mean, I keep thinking I should be putting in money and I should be really thinking about retirement, but the truth is, I'm not.

In contrast, another woman discussed the thorough consideration she and her partner have invested into retirement planning:

> I think we've done a lot. We have an accountant that we like and trust. We have ourselves insured so that should one of us pass away, the house would immediately be paid for.... We both have our retirement plans, and we've recently been going through financial planning training with our accountant. We've paid off a tremendous amount of debt in the last six months, and hopefully plan to live debt free for the rest of our lives. So, I think we're well on our way to making sure that all of our bases our covered.

Similarly, one man explained how he and his partner prepared for retirement together: "We each have our own IRA plans.... [My partner] has a great deal of money invested in various places.... I have my IRA, I have stock. You know, we make a good living.... We have sufficient funds put away."

Although not all had retirement plans as extensive as those just described, some of those interviewed had a life insurance policy through their workplace, with their partner listed as the beneficiary. Thus, even among those who were not planning extensively for retirement, there were easily accessible ways that people in same-sex relationships compensated for the policy inequities.

## Being in a Relationship

Being in a committed relationship made some more likely to consider retirement planning and make plans for the future with their partners. One man explained how he began to think of his future differently since entering into a long-term partnership:

> My partner…has gotten me more involved with financial planning…. [He] is much more aware of that…. But I think a lot of that personally has to do with being single for so many years, the thought was well hey, when I die who really cares? Having a partner has made me more aware that I've got to plan for what happens if he dies first or if I die first how we're going to keep, continue to have what we currently have and so on.

Women we interviewed also discussed the influence of being in a committed relationship. As shown in the correlational analyses (table 9.2), relationship satisfaction was significantly associated with greater planning for same-sex couples but not other couple types. In-depth interview responses paralleled our prediction for the quantitative analyses that relationship satisfaction would be an important indicator of future prospects for same-sex couples and would also be associated with greater financial and lifestyle planning.

## Family Matters and Coming Out

Challenging retirement and end-of-life issues exist that are unique to sexual minority adults (see chapter 12, this volume). One respondent faced one of these considerations in the drafting of his will when his family did not know about his sexual orientation or his partner:

> It's a bit difficult sometimes because, you know, the problem comes up of wills and all that…. We have siblings, and they have children and that kind of thing. It becomes a little bit of a dilemma as to just what you can do without hurting other people's feelings…. or forcing them to make judgments. I have one sister-in-law who I have discussed being gay with. My parents, never. I mean, I can't imagine that they don't know it after all these years, but we have never said the words, and so it's just very difficult to say to my mother or father, "Well, yeah, I'm going to leave everything to my partner." It would force them to make a judgment that I just don't want them to have to make.

Thus, for same sex–attracted adults aging together, being in a relationship provides companionship but also raises potential challenges.

## Lifestyle Planning and Aging Together

Although couples made financial plans unilaterally or interdependently, when they spoke about lifestyle planning, nearly all considered their future lifestyles in tandem with their partners. As one woman described, "I'd like to paint... and [my partner] will have her writing and we'll just explore the creative side of life." Another man bought a vacation home with his partner, and they plan to move there in retirement: "We already own the home we live in right now... but we do have a mortgage on our vacation home.... What we were planning on doing is selling this house and moving there when we retire. So, you know, that's where we plan on going right now anyway."

The women and men interviewed made distinctions between lifestyle and financial planning. For example, many could better articulate how lifestyle plans would mesh with their partner's lifestyle plans than the ways their financial plans were being made. When asked whether she and her partner were planning for housing in later life, one woman answered, "We own the home that we're in and...I'm saying *we* because that is the way I look at it, but the truth is I'm the only name on the deed." She anticipated retiring with her partner and sharing their home, indicative of shared lifestyle planning for retirement. However, they had not formalized their financial interdependence; her partner was not a legal owner of the house. This couple considered their partnership to be a lifetime commitment, but they do not have the same financial and legal bonds of a legally married couple. If this woman were to pass away, her partner probably would not have the legal right to remain in their house. Their case is one example of a same-sex couple that made joint lifestyle plans for retirement without creating specific financial plans for retirement.

Other couples exhibited a greater coordination of lifestyle planning for retirement than financial planning. For example, one man spoke about his financial plans for retirement, noting only his own saving and investing: "I started a little late but I started saving a lot more, investing in some stocks and things... and then I've got a pension at [my workplace] too." However, he and his partner will make compromises to retire at the same age: "He'd like to go [retire] now...but...I'd like to stay long enough to...see myself...through to...a pension. I think he'll wait, you know." This couple had made joint decisions about the timing for retirement but kept financial planning separate.

Overall, though, many couples had both interdependent lifestyles and financial plans for retirement. Nearly all respondents (16 of 20) articulated specific lifestyle plans for their retirement with their partner. These plans spanned a wide range, and moving to a new location was the most frequently mentioned (8 of the 20 interviewed). For example, one man explained, "We want to sell this house and buy...a condominium in San Francisco.... We've had discussions already about investing and having multiple dwellings and ultimately we don't like that idea.... We need one place to live and that is sufficient." Of the other plans specified, 5 of 20 spoke about volunteering; 4 mentioned starting a small business; working on creative projects, traveling, and coordinating the timing of the retirement transition were each mentioned three times. One woman noted concrete future plans with her partner: "We definitely have plans for retirement.... We'd like to move back down to New Mexico, we'd like to move someplace with a little bit of land and we'd also like to do some traveling together, which we haven't had an opportunity to do." Another man negotiated moving after retirement with his partner so that he could care for his mother: "He would like to move and if we move...either we will have to stay here until my mother passes away or we're taking my mother with us. We haven't decided, we can't agree on where to go." Similar to that of many people in the sample, this man's lifestyle planning with his partner conveyed a sense of relationship longevity and an implicit assumption that they would spend the rest of their lives together.

## Summary

In this study, we examined the ways in which those in same-sex relationships follow typical patterns of retirement planning and the ways in which they diverge. Although there were suggestively similar patterns across couple types in the correlational analyses, these associations often were significant only among the same-sex couples. For example, women had a significantly lower rating of retirement planning than men, but this association was significant only among those in same-sex relationships. In addition, evidence of an amplification effect of gender patterns among same-sex couples was suggested by the qualitative results that women were most likely to describe their plans as interdependent, whereas men were most likely to mention unilateral plans.

In another example of how same-sex couples differed from legally married couples, the association between relationship satisfaction and retirement planning was strongest for those in same-sex relationships and lowest for those in the married group; the cohabiting group was in between the two. It appears that the cohabitants may occupy an intermediary stage between the same-sex and the married groups, suggesting that although relationship satisfaction has an impact on their plans, it might be tempered by the potential that they could marry and be guided by other legal bonds. In contrast, same-sex couples can rely only on financial and legal planning. Perhaps as a buffer against the lack of societal and legal support, the sexual minority women and men spoke about how being in a relationship made them more future oriented and often heightened their awareness of retirement planning issues. Often, this increased awareness of retirement issues was triggered by both considerations of the practicalities of a future that will be spent with their partners and the influence of a partner with greater knowledge of retirement issues.

To summarize results for those in same-sex relationships from both the quantitative and qualitative analyses, women plan less than men, women are likely to make plans interdependently with their partners, for both men and women relationship satisfaction and retirement planning are linked, and being in a relationship is associated with a consideration of the need to make plans for the future.

These results suggest both risks and opportunities for the retirement planning of same-sex couples. First, although some of the women interviewed described thorough financial and lifestyle retirement plans, the quantitative results suggest that, in general, women's degree of planning is lower than that of men. Women should be encouraged to seek out retirement planning information and assistance. Second, women's planning style—interdependence—suggests that information seeking and implementing retirement plans might be best done with their partners. Third, the link between relationship satisfaction and planning suggests for both men and women that planning together goes hand in hand with greater relationship satisfaction. Fourth, in the interviews, both women and men discussed how being in a relationship increased their planning, either because their partners were knowledgeable about retirement planning or because being in a relationship made them more future oriented. Thus, LGBT adults who are single might need assistance and motivation to think about their future plans and examine their retirement options.

## Conclusion

Because of the small sample size, particularly the low number of men, the results should be interpreted cautiously. Because participants were identified as being in a same-sex relationship solely by the gender of their partner, not through any questions assessing sexual orientation or identity, we cannot discern whether it is sexual identity or sexual orientation that accounts for our findings. However, these limitations are offset to some extent by two factors. First, unlike much research with LGBT samples, these data are from a normative sample drawn from a larger study. Second, we have both quantitative and qualitative data that allowed a multimethod analysis. Furthermore, our results suggest that the experiences of single LGBT adults might differ from those in relationships. Finally, our sample is of adults who lived in central New York State in the late 1990s. The experiences of those living in other countries that legally recognize same-sex relationships might be expected to be more similar to those of heterosexual married couples.

These limitations suggest potential questions for further research. For example, what are the retirement plans of LGBT singles? How does being in a prior heterosexual married relationship influence the retirement plans of single or cohabiting LGBT adults? Given the gender differences found for retirement planning, what are the implications for transgender adults? Are transgender adults who can in some cases legally marry more like heterosexual adults than same sex–attracted adults in their patterns of retirement planning? Taken with the results presented here, further work will add to our understanding of the commonalities and unique paths of LGBT retirement planning.

## ACKNOWLEDGMENTS

This research was supported by grants from the Alfred P. Sloan Foundation (Grant Nos. Sloan FDN 96-6-9 and 99-6-3), Phyllis Moen, principal investigator. We gratefully acknowledge the Ecology of Careers Study participants and, in particular, the women and men who participated in the in-depth interviews.

## NOTES

1. In year 2000 U.S. Census, the percentage of married couple households with children under 18 declined to 23.5% of all households in 2000, from 25.6% in 1990 and from 45% in 1960 (Schmitt, 2001). Additionally, in the 2000 Census 601,209 households were headed by same-sex unmarried partners (Smith & Gates, 2001). Because 3–8% of adults have predominantly same-sex attractions (Laumann et al., 1994), roughly 4 million Americans who will be over the age of 65 by 2030 are likely to be attracted to the same sex.

2. See Moen, Sweet, and Townsend (2001) for a detailed description of sampling methods and study design.

3. An additional study was conducted to further examine correlates of the financial planning scale. With a sample of 55 adults (age, $M = 39.27$, $SD = 10.99$; 26 women), the financial planning scale was moderately correlated with both percentile rating of a comparison of one's financial planning to one's peers, where $0$ = lowest and $100$ = highest ($r = .43$, $p \leq .05$), and to objective retirement planning behavior, particularly discussing financial planning with an accountant or retirement planning specialist ($r = .46$, $p \leq .05$). In a linear regression model, participants' percentile ratings of their financial planning and discussing financial planning with an accountant accounted for 23% of the variance of the financial planning variable (adjusted $R^2 = .23$, $F = 8.42$, $p \leq .01$).

## REFERENCES

Bennett, L. (2002). *The state of the family: Laws and legislation affecting gay, lesbian, bisexual, and transgender families.* Washington, DC: Human Rights Campaign.

Blood, R. O., & Wolfe, D. M. (1960). *Husbands and wives: The dynamics of married living.* Glencoe, IL: The Free Press.

Blumstein, P., & Schwarz, P. (1983). *American couples: Money, work, sex.* New York: William Morrow.

Brines, J., & Joyner, K. (1999). The ties that bind: Principles of cohesion in cohabitation and marriage. *American Sociological Review, 64,* 333–335.

Cahill, S., & South, K. (2002). Policy issues affecting lesbian, gay, bisexual and transgender people in retirement. *Generations, 26,* 49–54.

Cahill, S., South, K., & Spade, J. (2000). *Outing age: Public policy issues affecting gay, lesbian, bisexual, and transgender elders.* New York: National Gay and Lesbian Task Force.

Caldwell, M. A., & Peplau, L. A. (1984). The balance of power in lesbian relationships. *Sex Roles, 10,* 587–600.

Carrington, C. (1999). *No place like home: Relationships and family life among lesbians and gay men.* Chicago: University of Chicago Press.

Clarkberg, M., Stolzenberg, R. M., & Waite, L. J. (1995). Attitudes, values, and entrance into cohabitational versus married unions. *Social Forces, 74,* 609–632.

Cross, S. E., & Madson, L. (1997). Models of the self: Self-construals and gender. *Psychological Bulletin, 122*(1), 5–37.

Dolan, E. M., & Stum, M. S. (1998). Economic security and financial management issues facing same-sex couples. *Journal of Family and Economic Issues, 19,* 343–365.

Esterberg, K. G., & Savin-Williams, R. C. (2000). Lesbian, gay, and bisexual families. In D. H. Demo & K. R. Allen (Eds.), *Handbook of family diversity* (pp. 197–215). New York: Oxford University Press.

Fairchild, S. K., Carrino, G. E., & Ramirez, M. R. (1996). Social workers' perceptions of staff attitudes toward resident sexuality in a random sample of New York State nursing homes: A pilot study. *Journal of Gerontological Social Work, 26*, 153–169.

Ginn, J., & Arbor, S. (1996). Patterns of employment, gender and pensions: The effect of work history on older women's non-state pensions. *Work, Employment, and Society, 10*, 469–490.

Green, R. J., Bettinger, M., & Zacks, E. (1996). Are lesbian couples fused and gay male couples disengaged?: Questioning gender straightjackets. In J. Laird & R. Green (Eds.), *Lesbians and gays in couples and families: A handbook for therapists* (pp. 185–230). San Francisco: Jossey-Bass/Pfeiffer.

Han, S. K., & Moen, P. (1999). Clocking out: Temporal patterning of retirement. *American Journal of Sociology, 105*, 191–236.

Henkens, K. (1999). Retirement intentions and spousal support: A multi-actor approach. *Journal of Gerontology: Social Sciences, 54B*, S1–S19.

Henretta, J. C., O'Rand, A. M., & Chan, C. G. (1993). Joint role investments and synchronization of retirement: A sequential approach to couples' retirement timing. *Social Forces, 71*, 981–1000.

Kurdek, L. A. (1993). The allocation of household labor in gay, lesbian, and heterosexual married couples. *Journal of Social Issues, 49*(3), 127–139.

Kurdek, L. A. (1998). Relationship outcomes and their predictors: Longitudinal evidence from heterosexual married, gay cohabiting, and lesbian cohabiting couples. *Journal of Marriage and the Family, 60*, 553–568.

Laumann, E., Gagnon, J. H., Michael, R. T., & Michaels, S. (1994). *The social organization of sexuality: Sexual practices in the United States.* Chicago: University of Chicago Press.

Mock, S. E., & Cornelius, S. W. (2001). *Couples' retirement planning and timing: A life course analysis of diverse couple types.* Working Paper No. 02-15. Ithaca, NY: Cornell University, Bronfenbrenner Life Course Center.

Mock, S. E., & Cornelius, S. W. (2003). The case of same-sex couples. In P. Moen (Ed.), *It's about time: Couples' career strains, strategies, and successes* (pp. 275–287). Ithaca, NY: Cornell University Press.

Moen, P. (2001). *The career quandary.* Reports on America No. 2/1. Washington, DC: Population Reference Bureau.

Moen, P., Kim, J. E., & Hofmeister, H. (2001). Couples' work/retirement transitions, gender, and marital quality. *Social Psychology Quarterly, 64*, 55–71.

Moen, P., Sweet, S., & Swisher, R. (2001). *Customizing the career clock: Retirement planning and expectations.* Working Paper No. 01-08. Ithaca, NY: Cornell University, Bronfenbrenner Life Course Center.

Moen, P., Sweet, S., & Townsend, B. (2001). Appendix B: Characteristics of participants. In P. Moen, S. Sweet, & B. Townsend (Eds.), *How family friendly is upstate New York?* (pp. 103–106). Ithaca, NY: Cornell University, Bronfenbrenner Life Course Center.

O'Rand, A. M., Henretta, J. C., & Krecker, M. L. (1992). Family pathways to retirement. In M. Szinovacz & D. J. Ekerdt (Eds.), *Families and retirement* (pp. 81–98). Thousand Oaks, CA: SAGE.

Patterson, C. J. (1995). Sexual orientation and human development: An overview. *Developmental Psychology, 31,* 3–11.

Peplau, L. A. (1991). Lesbian and gay relationships. In J. C. Gonsiorek & J. D. Weinrich (Eds.), *Homosexuality: Research implications for public policy* (pp. 177–196). Thousand Oaks, CA: SAGE.

Quick, H. E., & Moen, P. (1998). Gender, employment, and retirement quality: A life course approach to the differential experiences of men and women. *Journal of Occupational Health Psychology, 3,* 44–64.

Rutter, V., & Schwartz, P. (2000). Gender, marriage, and diverse possibilities for cross-sex and same-sex pairs. In D. H. Demo, K. R. Allen, & M. A. Fine (Eds.), *Handbook of family diversity* (pp. 59–81). London: Oxford University Press.

Savin-Williams, R. C. (2001a). A critique of research on sexual-minority youths. *Journal of Adolescence, 24,* 5–13.

Savin-Williams, R. C. (2001b). Suicide attempts among sexual-minority youths: Population and measurement issues. *Journal of Consulting and Clinical Psychology, 69,* 983–991.

Savin-Williams, R. C., & Diamond, L. M. (1999). Sexual orientation. In W. K. Silverman & T. H. Ollendick (Eds.), *Developmental issues in the clinical treatment of children* (pp. 241–258). Needham Heights, MA: Allyn & Bacon.

Schmitt, E. (2001, May 15). For first time, nuclear families drop below 25% of households. *The New York Times,* p. A1.

Smith, D. M., & Gates, G. J. (2001). *Gay and lesbian families in the United States: Same-sex unmarried partner households.* Washington, DC: Human Rights Campaign.

Smith, D. B., & Moen, P. (1998). Spousal influence on retirement: His, her, and their perceptions. *Journal of Marriage and the Family, 60,* 734–744.

Szinovacz, M., & DeViney, S. (2000). Marital characteristics and retirement decisions. *Research on Aging, 22,* 470–498.

Szinovacz, M. E., DeViney, S., & Davey, A. (2001). Influences of family obligations and relationships on retirement: Variations by gender, race, and marital status. *Journal of Gerontology, 56B,* S20–S27.

Webster, C., & Reiss, M. C. (2001). Do established antecedents of purchase decision-making power apply to contemporary couples? *Psychology and Marketing, 18,* 951–972.

# Lesbian and Bisexual Women as Grandparents
## *The Centrality of Sexual Orientation in the Grandparent-Grandchild Relationship*
### Nancy Orel

More than 10 million children currently live with 3 million gay, lesbian, or bisexual parents in the United States (Mercier & Harold, 2003), and the number of lesbian, gay, and bisexual parents has rapidly increased in the last two decades (Flaks et al., 1995; Johnson & O'Connor, 2002). The literature is rich with information about the common concerns and issues facing young lesbians and bisexual women who are parents. However, few studies have documented the common issues and concerns of middle-aged and older lesbians and bisexual women who have been parents for decades. More significantly, little is known about lesbian and bisexual grandmothers. This chapter reports on a study of lesbian and bisexual grandmothers.

Historically, research on grandparents and grandchildren has used primarily white, well-educated, and middle-class samples and has assumed that the grandparents were heterosexual. Only one published study has explored the grandmother's role as experienced by lesbian women (Whalen, Bigner, & Barber, 2000). However, this study did not explore the effect of the grandmother's sexual orientation on the grandparent–grandchild relationship. Instead, grandmothers were asked to define what makes a good grandmother, and respondents indicated that in their role as grandmothers they provided emotional support, varied experiences outside the nuclear family, and support for the parents of their grandchildren.

Because most parents in the United States expect to become grandparents, lesbian, gay, bisexual, and transgender (LGBT) parents probably will become grandparents and great-grandparents. Accurate estimates of the current number of LGBT grandparents are not available. However, it is known that 94% of older Americans with children are grandparents, and it is estimated that 50% of older adults with children will become great-grandparents (Kornhaber, 1996). Applying these statistics to the estimated 3 million lesbian and gay parents, a conservative range of 1 to 2 million lesbians and gay men are (or will soon become) grandparents. Research focusing on the common concerns and issues facing LGBT grandparents is necessary.

This chapter highlights the findings from a qualitative research study that explored the perceptions of lesbian and bisexual grandmothers. It is important to note that gay fathers were not purposely omitted from this research, but as is common in most research on gay and lesbian parenting, fewer gay fathers than lesbian mothers are available as research participants. Additionally, although many of the experiences of lesbian and bisexual grandmothers may also characterize the experiences of gay grandfathers, there are unquestionably significant differences because of dissimilar cultural expectations concerning the roles and responsibilities of grandfathers and grandmothers. These culturally ascribed gender differences in the grandparent–grandchild relationship may compound the existing differences between lesbian or bisexual grandmothers and heterosexual grandmothers. Therefore, this study focuses on the experiences of one gender only, and parallel research will be conducted in the future with gay grandfathers. Likewise, the experiences of transgender grandparents are unique and merit a distinct and separate inquiry in future research.

The existing research and literature on grandchildren and grandparents suggest that the relationship between grandparents and their grandchildren is vital and significant and "has the potential for affecting the development of children in a way that cannot be duplicated in any other relationship" (Wilcoxon, 1987, p. 289). Relationships between grandparents and their grandchildren are becoming increasingly important because of the increasing longevity of family members and the changing demographic structure of American families (e.g., increases in divorce rates and the number of single-parent households). Because of these changing societal and family age structures, "intergenerational relationships—in terms of help given or received, solidarity or conflict or both—will be of increasing importance for family life in the future" (Bengtson, 2001, p. 6).

Previous research has indicated that the grandparent–grandchild connection is valuable, either directly or indirectly for both grandparents and grandchildren (Bengtson & Roberto, 1985). However, the actual value derived varies widely depending on many factors that contribute to the quality of the relationship. The grandparent–grandchild relationship is influenced by the age and gender of the grandparent and grandchild (Hagestad, 1985; Hodgson, 1998; Kivett, 1991), socioeconomic variables such as employment status, educational level, and economic resources (Cherlin & Furstenberg, 1986; Hunter, 1997), geographic proximity and frequency of contact between grandparent and grandchild (Kivett, 1985; Mueller, Wilhelm, & Elder, 2002), psychosocial compatibility (Kornhaber, 1996), personality characteristics (Kornhaber, 1996), disruptive life events (Barranti, 1985; Kornhaber & Woodward, 1981), and the mediating effects of parents (Mueller & Elder, 2003; Whitbeck, Hoyt, & Huck, 1993).

## Lesbian and Bisexual Grandmother Study

Although numerous studies have explored the grandparent–grandchild relationship and the variables that affect this vital relationship, lesbian and bisexual grandmothers have been neglected in the research. Despite national recognition of the important role grandmothers play in their grandchildren's lives in the United States, it was not known whether the grandmother's sexual orientation is related to this role. This study was undertaken to investigate lesbian and bisexual grandmothers' perceptions of their relationships with their grandchildren and whether this relationship is affected by their sexual orientation. The goal of this research was to obtain a deeper appreciation, understanding, and awareness of the grandmother–grandchild relationship when the grandmother defined her sexual orientation as lesbian or bisexual. It is important to note that *lesbian* and *bisexual* are sociocultural and historical constructs with a wide variety of personal, interpersonal, emotional, behavioral, and contextual meanings (Broido, 2000; Kitzinger & Wilkinson, 1995). People vary widely in the extent to which their sexuality and sexual orientation are salient components of their identity. Therefore, participants in this study provided the definition of their sexual orientation and self-identified as either lesbian or bisexual.

## *Participants*

A total of 16 grandmothers shared their perceptions of their relationship with their grandchildren. The 12 (75%) self-identified lesbian grandmothers and 4 (25%) self-identified bisexual grandmothers ranged in age from 44 to 75, with a mean age of 60.9 years. Twelve (75%) of the participants were Caucasian, three (19%) were African American, and one (6%) participant identified herself as "other" (Native American and Latino). Slightly more than half (56%) of the participants were currently employed. Using the International Standard

Classification of Occupations, four (44% of employed grandmothers) were classified as holding professional jobs; three (34%) held service-related positions, and two (22%) were in managerial positions. Seven (44%) of the grandmothers were retired from a variety of positions (professional jobs, 45%; labor, 27%; managerial, 16%; and service, 12%). In terms of educational attainment, one participant did not finish high school, 57% had a high school education, 12% had some college, and 25% had a college degree.

At the time of the study, nine (56%) of the grandmothers were in a partnered relationship with women. The length of these relationships ranged from 18 months to 23 years, with a mean of 8.8 years. Fourteen grandmothers (87.5%) were previously married in a heterosexual union, with the remaining two participants partnering with a man but never legally marrying. Twelve of the 14 marriages ended in divorce, and the remaining two ended with the death of the spouse. Among the 16 participants there were 31 adult children, who ranged in age from 21 to 53 years old (mean = 40.2), and 48 grandchildren, who ranged in age from 2 to 38 years old (mean = 18). Although not the primary focus of this study, 6 of the participants also had great-grandchildren ($n = 26$). Great-grandchildren ranged in age from 6 months to 20 years old. Collectively, there were 29 granddaughters, 19 grandsons, 11 great-granddaughters, and 15 great-grandsons. According to the participants, all 31 of the adult children (21 women and 10 men) were heterosexual.

## Procedure

Given the exploratory nature of this investigation, qualitative procedures were the most favored and appropriate method. Participants for this study were recruited using a modified snowball sampling method (Patton, 1990). That is, potential lesbian and bisexual grandmothers were identified and contacted through identified colleagues and agents. Identified colleagues recruited participants who belonged to middle-aged and older lesbian friendship networks, support groups, and religious organizations. Agents were people known to this researcher who had access to other potential respondents who were not members of political or social gay, lesbian, or bisexual organizations. This method ensured that participants included both out lesbian and bisexual grandmothers and grandmothers whose sexual orientation had not been disclosed. To protect participant confidentiality, interested women identified by agents and colleagues contacted the researcher by telephone. Potential participants were screened for eligibility by telephone. Eligible participants were lesbian and bisexual grandmothers with at least one biological or legally recognized grandchild. These participants had sons and daughters through previous heterosexual relationships or adoption, and these sons and daughters had legally recognized children. For reasons of statistical independence, domestic partners of women already participating in the study were not included so that only one grandmother per family was interviewed. Geographically, participants were recruited from the Midwest, specifically from northwestern Ohio and southeastern Michigan.

Eligible women were interviewed using a face-to-face semistructured in-depth interview. A total of 16 grandmothers participated. It was the goal of this researcher to approach the interviews with the intent of engaging in an informal collaborative process with the respondents. An interview guide was used as an outline of topics of potential theoretical importance to be covered in the interview (e.g., the relationship between their lesbian or bisexual identity and their identity as grandmothers), but participants were not discouraged from pursuing other areas. Each interview was approximately 90 to 120 minutes long, and all interviews were audiotaped.

## Data Analysis

Interviews were transcribed verbatim from the audiotapes. Using the grounded theory approach (Strauss & Corbin, 1994), data that were systematically generated were analyzed in an ongoing reiterative process to identify integrative connections. Following the recommendations of Marshall and Rossman (1995), data analysis included organizing the data, generating themes and patterns, testing the emergent hypotheses against the data, and searching for alternative explanations of the data. The data collected were verified through two procedures. First, after the interviews were transcribed, participants were asked to review portions of their transcribed interviews to verify that their responses accurately captured the points they wanted to make. Secondly, colleagues with expertise working with LGBT elders or multigenerational families reviewed the data.

## Results

Themes emerged from the data that represented recurring patterns and relationships between the narratives provided by the participants. Lesbian and bisexual grandmothers' perceptions of the grandparent–grandchild relationship consisted of four themes: the formation of a lesbian or bisexual grandmother identity, the centrality of sexual orientation in the grandmother–grandchild relationship, the impact of externalized or internalized homonegativity on the grandmother–grandchild relationship, and the mediating role of the parents in the grandmother–grandchild relationship. Each of these themes will be discussed in the following section, and quotes from the interview transcripts will be provided where appropriate to illustrate the analytic patterns. Pseudonyms are used to protect the identity of the participants.

## Formation of a Lesbian or Bisexual Grandmother Identity

All participants in this study had the previous experience of meshing their lesbian and bisexual identities with the important identity of being a mother. There were differences among the women as to when they identified themselves as lesbian or bisexual and the timing of the birth of their children. Ten grandmothers indicated that they did not identify themselves as lesbian or bisexual until after many years of being married and being a mother. For example,

> I really didn't explore the issue of being straight or gay. I just did what you were supposed to do…get married, have kids and own the house with the white picket fence. Back then you didn't talk about sex and if you did it was only in the context of men and women. I learned about sex when I was on my honeymoon with my husband. Likewise, I learned about true love when I fell in love with a woman.

As this quote illustrates, previously married grandmothers described what they perceived to be the cultural and financial need to enter into a marital relationship with a man and start a family. This was also evident in the following comment from the oldest grandmother in this study: "Back then you didn't even consider not marrying. The only question was whether or not you would finish high school before you got married."

The social conditions that encouraged the participants to marry and bear children also made it difficult for them to question their decisions to marry and have children and to question issues related to their sexual orientation. Grandmothers described the realization that they were in relationships that were not consistent with their true sexual orientation as being psychologically difficult and painful. They indicated that the difficulty was intensified by their sense of isolation and aloneness in a nonsupportive culture. For example,

When I was growing up, being gay was not something that you talked about. Kids today have it so much easier. I couldn't talk to anyone. I used to be able to talk to my mom about everything, but I couldn't tell her that I was questioning my marriage because I wanted to be with a woman.

Another grandmother believed that the lack of general discussion on sexual orientation when she was growing up prevented her from fully exploring her own sexual orientation. However, for other participants, their roles as mothers and wives were viewed as being demanding enough to prevent any introspection about issues related to sexual orientation. As one participant said, "Being a mother kept my focus on raising my kids. I didn't have time or energy to think about how my marriage wasn't working or why it wasn't working."

For all 16 participants, "becoming lesbians" or engaging in sexual activities with a woman was a significant event. Fourteen participants indicated that before their first physical encounter with other women, they engaged in an ongoing internal dialogue concerning their sexual orientation. However, two participants indicated that they did not go through a questioning period; instead it seemed to them that one day they were "straight" and the next day they defined themselves as being "gay." As one said,

I never went through that questioning period that a lot of lesbians talk about. One day I was straight and then this woman seduces me and "wow." I knew at that moment that this was what I was missing all my life and suddenly it made sense why I was never content in my marriage. So ... I went from not being gay to being gay in a matter of seconds.

All 16 women in this study discussed the psychological importance of being able to self-identify as being either lesbian or bisexual. The ability to identify as lesbian was viewed as freeing, but there was anxiety and fear related to ending the marriage and the security that the heterosexual union provided. The women also reported grieving for the "years lost." Many indicated that cultural and social constraints prevented them from fully investigating their sexual orientation earlier in their lives and that negative cultural attitudes about homosexuality prevented them from "fully living their lives as lesbians." As one of the grandmothers said,

I realized that I was a lesbian and didn't want to be married any longer, but I never told my husband the exact reason I wanted out of the marriage. Back then, it was hard enough being a divorced mother, let alone a divorced lesbian mother. I had to get a job and support me and my two kids. I needed my mother to help watch the kids during the day so that I could work. I couldn't risk telling her I was gay. In fact I couldn't risk being openly gay. I heard too many horror stories from other women. What if they wanted to take the kids away from me? That I couldn't live with.

Previously married participants indicated that ending their marital relationships with a divorce decree was in many ways both a personal and social marker of their acceptance of their homosexuality. Another very significant marker was disclosing their sexual orientation to their children. The decision-making process and subsequent ability to come out to their children was reported as a significant event for all 12 of the grandmothers who had done so. The actual process of coming out to their children varied. Likewise, the type and range of responses that participants received from their children were just as varied. One participant combined coming out to her child with another significant event in the family. She was the only respondent who reported that she received a very negative response.

When I told my 13 year old son that Sally was going to be moving in with us, he asked if we were lesbians. I assumed that he was ready for the information if he was asking the question. When I told him that I was, he ran up to his room and called his father. The next day he left to go live with his father. He didn't want to talk to me for about 3 months. We haven't been close since.

Although they saw coming out to their children as a significant event, most respondents indicated that disclosing their sexual orientation to their children was an indirect process rather than a defining event. The grandmothers indicated that they calculated behaviors and dialogue in order to ease into the topic of their sexual orientation. For example,

It wasn't as if one day I decided to sit my children down and say, "Hey kids, did you know that your mom is a lesbian?" Instead, from the time they were born, I would try to introduce tolerance of others who were different and to stress to them that you have to be open about differences. I would make sure that if a certain movie was out that had positive gay roles that we would go see it. Eventually, the kids just knew.

For participants who believed that they were open and honest about their sexual orientation with their young and adolescent children (75%), this level of honesty was viewed as a key factor in the maintenance of an intimate and warm relationship with their now adult children. In turn, participants reported that this heightened level of affection and intimacy with their adult children facilitated the establishment of an affectionate relationship with their grandchildren. The grandmothers firmly believed that unless their relationships with their adult children were strong, they would never have had the opportunity to establish strong bonds with their grandchildren. Grandmothers also reported that their relationships with their adult children often determined the specific role they would enact as grandmothers. All grandmothers also believed that cultural gender expectations determined their role as grandmothers. There were cultural expectations that grandmothers would assume a parent-like nurturing role with their grandchildren. Lesbian and bisexual grandmothers also indicated that although they participated in a wide range of activities with their grandchildren, often the type of activities requested by the grandchildren were gender stereotypic (e.g., going shopping, baking). However, four grandmothers specifically indicated that they viewed their role as providing strong messages of gender flexibility and participated in activities with their grandchildren that represented this flexibility in gender roles.

Although the grandparenting roles among the grandmothers were diverse, grandmothers conceptualized these roles according to how a particular role satisfied their needs, the needs of their adult children, and the needs of their grandchildren. All grandmothers expressed the desire to support the parents of their grandchildren. All grandmothers reported that their relationships with their grandchildren brought purpose and meaning to their lives, and the grandmothers assumed that they were meeting their grandchildren's need for love and attention.

## The Centrality of Sexual Orientation in the Grandmother-Grandchild Relationship

The second theme that emerged from the data was the centrality of sexual orientation in the grandparent–grandchild relationship. In the analysis of the grandmothers' narratives concerning their level of satisfaction obtained from the grandparenting role, a prominent difference emerged between the grandmothers who were out and the grandmothers who had not disclosed their sexual orientation to their adult children or grandchildren. Sexual orientation was an issue that repeatedly surfaced in their descriptions of their relationships with their grandchildren.

Four of the 16 participants (25%) in this study were completely secretive about their sexual orientation; neither their adult children nor their grandchildren knew of their self-identifications as lesbian or bisexual. Two additional grandmothers had not disclosed their sexual orientation to their grandchildren, for a total of six (38%). Six of the sixteen grandmothers (38%) were out to both their adult children and all of their grandchildren, and another four grandmothers (25%) were out to their adult children and assumed that their grandchildren knew about their sexual orientation but could not confirm this assumption.

Grandmothers' explanations for being open or secretive about their sexual orientation varied, with age or developmental level of the grandchild being a primary factor. Additionally, two grandmothers who were out to their adult children but remained closeted with their grandchildren indicated that they were honoring their adult children's request to remain silent. One grandmother indicated that she did not disclose her sexual orientation to her grandchildren for "protection." She assumed that her grandchildren would have it easier if they did not know that their grandmother was a lesbian. "I didn't want her [her granddaughter] to have to explain to her friends what a lesbian grandmother was. I'm afraid that her friends would tease her if they knew that she had a grandmother who was a lesbian."

As previously indicated, six of the grandparents reported that their grandchildren did not know about their sexual orientation. However, it is important to note that this often was an assumption on the part of the grandparents. When asked, "How do you know this?" the grandmothers indicated that they just assumed that their grandchildren did not know. Similarly, some grandmothers assumed that their grandchildren knew. As one grandmother said, "They must know. They see me all the time with Jane [her partner]. I mean, how could they not know? I've been with Jane for fifteen years."

Grandmothers who did not disclose their sexual orientation to their grandchildren reported a sense of dishonesty and distance between themselves and their grandchildren. The grandmothers also reported that it was extremely stressful for them to hide their sexual orientation, that the effort necessary to maintain the illusion of heterosexuality was almost unbearable. They also voiced concerns regarding how their grandchildren would react to the knowledge of them being lesbian or bisexual. However, these grandmothers also indicated that they wondered whether their grandchildren would react negatively to their homosexuality or just react negatively to their grandmothers being sexual. As one grandmother said, "I think my granddaughter would be more upset knowing that her grandmother was still having sex. She would probably say that was gross."

The grandmothers' level of concern about grandchildren learning about their homosexuality was related to their adult children's knowledge and acceptance of their homosexuality. Again, this speaks to the influence of the parent in the grandparent–grandchild relationship. Grandmothers indicated that their concerns about their grandchildren were tempered by the fact that their adult children were comfortable with their homosexuality. "I'm assuming that if my granddaughter did have difficulty with my lesbianism, my daughter would set her straight—no pun intended." Another grandmother believed that her grandchildren were accepting of her homosexuality because she was comfortable with her self-identification as a lesbian. She elaborated on this when she said,

> I'm comfortable with who I am. If I wasn't, I think my grandkids would pick that up and view my relationship with my partner as something negative. It [her lesbian sexual orientation] has to be presented in a positive light. I've had friends who told their kids in such a way as if they were apologizing for being gay. You have to be proud of who you are before you can expect your grandchildren to be proud of you. That goes with everything, from what career you had, to how you think, your opinions, and what not. I've lived too many years and been through too much to not be comfortable with who I am now.

Generally, grandmothers indicated that their sexual orientation per se was not significant in regard to their relationships with their grandchildren. As one grandmother said, "I'm a mother first, then a grandmother, and lastly a lesbian. My lesbianism is such a small part of who I am, and being a lesbian doesn't make me a good grandmother." Another grandmother said, "Honestly, my homosexuality is not an issue as far as my grandchildren are concerned. It's important to me as an individual, but in my role as a grandmother it makes no difference."

The actual significance of sexual orientation on the grandparent–grandchild bond was related to how a grandparent's sexual orientation affected the level of honest discourse that took place with her grandchildren. This level of honesty was severely compromised when the grandparent was fearful of disclosing an important personal dimension of her identity: her sexual orientation. However, the fear was created and fueled by the heterosexist and homophobic context in which the lesbian or bisexual grandmother-grandchild relationship existed. This was evident in the following statement that was echoed by all grandmothers: "My sexual orientation shouldn't matter, but our culture makes it matter."

What was evident in each grandmother's statements concerning the centrality of her sexual orientation in the grandparent–grandchild relationship was the impact of heterosexism and homonegativity on her ability to have an open, honest, and influential relationship with both her adult children and her grandchildren. Therefore, the impact of externalized and internalized homonegativity on the grandmother–grandchild relationship was the third theme to emerge from the data.

## The Impact of Externalized and Internalized Homonegativity on the Grandmother-Grandchild Relationship

The grandmothers in this study all indicated that any personal conflicts that they had concerning their role as a lesbian or bisexual grandmother or conflicts with their identity as a lesbian or bisexual woman reflected societal attitudes toward homosexuals and societal oppression of women in general. The older grandmothers specifically discussed the era in which they were raised and how they internalized the culture's negativity toward homosexuals. The oldest grandmother in this study was in her early 40s when the gay civil rights movement began with the 1969 Stonewall Inn riots. Her childhood and adolescent memories of issues related to homosexuality were fraught with negativity. It was not surprising that the older participants struggled to view themselves positively as lesbians or bisexual women.

Because of the differences in the sociocultural and sociopolitical context of the grandmothers' lives, the older grandmothers were less likely to be out to all family members (e.g., daughters, sons, siblings, ex-husbands, grandchildren) than were the younger grandmothers. Older grandmothers spoke of how the decision to remain silent about their sexual orientation was based on fears of becoming estranged from their families of origin. This was especially true for two of the grandmothers who were never married and were not currently in a relationship. Likewise, two of the grandmothers who lost their spouses to death indicated that they were less likely to disclose their homosexuality because, as one said, "There's status in being a widow. There's no status in being a lesbian."

The younger grandmothers' adolescent and early adulthood memories of issues related to homosexuality were still negative, but included in these cognitions were messages of societal acceptance, tolerance, and gay pride. This is reflected in the statement made by one grandmother when she said,

I refuse to stay in the closet or pretend that I'm straight. My daughter's openness to my homosexuality is because I didn't internalize the culture's anti-gay attitudes and pretend that I was something that I wasn't when she was growing up.... . Now that I'm a grandmother, I'm not going to pretend that I'm straight for my grandkid.

The lesbian and bisexual grandmothers in this study discussed the ways in which they have confronted homophobia and the ways in which they have come to live with it. The lesbian and bisexual grandmothers found emotional and social support from their families of choice and from the gay and lesbian community. All of the grandmothers provided detailed descriptions of the relationships they had with members of their families of origin, families of creation, and families of choice. Although three of the grandmothers forged families of choice because of estrangement from biological family members, two grandmothers indicated that geographic distance from their biological families was the primary motivator in establishing close family-like networks.

The grandmothers indicated that they made conscious decisions on the type of familial and social support that they would establish and maintain. Some grandmothers believed that their involvement in the gay and lesbian community was instrumental for their psychological well-being. However, other grandmothers viewed involvement in the LGBT community as conflicting with their ability to be involved with their biological families. For example, one grandmother indicated that although she would like to be more politically active, she had concerns about "being really out" and how this would affect her relationships with her grandchildren.

The nine currently partnered grandmothers (56%) provided the most poignant narratives that illustrated the impact of externalized and internalized homonegativity on the grandparent–grandchild relationship. These grandmothers reported the difficulties they have with their partners' status as a co-grandmother. They noted that the nonbiological grandmother's role in relation to the grandchild was far less visible than the role of the biological grandmother, and the nonbiological grandmother's role was completely invisible within a heterosexist culture. This invisibility of the nonbiological grandmother's role caused conflicts for the lesbian couples with grandchildren. Often, the biological grandmothers were jealous of the co-grandmother's freedom from the assumed responsibilities of being a grandparent, but at other times, biological grandparents were angry at their partner's lack of interest in the grandchildren. Because our culture has not recognized same-gender relationships, the biological grandmothers and co-grandmothers had unequal status with regard to the grandchildren. Likewise, if the adult children or grandchildren were unaware of the biological and nonbiological grandmothers' partnered relationship, the adult children and grandchildren sometimes inadvertently disregarded the feelings of the co-grandmother. As one grandmother said,

> Me being the blood mother–grandmother does make me feel completely different from my partner at times. I know there are times when she feels like I disregard her feelings, but as the mom–grandma, I can only make decisions that I feel I can live with. I never want her to feel like she doesn't matter or that her feelings aren't important, especially since society does that already. When we went to my ... oops, our granddaughter's play at school, me and all the other grandmas were bragging about our grandkids. I felt bad for my partner because she can't brag even though she's the grandma too. Even my own grown daughter doesn't acknowledge her as a grandmother. I know that hurts her the most and it makes it hard for her to really have a close relationship with my, our granddaughter.

This particular quote illustrates again the influence that the middle generation (adult children) has in the formation and maintenance of the grandparent–grandchild relationship. Because the term *mediating* historically has been used in the grandparent–grandchild literature to characterize the influence of the middle generation, the label given to the fourth broad term to emerge from the data was "the mediating role of the parents in the grandmother-grandchild relationship."

## The Mediating Role of the Parents in the Grandmother-Grandchild Relationship

The grandmothers reported that their adult children often determined the amount of access that they, or in some cases their partners, would have to their grandchildren. Grandmothers believed that the level of access ultimately affected the nature and quality of the grandparenting roles. The adult children (parents) facilitated and in some cases discouraged the development of an emotionally intimate relationship between the grandparents and grandchildren. What was also evident in the grandmothers' accounts was the influence of family relationship histories on the behavior between grandmothers and grandchildren. Specifically, early family interactions (e.g., warmth, affection, and respect between members), negative feelings between generations, and significant family disruptions (e.g., divorce) set in motion a chain of events that affected the interaction styles and expectations across the three generations. For example, grandmothers explained that their adult children who perceived their early family experiences as positive encouraged the formation of a strong grandparent–grandchild relationship through frequent access. Conversely, adult children who were described by the grandmothers as still "holding a grudge about the divorce" discouraged the formation of the grandparent–grandchild relationship and limited access. As one grandmother said,

I really believe that the reason I don't see my grandchildren often goes all the way back to the divorce. He was only seven at the time and it was hard explaining to him why daddy was leaving. I know he blamed me for the divorce. Our relationship has always been rocky. He was into drugs and alcohol and no matter what I did, it wasn't good enough. Likewise, my daughter and I haven't been close.

However, the majority of grandmothers in this study spoke very fondly of their affectionate and intimate relationships with their adult children. They also reported that these positive ongoing close relationships have been instrumental in their close relationships with their grandchildren. Two examples included the following:

I couldn't love my grandkids any more. They mean everything to me and my son knows that. He's great about bringing them over here to visit me and I'm always included in all the family gatherings and what nots.... But we have always been close. To this day, my son still always asks me for advice and he's taught his kids to come to me for advice.

I really believe that my daughters want me to have good relationships with their children. Me and my partner are invited to all the family gatherings. In fact, the last family gathering was quite a scene. My ex-husband was there with his third wife, and his kids from his marriage to his second wife. My ex-husband's brother was also there with his second wife and all her kids from her first marriage. My uncle, who is gay was there with his partner of over fifty years. There were kids everywhere! These kids have been exposed to diversity from day one. Having a lesbian for a grandmother is no big deal.

This last quote also illustrates the ongoing influence of grandmothers' ex-husbands on the role of the parent in the grandparent–grandchild relationship.

All 12 of the divorced grandmothers maintained relationships with their ex-husbands. The majority (84%) reported that these ongoing relationships have been favorable. However, two grandmothers indicated that their conflictual relationships with their ex-husbands have led to conflicts with their adult children.

> I know he [her ex-husband] has said some terrible things about me. He was the one who told my grandkids that I was a lesbian and ever since my relationship with my grandkids hasn't been the same. But I'm more upset with Steve [her eldest son] for siding with him against me. But it's been that way for as long as I can remember. It's just not fair to me. It's sad. It breaks my heart.

The grief illustrated by this grandmother's account concerning her estranged relationship with her grandson was the exception to the sentiments expressed by the majority of the grandmothers in this study. During interviews, grandmothers' articulate reports of their grandchildren were coupled with photographs of their grandchildren or poignant stories of their accomplishments. The majority of the grandmothers expressed profound joy when describing their relationships with their grandchildren and seemed reticent to discuss any ill effects they think their sexual orientation may have had or could have on their future relationships with their grandchildren. However, grandmothers were aware of the impact their sexual orientation had on their relationships with their adult children and subsequently on their relationships with their grandchildren. The grandmothers who decided to remain silent about their sexual orientation expressed fears concerning loss of contact with children and grandchildren if their homosexuality or bisexuality was known. Conversely, the grandmothers who were open about their sexual orientation saw this level of honesty as significant in the formation and maintenance of strong familial relationships with adult children and grandchildren.

## Conclusion

The grandmothers' narratives provided additional insights into the variables that affect the grandparent–grandchild relationship and the significance of this dyadic relationship when the eldest matriarchal figure is lesbian or bisexual. Significantly, the grandmothers always described their relationships with their grandchildren in the context of their ongoing relationships with their adult children. A primary finding was that adult children either facilitated or discouraged the development of an emotionally intimate relationship between their parents (grandmothers) and children (grandchildren). As has been documented in previous research, the grandparent–grandchild connection should be conceptualized as an indirect one with parents as intermediaries (Mueller, Wilhelm, & Elder, 2002; Orel & Dupuy, 2002; Whitbeck, Hoyt, & Huck, 1993). In the current study, grandmothers who had a strong, intimate relationship with their adult children were more likely to have a close relationship with their grandchildren.

Lesbian and bisexual grandmothers believed that they were a key source of emotional support for their grandchildren and provided emotional and instrumental support to their adult children. The grandmothers enacted numerous roles that were dynamic, varied, flexible, complementary, ever-changing, and adapted to the developmental changes of their grandchildren. These same grandparenting roles have been previously identified in the gerontological literature for heterosexual grandparents (Kornhaber, 1996; Mueller, Wilhelm, & Elder, 2002). Likewise, the results of this study paralleled the findings of Whalen, Bigner, and Barber (2000), who explored the grandmother role as experienced by nine lesbian women.

Managing disclosure about sexual orientation was a primary issue for all of the grandmothers in this study, and participants' decisions to come out or remain closeted took into consideration the level of sexism, heterosexism, and homonegativity in their particular setting and context. There were important differences between the grandmothers who had and those who had not disclosed their sexual orientation to their adult children or grandchildren. Although the differences depended on their adult children's attitudes toward their sexual orientation, grandmothers who were open about their sexual orientation believed that this self-disclosure was a key factor in forming and maintaining emotionally strong relationships with their grandchildren. However, a limitation of this study was in its reliance on the reports of only one generation when exploring the grandparent–grandchild relationship. Because each generation may view the relationship differently (Bengtson et al., 2000), future research should explore the perceptions of grandchildren of lesbian and bisexual grandparents.

Other limitations of this study must be acknowledged. The results of this study cannot be generalized to the broader population of lesbian and bisexual grandmothers because of the small sample and nonrandom sampling procedures. Future research with a larger and more diverse representative sample is suggested. This study especially needs to be replicated with gay men, bisexual men, and transgender grandparents. Another important area of inquiry is the experiences surrounding grandchildren's relationships with the co-grandparents or partners of LGBT grandparents. As has been reported for lesbian couples with children (Hequembourg & Farrell, 1999), it may be found that a potential source of conflict for partnered lesbian grandmothers is the issue of asymmetries in their grandparental relationships. Nonbiological grandmothers may have a less visible and recognizable role than the biological grandmother. This invisibility would be compounded if the nonbiological grandmother is also closeted. This invisibility could be especially problematic for lesbian stepgrandmothers. The role of LGBT grandparents in stepfamilies and other unique familial configurations (e.g., extended families, blended families) merits exploration. This exploration would also include LGBT grandparents' relationships with their grandchildren when familial configurations are altered by death, divorce, or broken commitments.

Despite the limitations of the present study, the findings offer an important initial investigation of the role of grandparenting in the lives of lesbian and bisexual women. These data add to the current understanding of the importance of the grandparent–grandchild relationship for all three generations and to the current understanding of the importance of familial relationships for middle-aged and older lesbians and bisexual woman. The results of this research can be used to acknowledge and accentuate the mutually beneficial aspects of the grandparent–grandchild relationship.

Previous research indicated that strong grandparent–grandchild relationships influence grandchildren's subsequent attitudes toward the aged (Pecchioni & Croghan, 2002; Ponzetti & Folkrod, 1989). Specifically, grandchildren who experienced an intimate, positive, and meaningful relationship with their grandparents had a more positive attitude toward the aged and the aging process. Similarly, it would be interesting to determine whether strong grandparent–grandchild relationships with LGBT grandparents reduces the level of homonegativity in the grandchildren.

## REFERENCES

Barranti, C. C. (1985). The grandparent–grandchild relationship: Family resource in an era of voluntary bond. *Family Relations, 34,* 343–352.

Bengtson, V. (2001). Beyond the nuclear family: The increasing importance of multigenerational bonds, *Journal of Marriage and Family, 63,* 1–16.

Bengtson, V., Giarrusso, R., Silverstein, M., & Wang, Q. (2000). Families and intergenerational relationships in aging societies. *International Journal of Aging, 2*(1), 3–10.

Bengtson, V., & Roberto, J. (Eds.). (1985). *Grandparenthood.* Beverly Hills, CA: SAGE.

Broido, E. (2000). Constructing identity: The nature and meaning of lesbian, gay, and bisexual identities. In R. M. Perez, K. A. DeBond, & K. J. Bieshke (Eds.), *Handbook of counseling and psychotherapy with lesbian, gay, and bisexual clients* (pp. 13–33). Washington, DC: American Psychological Association.

Cherlin, A. J., & Furstenberg, F. (1986). *The new American grandparent.* New York: Basic Books.

Flaks, D., Ficher, I., Masterpasqua, F., & Joseph, G. (1995). Lesbians choosing motherhood: A comparative study of lesbian and heterosexual parents and their children. *Developmental Psychology, 37,* 105–114.

Hagestad, G. (1985). Continuity and connectedness. In V. L. Bengtson & J. F. Robertson (Eds.), *Grandparenthood* (pp. 31–48). Beverly Hills, CA: SAGE.

Hequembourg, A., & Farrell, M. (1999). Lesbian motherhood: Negotiating marginal mainstream identities. *Gender and Society, 13,* 540–557.

Hodgson, L. (1998). Grandparents and older grandchildren. In M. Szinovacz (Ed.), *Handbook on grandparenthood* (pp. 169–183). Westport, CT: Greenwood.

Hunter, A. G. (1997). Counting on grandmothers: Black mothers' and fathers' reliance on grandmothers for parenting support. *Journal of Family Issues, 18,* 251–269.

Johnson, S., & O'Connor, E. (2002). *The gay baby boom: The psychology of gay parenthood.* New York: New York University Press.

Kitzinger, C., & Wilkinson, S. (1995). Transitions from heterosexuality to lesbianism: The discursive production of lesbian identities. *Developmental Psychology, 31,* 95–104.

Kivett, V. (1985). Grandfathers and grandchildren: Patterns of association, helping, and psychological closeness. *Family Relations: Journal of Applied Family & Child Studies, 34,* 565–571.

Kivett, V. (1991). The grandparent–grandchild connection. *Marriage and Family Review, 16,* 267–290.

Kornhaber, A. (1996). *Contemporary grandparenting.* Thousand Oaks, CA: SAGE.

Kornhaber, A., & Woodward, K. L. (1981). *Grandparents/grandchildren: The vital connection.* Garden City, NY: Anchor Press.

Marshall, C., & Rossman, G. (1995). *Designing qualitative research* (2nd ed.). London: SAGE.

Mercier, L., & Harold, R. (2003). A feminist approach to exploring the intersection of individuals, families, and communities: An illustration focusing on lesbian mother research. *Journal of Human Behavior in the Social Environment, 7*(3–4), 79–95.

Mueller, M., & Elder, G. (2003). Family contingencies across the generations: Grandparent–grandchild relationships in holistic perspective. *Journal of Marriage and Family, 65,* 404–417.

Mueller, M., Wilhelm, B., & Elder, G. (2002). Variations in grandparenting. *Research on Aging, 24,* 360–388.

Orel, N., & Dupuy, P. (2002). Grandchildren as auxiliary caregivers for grandparents with cognitive and/or physical limitations: Coping strategies and ramifications. *Child Study Journal, 32*, 193–213.

Patton, M. W. (1990). *Qualitative evaluation and research methods* (2nd ed.). Newbury Park, CA: SAGE.

Pecchioni, L., & Croghan, J. (2002, December). Young adults' stereotypes of older adults with their grandparents as the targets. *Journal of Communication, 52*, 715–730.

Ponzetti, J., & Folkrod, A. (1989). Grandchildren's perceptions of their relationships with their grandparents. *Child Study Journal, 19*, 41–50.

Strauss, A., & Corbin, J. (1994). Grounded theory methodology: An overview. In K. Denzin & Y. S. Lincoln (Eds.), *Handbook of qualitative research* (pp. 273–285). Thousand Oaks, CA: SAGE.

Whalen, D., Bigner, J., & Barber, C. (2000). The grandmother role as experienced by lesbian women. *Journal of Women and Aging, 12*(3–4), 39–57.

Whitbeck, L., Hoyt, D., & Huck, S. (1993). Family relationship history, contemporary parent–grandparent relationship quality, and the grandparent–grandchild relationship. *Journal of Marriage and the Family, 55*, 1025–1035.

Wilcoxon, S. (1987). Grandparents and grandchildren: An often neglected relationship between significant others. *Journal of Counseling and Development, 65*, 289–290.

# Legal Concerns of LGBT Elders

*Matthew R. Dubois*

*I*ssues of gender identity and sexual orientation in the U.S. elder population cannot be ignored. Professional and institutional heterosexist assumptions are receding. The need for the aging closet is becoming less acute. These advances are evidenced by frank discussions among elder professionals (Butler, 2002), by rapid advances in the laws directly affecting gays and lesbians (see *Lawrence v. Texas,* 2003, and *Goodridge et al. v. Department of Public Health,* 2003), and by demographics that show increasing numbers of nontraditional households, particularly among the elderly (Burda, 2002). Treatment of gays and lesbians in the law is improving but remains in turmoil.

## Introduction to Legal Concerns of LGBT Elders

Elder benefits and rights are defined most often by federal laws and regulations including Social Security benefits and entitlements, Medicaid, Medicare, and retirement plan rules that do not recognize gay and lesbian relationships, elderly or otherwise. The majority of gay and lesbian elders in the United States still cannot access most basic family rights and protections, which flow from the federal "elder safety net." Elderly life partners may have spent their lives relying on each other, but in old age they will not receive most of the benefits available to their heterosexual counterparts. Concurrent with the writing of this chapter, Massachusetts approved and implemented the first legal marriages in the United States; many of the first couples married were elders. However, the legal future of these marriages is unsettled, and they do not provide the bulk of marriage-related rights and protections offered to heterosexuals under federal law. Indeed, recognition of gay and lesbian marriages is currently prohibited by the federal Defense of Marriage Act.

However, a generation of gays and lesbians who have struggled for acceptance are working in elder service professions and approaching retirement age themselves. Despite many of the nation's older elders remaining in a web of closet privacy, a defense strategy necessitated by past homophobia and continuing perceptions of heterosexism (Butler, 2002), the invisibility and insensitivity associated with being gay and old is disappearing in both the public consciousness and in the law. Individual elders must protect themselves in this time of significant social upheaval; although legal protections are a patchwork at best, legal tools are available, and private legal planning can provide some protections for gay seniors.

The process of more pervasive legal change that creates equality for sexual minorities, following the U.S. Supreme Court's rejection of all laws criminalizing sodomy (*Lawrence v. Texas,* 2003), will be slow but sure (Coyle, 2003, p. 24). For the most part, however, statutory protections, regulatory policy, and both public and private assistance programs for the elderly remain geared toward traditional models of family and either assume heterosexuality or are sexual orientation neutral.

The wide discrepancy in federal, state, and local laws affecting gays and lesbians necessarily means that for at least a few more generations, gay and lesbian elders must continue to engage in deliberate advance legal planning to protect themselves, their families, and their property (Dubois, 1999). Planning ahead for the elder years is of vital importance for gays, lesbians, bisexuals and transgendered (LGBT) individuals and couples. They should think about issues such as incapacity and estate planning long before most people ponder these issues. Although many areas of law affect gays and lesbians (including criminal protections against hate-motivated threats or harassment, housing discrimination, family law, and HIV and AIDS policy), some specific areas of the law by their nature implicate aging issues, and LGBT elders must take care to protect their interests in these areas.

## Incapacity Planning

It is essential that gay and lesbian elders choose agents to assist them with their legal and financial affairs in the event of their incapacity. This person is not a personal assistant, home care provider, or health aide; this is a person who will substitute his or her judgment, in a legally binding manner, as a fiduciary and as a health care proxy in making decisions about an elder's life and affairs. Spouses and some biological relatives automatically receive authority for some decisions; life partners, children of life partners, or other nontraditional family members do not. It is particularly important to the gay elder to appoint an agent to make these decisions because of general intolerance, the inability to marry a life partner, or hostile biological family members. The authority to act as a fiduciary or health care proxy can also be granted by a court, usually a probate court, in an adult proceeding for guardianship or conservatorship.

However, it is possible to avoid court proceedings by making agent nominations in writing, in a durable financial power of attorney and a power of attorney for health care (also known as an advance directive or health care proxy). Laws regarding agency under durable powers of attorney differ from state to state, and an attorney licensed in the elder's state of primary residence should be consulted. However, there are a number of commonalities that should be addressed on behalf of LGBT elders in these advance directives.

A health care power of attorney for LGBT elders should contain strong language to ensure that the agent named in the document will be respected despite lack of biological ties. Consider that although an agent under a health care power of attorney may have access to the principal and his or her records, the agent's authority to make decisions may be limited to the express language of the document. The right to make decisions regarding ability and priority of visitation is an example of a right taken for granted, often not included in powers of attorney, that without express authority may be denied to a nonrelated agent in favor of the wishes of biological family.

Nontraditional couples have concerns about having access to each other in medical or nursing care facilities. Durable powers of attorney should indicate the importance that the LGBT elder places on his or her agent and state a relationship of life partners obviously and clearly. Powers of attorney are not the place to hide your relationship with your agent; convincing closeted elders of the importance of this fact often is difficult and contradicts their long-held, well-developed coping mechanisms. If they want their agent and life partner to be treated as a married spouse, this wish should be stated at the beginning of the document.

Most state and regional laws regarding incapacitated and disabled people place spouses and biological family ahead of actual or chosen family when appointing a guardian or conservator. Despite signed advance directives, sometimes a disgruntled relation may file an adult guardianship proceeding. Therefore, advance directives should specifically nominate the agent or other person to serve as guardian or conservator if one becomes necessary. A written nomination usually has priority over the spousal and biological hierarchy in most state statutes. A few states have added domestic partners to the list of appointment priority for guardian or conservator (California, Hawaii, Maine, and New Jersey); however, the definition and requirements for qualifying as a domestic partner vary by jurisdiction.

Finally, many state statutes have provisions regarding custody of remains at death. The agent or life partner's authority over bodily remains should be clearly stated in the health care power of attorney, the will, or a specific document as required by the law in the state of primary residence.

If possible, LGBT elders should discuss their advanced legal planning with a life partner, agent, children, and their family. Advocacy for LGBT elders regarding the importance of gay identity and respect for advance planning will be necessary with prospective long-term care providers or facilities. Agents and guardians for LGBT elders should be familiar with local nondiscrimination ordinances, abuse and neglect laws, and, when necessary, suitable litigation remedies. These laws differ from area to area, usually depending on municipal law, although more and more statewide protections are available.

## LGBT Retirement Planning

State and federal retirement entitlement programs including Social Security and Medicare and also many private retirement, insurance, and investment vehicles provide express protections for spouses based on marriage and for dependents based on biological ties. "Single" people, which under the Social Security and Medicare programs includes gay and lesbian life partners and their children, carry the largest financial burden in terms of personal contribution. When you begin to scrutinize the Social Security program, which is nominally work credit based, the term "equal work for equal pay" takes on new meaning (Peard, 1997). Through a variety of allowances married heterosexual couples get disproportionate benefits over "single" people. Although encouraging the formation of stable families may be a laudable goal, gay elders who have worked hard to contribute to Social Security and who may have created a family or had children do not receive the same benefits as their heterosexual counterparts and need to engage in specialized estate and retirement planning to protect themselves as they age (Dubois, 1999).

Because marriage (or civil unions) and second parent adoption are not available in most states, LGBT elders must affirmatively address their estate plan and retirement needs to provide for their family, guarantee retirement income, and pass their estate to intended beneficiaries. The inability to marry differentiates the approach in LGBT elder legal plans for retirement and the senior years. In contrast, financial, estate, and retirement planning for heterosexual couples is prevalent and encouraged by the legal profession, providing a continuity of support that allows heterosexual couples to develop extensive plans for retirement with more certainty. Tax benefits for married spouses are too numerous to mention here, but a significant amount of estate planning revolves around tax law. Even if marriage or civil union rights are obtained in some states, LGBT couples cannot rely on these protections, certainly not if they want to ensure comprehensive retirement security. As discussed earlier, the majority of elderly protections are based in federal law, and state-based protections will remain a patchwork of disjointed requirements. For example, retirement relocation or even travel plans may be important to consider because rights change from state to state. The residence of elders who become incapacitated by dementia, stroke, or other disability often is dictated by circumstance, finances, or the courts, so retirement and estate plans must be portable between states. Until LGBT marriage protections are extended through all U.S. jurisdictions, retirement benefits or legal protections available in one state (such as Massachusetts) may well not be available in or accessible from another state.

An understanding of what benefits gay and lesbian elder couples do not have is essential to creating legal solutions. LGBT elders may not have access to private medical and health benefits through a life partner unless the policy specifically provides for domestic partners and their children. Domestic partner coverage is available through some carriers but is entirely dependent on the goodwill of the employer because the cost usually is substantially greater than traditional family coverage. Even if it exists, domestic partner health insurance coverage may require a written statement by the insured about their status as domestic partners. It may be available only to same-sex couples or to both opposite- and same-sex couples depending on municipal or state law and regulation. It may require registration as a domestic partner under a municipal domestic partner ordinance or registry.

Under federal Social Security law and regulation, gay and lesbian couples do not have access to survivor benefits or spousal retirement benefits. Their children or dependent life partner will not have access to survivor or disability benefits in the event the nonbiological parent or life partner dies. Gay and lesbian life partners need to consider a loss of income if the higher-earning partner dies first. Widows or widowers have access to survivor's benefits and the larger of their own or their spouse's Social Security retirement amount. Alternative income sources from investments and life insurance must be available instead for a surviving gay or lesbian partner.

Similarly, protections under pension law and income tax law are geared toward married spouses. Gay and lesbian elders must consider that their retirement income and benefits probably will end upon their death, leaving little or nothing for their same-sex partner or nonbiological family. The protections of traditional employer-provided retirement plans must be replaced with personal retirement investments that will provide benefits to the named beneficiary. Public employees may have greater access to domestic partner retirement benefits, and coverage terms differ greatly from state to state (Wriggins, 1994). Regulated employer contribution retirement plans such as 401(k) accounts must also be considered in planning for a gay or lesbian couple. The tax treatment and required distributions of such plans are significantly less advantageous for a surviving life partner than for a surviving spouse (Choate, 2003).

## Legal Concerns in LGBT Long-Term Care Financing

A significant difficulty for many middle-income gay and lesbian elders comes in the funding of their long-term care costs. Elders of moderate means, who do not have high-quality comprehensive long-term care insurance, will need to rely on public assistance with long-term care costs; the cost of nursing care is so high that only the wealthy can afford private nursing care for an extended time (Vogel, 2002). In the constantly changing area of Medicaid law, the only financial protections allowed under federal requirements are for married spouses. Unmarried couples who combine their finances are at great risk in the event of extended long-term care; this is unlikely to change in the near future. In fact, it is likely that the availability of Medicaid funds will be further restricted considering the budgetary and political pressures on the program. Because most of the financial protections in Medicaid law are marriage based, LGBT elders will be at highest risk when budget savings reductions are made in available long-term care financing assistance under the Medicaid program.

Gays or lesbians with a partner facing expensive or extended long-term care must consider the need to separate their finances well in advance of the Medicaid look-back period (currently 3 to 5 years in most jurisdictions) or risk exposing the assets of the partner living in the community to the drain of long-term care expenses. This financial examination and restructuring may include joint real estate or other assets held between LGBT elders, the full value of which may be available for payment of long-term care expenses while held jointly. A healthy life partner or dependent child, living in the community, can become severely impoverished because of the lack of protections for nontraditional family members in Medicaid law. An elder law attorney familiar with Medicaid law in the elder's state of primary residence should be consulted well in advance (3–5 years) when planning for public assistance with long-term care costs will be needed.

Family finances may be significantly drained by a long illness, and protections including Social Security disability, Medicaid spousal allowances, and private insurance may be inaccessible for the family of the gay or lesbian elder. Appropriate investment, annuity, or insurance options to replace these missing protections should be part of a legal plan for a gay or lesbian elder. Because of the quality of care it can ensure, private sector long-term care financing is always preferred, if it is affordable (Vogel, 2002). A long-term care insurance policy, designed with appropriate benefits and coverage, may be a sound approach for many gay and lesbian elders who plan far enough in advance, particularly if they have unequal income or worth. It is important to work with a long-term care insurance professional who understands the needs of gay and lesbian elders and the complexities of long-term care insurance.

## Estate Planning and Probate

The need for detailed advance estate planning for LGBT elders cannot be stressed enough. The Uniform Probate Code and almost all state probate laws provide for personal representative (or executor) appointment, intestate (without a will) succession, and family protections based on marriage or biological ties. Express appointment of a life partner or other gay family member as personal representative or executor in the will affirms his or her importance to the decedent. LGBT wills can also show support of a surviving life partner or chosen family member by giving a power of appointment over the residuary of an estate or any testamentary trusts.

Some statutory estate protections, such as spousal and homestead allowances and elective spousal shares, cannot be obtained through execution of testamentary documents and must await statutory approval under marriage, civil union, or statewide domestic partner protections. These protections vary from state to state. However, all LGBT elders can create certain testamentary protections through a will to provide for a life partner and for succession that reflects their chosen as well as biological family ties. As in the durable powers of attorney, gays and lesbians should state at the beginning of a will their chosen familial relationships and the importance they place on them.

The default model of the marriage and biological family is almost always the model found in state statutes for intestate succession. The LGBT elder must have a will that expressly states otherwise; for example, it should state that a life partner is to be treated as if he or she were a married spouse for purposes of succession. LGBT elders with life partners should avoid waiting until after their death to come out to biological family in their will. A lack of open support for a partner will only increase the chances of a will challenge based on undue influence. A decedent's will can be challenged by any interested party, which typically includes biological family members who would be heirs at law if the decedent did not have a will.

Joint ownership of assets is a common desire among same-sex couples that affects their estate plan. Owning property jointly is a public statement of your commitment and trust. However, there are gift tax consequences of adding a partner to a real estate deed without consideration (an exchange of value) between the life partners or unequal payment of a security or mortgage obligation. Many LGBT elders and many attorneys not sensitive to these issues may inadvertently create joint ownerships that sabotage financial, estate, business, or retirement plans or create additional expense through unforeseen gift tax consequences.

In the area of federal gift tax law, the marital exemption for lifetime gifts between spouses is not available for gay and lesbian life partners. This complicates the common strategy of evening out assets between the life partners to take full advantage of both partners' gift and estate tax exclusions. Large lifetime transfers of assets between same-sex partners for estate planning purposes, above the annual exemption amount (currently $11,000), will create reportable taxable gifts in the year made.

Gay and lesbian couples with taxable estates will have difficulty providing for liquidity to pay estate taxes at death if their estate is illiquid (e.g., real estate or shares in a closely held business). Commonly, estate planning attorneys for married couples use "second to die insurance" to provide liquidity for estate tax payments, which is not available to gay life partners. Gay and lesbian couples who fail to do adequate estate planning may have difficulty in paying their deceased partner's tax obligations. Irrevocable life insurance trusts, annuity trusts, charitable trusts, and survivor's insurance can be used to partially address these concerns if a gay couple has a taxable estate. Many people are misinformed regarding the "repeal" of the federal estate tax laws and believe they will not have a taxable estate. An estate that is valued (or will be at death) at more than $1 million may have an estate tax liability. With the passage of the 2001 federal tax law changes, many states dispensed with their "sponge" inheritance tax and instituted an exemption of less than $1 million. Absent further changes to federal inheritance tax laws, the estate tax lifetime exemption amount will return to $1 million in 2011 and, of particular concern to LGBT elders who may have added a partner to a deed or two over the years, the gift tax lifetime exemption remains set at $1 million (Zaritsky, 2001). Many LGBT elders may unexpectedly find that they have assets beyond these totals and should have instituted an estate plan with their attorney.

Often gay and lesbian elders are concerned with privacy. Probate is a public proceeding with publicly available records. Mirror revocable living trusts may be advisable when an elder is concerned with privacy or hostile biological family. Estate planning tools such as those discussed here have specific uses and consequences for your financial and retirement plans that may not be readily apparent. Gay and lesbian elders should consult with an attorney familiar with both estate planning and LGBT issues.

## Transgender Elders and the Law

Transgender elders deserve special mention because they are generally excluded from legal protections and advances. Although the extension of privacy rights by the *Lawrence* case protects individuals from criminal charges arising from specific sexual conduct, it represents the current extent of our societal consciousness and ability to affirmatively address the role of sexual identity in conjunction with equal rights. The unique needs of aging transgendered people and any discussion of gender identity are lacking in the discourse of legal or long-term care professionals, with notable exceptions (Witten, 2002).

Because of their unique medical needs, and in part because of their "minority within a minority" status, advance planning for aging and incapacity is doubly important for transgendered elders. The length of time spent in the contragender role, administrative law proof requirements, and the jurisdictional quirks of state law in the areas of personal identification, name change, and family law often affect the rights of the transgendered elder. Even changing the gender on a birth certificate may be difficult because the legal procedure for this task may not be addressed in state law. Attorneys involved in educating the judiciary on these issues are available through legal networks such as Gay & Lesbian Advocates & Defenders of Boston and Lambda Legal (in many states, including New York and California; see the Web sites listed under References).

An advocate with appropriate authority through either agent appointment in a durable power of attorney or through adult guardianship in the event of aging-related incapacity may be appropriate depending on applicable state or even municipal laws and available protections. Investigation of appropriate LGBT community–based specialty retirement living and long-term care options may provide an appropriate placement where a transgendered elder can be open and receive care appropriate to his or her needs.

# Conclusion

Many legal concerns specific to LGBT elders can be overlooked by attorneys advising them. Even if the attorney is sensitive and open to the LGBT elder and has the best of intentions, the area is an unrecognized specialty; many issues may elude the general practitioner attorney.

With the significant and rising expense of health care and long-term care, every elder must be concerned about financial and legal advanced planning. Because of the rapidly changing area of LGBT rights, LGBT elders should consider regular legal consultations regarding appropriate legal documents and safeguards. LGBT people planning for their elder years should consider building a network of advocates, including attorneys, insurance advisors, accountants, elder care managers, physicians, and others. This will ensure that they have every advantage current law affords.

## REFERENCES

Burda, J. (2002, July–August). Nontraditional families, nontraditional estates. *GP-SOLO American Bar Association, 20*(5), 22–29.

Butler, S. (Ed.). (2002, Fall). Geriatric care management with sexual minorities. *Geriatric Care Management Journal, 12*(3), 2.

Choate, N. B. (2003). *Life and death planning for retirement benefits.* Boston: Ataxplan Publications.

Coyle, M. (2003, July 7). The fallout begins, gay rights. *The National Law Journal, 25*(45), 1, 24.

Dubois, M. (1999). Legal planning for gay, lesbian, and non-traditional elders. *Albany Law Review, 63*(1), 263–332.

*Goodridge v. Department of Public Health,* 440 Mass. 309 (2003).

*Lawrence v. Texas,* 123 S.Ct. 2472, 2480 (TX 2003).

Peard, P. A. (1997). Domestic partnership benefits: Equal pay for equal work. *Maine Bar Journal, 12,* 184–186.

Vogel, T. M. (2002). Private sector long-term care planning. *Elder's Advisor, 4*(2), 1–13.

Witten, T. (2002, Fall). Geriatric care and management issues for the transgender and intersex populations. *Geriatric Care Management Journal, 12,* 20–24.

Wriggins, J. (1994). Kinship and marriage in Massachusetts public employee retirement law: An analysis of the beneficiary provisions, and proposals for change. *New England Law Review, 28,* 991–1010.

Zaritsky, H. M. (2001). *Practical estate planning and drafting after the Economic Growth and Tax Relief Reconciliation Act of 2001.* New York: Warren, Gorham & Lamont.

## ADDITIONAL RESOURCES

Berkery, P. M. Jr. (1996). *Personal financial planning for gays & lesbians.* Burr Ridge, IL: Irwin.

Berkery, P. M. Jr. & Diggins, G. A. (1998). *Gay finances in a straight world.* New York: Macmillan.

Chasen, J. S. (2001). More estate and gift tax planning for nontraditional families. *Probate & Property, 15*(3), 54–58.

Chasen, J. S., & Schwartz, E. F. (2001). Estate and gift tax planning for nontraditional families. *Probate & Property, 15*(1), 6–10.

Choate, N. B. (2003). *Life and death planning for retirement benefits.* Boston: Ataxplan Publications.

Dubois, M. (2003, January 8). Elder law: Answers for gay and lesbian elders. *Maine Lawyers Review, 11*(1), 16–17.

Dubois, M. (2003, March 6). Elder law: When to use supplemental needs trusts for the disabled and the elderly. *Maine Lawyers Review, 11*(5), 20–21.

Dubois, M. (2004, June 3). Elder law: Adding "domestic partner" in Maine's probate code. *Maine Lawyers Review, 12*(11), 21–23.

## ADDITIONAL CASES

*Baehr v. Levin,* 852 P.2d 44 (Haw. 1993).

*Aff'd sub nom Baehr v. Miike,* 950 P.2d 1234 (Haw. 1996).

*Baker v. State,* 170 Vt. 194, 242 (VT 1999).

*Brause v. Bureau of Vital Statistics,* No. 3 AN-95-6562 CJ (Alaska Super. Ct. Feb. 27, 1998).

## WEB SITES

Gay & Lesbian Advocates & Defenders (GLAD): www.glad.org.

Human Rights Campaign (HRC): www.hrc.org.

Lambda Legal Defense and Education Fund: www.lambdalegal.org.

Lesbian and Gay Aging Issues Network (LGAIN): www.asaging.org/lgain.

# End-of-Life Issues for LGBT Older Adults

*Dean Blevins and James L. Werth, Jr.*

*T*his chapter extends current discussions of dying and death in the lesbian, gay, bisexual, and transgender (LGBT) community beyond HIV disease to describe the processes and issues faced by LGBT older adults near and at the end of life (EOL). Through a review of existing literature, we discuss several key issues and processes at the EOL, including morbidity, mortality, decision making, and issues of mental health and coping, overlaid with concerns about stigma, discrimination and prejudice (actual and potential), and legal issues that can influence the care accessed and provided at the EOL for LGBT elders. Areas in need of attention are considered throughout the chapter, and several priority areas are discussed for future research and improvements in professional practice.

## Context

The U.S. population is rapidly growing older as a consequence of advances in public health and medicine. As of 2001, life expectancy at birth was 77.2 years, and at age 65 this rises to 82.9 years (National Center for Health Statistics [NCHS], 2003). When death does occur, 69.6% of people can expect it to be a consequence of one of the five leading causes of mortality: heart disease, cancer, cerebrovascular diseases, respiratory diseases, or accidents, with the foremost two accounting for 53.2% of deaths (NCHS, 2003). These trends have important implications for any discussion of dying and death. First, most people who die are older adults. Second, the chronicity of the leading causes of death often involves a prolonged period during which people become increasingly frail before death (Covinsky et al., 2003).

A focus on EOL issues for people who are dying and their significant others has only recently gained significant attention. However, the LGBT community has received spotty attention at best. When EOL issues have been discussed for the LGBT population, attention has centered largely on HIV, AIDS, or the inclusion of sexual orientation as a distinct culture (Blevins & Papadatou, 2006). Although the LGBT community has been disproportionately affected by the HIV pandemic, the majority of older LGBT adults experience morbidity and mortality as a result of the same conditions as the rest of the population (Gay and Lesbian Medical Association [GLMA], 2001). The present review integrates the death and dying literature with issues pertinent to aging and the LGBT community to discuss the key areas of morbidity and mortality, decision making, grief and bereavement, caregiving, and psychosocial issues. Throughout the chapter, legal and ethical issues are addressed for LGBT elders near the EOL.

## Morbidity

Morbidity among older adults has been extensively researched by gerontologists over the last half century, with the general conclusion that no bodily system is unaffected by factors associated with aging (Masoro & Austad, 2001). This is not meant to be pessimistic; most age-associated changes are a nonpathological part of aging to which older adults adapt or compensate for quite well (Baltes & Kliegl, 1992). Pathological conditions such as rheumatoid arthritis, Alzheimer's disease, and Parkinson's disease are not a normal part of aging. To our knowledge, no diseases have been shown to be more or less biologically likely in LGBT elders than in non-LGBT adults; however, no national data exist on the general health and well-being of LGBT adults (Dean et al., 2000; Sell, 1997; Solarz, 1999).

Among transgendered older adults, questions have arisen about the potential effects of long-term hormone use and the use of silicone breast implants on rates of cancer. There is no evidence that either influences cancer rates (Cascio, 2001; Wilkerson, 2001). A person's natal biological sex should determine the physical health preventive measures one takes. For example, sexual reassignment surgery for a male-to-female (MTF) person does not remove the prostate, and so regular prostate exams are necessary with age.

These and other issues are discussed in a companion document of the third installment of the national public health initiative, *Healthy People 2010*. The GLMA was consulted to identify and discuss health objectives relevant to the

LGBT community. The group's final report, *Healthy People 2010 Companion Document* (GLMA, 2001), discusses 110 objectives in 12 focus areas, which should be a basis for efforts at data collection and health promotion for the LGBT community at the local and national levels.

# Mortality

As of 2001, 86% of girls and 77% of boys can expect to reach age 65, which is quite an advance over the 43% and 39%, respectively, in 1900 (Centers for Disease Control and Prevention [CDC], 2001). The majority of deaths in 2001 among people over 65 occurred as a result of heart disease or cancer, followed by stroke, chronic obstructive pulmonary diseases, and pneumonia and influenza. For African Americans and Native Americans, diabetes is one of the five leading causes of death (CDC, 2001).

Although the proportion of heterosexual HIV and AIDS cases in the United States is increasing, the majority of cases are still among men who have sex with men (CDC, 2003). People over age 50 accounted for 8% of all AIDS-related deaths reported to the CDC and have consistently made up about 10% of all HIV and AIDS cases in the United States (CDC, 2003). With the widespread use of antiretroviral therapy since 1996, AIDS deaths have decreased in all age groups. Consequently, prevalence rates (the numbers of people living with HIV and AIDS) have continued to rise (CDC, 2003). As the most heavily infected segments of the population continue to age, it is likely that a growing number of AIDS-related deaths will be among LGBT people over age 50. In fact, in 2002 approximately 190,000 people between the ages of 35 and 54 in the United States were living with HIV or AIDS, many of whom will reach advanced age before death (CDC, 2003; Linsk, 2000).

Another important consideration is that the wish that death will be quick and in one's own home is contrary to how most deaths occur. In fact, 65–70% of older adults die in institutions (Brock & Foley, 1998; Covinsky et al., 2003), and with the increasing age at which people die, there is a trend toward greater use of skilled medical and nursing care facilities at the EOL (Steinhauser et al., 2000). Issues surrounding this profile of morbidity and mortality raise many issues relevant to the planning of EOL care. The contemporary health care system and sociocultural environment within which LGBT elders will confront these issues necessitate careful advanced consideration to ensure that one's wishes are respected near and at the EOL.

## Decision Making at the End of Life

Traditionally, EOL is defined as the point at which aggressive curative care is stopped, often within the last 6 months of life; however, there is no definitive method of determining life expectancy prospectively. Thus, using a marker such as a 6-month prognosis is inherently problematic. Moreover, the majority of people die of chronic illnesses that do not have a reliable (and hence predictable) course. Figure 12.1, from the work of Lunney and colleagues, illustrates four trajectories of dying (Lunney, Lynn, & Hogan, 2002; Lunney et al., 2003). The frame labeled *Terminal Illnesses* is the pattern that has historically been

FIGURE 12.1

Self-Identification: Men by Age Group

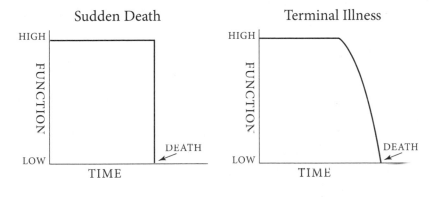

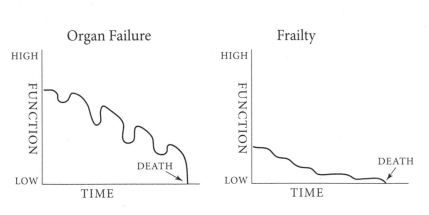

SOURCE: J. R. Lunney, et al. (2003, p. 2388)

the focus of specialized EOL services such as hospice. Although some forms of cancer have this predictable course of decline, most conditions fall within one of the bottom two frames of *Organ Failure* or *Frailty.*

These difficulties in prognostication have two important implications for older adults, which may be especially important for LGBT elders. First, advanced care planning is critical to increase the chance that care preferences will be respected at the EOL. No assumptions can be made about how others in our lives will respond to the challenges of health care decision making should we lose the cognitive capacity to make our own choices. Second, issues concerning burial, final arrangements, and inheritance affect our loved ones after we die. Countless laws exist governing the process and manner of health care decision making and postmortem inheritance; however, LGBT couples are not granted the same rights as heterosexual partners. Advanced planning may not offer a guarantee that wishes will be respected, but it is the best step to increase the odds that they will be (see chapter 11, this volume).

## *Decision Making*

The long trajectories of dying that are common among older adults today mean that critical decisions will be needed at many points in care delivery. At what point is aggressive, curative treatment replaced with palliative care? Under what conditions does one decide to forgo cardiopulmonary resuscitation or artificial nutrition and hydration? We cannot predict exactly what medical care we will need in advance, and often such decisions must be made quickly, under stress, and by others if we lose cognitive capacity. Who, then, do we trust to make these decisions? Will the authority rest with our physicians, a biological family member, a significant other? A person may not always be able to determine exactly how she or he will die, but there are means to influence how she or he will *not* die.

In the ideal situation, patients make their own health care decisions, but this requires that they have the cognitive capacity to do so; are not being influenced by fear, anxiety, depression, or other psychosocial pressures; and have accurate, intelligible, and timely information from health care providers. Rarely are all of these conditions met when a person is called on to make a critical health care decision. Consequently, health care professionals are extremely important as educators and assessors of decisions that fit with patient and family preferences. When, what, and how to engage in this process can be different for each individual, and at the same time there are separate and interacting cultural issues that must be determined on a case-by-case basis (Blevins & Papadatou, 2006).

An additional issue concerns the person who will make medical decisions if the patient chooses not to be the primary decision maker or loses capacity to do so. Most people near the EOL have not completed any form of advance directive (AD) designating a decision maker in such a circumstance (SUPPORT Principal Investigators, 1995). Multiple influences can impair or manipulate the decision-making process (Werth & Gordon, 1998; Werth, Gordon, & Johnson, 2002). The health care providers' role in such situations includes the use of objective assessment methods to determine that the decision-making process is sound, whether or not they agree with the ultimate choice of patients and their loved ones (see Werth & Kleespies, 2006).

## Advance Directives

Federal legislation (e.g., The Patient Self-Determination Act of 1990, 1994), judicial decisions (e.g., *Cruzan v. Director, Missouri Department of Health,* 1990), and state laws (e.g., the Oregon Death with Dignity Act; Oregon Health Division, 2001) have accumulated in recent years to reaffirm the rights of patients to determine the manner and timing of medical care and death. It is estimated that 70% of deaths are negotiated in one manner or another (*In re L.W.,* 1992). ADs are the legal embodiment of patients' wishes concerning the extent of and type of EOL care desired, including living wills and the designation of a proxy decision maker for health care and for finances (see Ditto, 2006).

These documents are critical for LGBT elders because they are the only legal means of safeguarding the authority of a significant other in situations of medical decision making. State laws determine the specific documents and procedures that must be in place to grant a nonmarried partner authority to make decisions for another. One cannot assume that family members will respect a same-sex relationship as one would a heterosexual married couple. In the absence of ADs specifically granting a life partner legal authority over one's medical care and estate, there is little legal recourse for a life partner who wants to be involved in care provision.

This is not to say that ADs will guarantee that LGBT elders' wishes will be followed. In the largest EOL research project to date (SUPPORT Principal Investigators 1995), an intervention specifically designed to enhance the use of ADs failed. It was found that ADs are not communicated between providers, patients do not tell providers about them, and they are sometimes blatantly ignored.

Another issue with ADs concerns the proxy named to make decisions on behalf of the patient. A substantial body of literature has documented the poor correspondence between the decisions proxies make and the decisions that patients would make for themselves (Ditto et al., 2001; Ditto, 2006). Finally, it must be emphasized that although ADs often are discussed in the context of indicating what treatment is not wanted, they can also be used to document the person's wishes to have treatment provided; this is especially important for members of religious or ethnic groups who do not want to do anything that might be perceived as limiting care (Werth, Blevins, et al., 2002). Even with the problems of ADs, it is important to reemphasize that they are the only legal means of protecting the ability of chosen loved ones to play a role in EOL decisions if biological relatives challenge or fail to acknowledge the role of a life partner.

## *Hastened Death*

Hastened death includes actions or nonactions that will affect the manner and timing of death. It includes suicide, physician-assisted death (in which the physician provides the means of ending life but does not actually participate in the process; this is explicitly legal only in Oregon), and active euthanasia (in which another person is the direct cause of a patient's death; this is not legal in the United States). We also believe that other more typical actions such as withholding and withdrawing treatment (e.g., not going on a ventilator; discontinuing dialysis) also can be considered forms of hastened death.

Laws pertaining to withholding and withdrawing treatment are very complex and often contrary to common practice in medicine. State laws vary in how and when these actions are permissible. Because of the complexity of the legal system across the United States, it is imperative that same-sex couples consult an authority in such matters before the onset or occurrence of a terminal illness.

Because maximizing the quality of life usually is the primary goal of EOL care, some situations might warrant consideration of hastened death. Although it is beyond the scope of this chapter to discuss the many ethical, legal, and cultural issues that surround "rational suicide" and assisted death (see Werth, 1999, 2002), it is important to note that LGBT elders may be a particularly high-risk group for suicide (Paul et al., 2002). Studies have documented that suicide completion is higher in the elderly than any other age group and higher among men than women (CDC, 2001; NCHS, 2003). Suicide ideation and attempts have also been particularly high among the transgendered (see Wilkerson, 2001, for a review) and among people dying of AIDS-related conditions (Paul et al., 2002;

Schneider et al., 1991). Although reports on suicide by gays and lesbians have been published (e.g., D'Augelli, Hershberger, & Pilkington, 2001; Paul et al., 2002), there have been no studies specifically on LGBT elder suicide. Medical and mental health providers must be aware of the potential interaction of risk factors for suicide (e.g., depression, being LGBT, elderly male, diagnosed with a terminal illness). The most important role for providers is to ensure that patients are engaging in sound decision-making processes and not being unduly influenced by mental health conditions or by the pressures of other people.

## Bereavement and Grief

The majority of people who die in the United States are older adults. Whereas *bereavement* is a term used to represent the entire objective experience of losing someone to death, *grief* is the process and cluster of individual reactions (physiological and psychological) to cope with that loss (Stroebe et al., 2001). With a few exceptions (e.g., Moss, Moss, & Hansson, 2001), most discussions of bereavement have not allocated much attention to the specific issues confronted by older adults. Furthermore, the literature on LGBT bereavement has been limited largely to the experiences of partners or caregivers of those who have died with AIDS.

The classic work of Holmes and Rahe (1967) illustrates that loss from death, especially of a partner or spouse, is the most stressful situation faced in life. Recent evidence also suggests similar grief reactions of people who lose siblings (Hays, Gold, & Pieper, 1997) or grandchildren (De Vries et al., 1997; Fry, 1997). The timing of death is especially important to grieving. With advancing age, death becomes more likely, and these deaths are viewed as "on time" and thus, more acceptable than "off-time" deaths (i.e., deaths among younger adults). Although some evidence supports the idea that elder deaths are more easily grieved, such criteria (i.e., on-time or off-time) should never be used to define how a person should grieve.

Most explorations of bereavement and grief adopt a stage- (Kubler-Ross, 1969) or task-based (Worden, 2001) approach in which priority areas are specified to which coping efforts are directed. Both approaches have been increasingly called into question because of the great diversity in grief reactions between people, the frequent misapplication of such models, and the cultural specificity of any given theory (Blevins & Papadatou, 2006). Others have cautioned that discussing a natural phenomenon such as grief in terms of signs and symptoms medicalizes the process and suggests that treatment is necessary to "cure" it (Casarett, Kutner, & Abrahm, 2001). All of these criticisms are related and concern primarily the neglect of individual resources (personal and social) used to cope with the death of a loved one and characteristics that surround the death (e.g., occurrence of multiple deaths close in time, emotional and physical proximity to the deceased).

## Anticipatory Grief

As noted earlier, grief is a method of coping with loss and coming to terms with the changes that accompany the death of a loved one. Although reviews of the literature have been mixed regarding the authenticity of the concept of anticipatory grief (e.g., Rando, 2000), many in the field believe it is a real phenomenon that is distinguishable from other conditions such as depression (Duke, 1998; Meuser & Marwit, 2001). Anticipatory grief, when present, usually manifests with physical and psychological symptoms very similar to those of postmortem bereavement (Gilliland & Fleming, 1998). It is multifaceted and can include symptoms of anger, guilt, anxiety, irritability, and functional difficulties. Anticipatory grief can facilitate the bereavement of loved ones by essentially providing a "head start" on grief and, if it is recognized, can be used to seek individual patterns of closure necessary before the death of a patient that will not be possible postmortem (e.g., completing unsettled discussions).

No research has specifically explored how older LGBT people experience and cope with loss through anticipatory grief; however, being involved in caregiving of loved ones or others who are dying does seem to facilitate bereavement. Especially for prolonged illnesses, it is critical that health care providers be able to recognize and distinguish between normal anticipatory grief and potential clinical mental health disorders because these are likely to complicate postmortem bereavement. Actions that loved ones may take to prepare for a death have the potential to affect their relationship with the dying person. Although the action may be positive (e.g., increased communication), it may also implicitly have negative effects in that it may prematurely distance one from the dying person and reduce interpersonal support.

## Disenfranchised Grief

Many relationships between older LGBT adults are as loving and long-term as those in traditionally married heterosexual couples (Quam & Whitford, 1992).

Consequently, there is no reason to assume that when a partner in an LGBT relationship dies, there will be any less emotional and physiological reaction to the death. However, there is good reason to be concerned that partner grief among LGBT elders will be more difficult because cultural perspectives often fail to recognize and respect the genuineness of same-sex relationships (Lennon, Martin, & Dean, 1990; Rosen, 1989). Disenfranchised grief has been referred to in the literature as being the result of societal denial of the right to mourn a "forbidden" relationship, especially because most U.S. states and employers do not grant rights of survivorship to same-sex couples (Cahill, South, & Spade, 2000; Rosen, 1989). Thus, in addition to the lack of emotional recognition and validation of a significant other, the heterosexist policies common in the United States may reduce personal resources to cope with a loved one's death.

For example, for heterosexual couples the widowed spouse is entitled to a certain percentage of the deceased partner's Social Security benefits; this is not granted to same-sex couples, even if all states were to legally recognize same-sex unions, because Social Security is a federal program. Similarly, biological family members may (and have) successfully claimed full rights to the deceased person's estate, despite LGBT relationships that have existed for many years. Such additional financial strains may make the grieving process especially difficult. Several court cases have invalidated the marriages of men who underwent sexual reassignment surgery (having subsequently become legally married to a man), thus denying the surviving spouse the legal benefits of heterosexual marriage (Cahill, South, & Spade, 2000; Human Rights Campaign, 2003).

Although the majority of AIDS deaths have been among younger adults, survival with HIV or AIDS into old age is a trend that is expected to continue into the future (CDC, 2003; Linsk, 2000). Studies of surviving partners of those who died from AIDS-related illnesses have shown evidence of survivor guilt (Boykin, 1991), negative impacts on self-esteem and identity (Biller & Rice, 1990), and, especially among HIV-positive partners, deteriorated health (Lennon, Martin, & Dean, 1990; Martin & Dean, 1993), death anxiety (Bivens et al., 1994; Franks et al., 1991), and suicidal ideation (Schneider et al., 1991). Social support, from the community and family, often is critical to successful coping and grief work (Biller & Rice, 1990; Lennon, Martin, & Dean, 1990).

## *Life Span Developmental Issues*

The LGBT community became intimately familiar with the issues of bereavement and grief with the onset of the HIV pandemic. Although such medical treatment advances as antiretroviral therapy have dramatically increased the expected survival time for people with HIV or AIDS, the air of unnatural and untimely death and morbidity still weighs heavily on the entire LGBT community (Worden, 1991). Therefore, when discussing societal influences on grief among LGBT elders, it is important to recognize that there are direct effects and indirect effects, in addition to the historical, cumulative effects of more than two decades of AIDS-related losses.

Consideration of loss over time is especially important for LGBT elders. Older adulthood often is characterized as a period of loss: decreased physical functioning, role loss with retirement, relationship loss with the increasing commonness of deaths from friends and relatives, and, in the case of significant illness, social commitments and involvements. For LGBT elders, these losses include the many who have died of AIDS. Studies have demonstrated that there can be a cumulative negative effect of multiple losses as a consequence of AIDS, the extent of the effect depends on such factors as the time between losses, intensity of the relationship with those who have died, the degree of social stigma surrounding an AIDS death, and the survivor's own health status (Biller & Rice, 1990; Lennon, Martin, & Dean, 1990; Neugebauer et al., 1992; Viney et al., 1992). Thus, added to the effects of cumulative AIDS losses are those that naturally accompany older adulthood. However, among the LGBT community, uncomplicated bereavement is facilitated by social integration into the community (Boykin, 1991) and participating in caregiving of the dying (Lennon, Martin, & Dean, 1990; McGaffic & Longman, 1993).

The extent to which older adults are (and can be) out in their personal and work lives may be a critical factor in their experiences of multiple losses. It is very common for older adults to have lived their entire lives without full disclosure of their sexual orientation or true gender identity. Professional caregivers of LGBT elders needing home-based or institutionalized services have to respect this preference but be aware of the potential deleterious effects the choice could have on physical and mental health status.

## Living Arrangements and Caregiving

One of the consequences of the progressive frailty of many older adults before death is the increased likelihood of institutionalization. Although only 4% of people over 65 are in nursing homes at any given time (NCHS, 2003), the probability of nursing home residence and likelihood of dying there dramatically increase with each successive decade (see Blevins & Deason-Howell, 2002, for a review). Thus it is not surprising that professional nursing staff, rather than family members and friends, will provide the majority of EOL caregiving.

Friendship networks are critical to maximizing the independence of frail elders and increase the chances of remaining in one's home until death. However, friends often are of similar age and may be in similar need of assistance. Most caregiving in the United States falls to the adult daughters and granddaughters in heterosexual-parented families (Lawrence et al., 2002). Although many LGBT elders have children and friends to whom they can turn for caregiving needs (Berger, 1982; Kelly, 1977), many do not.

Quam and Whitford (1992) surveyed 80 gays and lesbians (aged 50–73) on demographic variables, life satisfaction, and integration in the gay community. Although only 36.6% were in a relationship, most expressed high life satisfaction, 58.7% had children, and participation in the gay community was highly valued (which was a source of social support among AIDS caregivers). A family of choice had been constructed, substituting for the heterosexual family structure. However, this was not a representative sample of older gays and lesbians and did not include those identified as bisexual and transgendered. Furthermore, such a high percentage with children may or may not be a trend for older adults in future cohorts. Finally, research has not explored the supportive nature and caregiving roles of those balancing the support of biological and chosen family members.

The Quam and Whitford study also reflected a trend that has continued over the past decade in asking about preferred living arrangements, although responses were not specific to EOL situations. The majority (62%) expressed an interest in moving into a lesbian-only or gay men-only retirement community. Since this study, several such communities have been created and are in various stages of development (see the American Society on Aging's Lesbian and Gay Aging Issues Network Web site at www.asaging.org/networks/lgain/lgainhome.cfm; see also chapter 14, this volume). The chief concern for many who express an interest in these living environments is one of fitting into a nonjudgmental setting; however, such environments will not protect one from the sometimes rampant prejudices of health care providers if major medical issues arise, as is common at the EOL (Preston, Koch, & Young, 1991; Schantz & O'Hanlan, 1994). As a result of the influx of people with AIDS into hospices across the United States, many hospice providers became actively engaged in changing their organizational culture to avoid the assumption of heterosexuality (Barbour, 1995; Lew-Napoleone, 1992). Although such changes in other health care settings providing EOL care have not been common, some models do exist (Cherin et al., 2000).

## Psychosocial Issues

Psychosocial issues are paramount in EOL care for all older adults and include the "emotional, intellectual, spiritual, interpersonal, social, cultural, and economic dimension of the human experience" (International Work Group on Death, Dying, and Bereavement, 1993, p. 29, as cited in Werth, Gordon, & Johnson, 2002, p. 402). A tremendous body of literature has accumulated indicating the importance of attending to the whole person at the EOL because the current medical model of care tends to focus exclusively on physical symptoms, neglecting psychosocial matters. Although it is not possible to discuss all psychosocial issues in detail (see Werth, Gordon, & Johnson, 2002; Werth & Blevins, 2006), the following sections highlight several issues that have been shown or have the potential to be uniquely important for LGBT elders at the EOL.

### *Stigma*

The stigma associated with homosexuality, bisexuality, and being transgendered is a ubiquitous concern at the EOL and throughout the health care system. Homophobic and discriminatory practices are common among health care professionals (Kovacs & Rodgers, 1995; Preston, Koch, & Young, 1991; Schantz & O'Hanlan, 1994; Tehan, 1991; Wilkerson, 2001) and can significantly affect access and quality of care for LGBT elders. The primary issues of stigma in EOL care for LGBT elders are deficits in knowledge (to respect and provide for unique needs among LGBT elders and to avoid misinformed assumptions about the lifestyle implications of being LGBT) and deficits in legal protections associated with health care for the LGBT community (Cahill, South, & Spade, 2000). Stigma is also important as a potential barrier for many LGBT elders confronting situations that foster life review and other intrapsychic processes that can be critical to the coping efforts of the terminally ill.

Tehan (1991) explored organizational barriers to accessing hospice care for those with AIDS. Providers expressed reluctance to market to those dying of AIDS in communities that are more conservative or those less affected by the pandemic. Results also suggested that the misperception that providing EOL care for people with AIDS is more expensive might be largely a function of the efficiency and effectiveness of care gained through experience (see also Hellinger, 1998), in addition to fear of HIV transmission (Barbour, 1995). As was discussed earlier with the issue of decision making, there are few legal protections for unique LGBT rights and needs; horror stories of denied access to care, inappropriate care, and inadequate care are common among out LGBT elders (see Cahill, South, & Spade, 2000; Wilkerson, 2001). Therefore stigma of LGBT elders at the EOL is an extremely important concern, especially as baby boomers (who are much more open about their sexuality than current older adults) begin to move into the older adult age group. Only concerted efforts (e.g., in professional training and education, expanded hate crime legislation) will increase the likelihood that LGBT elders receive appropriate and timely EOL care.

Stigma can also become a barrier to adaptive coping to one's own death and to that of peers and significant others. As discussed earlier, the inability of elders to mourn the loss of loved ones and friends can result in disenfranchised grief. A similar situation can occur for the dying person who is prevented from expressing her or his true identity in an open and accepting environment, increasing the chances of developing or exacerbating diagnosable mental health conditions (e.g., clinical depression, anxiety; see Cadwell, 1991). Hospice, with a history of caregiving for people with HIV or AIDS, usually men who have sex with men, has developed and refined caregiving for the LGBT population (though not necessarily for LGBT elders) that is based on the philosophy of acceptance and respect for cultural differences among patients, their loved ones, and care choices at the EOL (see Barbour, 1995; Lew-Napoleone, 1992).

## Religion and Spirituality

Religion and spirituality have long been recognized in the gerontological literature as particularly potent resources for coping with loss in older adulthood (Koenig, 2002). However, in the LGBT community, religion may be an additional source of stress and complicate the grieving process, depending on how doctrine is interpreted and internalized (Bivens et al., 1994; Franks et al., 1991). If grieving people view a same-sex relationship as having been condemned by their own religious beliefs, this may further complicate the process of validating the relationship with the deceased. This is another example of how societal belief systems (i.e., those disavowing the sanctity of a same-sex union) may make grieving more laborious and increase the risk that LGBT elders will experience significant and enduring psychosocial distress after the death of loved ones. It is important for health care providers to be aware of the psychosocial distress that could be caused by certain belief systems and to refer those experiencing spiritual problems to professionals who can appropriately respect their beliefs while also offering guidance related to the issues confronted at or near the EOL.

## Diagnosable Mental Health Conditions

Although diagnosable mental health conditions are not a normal part of aging (Kennedy, 2000) or dying (Werth, Gordon, & Johnson, 2002), they can coexist with a terminal illness or be caused or complicated by one, and they require treatment. The general theme of mental health care for older adults and for dying people is that there is a disturbing paucity of attention to these issues in mainstream social science (e.g., Werth et al., 2003) and medical (e.g., GLMA, 2001) literature. In addition to the personal distress caused by untreated and unnecessary mental conditions, severe bouts of depression and anxiety can interfere with the ability of terminally ill people to make rational decisions. Such conditions have been suggested to be more common in some members of the LGBT community (Barbour, 1995; Paul et al., 2002; Schneider et al., 1991; Wilkerson, 2001) and therefore should be a particular concern in research and in the foci of caregiving efforts from front-line professionals. With age and certain terminal illnesses (e.g., AIDS), some conditions such as dementia and delirium become more likely, raising particular concerns about appropriate assessment and treatment (see Gibson et al., 2006), in addition to issues of advanced care planning and decision making (see Werth, Gordon, & Johnson, 2002, for a discussion).

## Future Research and Practice Issues

A consistent theme throughout this chapter has been the lack of data that specifically examine questions pertaining to LGBT elders, including the needs and issues confronted at or near the EOL. The only national data available on LGBT health are collected through the CDC in its efforts to monitor the HIV pandemic in the United States. A significant difficulty in collecting national data concerns the well-reasoned reluctance of respondents to self-identify as LGBT in surveys (mail and phone); this is even more of an issue among older adults, who have often lived their entire lives under a cloak of heterosexuality. The unwillingness of LGBT elders to self-identify, whether out of fears of condemnation, issues of internalized homophobia, or simply personal choice, necessitates the extrapolation of evidence on EOL issues from a very narrow domain of EOL research (i.e., HIV and AIDS research) or from research with unrepresentative samples of volunteers. Therefore the most critical research issue is the development of nationally representative data on LGBT elder health, including dying and death.

Specific to EOL issues, there are many potential avenues in which greater information and understanding are needed. Although it would be too extensive to discuss all possible topics, it is instructive to consider the topics for which LGBT elders may warrant unique considerations in care provision near the EOL. Foremost of these are systemic level studies examining the influence of stigma and attitudes about the LGBT community on the access, type, quality, and extent of EOL care by providers and policy makers and attitudes of the LGBT community by the potential patients themselves and the potential care decision makers (e.g., significant others, family, friends). Such research addresses issues of equality in care and respect for the LGBT identity and specific needs of this distinct cultural subgroup.

Clinical studies exploring the potential differences in morbidity, mortality, disease manifestations (e.g., symptom experiences), and the interactions between physical and psychosocial experiences of dying people are also needed to inform providers and promote development of evidenced-based practices for LGBT elders.

Finally, research should accommodate the diversity within the LGBT community; subpopulations even within the omnibus LGBT label may have different needs. Additionally, these differences are not likely to be static but will vary over time. Thus, in thinking about the research necessary to explore and improve the EOL experiences of LGBT elders, research methods that have been commonly used with other cultural groups, including techniques for recruiting study participants for sensitive topics and interdisciplinary research frameworks, should be considered.

# Conclusion

Although most issues at the EOL are similar regardless of one's sexual orientation and gender identity, many unique situations may decrease elders' quality of life and quality of care in the U.S. health care system. Issues concerning morbidity, mortality, decision making, mental health, and coping are overlaid with concerns about stigma, discrimination and prejudice (actual and potential), and legal issues that can influence the care accessed and provided at the EOL for LGBT elders. The importance of advanced planning for LGBT elders and the complex legal issues that are involved in EOL decisions warrant careful thought. Several research issues were also presented that would enhance our understanding of the experience of dying and death among the LGBT community and ultimately ensure appropriate and effective EOL care.

## REFERENCES

Baltes, P. B., & Kliegl, R. (1992). Further testing of limits of cognitive plasticity: Negative age differences in a mnemonic skill are robust. *Developmental Psychology, 28,* 121–125.

Barbour, R. S. (1995). Responding to a challenge: Nursing care and AIDS. *International Journal of Nursing Studies, 32,* 213–223.

Berger, R. M. (1982). The unseen minority: Older gays and lesbians. *Social Work, 27,* 236–242.

Biller, R., & Rice, S. (1990). Experiencing multiple loss of persons with AIDS: Grief and bereavement issues. *Health and Social Work, 15,* 283–290.

Bivens, A. J., Neimeyer, R. A., Kirchberg, T. M., & Moore, M. K. (1994). Death concern and religious beliefs among gays and bisexuals of variable proximity to AIDS. *Omega, 30,* 105–120.

Blevins, D., & Deason-Howell, L. M. (2002). End-of-life care in nursing homes: The interface of policy, research, and practice. *Behavioral Sciences and the Law, 20,* 271–286.

Blevins, D., & Papadatou, D. (2006). The effects of culture in end-of-life situations. In J. L. Werth Jr. & D. Blevins (Eds.), *Psychosocial issues near the end of life: A resource for professional care providers.* (pp. 27–56). Washington, DC: American Psychological Association.

Boykin, F. F. (1991). The AIDS crisis and gay male survivor guilt. *Smith College Studies in Social Work, 61,* 247–259.

Brock, D. B., & Foley, D. J. (1998). Demography and epidemiology of dying in the U.S. with emphasis on deaths of older persons. *The Hospice Journal, 13,* 49–60.

Cadwell, S. (1991). Twice removed: The stigma suffered by gay men with AIDS. *Smith College Studies in Social Work, 61,* 236–246.

Cahill, S., South, K., & Spade, J. (2000). *Outing age: Public policy issues affecting gay, lesbian, bisexual and transgender elders.* Retrieved August 1, 2003, from www.ngltf.org/downloads/outingage.pdf.

Casarett, D., Kutner, J. S., & Abrahm, J. (2001). Life after death: A practical approach to grief and bereavement. *Annals of Internal Medicine, 134,* 208–215.

Cascio, J. (2001). Cancer risks in the trans community. *Trans-Health, 1.* Retrieved August 9, 2003, from www.trans-health.com/Iss3Vol1/cancer.htm.

Centers for Disease Control and Prevention (CDC). (2001). *Trends in causes of death among the elderly.* Retrieved July 10, 2003, from www.cdc.gov/nchs/data/agingtrends/01death.pdf.

Centers for Disease Control and Prevention (CDC). (2003). *HIV/AIDS surveillance report: Cases of* HIV *and* AIDS *in the United States, 2002.* Retrieved November 1, 2003, from www.cdc.gov/hiv/stats/hasr1402/2002SurveillanceReport.pdf.

Cherin, D. A., Huba, G. J., Melchoir, L. A., Enguidanos, S., Simmons, W. J., & Brief, D. E. (2000). Issues in implementing and evaluating a managed care home health care system for HIV/AIDS: Visiting Nurse Association Foundation of Los Angeles. *Drugs & Society, A Journal of Contemporary Issues, 16,* 203–222.

Covinsky, K. E., Eng, C., Lui, L. Y., Sands, L. P., & Yaffe, K. (2003). The last 2 years of life: Functional trajectories of frail older people. *Journal of the American Geriatrics Society, 51,* 492–498.

*Cruzan v. Director, Missouri Department of Health, 497* U.S. 261 (1990).

D'Augelli, A. R., Hershberger, S. L., & Pilkington, N. W. (2001). Suicidality patterns and sexual orientation-related factors among lesbian, gay, and bisexual youth. *Suicide and Life Threatening Behavior, 31,* 250–264.

Dean, L., Meyer, I. H., Robinson, K., Sell, R. L., Sember, R., Silenzio, V. M. B., et al. (2000). Lesbian, gay, bisexual, and transgender health: Findings and concerns. *Journal of the Gay and Lesbian Medical Association, 3,* 101–151.

De Vries, B., Davis, C. G., Wortman, C. B., & Lehman, D. R. (1997). Long-term psychological and somatic consequences of later life parental bereavement. *Omega, 35,* 97–117.

Ditto, P. H. (2006). Self-determination, substituted judgment, and the psychology of advance medical decision making. In J. L. Werth Jr. & D. Blevins (Eds.), *Psychosocial issues near the end of life: A resource for professional care providers.* (pp. 89–110). Washington, DC: American Psychological Association.

Ditto, P. H., Danks, J. H., Smucker, W. D., Bookwala, J., Coppola, K. M., Dresser, R., et al. (2001). Advance directives as acts of communication. *Archives of Internal Medicine, 161,* 421–430.

Duke, S. (1998). An exploration of anticipatory grief: The lived experience of people during their spouses' terminal illness and in bereavement. *Journal of Advanced Nursing, 28,* 829–839.

Franks, K., Templer, D. I., Cappelletty, G. G., & Kauffman, I. (1991). Exploration of death anxiety as a function of religious variables in gay men with and without AIDS. *Omega, 22,* 43–50.

Fry, P. S. (1997). Grandparents' reactions to the death of a grandchild: An exploratory factor analysis. *Omega, 35,* 119–140.

Gay and Lesbian Medical Association (GLMA). (2001). *Healthy People 2010 companion document for lesbian, gay, bisexual, and transgender (LGBT) health.* Retrieved July 23, 2002, from www.glma.org/policy/hp2010/index.html.

Gibson, C. A., Breitbart, W., Tomarkin, A., & Nelson, C. J. (2006). Psychosocial issues near the end of life. In J. L. Werth Jr. & D. Blevins (Eds.), *Psychosocial issues near the end of life: A resource for professional care providers.* (pp. 137–162). Washington, DC: American Psychological Association.

Gilliland, G., & Fleming, S. (1998). A comparison of spousal anticipatory grief and conventional grief. *Death Studies, 22,* 541–569.

Hays, J. C., Gold, D. T., & Pieper, C. F. (1997). Sibling bereavement in late life. *Omega, 35,* 25–42.

Hellinger, F. J. (1998). Cost and financing of care for persons with HIV disease: An overview. *Health Care Financing Review, 19,* 5–18.

Holmes, T. H., & Rahe, R. H. (1967). The Social Readjustment Rating Scale. *Journal of Psychosomatic Research, 11,* 213–218.

Human Rights Campaign. (2003). *Equality in the states: Gay, lesbian, bisexual and transgender Americans and state laws and legislation in 2003.* Retrieved July 10, 2003, from www.hrc.org.

*In re L.W.,* 482 N.W.2d 60 (Wis. 1992).

Kelly, I. (1977). The aging male homosexual: Myth and reality. *The Gerontologist, 77,* 328–332.

Kennedy, G. J. (2000). *Geriatric mental health care: A treatment guide for health professionals.* New York: Guilford.

Koenig, H. G. (2002). A commentary: The role of religion and spirituality at the end of life. *The Gerontologist, 42*(Special Issue III), 20–23.

Kovacs, P. J., & Rodgers, A. Y. (1995). Meeting the social service needs of persons with AIDS: Hospices' response. *The Hospice Journal, 10,* 49–65.

Kübler-Ross, E. (1969). *On death and dying.* New York: Macmillan.

Lawrence, J. A., Goodnow, J. J., Woods, K., & Karantzas, G. (2002). Distributions of caregiving tasks among family members: The place of gender and availability. *Journal of Family Psychology, 16,* 493–509.

Lennon, M. C., Martin, J. L., & Dean, L. (1990). The influence of social support on AIDS-related grief reaction among gay men. *Social Science & Medicine, 31,* 477–484.

Lew-Napoleone, S. (1992). Hospice service and AIDS. In H. Land (Ed.), *AIDS: A complete guide to psychosocial intervention* (pp. 65–77). New York: Springer.

Linsk, N. L. (2000). HIV among older adults: Age-specific issues in prevention and treatment. *The AIDS Reader, 10,* 430–440.

Lunney, J. R., Lynn, J., Foley, D. J., Lipson, S., & Guralnik, J. M. (2003). Patterns of functional decline at the end of life. *Journal of the American Medical Association, 289,* 2387–2392.

Lunney, J. R., Lynn, J., & Hogan, C. (2002). Profiles of older Medicare decedents. *Journal of the American Geriatrics Society, 50,* 1108–1112.

Martin, J. L., & Dean, L. (1993). Effects of AIDS-related bereavement and HIV-related illness on psychological distress among gay men: A 7-year longitudinal study, 1985–1991. *Journal of Consulting and Clinical Psychology, 61,* 94–103.

Masoro, E. J., & Austad, S. N. (Eds.). (2001). *Handbook of the biology and aging* (5th ed.). Orlando, FL: Academic Press.

McGaffic, C. M., & Longman, A. J. (1993). Connecting and disconnecting: Bereavement experiences of six gay men. *Journal of the Association of Nurses in AIDS Care, 4,* 49–57.

Meuser, T. M., & Marwit, S. J. (2001). A comprehensive, stage-sensitive model of grief in dementia caregiving. *The Gerontologist, 41,* 658–670.

Moss, M. S., Moss, S. Z., & Hansson, R. O. (2001). Bereavement and old age. In M. S. Stroebe, R. O. Hansson, W. Stroebe, & H. Schut (Eds.), *Handbook of bereavement research: Consequences, coping, and care* (pp. 241–260). Washington, DC: APA Books.

National Center for Health Statistics (NCHS). (2003). *Health, United States, 2003.* Retrieved October 30, 2003, from www.cdc.gov/nchs/data/hus/hus03.pdf.

Neugebauer, R., Rabkin, J. G., Williams, J. B., Remien, R. H., Goetz, R., & Gorman, J. M. (1992). Bereavement reactions among homosexual men experiencing multiple losses in the AIDS epidemic. *American Journal of Psychiatry, 149,* 1374–1379.

Oregon Health Division. (2001). *Oregon's Death with Dignity Act.* Retrieved January 10, 2002, from www.ohd.hr.state.or.us/chs/pas/ors.htm.

*Patient Self-Determination Act of 1990.* 42 U.S.C. §§ 1395cc(f) & 1396a(w) (1994).

Paul, J. P., Catania, J., Pollack, L., Moskowitz, J., Canchola, M. S., Mills, T., Binson, D., & Stall, R. (2002). Suicide attempts among gay and bisexual men: Lifetime prevalence and antecedents. *American Journal of Public Health, 92,* 1338–1345.

Preston, D. B., Koch, P. B., & Young, E. W. (1991). AIDS: Experiences and attitudes of nurses from rural communities in Pennsylvania and New York. *The Hospice Journal, 4,* 109–125.

Quam, J. K., & Whitford, G. S. (1992). Adaptation and age-related expectations of older gay and lesbian adults. *The Gerontologist, 32,* 367–374.

Rando, T. A. (2000). *Clinical dimensions of anticipatory mourning: Theory, and practice in working with the dying, their loved ones, and their caregivers.* Champaign, IL: Research Press.

Rosen, E. J. (1989). Hospice work with AIDS-related disenfranchised grief. In K. J. Doka (Ed.), *Disenfranchised grief: Recognizing hidden sorrow* (pp. 301–311). Indianapolis, IN: Wiley.

Schantz, B., & O'Hanlan, K. (1994). *Anti-gay discrimination in medicine: Results of a national survey of lesbian, gay and bisexual physicians.* San Francisco: American Association of Physicians for Human Rights.

Schneider, S. G., Taylor, S. E., Hammen, C., Kemeny, M. E., & Dudley, J. (1991). Factors influencing suicide intent in gay and bisexual suicide ideators: Differing models for men with and without human immunodeficiency virus. *Journal of Personality and Social Psychology, 61,* 776–788.

Sell, R. L. (1997). Defining and measuring sexual orientation: A review. *Archives of Sexual Behavior, 26,* 643–658.

Solarz, A. L. (Ed.). (1999). *Lesbian health: Current assessment and directions for the future.* Washington, DC: National Academy Press.

Steinhauser, K. E., Christakis, N. A., Clipp, E. C., McNeilly, M., McIntyre, L., & Tulsky, J. A. (2000). Factors considered important at the end of life by patients, family, physicians, and other care providers. *Journal of the American Medical Association, 284,* 2476–2482.

Stroebe, M. S., Hansson, R. O., Stroebe, W., & Schut, H. (2001). Introduction: Concepts and issues in contemporary research on bereavement. In M. S. Stroebe, R. O. Hansson, W. Stroebe, & H. Schut. (Eds.), *Handbook of bereavement research: Consequences, coping, and care* (pp. 3–22). Washington, DC: APA Books.

SUPPORT Principal Investigators. (1995). A controlled trial to improve care for seriously ill hospitalized patients. *JAMA, 274,* 1591–1598.

Tehan, C. (1991). The cost of caring for patients with HIV infection in hospice. *The Hospice Journal, 4,* 41–59.

Viney, L. L., Henry, R. M., Walker, B. M., & Crooks, L. (1992). The psychosocial impact of multiple deaths from AIDS. *Omega, 24,* 151–163.

Werth, J. L. Jr. (Ed.). (1999). *Contemporary perspectives on rational suicide.* Philadelphia: Brunner-Mazel.

Werth, J. L. Jr. (2002). Legal and ethical considerations for mental health professionals related to end-of-life care and decision-making. *American Behavioral Scientist, 46,* 373–388.

Werth, J. L. Jr., & Blevins, D. (Eds.). (2006). *Psychosocial issues near the end of life: A resource for professional care providers.* Washington, DC: American Psychological Association.

Werth, J. L. Jr., Blevins, D., Toussaint, K., & Durham, M. R. (2002). The influence of cultural diversity on end-of-life care and decisions. *American Behavioral Scientist* 46: 204–219.

Werth, J. L. Jr., & Gordon, J. R. (1998). Helping at the end of life: Hastened death and the mental health professional. In. L. VandeCreek, S. Knapp, & T. L. Jackson (Eds.), *Innovations in clinical practice: A source book* (Vol. 16, pp. 385–398). Sarasota, FL: Professional Resource Press.

Werth, J. L. Jr., Gordon, J. R., & Johnson, R. R. Jr. (2002). Psychosocial issues near the end of life. *Aging and Mental Health, 6,* 402–412.

Werth, J. L. Jr., & Kleespies, P. M. (2006). Ethical considerations in providing psychological services in end-of-life care. In J. L. Werth Jr. & D. Blevins (Eds.), *Psychosocial issues near the end of life: A resource for professional care providers.* (pp. 57–88). Washington, DC: American Psychological Association.

Werth, J. L. Jr., Kopera-Frye, K., Blevins, D., & Bossick, B. (2003). Older adult representation in the counseling psychology literature. *The Counseling Psychologist, 31,* 789–814.

Wilkerson, G. J. (2001). What we don't know: The unaddressed health concerns of the transgendered. *Trans-Health, 1.* Retrieved September 10, 2003, from www.trans-health.com/Iss1Vol1/dont_know.htm.

Worden, J. W. (1991). Grieving a loss from AIDS. *The Hospice Journal, 4,* 143–150.

Worden, J. W. (2001). *Grief counseling and grief therapy: A handbook for the mental health practitioner* (3rd ed.). New York: Springer.

# 13

# Community Needs Assessment
## *Documenting the Need for Affirmative Services for LGB Older Adults*
### Nancy Orel

———————— ∽∞∾ ————————

While the overall U.S. population has tripled in the past century, the number of people aged 65 and older has increased elevenfold (U.S. Census Bureau, 2000). Currently, nearly 35 million Americans are aged 65 and older, representing 13% of the population, or one in eight Americans. During the next 25 years, as baby boomers age, the number of American elders will double, from 34.7 million to 69.4 million. It is estimated that in 2030, one in five Americans will be 65 years of age or older.

Paralleling the overall older adult population, it is assumed that the number and proportion of lesbian, gay, bisexual, and transgender (LGBT) older adults will significantly increase. Although obtaining accurate estimates of the present and projected LGBT elder population has been problematic because of the "invisibility" of this population, the National Gay and Lesbian Task Force Policy Institute (1999) estimates that currently 1–3 million Americans aged 65 and older are lesbian, gay, or bisexual (LGB).

Although the LGBT senior population is growing, little attention has been given to identifying and understanding the needs and concerns of this growing population (Quam & Whitford, 1992). The paucity of research on the needs and concerns of LGBT elders has been attributed primarily to perceived hostility against gays and lesbians, which discouraged many LGBT elders from participating in research that would require that they self-identify (Kochman, 1997). Current cohorts of LGBT elders remain silent and invisible for self-preservation and survival, having come of age at a time when keeping one's sexual orientation hidden was a prominent coping mechanism (Cook-Daniels, 1997; Kimmel, 1978; Kochman, 1997; Rosenfeld, 1999).

Several studies have reported psychological resiliency among the current cohort of lesbian and gay elders, however. These elders deconstructed the negative images associated with heterosexism and disclosed their sexual identification as lesbians and gays. In the process, they developed adaptive coping mechanisms, which later assisted them in coping with the stigma that often accompanies aging. These psychologically resilient older gay men and lesbians adjusted to aging more successfully than their heterosexual counterparts, and they reported higher levels of life satisfaction, greater flexibility and fluidity in gender role definition, lower self-criticism, and fewer psychosomatic problems (Adelman, 1991; Barranti & Cohen, 2000; Berger, 1980; Berger & Kelly, 1996; D'Augelli, 1994; Friend, 1980, 1990; Humphreys & Quam, 1998; Kimmel, 1978).

Although the previous research on lesbian and gay elders focused primarily on issues related to identity, stigma, and adjustment to aging, the current body of literature is focusing on the variables that facilitate successful aging. "Successful aging implies that individuals are satisfied or contented with their lives—that they have found ways of maximizing the positive of their lives while minimizing the impact of inevitable age-related losses" (Morgan & Kunkel, 1998, p. 146). Researchers have identified factors that are associated with successful aging for lesbian and gay elders. These factors include good health, the avoidance of unhealthy behaviors, the ability to stay in one's own home, financial resources, higher levels of education, the presence of a life partner, and a broad social network (Hamburger, 1997; Kimmel, 1995; Lee, 1987; Sharp, 1997; Wahler & Gabbay, 1997).

Friend's (1990) study of successful aging for lesbians and gay men found that a social network of friends and family that is closely identified with or supportive of the lesbian and gay experience is essential for healthy and successful aging. Historically, LGBT elders often had to create their own social support networks in order to receive the support and assistance that were not available to them because of their sexual orientation (Grossman, D'Augelli, & Hershberger, 2000; Kimmel, 1978). The quality and extent of social support networks are related to the level of comfort with their sexual orientation, degree of external community heterosexism, and availability of an LGBT community (Barranti, 1998; Patterson, 2000). The lack of a supportive LGBT community and fear of experiencing discrimination from the larger community can socially isolate LGBT older adults. This in turn can decrease the LGBT elder's quality of life (Herdt, Beeler, & Rawls, 1997; Quam & Whitford, 1992).

Discrimination and intolerance create numerous obstacles for LGBT elders. Many services and programs available to heterosexuals are difficult to obtain or are denied to LGBT elders. For example, Social Security's treatment of same-sex couples is perhaps the most blatant form of institutionalized heterosexism in federal policy (Coons, 2003). Additionally, although the LGBT identity is no longer labeled as a mental illness, research indicates that many professionals still hold this view (Garnets et al., 1991; Phillips & Fischer, 1998). Research by the Gay & Lesbian Medical Association found that two-thirds of physicians and medical students polled were aware of biased care by medical professionals, and approximately 90% heard disparaging remarks about LGB patients. "Research suggests that LGBT people have justifiable concerns about negative views held by professionals and the impact of these views on their health care and receipt of social services" (Coons, 2003, p. 9).

Empirically based information and analysis on the obstacles facing LGBT elders in accessing programs and services is needed. Without an accurate knowledge and understanding of their needs, concerns, and obstacles, effective programs and services for LGBT elders cannot be planned and implemented. In recognition of the need for empirically based information, this author, with faculty assistance from Case Western Reserve University and Eastern Michigan University, developed a wide-ranging needs assessment instrument to identify the areas of concern for LGBT older adults. As a first step in the development of the needs assessment instrument, qualitative methodological strategies (e.g., focus groups, in-depth interviews) were used to isolate the variables included in the final needs assessment instrument. The primary purpose of the focus group research was to identify the diverse perceptions regarding the needs, concerns, and issues affecting a select group of LGBT older adults. Another objective of the focus group discussions was to gather LGBT elders' perceptions about aging in the LGBT community and the use of aging services by LGBT older adults. It was assumed that the focus group discussions would illustrate the unmet needs among LGBT elders and provide direction for the planning of services and programs. The second step was to administer the measure.

There are three aims of this chapter. First, the results from a series of focus groups and in-depth interviews with LGB elders from three select areas in the Midwest (northeastern Ohio, northwestern Ohio, and southeastern Michigan) are presented. Second, the LGB Elders Needs Assessment Scale is introduced, and preliminary findings from the returned surveys are discussed. Third, recommendations for affirmative programs and services that would address the unique concerns of LGBT elders are provided.

## LGB Elders: Expressed Needs and Concerns
## Across Focus Groups

A brief description of the methods and findings of the three focus groups is presented. A more detailed description of the sample, procedures, and results (including narratives) is available in Orel (2004) or may be obtained by contacting the author.

## *Methods*

### Sample

A variety of methods were used to recruit potential participants for the three focus groups. This researcher, identified colleagues, and agents (e.g., people who had access to the LGBT community) personally recruited participants who belonged to older gay and lesbian friendship networks, support groups, and religious organizations. It is important to note that participation in the focus groups was limited to people over the age of 65 who self-identified as lesbian, gay, bisexual, or transgender. Although much effort was made to recruit transgender elders, recruitment methods were not successful. Therefore, the experiences of transgender older adults are not included in the current study. Future research will emphasize the inclusion of transgender elders because the perceptions and points of view of transgender elders are unique enough to merit a distinct and separate inquiry (chapter 2, this volume).

A total of 26 self-identified LGB elders participated in three focus groups of 7–10 people in three different areas (northwestern Ohio, northeastern Ohio, and southeastern Michigan). There were 10 gay men, 13 lesbians, and 3 bisexual women, based on their own identified sexual orientation. Participants ranged in age from 65 to 84, with a mean age of 72.3. Collectively, the three focus groups consisted of LGB elders of various ethnic groups (African Americans [$n = 6$], European Americans [$n = 17$], Asian Americans [$n = 1$], Latinos and Latinas [$n = 2$]), socioeconomic statuses (low income [$n = 5$], middle income [$n = 15$], upper income [$n = 6$]), and educational levels (less than 8th grade education [$n = 2$], high school graduates [$n = 17$], college graduates [$n = 5$], advanced degrees [$n = 2$]).

### Procedure and Instrument

All focus group participants were informed, in writing, of the general nature of the research project and the voluntary and confidential nature of his or her participation. Focus groups were conducted over a period of 6 months, and the length of each focus group was from 90 minutes to 2 hours. Focus group discussions were audiotaped and transcribed. The focus groups were conducted at preidentified gay-friendly sites.

This focus group moderator and researcher received assistance from an observer (a self-identified lesbian elder) who took detailed notes during the focus group discussions. A question route (e.g., a prepared series of questions) was used to guide the discussion. The questions reflected the common themes in the previous literature on LGBT older adults. Additionally, the question route was tested on people with characteristics similar to those of the participants before any focus groups were conducted. The question route was flexible to allow the group to direct the discussion toward the issues they viewed as being important, yet it had enough structure to prevent the group from moving too far from the topic of interest. Generally, the focus group participants were asked to discuss their unique needs and concerns as older LGB people and the extent to which they were satisfied with service providers. Examples of specific questions posed to focus group participants included, "What are your primary concerns about aging?" "What are your primary concerns about being an LGB elder?" and "How has your sexual orientation affected the types of governmental assistance that you are either eligible for or are presently receiving?"

## Data Analysis

Analysis of focus group data was an ongoing process and was performed at a range of levels. Beginning with the conceptualization of the focus group questions, preliminary analysis took place. During the interim phase, audiotapes and field notes were transcribed, sorted, and summarized. Analysis of the transcripts was the most formal process, whereby information was examined, categorized, coded, and tabulated. Two colleagues also coded the focus group transcripts independently to enhance reliability. Differences between researchers in the coding of statements were discussed until consensus was reached.

## *Results and Findings*

Content analysis of the expressed beliefs, attitudes, and opinions from participants revealed that there were seven major areas of importance for LGB elders: physical health, housing, legal rights, mental health, spirituality, LGB-affirmative services, and family and social networks. Each of these areas is discussed briefly in the following sections.

## Physical Health

All 26 focus group participants indicated that their physical health and health care needs were a primary source of concern. Like others in the general older adult population, LGB elders expressed concern about rising health care costs and their failing health. A unique health care concern that LGB focus group elders emphasized was the discrimination and bias that they have experienced in health care settings. Focus group participants discussed their frustrations with medical personnel who assumed heterosexuality when assessing issues related to sexual activity, if sexual activity was discussed at all.

Frustration with the health care system was heightened for LGB older adults who did not share their sexual orientation with their health care provider. More than half of the participants indicated that they were not out to medical practitioners, and they feared the reactions they would receive if they did share their sexual orientation. These same LGB elders indicated that because of their lack of self-disclosure, they have been prevented from visiting their life partners in hospitals or participating in discussions about their partners with medical personal. Conversely, the LGB elders who shared their sexual orientation with their primary care physicians reported more positive experiences. For example, participants who disclosed their sexual orientation to their physicians believed that this honesty facilitated a more trusting and open patient–doctor relationship. Likewise, other participants reported that their partners were included in health care discussions with their physicians.

Another primary medical concern for focus group participants was the financial constraints in seeking medical attention. Although all participants had some type of medical insurance, the degree to which this insurance covered health-related expenses varied tremendously. Participants who relied solely on government-sponsored programs (e.g., Medicare) reported the greatest difficulty in meeting medical expenses, especially prescription drug costs.

All participants expressed concern about providing caregiving services to their long-term partners, if needed in the future. Specifically, they were concerned about employing home health care personnel who would not discriminate against them because of their sexual orientation. This same level of concern was expressed when participants discussed the likelihood that they would need caregiving services in the future. Participants assumed that their partners or friends would provide the necessary care but were also aware that this assumption may be unrealistic if their health care concerns became problematic for their partners or friends. This realization of the possible need for long-term care services led to the discussion of nursing homes and general housing needs and concerns.

## Housing

Focus group participants indicated that their present homes would not meet their needs if they developed major physical limitations. Although all participants expressed the desire to "age in place" and remain in their own homes, they also recognized the potential need for long-term care in a nursing home. Participants expressed their desires for LGBT-only nursing homes. Likewise, the majority of the participants (67%) voiced their preference for LGBT-only retirement communities. The primary reason stated was the belief that if their sexual orientation were known, they would not be welcomed in existing retirement communities (see chapter 14, this volume, for similar data). Other reasons given for this preference included similar interests, a sense of family, and a greater likelihood of meeting a potential intimate partner for those who were single. One participant indicated that his primary concern regarding nursing home placement was whether his current partner would have the same visitation rights and privileges that heterosexual residents have. This comment paralleled the repeatedly voiced concern that same-sex couples are denied benefits married heterosexual couples take for granted.

## Legal Rights

All focus group participants voiced their frustrations that people in same-gender long-term relationships do not have the same rights as married couples. Benefits available to married couples in the United States that are not available to same-gender partnered relationships include spousal benefits through Social Security or other pension plans, status of next of kin for hospital visits and medical decisions, automatic inheritance of jointly owned real and personal property, dissolution and divorce protections, domestic violence protection orders, immigration and residency for partners from other countries, joint leases with automatic renewal rights in the event one partner dies, spousal exemption to property tax increases upon the death of one partner, joint filing of income tax returns, bereavement or sick leave to care for a partner, and decision-making power with respect to burial or cremation (see also chapter 11, this volume).

Focus group participants who were in partnered relationships reported that they have had to make special and creative legal arrangements to obtain many of the aforementioned benefits intrinsic in heterosexual marriages. These special legal arrangements included setting up personal partnership agreements; signing durable financial powers of attorney, health care proxies, and consents to priority visitation; and executing living wills and last wills.

Forty-three percent of the focus group participants voiced their concerns that despite the special legal arrangements that they had made, their desires could still be questioned, especially if their competency was challenged by estranged biological family members. An important area of discussion among participants was the likelihood of developing Alzheimer's disease and their fears of being labeled "incompetent," "senile," or "crazy" by mental health professionals. Mental health needs were the next topic of discussion.

## Mental Health

Half of the participants had used formal mental health services in the past to address issues related to depression, anxiety, or substance abuse. One explanation for the high use of mental health services by this select group of LGB elders was the fact that 7 of the 26 focus group members were previously employed in mental health professions. These members were aware of and comfortable with counseling. Participants who used mental health services emphasized the importance of finding gay-friendly therapists.

The majority of focus group participants perceived themselves as being healthy, happy, well-adjusted, and able to negotiate the challenges of aging. Many of the participants expressed the idea that the psychological resiliency necessary for coming out prepared them for the psychological difficulties of aging. Other participants credited their spiritual beliefs for their psychological well-being.

## Spirituality

All participants indicated that their spiritual beliefs became more important to them with advancing age but that their involvement in religious organizations had not increased. All participants indicated that they would be more active in religious organizations if the bias against homosexuality did not exist in those organizations. Focus group members discussed how they sought out religious organizations that were accepting of LGBT people. It was in these gay-friendly religious organizations that they felt affirmed and accepted.

## LGBT-Affirmative Services

All focus group participants expressed the importance of their membership in the LGBT community. Participants indicated that it was because of the LGBT community and other social networks that they were able to be comfortable with their own sexual orientation. Establishing accepting social networks and maintaining strong familial relationships was a theme that emerged repeatedly. The participants also desired membership in organizations that serve primarily elders, but they expressed concern that if their sexual orientation was known, they would not be accepted. Although focus group members initially expressed their desire to have gay-only senior centers, they later concluded that senior centers that were accepting probably would meet more of their needs because of the expansive services currently in place at government-sponsored senior centers.

## Family and Social Networks

All focus group participants discussed the importance of familial relationships, but key differences emerged for out participants and those who had not disclosed their sexual orientation to family members. For closeted participants (38%), there was an overwhelming sense that this nondisclosure prevented them from feeling emotionally close to family members. Conversely, out and accepted participants reported that familial support was extremely important for their sense of happiness and well-being. This familial support included adult children from previous heterosexual unions, grandchildren, and siblings.

Families of choice were another very important source of emotional support for the participants. A surprising finding was that many LGB elders reported that they expanded their social networks as they aged. During their adolescence, early adulthood, and middle adulthood, most of the participants' social needs were met through members of the LGBT community. Out of necessity (e.g., death of friends, ageism), many have extended their social networks outside the LGBT community (see chapter 4, this volume, for similar data).

## Development of the Needs Assessment Scale

Focus group members identified their specific issues of importance as older LGB men and women. Six of these seven areas (physical health, housing, legal rights, mental health, spirituality, family and social networks) have been previously identified in the gerontological literature as being areas of importance for heterosexual older men and women (Ferrini & Ferrini, 2000). Unlike their heterosexual counterparts, LGB older adults identified the need for LGBT-affirming services. The need for affirming services reflects the discrimination that focus group members collectively experienced and the barriers they faced in accessing and using services.

The focus groups were a very effective method for exploring many aspects of older LGB people's beliefs, attitudes, and opinions. Of course, because of the small number of focus group participants and the convenience nature of participant recruiting practices, the results cannot be generalized to a larger population. However, it was not the goal to generalize the findings. As previously indicated, the second step was to develop and distribute a survey instrument that specifically contained questions addressing the seven areas identified in the focus group discussions (physical health, housing, legal rights, mental health, spirituality, LGBT affirmative services, and family and social networks).

## Method

### Procedure and Instrument

An extensive 150-item self-report survey instrument was developed that contained both project-specific items and a standardized questionnaire. Specific questions for the self-report survey instrument were generated from the needs, concerns, range of issues, common issues, opinions, and attitudes expressed across focus groups. Both forced-response and open-ended questions in the Lesbian, Gay, and Bisexual Elders Needs Assessment Scale assess the perceived needs, concerns, and issues in the seven areas identified as important by focus group members. The Needs Assessment Scale also explores respondents' perceptions of needs not being met and their level of involvement and satisfaction with agencies or organizations that provide services to either older adults or LGBT people. Additionally, respondents are asked to provide sociodemographic information (e.g., age, gender, socioeconomic status, race, ethnicity, religion, relationship status, work history, education, housing, familial relationships) and complete a modified Outness Inventory (Mohr & Fassinger, 2000) that assesses their level of outness and their level of comfort with their sexual orientation.

The Lesbian, Gay, and Bisexual Elders Needs Assessment Scale was distributed to self-identified LGB individuals over age 65 living in adjoining Midwestern states (e.g., Ohio, Michigan). The questionnaire was available at LGBT organizations and agencies and at mainstream older adult service providers in order to include LGB elders who are not active in the LGBT community. To ensure anonymity and protect the confidentiality of the respondents, the survey instrument did not request any identifying information, and respondents could complete the survey in their homes or apartments. Respondents were provided with a preaddressed, prepaid envelope for the return of their completed surveys.

## Data Analysis

It is anticipated that the analysis of the responses from the Lesbian, Gay, and Bisexual Elders Needs Assessment Scale will bring a new awareness to the issues, concerns, and needs facing LGB older adults. Focus group participants have been contacted again to assist in the analysis because they will be instrumental in pursuing exploratory aspects of the analysis and explaining potential unanticipated results.

The analysis of the codified responses and responses to the open-ended questions has been an ongoing process. To date, approximately 2,000 questionnaires have been distributed, and slightly more than half have been returned ($n = 1,150$). Although definitive results depend on the return of additional questionnaires, some preliminary observations can be provided.

## *Results and Findings*

Respondents range in age from 64 to 88 years of age (mean = 73), and 83% live in an urban setting. There are 414 gay men (36%) and 736 women who identified their sexual orientation as lesbian or bisexual (64%). More than 52% ($n = 601$) are in a partnered relationship, and 68% ($n = 782$) are active in the LGBT community. Most respondents (73%) indicated that they are out and comfortable with their self-identified lesbian, gay, or bisexual label. Approximately 91% of the respondents ($n = 1,045$) are Caucasian, 8% are African American ($n = 91$), and less than 2% ($n = 14$) are Latino or Latina. It is apparent from the preliminary analysis that greater emphasis must be placed on reaching a more diverse sample of LGB older adults.

The responses to questions that assessed their use of programs and services indicated that eligible respondents were recipients of federal, state, and local services for older adults (e.g., Medicare, Medicaid, Social Security, government-sponsored meal programs, hospice services). However, the responses to the questions that assessed their perceptions of these services and programs revealed that slightly more than 53% ($n = 615$) were dissatisfied with the services. Many respondents indicated that the available services, especially senior centers, did not meet their unique needs as LGB elders. For example, one respondent on an open-ended question indicated that although the staff at the local senior center plans numerous educational programs, when she requested an educational program on aging in the LGBT community she was told that this type of program was "not needed at this particular senior center." The respondent also indicated that when she approached a local LGBT nightclub and requested social programs specifically for LGBT older adults, she was told that "there would not be enough interest." However, the preliminary results from this survey indicate that most respondents (83%) are interested in participating in social groups exclusively for LGBT people over the age of 60.

## Affirmative Programs to Address the Unique Concerns of LGBT Elders

Affirming services for LGBT elders must be available on multiple levels, from individuals to organizations, communities, and overarching policies. To illustrate the type of services and programs that are needed for LGBT elders, table 13.1 lists the continuum of services and programs that are currently available for the older adult population. The table was developed using multiple data sets. That is, the services are listed according to the areas of concern identified by LGB elder focus group participants, themes suggested by the gerontologic and LGBT literature, and responses to forced-choice and open-ended questions from the LGB needs assessment scale. It is important to note that the actual type or number of services that an older adult will need varies according to a variety of factors, with the most significant being level of physical health or cognitive abilities and the availability of personal support from family, friends, neighbors, and community.

Unfortunately, ageist and heterosexist attitudes continue to exist. One example of ageist attitudes held by society at large is the misperception that older adults do not engage in sexual activities. Because of this misperception, if one aspect of sexual orientation is defined by sexual behaviors, and if the belief is that older adults are no longer sexual, then a conclusion could be made that older LGB people do not exist. Because our culture fails to acknowledge that elders (aging parents, grandparents, and great grandparents) are sexually active,

TABLE 13.1

## Continuum of Services and Programs Currently Available for Older Adults

| General Area | Specific Service or Program Available |
|---|---|
| Physical health | Dental services |
| | Emergency assistance |
| | Geriatric assessments |
| | Health care information services |
| | Health promotion |
| | Health screening |
| | Hearing and vision services |
| | Home health services |
| | Hospice services |
| | Hospital services (inpatient, outpatient) |
| | Medical treatment |
| | Medicare and Medicaid |
| | Nutrition services (congregate, food stamps, home-delivered meals) |
| | Restorative services |
| | Speech therapy |
| | Transportation services for medical care |
| Housing | Adult foster care |
| | Assisted living sites |
| | Chore services |
| | Congregate living sites |
| | Energy assistance |
| | Homemaker services |
| | Home repair services |
| | Housing information |
| | Long-term care facilities |
| | Property tax assistance |
| | Retirement communities |
| | Shared housing |
| | Utility programs (e.g., utility assistance, weatherization) |
| Legal rights | Advance directives |
| | Advocacy, legal and self-empowerment |
| | Conservatorship |
| | Consumer help information |
| | Disability and rehabilitation services |
| | Financial assistance and estate planning |
| | Funeral planning |
| | Guardianship |

*(continued on next page)*

(Table 13.1 *continued*)

|  | Health-related agencies and services |
|---|---|
| | (e.g., AIDS and HIV, Alzheimer's, cancer) |
| | Holistic health and wellness programs |
| | Insurance counseling |
| | Living trusts and wills |
| | Medical equipment and adaptive devices |
| | Medicare and Medicaid |
| | Powers of attorney |
| | Social Security |
| **Mental health** | Bereavement counseling |
| | Counseling services |
| | Education and leisure programs |
| | Emergency response |
| | Geropsychiatric assessments |
| | Protective services |
| | Psychiatric services (inpatient, outpatient) |
| | Safety and security programs (e.g., adult protective services) |
| **Spirituality** | Religious organizations |
| | Supportive services through religious organizations |
| **LGB-affirmative services** | Aging Initiative of the National Gay and Lesbian Task Force |
| | American Society on Aging's Lesbian and Gay Aging Issues Network |
| | Family Caregiver Alliance: LGBT Caring Community Program |
| | Gay and Lesbian Medical Association |
| | Lambda Legal Defense Fund |
| | LGBT community organizations |
| | Local and national LGBT elder resource directories |
| | National Association on HIV over Fifty |
| | National Center for Lesbian Rights |
| | National Gay and Lesbian Task Force |
| | Old Lesbians Organizing for Change |
| | Pride Senior Network |
| | Services and Advocacy for GLBT Elders (SAGE) |
| **Family and social networks** | Adult day care services |
| | Caregiver services |
| | Companionship services |
| | Educational opportunities |
| | Employment opportunities |
| | Multipurpose senior centers |
| | Outreach programs |
| | Respite services |
| | Support groups |
| | Telephone reassurance programs |
| | Volunteer opportunities |

same-gender sexual behaviors among older adults are perceived as implausible. Sadly, many younger LGB people have internalized societal ageist attitudes and discount the possibility of older people being lesbian, gay, or bisexual.

Because of the prevailing heterosexist and ageist attitudes, many LGBT elders have internalized these negative cultural attitudes and beliefs (Adelman, 1991; Morrow, 2001). LGBT people currently over the age of 65 were at least in their early 30s when the gay civil rights movement began with the 1969 Stonewall Inn riots. For these LGBT elders, childhood and adolescent memories of issues related to homosexuality are generally negative. Before the gay civil rights movement, "homosexuals were viewed as 'perverted' by society, 'evil' by the church, 'sick' by the medical and psychiatric professions, and 'criminals' by the police" (Reid, 1995, p. 217). It is not surprising then that LGBT elders struggle to view themselves positively as homosexual, bisexual, or transgender. Empirical studies have found higher rates of depression, stress, addictions, and suicide for LGBT elders who did not challenge internalized, extremely negative heterosexist beliefs (Bradford, Ryan, & Rothblum, 1994; Grossman, Hershberger, & O'Connell, 2001; Ritter & Terndrup, 2002).

Reviews of the professional literature have been unable to identify the perfect solution for eradicating heterosexism and homonegativity in the network of aging service providers. However, several promising programs and groups have been effective in addressing the discrimination faced by LGBT elders. For example, Services and Advocacy for GLBT Elders (SAGE) has developed comprehensive staff training programs designed to sensitize social service providers to the unique needs and concerns of LGBT elders (chapter 15, this volume). A variety of researchers have documented the success of these and other staff training programs (Metz, 1997; Nystrom & Jones, 2003; Slusher, Mayer, & Dunkle, 1996; van Wormer, Wells, & Boes, 2000).

The Gray Pride Interagency Taskforce on Gay and Lesbian Aging in Cleveland, Ohio is another example of a group whose mission is to raise awareness about the needs and issues facing LGBT elders in the hopes of stimulating change at organizational and community levels. Through a series of community dialogues, a comprehensive list of action strategies was developed to address the concerns of LGBT elders living in Ohio (table 13.2). This type of local effort must take place in cities and communities across the United States. On the national level, the Aging Initiative of the National Gay and Lesbian Task Force is working with key groups at the federal, state, and local levels to implement a variety of political action strategies to address the needs and concerns of LGBT elders across the United States.

**TABLE 13.2**

## Action Strategies to Address the Issues and Concerns of LGBT and Older Adults

*Community Involvement and Activism*

- Expand Gray Pride Interagency Taskforce's mission of advocacy, education, and programming on behalf of LGBT elders.
- Involve key aging service organizations in Taskforce's mission.

*Research and Information*

- Initiate applied research and needs assessment activities to increase knowledge on issues of importance for LGBT elders.
- Compile and distribute resource directories of local services and programs offered for LGBT elders.

*Funding*

- Secure Federal, State, and local funding to develop and implement programs for LGBT elders.
- Ensure that currently funded services/programs for older adults include LGBT elders in their service efforts.

*Employment and Volunteer Policies and Practices*

- Encourage the recruitment and hiring of LGBT employees and volunteers for positions within established aging organizations.
- Promote an organizational culture that supports diversity and encourages non-discriminatory practices in hiring, promotion, and termination.

*Education and Training*

- Develop and implement on going education and training about LGBT adding issues for service organizations.
- Involve LGBT elders in the planning and delivery of educational programs.

*Service Delivery Practice and Policies*

- Examine current policies and if necessary provide non-discriminatory policy statements.
- Examine current programs/services offered through the aging network and LGBT community, and if necessary modify to be more inclusive/sensitive to LGBT elders.
- Develop and sponsor, in collaboration with established aging organizations new programs/services directed to the needs of LGBT elders.
- Conduct extensive outreach activities to reach the hidden population of LGBT elders.

*Advocacy Efforts*

- Engage in legislative advocacy and community advocacy to raise awareness of LGBT aging issues.

SOURCE: Gray Pride Interagency Taskforce on Gay and Lesbian Aging (2003).

Until major changes take place in attitudes toward and laws protecting the rights of LGBT people, most communities will need to develop and implement their own affirming programs and services for LGBT elders. This has occurred in major urban areas across the United States. Cities such as San Francisco, Los Angeles, New York, Washington, Boston, Fort Lauderdale, and Cleveland have developed or are in the process of developing retirement communities that are specifically tailored for LGBT elders (see chapter 14, this volume).

Just as the aging network needs to address the existing heterosexist attitudes that have prevented LGBT elders from using existing elder care services, the LGBT community must also address the prevailing ageist attitudes that have prevented many LGBT elders from using the supportive services that are available through the LGBT community. This would include conducting in-service training for national and local staff and volunteers at LGBT community sites on the unique needs of LGBT elders.

All of us must become more proactive in eradicating ageism, especially because all of us have the potential to be targets of ageism. According to Greene (2002, p. 162), "unlike ethnicity, the aged represent a stigmatized group with permeable group boundaries; a group to which, if we live long enough, we will all eventually belong. Unlike people with disabilities, a group to which potentially any of us *could* belong, or specific ethnic group to which we cannot belong unless we are born into them, all human beings go from not belonging to this group to belonging to it." Therefore all of us must become more politically involved in supporting legislation that would benefit not only LGBT elders but elders in general.

The aging of the American population will result in a greater need and demand for services and programs. Therefore, collaborative endeavors between the aging network and the LGBT community are needed to develop appropriate, adequate, and affirming services for LGBT elders. Together these two entities can address the interplay of ageism and heterosexism that has historically prevented the provision of needed services for LGBT elders. All of these efforts will enable LGBT elders to age with dignity instead of discrimination.

## REFERENCES

Adelman, M. (1991). Stigma, gay lifestyles, and adjustment to aging: A study of later-life gay men and lesbians. *Journal of Homosexuality, 2*(3–4), 7–32.

Barranti, C. (1998). Social work practice with lesbian couples. In G. Mallon (Ed.), *Foundations of social work practice with lesbian and gay persons* (pp. 183–207). New York: Harrington Park Press.

Barranti, C., & Cohen, H. (2000). Lesbian and gay elders: An invisible minority. In R. Schneider, N. Kropt, & A. Kisor (Eds.), *Gerontological social work: Knowledge, service settings and special populations* (2nd ed., pp. 343–367). Belmont, CA: Wadsworth.

Berger, R. (1980). Psychological adaptation of the older homosexual male. *Journal of Homosexuality, 5*(3), 161–175.

Berger, R., & Kelly, J. (1996). Gay men and lesbians grown old. In R. Cabaj & T. Stein (Eds.), *Textbook of homosexuality and mental health* (pp. 305–316). Washington, DC: American Psychiatric Press.

Bradford, J., Ryan, C., & Rothblum, E. (1994). National lesbian health care survey: Implications for mental health care. *Journal of Consulting and Clinical Psychology, 62*, 228–242.

Cook-Daniels, L. (1997). Lesbian, gay male, bisexual, and transgendered elders: Elder abuse and neglect issues. *Journal of Elder Abuse and Neglect, 9*, 35–49.

Coons, D. (2003). *Lesbian, gay, bisexual, and transgender (LGBT) issues and family caregiving.* San Francisco: Family Caregiver Alliance.

D'Augelli, A. (1994). Lesbian and gay male development: Steps toward an analysis of lesbians' and gay men's lives. In B. Greene & G. Herek (Eds.), *Lesbian and gay psychology: Theory, research, and clinical applications* (pp. 118–131). Thousand Oaks, CA: SAGE.

Ferrini, A., & Ferrini, R. (2000). *Health in the later years* (3rd ed.). New York: McGraw-Hill.

Friend, R. (1980). Gaying: Adjustment and the older gay male. *Alternative Lifestyle, 3*, 231–248.

Friend, R. (1990). Older lesbian and gay people: A theory of successful aging. *Journal of Homosexuality, 20*(3–4), 99–118.

Garnets, L., Hancock, K., Cochran, S., Goodchilds, J., & Peplau, L. (1991). Issues in psychotherapy with lesbians and gay men: A survey of psychologists. *American Psychologist, 46*, 964–972.

Gray Pride Interagency Taskforce on Gay and Lesbian Aging. (2003). *Gray and gay: Our community responds—Issues and action strategies.* Proceedings from the Greater Cleveland Dialogue Series. Cleveland, OH: Author.

Greene, B. (2002). Older lesbians' concerns and psychotherapy: Beyond a footnote to the footnote. In F. K. Trotman & C. Brody (Eds.), *Psychotherapy and counseling with older women: Cross-cultural, family, and end-of-life issues* (pp. 161–174). New York: Springer.

Grossman, A., D'Augelli, A., & Hershberger, S. (2000). Social support networks of lesbian, gay, and bisexual adults 60 years of age and older. *Journal of Gerontology, 55B*, P171–P179.

Grossman, A., Hershberger, S., & O'Connell, T. (2001). Aspects of mental health among older lesbian, gay, and bisexual adults. *Aging & Mental Health, 5*(2), 149–158.

Hamburger, L. (1997). The wisdom of non-heterosexuality based senior housing and related services. *Journal of Gay and Lesbian Social Services, 6*(1), 11–25.

Herdt, G., Beeler, J., & Rawls, T. (1997). Life course diversity among older lesbians and gay men: A study in Chicago. *Journal of Gay, Lesbian, and Bisexual Identity, 2*, 199–230.

Humphreys, N., & Quam, J. (1998). Middle-aged and old gay, lesbian, and bisexual adults. In G. Appleby & J. W. Anastas (Eds.), *Not just a passing phase: Social work with gay, lesbian, and bisexual people* (pp. 245–267). New York: Columbia University Press.

Kimmel, D. (1978). Adult development and aging: A gay perspective. *Journal of Social Issues, 34*(3), 113–120.

Kimmel, D. (1995). Lesbians and gay men also grow old. In L. Bond, S. Cutler, & A. Greene (Eds.), *Promoting successful and productive aging* (pp. 289–303). Thousand Oaks, CA: Sage.

Kochman, A. (1997). Gay and lesbian elderly: Historical overview and implications for social work practice. *Journal of Gay and Lesbian Social Services, 6*(1), 1–10.

Lee, J. (1987). What can homosexual aging studies contribute to theories of aging? *Journal of Homosexuality, 13*(4), 43–71.

Metz, P. (1997). Staff development for working with lesbian and gay elders. *Journal of Gay and Lesbian Social Services, 6*(1), 35–44.

Mohr, J., & Fassinger, R. (2000). The outness inventory. *Measurement and Evaluation in Counseling and Development, 33*, 66–90.

Morgan, L., & Kunkel, S. (1998). *Aging: The social context.* Thousand Oaks, CA: Pine Forge.

Morrow, D. (2001). Older gays and lesbians: Surviving a generation of hate and violence. *Journal of Gay & Lesbian Social Services, 13*(1–2), 151–169.

National Gay and Lesbian Task Force Policy Institute. (1999). *Aging initiative.* Washington, DC: Author.

Nystrom, N., & Jones, T. (2003). Community building with aging and old lesbians. *American Journal of Community Psychology, 31*, 293–300.

Orel, N. (2004). Gay, lesbian, and bisexual elders: Expressed needs and concerns across focus groups. *Journal of Gerontological Social Work, 43*(2–3), 57–77.

Patterson, C. J. (2000). Family relationships of lesbians and gay men. *Journal of Marriage and the Family, 62*, 1052–1069.

Phillips, J., & Fischer, A. (1998). Graduate students' training experiences with lesbian, gay, and bisexual issues. *Counseling Psychologist, 26*, 712–734.

Quam, J., & Whitford, G. (1992). Adaptation and age-related expectations of older gay and lesbian adults. *The Gerontologist, 32*, 367–374.

Reid, J. D. (1995). Development in late life: Older lesbian and gay lives. In A. R. D'Augelli & C. J. Patterson (Eds.), *Lesbian, gays, and bisexual identities over the lifespan: Psychological perspectives* (pp. 215–240). New York: Oxford University Press.

Ritter, K., & Terndrup, A. (2002). *Handbook of affirmative psychotherapy with lesbians and gay men.* New York: Guilford.

Rosenfeld, D. (1999). Identity work among lesbian and gay elderly. *Journal of Aging Studies, 13*, 121–143.

Sharp, C. E. (1997). Lesbianism and later life in an Australian sample: How does development of one affect anticipation of the other? *Journal of Gay, Lesbian, and Bisexual Identity, 2*, 251–262.

Slusher, M., Mayer, C., & Dunkle, R. (1996). Gays and lesbians older and wiser: A support group for older gay people. *The Gerontologist, 36,* 118–123.

U.S. Census Bureau. (2000). *Statistical abstract of the United States.* Washington, DC: Government Printing Office.

van Wormer, K., Wells, J., & Boes, M. (2000). *Social work with lesbians, gay, and bisexuals: A strengths perspective.* Needham Heights, MA: Allyn & Bacon.

Wahler, J., & Gabby, S. (1997). Gay male aging: A review of the literature. *Journal of Gay & Lesbian Social Services, 6*(3), 1–20.

# 14

# openhouse

## Community Building and Research in the LGBT Aging Population

*Marcy Adelman, Jeanette Gurevitch, Brian de Vries, and John A. Blando*

―――――――――――――――⟨≈≈≈⟩―――――――――――――――

C ahill, South, and Spade (2000) estimate that the current LGBT elderly population in the United States is perhaps as large as 3 million people. Locally, the San Francisco Commission on Aging estimates that based on 1990 U.S. Census figures, the LGBT population 55 years and older in San Francisco may make up 10–20% of the total senior population (17,000 to 34,000 people). An oft-repeated phrase is equally applicable to both of these estimates: These numbers are sure to increase with the aging of the baby boomers and related demographic features. These features and this population demand our attention.

This chapter has three goals. The first goal is to introduce the reader to *openhouse*, an innovative grassroots effort to create and support housing for older LGBT people in San Francisco. A second goal is to report on the results of research that we have conducted to identify the needs and characterize the personal and social living environments of these people in support of this housing effort. The third goal, somewhat embedded in the first two, is to share some of the lessons learned in the process of developing and creating housing for older gay men and lesbians. Ultimately, this chapter sheds light on the role of research in the development and support of both community and community projects.

## The Need for LGBT Housing

The legacy of discrimination and harassment endured by many of the older members of today's LGBT community cannot be overstated. Perhaps nowhere is this legacy more pronounced than in health care settings, where institutionalized heterosexism (Cahill, 2002) and related negative experiences—which may have included involuntary medical interventions (Brotman, Ryan, & Cormier,

2003)—have led to feelings of shame and guilt (Kaufman & Raphael, 1996) and reasonable apprehension and suspicion on the part of the elders as they access care. Thus, older lesbians and gay men often are less likely than their heterosexual peers to seek out health care services (Harrison & Silenzio, 1996). When gay and lesbian support and services are available (which is rare), research suggests that such resources are used more often than generic senior services (Quam & Whitford, 1992) and are evaluated more positively (Jacobs, Rasmussen, & Hohman, 1999).

Housing is clearly a prominent issue in this regard, particularly in the context of supportive services. Building senior housing with services is a welcome and increasingly common development in many communities. But for LGBT people, this kind of project is extraordinary and unprecedented. Older gay men and lesbians who have struggled to come out and live openly in a hostile environment "often find themselves having to back into hiding when they begin to require health care services" (Brotman, Ryan, & Cormier, 2003, p. 193).

Efforts to address the need for supportive housing recently have assumed a couple of forms. First, several efforts are under way to develop senior gay and lesbian housing; most of these units are reported to be accessible to those of higher income levels (Cahill, 2002). Second, Cahill proposes that the housing needs of low- and moderate-income LGBT older adults may be served through efforts to render existing housing gay-friendly and the passing of federal nondiscrimination laws. Recent developments in San Francisco are directed at integrating these two forms; a description of these efforts follows.

## *openhouse:* An Overview and History

San Francisco has long been associated with gay and lesbian issues. Not surprisingly, efforts to develop housing for older members of the LGBT community began as early as the 1970s and 1980s. The AIDS crisis, hitting San Francisco early and particularly hard, arrested these efforts as the community dealt with significant loss of life and struggled to develop supportive services and demand the resources that were needed. An earnest revisiting of these efforts took place in the late 1990s, leading to what is now known as *openhouse,* a San Francisco–based nonprofit organization dedicated to creating and sustaining senior housing and services that welcomes all seniors and that honors lesbian, gay, bisexual, and transgender (LGBT) people. After Rainbow Adult Community Housing (RACH) was founded in 1998, several years of careful study (some of the results of which are presented below) and community and neighborhood discussions were undertaken, culminating in preparations to build a neighborhood complex or village of 225 apartments. The goal is to build a multicultural, active urban retirement community in San Francisco that provides housing for LGBT seniors and offers a menu of care for residents across all income levels.

Moreover, the *openhouse* retirement village will be a service hub that offers a wide range of LGBT-sensitive services, programs, and events to both residents and nonresidents. A menu of services will be provided by experienced organizations in collaboration with existing programs to more than 300 residents and 2,100 community members. This development of a strong, inclusive, multicultural community allowing LGBT seniors to age in place and have access to services consistent with their changing needs will act as a model for other projects. *openhouse* is intent on building a new community institution fostering an intergenerational community that honors aging as well as youth. Further, *openhouse* will serve, and has already served, as the source to which existing programs turn for expert consultation and gay sensitivity training referrals. In this manner, *openhouse* is the synthesis of the two approaches to housing LGBT elders, as described earlier.

*openhouse* is in a unique position to make this project possible. San Francisco's LGBT community has strong political representation, and there are many people in the city and state governments who support and can facilitate access to public resources. The time is right to build on the strength created by a network of LGBT health, service, cultural, and political organizations to build institutions that further develop the LGBT community. *openhouse* will take a place at the civic table to advocate for LGBT senior housing needs and to sponsor senior housing and services.

*openhouse* was formed on the basis of several rational assumptions. Congruent with the results reported by Quam and Whitford (1992), *openhouse* assumed that LGBT seniors would choose LGBT-focused housing for safety and protection from discrimination and would seek access to LGBT-sensitive and affirming services. Comparable assumptions were made about community support of this effort. Specifically, it was proposed that the broader LGBT community would support development of this project, seeing it as community building, and that the San Francisco community would support this project through funding technical assistance from the city, foundations, and corporations. *openhouse* also assumed that LGBT seniors would choose to remain in San Francisco; after all, as Murray (1996, pp. 223–224) wrote, San Francisco is seen as a place "in which being gay is celebrated, accepted, or at least tolerated as 'no big deal'—whatever was enough to be 'better than where I am now.'" Finally, it was assumed that LGBT seniors would qualify for housing assistance from the city and federal governments.

A number of organizations and funders were approached, both LGBT and mainstream, to assess their support for the project. In these discussions, serious issues were raised, and these issues assumed several forms. For example, some issues were San Francisco–specific, including doubts about the financial feasibility of building a community housing development in an inflated housing market with little available land. Some of the issues were concerns about the feasibility of a single dwelling housing people representing a very diverse array of communities in terms of sexual orientation, gender, socioeconomic status, and race and ethnicity. Typically senior housing is either homogeneous faith-based or supported and constructed by affinity groups and is geared either to higher- or lower-income seniors. In addition, some of the issues were more about aging in general, including comments that the gay male community's ageism ultimately would present obstacles to fundraising and inhibit the overall success of the project.

In response to many of these concerns, *openhouse* investigated the possibility that a nonprofit developer would build mixed-income senior housing with services meeting the special needs of the LGBT community. Most developers expressed support for the project's goals but had their own missions that directed them to build in their own neighborhoods, for their own constituents, and only for the lowest-income groups. It was ultimately decided that only as a nonprofit organization could *openhouse* have access to public and private resources for planning and construction, share ownership, and ensure that this project continue into the future as LGBT-friendly.

Initially, San Francisco city government personnel raised serious challenges to the idea of housing targeted to LGBT seniors. Even in San Francisco, the prevailing assumption was that LGBT people were primarily middle class and wealthy homeowners and would not need or qualify for city assistance. When confronted with questions about housing resources for lower-income LGBT seniors the city asserted that LGBT seniors already live in senior housing developments, both market rate and subsidized by the city, and that there were no problems and no need for targeted housing or special services. The city also raised one of the most serious challenges, the Fair Housing laws. They questioned whether it would be possible to build a development exclusively for LGBT seniors.

*openhouse* devoted considerable energy to dealing with these concerns and has managed to resolve crucial issues through investigation, outreach, and negotiation. One of the first and most critical components of this was the realization that the LGBT community, the city, and *openhouse* all needed data on which to proceed. At this point, *openhouse* was able to persuade LGBT funders, particularly Horizons Foundation, that only an LGBT organization could sponsor this project and that the need for data to provide a profile of LGBT seniors and their social and housing needs was urgent. The results of this survey are presented here.

## The Older Lesbian and Gay San Francisco Community

The *openhouse* survey was designed and administered to gather demographic, psychosocial, and retirement housing information from LGBT people of all ages. The questions were derived on the basis of clinical experience, exploratory interviews, a review of the gerontological research, and a review of previous studies conducted in New York and San Francisco. The resultant survey was pilot tested with a group of 135 seniors from local gay and lesbian senior organizations. Results from this pilot test, including comments from respondents, were analyzed and used to shape the second and final version of the survey. The final survey included demographic questions (e.g., age, present and estimated retirement income, education, employment status, and occupation), health questions (e.g., perceived health, chronic health conditions, and disabilities), social network and social support questions (including to whom a person might turn in times of need), identity-based questions (including degree of disclosure), questions about living arrangements (including current and expected accommodation needs and size), and personal preference questions for neighborhood, social and recreational, and community factors.

The final survey was administered to 1,301 LGBT adults ranging in ages from 18 to 92. Respondents were recruited from large, racially and ethnically diverse public venues including the Gay, Lesbian, Bisexual, and Transgender Pride Festival and Parade (attracting more than 500,000 people annually), the Folsom Street Fair (attracting more than 100,000 people), and the Castro Street Fair (attracting more than 35,000 people). Additionally, respondents were recruited from other local organizations (e.g., churches, synagogues) in which presentations were made by members of *openhouse*. All of these groups were social or fraternal organizations. Finally, as the goals and efforts of *openhouse* became more publicly known, respondents contacted the organization, offering to participate. Responses to the questionnaire itself and to the goals of *openhouse* were uniformly positive. Respondents completed the surveys sincerely, adding comments to the structured questions to ensure clarity and to amplify points.

The overall pattern of results of the survey presents an image of resilience and strength paired with financial, health, and support vulnerability.

Notwithstanding concerted recruitment efforts, across the entire sample transgender adults numbered only 16; there were no transgender adults among those over the age of 60. Furthermore, there were 63 bisexual adults in the sample, only 10 of whom were over the age of 60. These numbers preclude meaningful inclusion in statistical age and gender-based comparisons, so transgender and bisexual adults were not included in the analyses in this chapter. In the total sample and among those in the age group 50 to 59, approximately 54% were male and 46% female; in the group of those over the age of 60, 64% were male and 36% were female. More than half of the total sample (almost 55%, or 709 participants) was at least 50 years old. Contrasts and comparisons are offered when related (local or national) demographic information was available. Comparing across data sets precluded statistical analyses, although such analyses are presented in the *openhouse* data set.

More than one-quarter of the sample identified as people of color: 5.8% of the sample identified as African American, and 5.8% identified as Latino. Just over 3% of the sample identified as Asian, and 1% identified as Indian. Interestingly, 8.3% of the sample identified as biracial or endorsed multiple racial categories.

The 2000 Census reported that 62% of people living in San Francisco County identified as Caucasian. Although the sample on which these analyses are based differs somewhat from the census data, the *openhouse* sample contains a higher percentage of people of color than is typically seen in community surveys. The *openhouse* sample is believed to be the largest and most inclusive sample of gay men and lesbians over the age of 50. Sample sizes of homosexual men and women of this magnitude are extremely rare, and this is even more the case for samples of gay men and lesbians in the second half of life. The richness of these data should not be understated. This broad representation stands as testimony to *openhouse*'s commitment to inclusion.

Nonetheless, as with almost every survey of the LGBT population, the representativeness of these respondents merits comment; after all, this sample comprises participants of large, public LGBT events and groups in San Francisco. The combination of these factors may distinguish these people from others elsewhere in the country or even from others who participate in such public events and venues in San Francisco. Add to this the effect of those who are reticent about their homosexuality or who may not yet identify as homosexual (keeping aside variations in the use of the many terms often applied to homosexuals), and the challenge of surveying this population becomes clear.

For example, in addition to the diversity introduced by gender and race is the diversity inherent in age and cohort in particular. Age and cohort differences were manifested in the terms or descriptors people used to characterize themselves (figs. 14.1 and 14.2). Respondents were asked to identify the terms they used in self-description from among the following (in alphabetical order): *bisexual, dyke, gay, heterosexual, homosexual, lesbian,* or *queer*. Although 13 terms (e.g., *gay* or *homosexual*) or combinations of terms (e.g., both *gay* and *homosexual*) were used by the 730 men of the survey, 3 were the most common, as presented in figure 14.1. Within these three are age differences ($\chi^2(4, N = 502) = 10.78, p < .05$), with older men favoring the term *homosexual* more than younger men and younger men favoring *gay* or *queer* more than older men (echoed in the findings of Rawls, 2004). The 540 women of the survey used 15 terms or combinations of terms, and the top 4 are presented in figure 14.2. Age differences were again noted ($\chi^2(6, N = 342) = 12.87, p < .05$), particularly around the use of the term *gay,* favored much more highly by older women than by younger women.[1]

A general question addressing how out respondents were also was included on the survey. Interestingly, there were no overall age and gender differences. Specifically, on a 5-point scale ranging from a value of 1 (not at all) to 5 (completely), respondents were asked to indicate how out they were as LGBT people. The mean

FIGURE 14.1

## Self-Identification: Men by Age Group

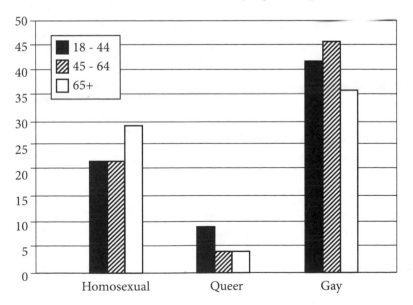

FIGURE 14.2

Self-Identification: Women by Age Group

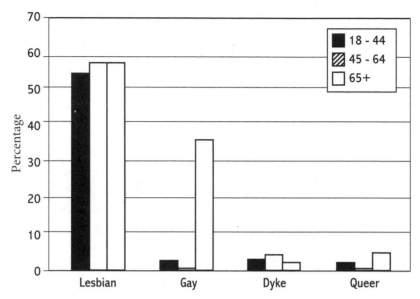

value on this scale was 4.25. Significant racial differences were noted, however, $F(7, 1{,}197) = 5.02$, $p < .001$. Caucasians rated themselves as more out (4.3) than did Latinos, African Americans, and Asians, with Asian participants rating themselves as least out (3.4). Like the terms people use in self-identification, these differences have implications for the extent to which homosexual men and women of varying ages and races will avail themselves of services for the LGBT community. Furthermore, knowing how respondents describe themselves allows organizations to provide appropriately tailored services with dignity and respect.

In related questions, respondents were asked about the kind of retirement housing complex they would prefer to live in, choosing from one of the following options: exclusively LGBT, mixed but mostly LGBT, mixed but mostly heterosexual, or don't know. There were no overall gender differences: 56% of men and just over 60% of women preferred mixed but mostly LGBT. Twenty-six percent of women and 24% of men chose exclusively LGBT. Very few chose mostly heterosexual (less than 5%), although almost 15% of men and 10% of women reported that they did not know. Age differences in such endorsements were few, although among the oldest women, a greater proportion reported that they did not know ($\chi^2(6, N = 501) = 15.86$, $p < .01$).

In this sample, gay men and lesbians were generally well educated and tended to be more highly educated than their heterosexual counterparts (as noted in available census data). (Similar data were reported by Black et al., 2000, in their analyses of data generated from random samples and the U.S. Census.) As shown in figure 14.3, approximately 75% of San Franciscans over the age of 45 had at least a high school education, according to census data; the comparable statistics for gay men and lesbians from the *openhouse* data were more than 95%. Likewise, about one-third of San Franciscans over the age of 45 had a bachelor's degree; the comparable percentage for lesbians and gay men in the area was about 65%. As in other samples, people of color in the sample tended

FIGURE 14.3

Educational Attainment:
San Francisco Census Data and *openhouse* Data by Age Group

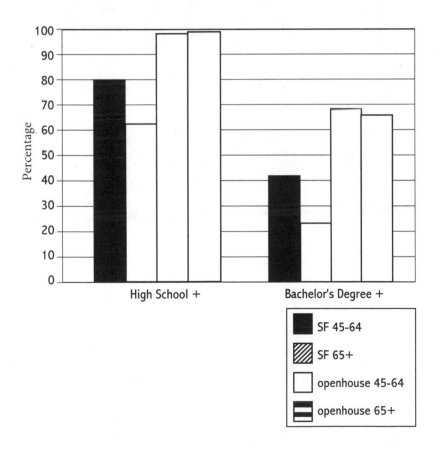

FIGURE 14.4

Percentage of Each Group in Four Income Levels:[a]
San Francisco Census Data and *openhouse* Data by Age Group

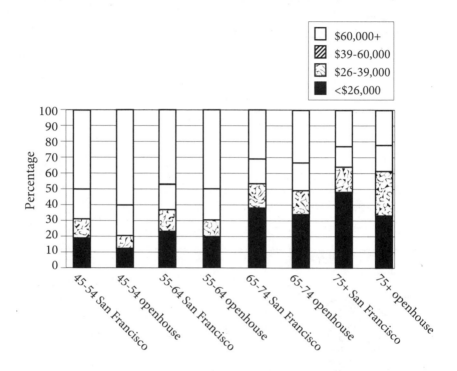

[a] Annual income shown in 4 groups: over $60,000; $39,000–$59,999; $26,000–$38,999; under $26,000.

to be overrepresented among those whose educational backgrounds culminated in secondary school and underrepresented among those with postgraduate degrees ($\chi^2(10, N = 1265) = 40.83, p < .001$).

The well-known link between education and income was not replicated in these data, however. That is, notwithstanding the apparently higher levels of educational attainment of the gay men and lesbians in this sample, income levels did not appear to differ between the general San Francisco population and the *openhouse* sample, as presented in figure 14.4.

Of particular interest from the standpoint of affordable housing, among lesbians and gay men aged 50–59, almost 40% earned less than $39,000 per year, including 20% who earned less than $26,000. Among those aged 60 and older, including over 42% who earned less than $39,000, almost 62% earned less than $26,000. Compared to Caucasians, people of color were more disadvantaged financially, with almost half (49.3%) earning less than $39,000 in contrast to 41% of Caucasians in the same income range, $\chi^2(3, N = 1224) = 8.07$, $p < .05$. The average income of participants in the *openhouse* sample is similar to that of their San Francisco heterosexual peers, rendering comparable the need for affordable housing. These data may at first appear surprising, given the prevalence and hardiness of the myth presenting primarily gay men (and also lesbians) as members of an affluent North American elite. Upon deeper reflection, these data conform neatly to those summarized by Badget (1998, p. 15) in a critical and comprehensive review of methodologically rigorous large-scale surveys, revealing that "lesbian, gay, and bisexual people are spread throughout the range of household income distribution, just as heterosexual people are."

In fact, the financial resources available to older gay men and lesbians may be significantly limited by the vastly greater proportion of those who live alone. According to census data, in San Francisco 3% of men over the age of 65 and just over 8% of women live alone; in the *openhouse* data, just under 24% of gay men and approximately 19% of lesbians reported living alone. In addition, almost three-quarters of gay men and almost half of the lesbians in this age group reported their relationship status as single. (This interesting juxtaposition of statistics—24% of gay men living alone compared with almost three-quarters reporting as single and 19% of lesbians living alone compared with almost half reporting as single—highlights the variability in the experience of couplehood in particular and relationship status more generally among gay men and lesbians; see de Vries and Blando, 2004.) Moreover, 72% of gay men and 43% of lesbians over the age of 65 reported having no children. These latter findings render the gay and lesbian group dramatically different from national statistics. The nonpartnered heterosexual man in later life is statistically rare (Huyck, 2001); and Himes (1992) estimates that approximately 80% of adults over the age of 60 have at least one living child. These differences have significant implications for social support, caregiving, and general health behaviors, as revealed in other chapters in this volume.

The need (current and potential) for care is made apparent in the surprisingly high numbers of respondents across the entire sample who reported a chronic condition or disability: almost 30%. As expected, this proportion increased when the focus was on those 60 years or older: just over 36% of gay men and almost 38% of lesbians, a significant age difference ($\chi^2(3, N = 1233) = 15.03$, $p < .01$). Overall, these percentages far exceed comparable data; for example, a recent report by the Federal Interagency Forum on Aging-Related Statistics (2000) revealed that, in 1994, about 16% of men over the age of 65 and 25% of women of comparable age had a chronic disability.

It is of significant interest, then, to identify to whom these LGBT older adults turn in times of need or crisis. In the absence of conventional family support systems, the primary providers of care to older adults (Stone, Cafferata, & Sangl, 1987), gay men and lesbians have come to place a high value on their friend-ships, what some authors call families of choice (Weston, 1991). These friends have a place of significance as the people to whom respondents would turn in times of crisis. More than 20% of gay men and just under 10% of lesbians would turn exclusively to their friends in times of need, $\chi^2(2, N = 1237) = 13.21$, $p < .001$ (fig. 14.5). An additional 25% of gay men and more than 40% of les-bians include friends in combination with others, $\chi^2(1, N = 1237) = 3.94$, $p < .05$. Partners are mentioned by just over 10% of gay men and 17% of lesbians. Given the smaller number of children reported by gay men and lesbians, they were relied on infrequently, except among Latinos, who reported a modestly

FIGURE 14.5

Persons To Whom Gay Men and Lesbians over Age 65
Turn in Times of Crisis by Gender

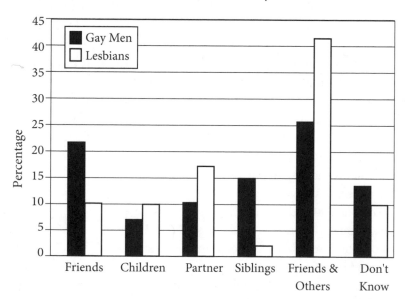

(nonsignificant) greater reliance on children. Siblings, exclusively, are mentioned significantly more often by gay men (14.8%) than by lesbians (2%), $\chi(2, N = 707) = 10.18, p < .01$. Together, these findings identify the constituents of the social networks of these respondents and their potential sources of support and care. An important point to temper these findings, however, is that almost 14% of gay men and just under 10% of lesbians reported that they did not know to whom they would turn in a time of crisis.

Moreover, this pool—these families of choice—from which the person may seek support and care exists largely outside social sanctions and legal support, limiting the work they can actually do. For example, several authors in primarily heterosexual contexts (Johnson, 1983) have noted the somewhat unreliable "fair-weather friend" phenomenon in contrast to the more stable "rainy day" kin. However, other authors (e.g., Barker, 2002), in similar contexts have commented on the success of these nontraditional caregiving relationships while addressing their vulnerabilities and the suspicion with which they are seen. Nontraditional caregivers remain an understudied and poorly understood issue.

The results of the *openhouse* survey, partially presented here, offer a snapshot of the older lesbian and gay population in San Francisco. Although the generalizability of these data may be questioned because they were collected in San Francisco and through public venues, the extent to which they support previously reported patterns revealed in random samples and census data stands them on comfortably solid ground. The older population mirrors the general older San Francisco population in some ways (e.g., income and to a lesser degree race) and dramatically differs in others (e.g., relationship status, parenthood status, disability rates). These differences are particularly important in that, together, they may be seen as increasing the risk of isolation in later life. That is, these older adults with greater proportions of disabilities and fewer traditional social resources on which to call may risk institutionalization or poor health maintenance. The individuals and communities on which they may call would greatly benefit from direction and support.

*openhouse* will offer such direction and support and provide the care and housing these people need. It will become the village in which care and community may be found. The research undertaken by *openhouse* both addresses these needs and offers a rare view of the social and personal worlds of older LGBT adults. This work is ongoing.

## State of the Project

*openhouse* has identified an excellent two-parcel, 2-acre site in San Francisco. One parcel is owned by the Mayor's Office of Real Estate, and the other is owned by the Redevelopment Agency. The parcels will become available for purchase through a Request for Proposal process in 2006. The site is the last available large vacant site near the Castro (the San Francisco neighborhood with the largest concentration of LGBT people). It is well situated between the Castro and the Civic Center (arts and public services) and within blocks of the LGBT Community Center and New Leaf Outreach to Elders (an LGBT community social and geriatric program). The site is in a neighborhood that is senior friendly and welcomes diversity. This site offers an ideal opportunity for the city to address the pressing needs of the LGBT senior community.

But land is at a premium in San Francisco. Although *openhouse* has strong LGBT community and neighborhood support, the success of securing this site is not certain. Consequently, *openhouse* has studied and continues to study many other sites throughout the city.

The preliminary planning effort for our development involved the active participation of members of *openhouse*'s board of directors, the project manager, public and private sector providers of senior services, LGBT community organizations and policymakers, and LGBT senior service consumers and members of community groups. Both this Community Planning Committee and surveys from the city's Department of Adult and Aging Services provided a preliminary inventory of existing local programs that serve LGBT seniors and identified service gaps. The committee identified opportunities for service collaboration and partnership that range from contracting for services to colocating existing programs at the *openhouse* site. A preliminary menu of potential services for the long-term care plan was also identified.

The completion of the *openhouse* survey was necessary to prepare the ground for *openhouse* service planning and to develop the integration of services with the architectural and operational program. *openhouse* survey data, data from interviews with consumer groups, and the work of the Community Planning Committee are now being used by the *openhouse* Service Planning Committee to finalize the service plan.

The completed service plan will inform the financial model that is to be developed by a company that specializes in financial consulting in the health care and senior living industry. The financial modeling program will assess the project's financial viability and assess the financial implications of various program diversification options. Completion of the financial model is timed to coincide with the results of a market study in the autumn of 2005. The results of these predevelopment studies will then be presented to the community for input and comment.

When the financial modeling, service planning, and community input are finalized, *openhouse* will be in a position to identify and select a lead service operator. When site control is achieved, *openhouse* will be able to develop an architectural concept that supports the service model and site constraints.

## Other LGBT Senior Housing Projects

*openhouse*'s unique vision is distinguished from those of other planned or completed LGBT senior housing projects in a variety of ways. There will be a mixture of incomes (low, moderate, and market rate) and a mixture of uses (housing, services, and retail businesses as well as a performing arts theater, wellness center, and restaurant) open to both residents and the public. The menu of planned LGBT-sensitive services will serve more than 300 residents and will be available to approximately 2,000 community members who choose to remain in their own homes. *openhouse*'s village is envisioned as an inclusive and vital community that fosters positive aging and integrates the LGBT senior community into the long-term care system in the city of San Francisco.

Other nonprofit projects are known to be planned in three cities: Hollywood, California; Boston, Massachusetts; and Portland, Oregon. In Hollywood, the project is a joint effort of the Gay and Lesbian Elder Housing Corporation, the City of Los Angeles, and a St. Louis–based developer that plans to build a 103-unit complex for a mixture of low- and very-low-income LGBT seniors (including homeless men and women and those at risk for being homeless) and seniors living with HIV and AIDS; it was expected to open in 2005. In Boston, Stonewall Communities has plans to build a hundred-unit residential community for middle- and upper-income lesbian and gay elders. Their plans call for a range of lesbian- and gay-sensitive health services and amenities. In Portland, Senior Housing and Retirement Enterprises (SHARE), another community-based nonprofit, is considering senior housing for primarily moderate-income LGBT seniors, with the possibility of some Section 8 housing. SHARE plans to complete their LGBT senior housing in 2008.

The for-profit resort market has also begun to take shape across the country. The Rainbow Vision Project in Santa Fe, New Mexico, opened a market rate project in 2005. They have a 12.7-acre site just south of Santa Fe on which they plan to build 146 units, mostly independent living with some assisted living apartments. Birds of a Feather Resort Communities in Pecos, New Mexico is lesbian only, and Paradise City Village in Northampton, Massachusetts is developing condominiums for lesbians and gay men in midlife and older. Both projects are designed as upper-income independent living resorts that are still in the development stage, with no opening date as of yet.

Existing lesbian and gay retirement or resort communities, all developed by for-profit companies for middle- and upper-income seniors, are the Palms of Manasota in Palmetto, Florida; the Resort on Carefree Boulevard in Fort Myers, Florida; the Pueblo in Apache Junction, Arizona; and Calamus Communities in Phoenix, Arizona. All of these communities are market rate and provide few or no basic health services.

The *openhouse* survey revealed that LGBT seniors, regardless of income, are more likely to be childless, single, and living alone than their heterosexual peers and with a significantly higher incidence of chronic illness or disability. We know that children and partners often act as primary caregivers and that living with a caretaker often is a major factor in accessing health care. Clearly the entire LGBT senior community, regardless of income, needs community support and assistance to ensure quality of life. *openhouse* is attempting to respond to the need for LGBT-sensitive resources and services for the entire community. However, the final plans for *openhouse*'s project will be determined by predevelopment studies, the acquisition of a suitable site, and the will of the city of San Francisco and the LGBT community to support *openhouse*'s project.


# Conclusion

*openhouse* is poised to make a difference in San Francisco and to offer a model to other communities around the county. This has been and remains a lengthy process requiring the coordination and commitment of health, service, cultural, and political organizations and, most importantly, the LGBT community. The great need and the high stakes sustain these individuals and groups through this effort. The importance of solid research to support these goals and to help dispel myths cannot be overstated.

## NOTE

1. In light of these data, the men and women of the sample are hereinafter referred to as gay men and lesbians, respectively.

## REFERENCES

Badget, M. V. L. (1998). *Income inflation: The myth of affluence among gay, lesbian, and bisexual Americans.* Washington, DC: The Policy Institute of the National Gay and Lesbian Task Force and the Institute for Gay and Lesbian Strategic Studies. Retrieved February 6, 2004, from www.ngltf.org/downloads/income.pdf.

Barker, J. (2002). Neighbors, friends, and other non-kin caregivers of community-living dependent elders. *Journals of Gerontology: Psychological Sciences and Social Sciences, 57,* S158–S167.

Black, D., Gates, G., Sanders, S., & Taylor, L. (2000). Demographics of the gay and lesbian population in the United States: Evidence from available systematic data sources. *Demography, 37,* 139–154.

Brotman, S., Ryan, B., & Cormier, R. (2003). The health and social service needs of gay and lesbian elders and their families in Canada. *The Gerontologist, 43,* 192–202.

Cahill, S. (2002). Long term care issues affecting gay, lesbian, bisexual and transgender elders. *Geriatric Care Management Journal, 12,* 4–8.

Cahill, S., South, K., & Spade, J. (2000). *Outing age: Public policy issues affecting gay, lesbian, bisexual, and transgender elders.* Washington, DC: National Gay and Lesbian Task Force Policy Institute.

de Vries, B., & Blando, J. A. (2004). The study of gay and lesbian aging: Lessons for social gerontology. In G. Herdt & B. de Vries (Eds.), *Gay and lesbian aging: Research and future directions* (pp. 3–28). New York: Springer.

Federal Interagency Forum on Aging-Related Statistics. (2000). *Older Americans 2000: Key indicators of well-being.* Washington, DC: U.S. Government Printing Office.

Harrison, A. E., & Silenzio, V. M. (1996). Comprehensive care of lesbian and gay patients and families. *Primary Care: Models of Ambulatory Care, 23,* 31–46.

Himes, C. L. (1992). Future caregivers: Projected family structures of older persons. *Journals of Gerontology: Social Sciences, 47,* S17–S26.

Huyck, M. H. (2001). Romantic relationships in later life. *Generations, 25*(2), 9–17.

Jacobs, R., Rasmussen, L., & Hohman, M. (1999). The social support needs of older lesbians, gay men, and bisexuals. *Journal of Gay and Lesbian Social Services, 9*(1), 1–30.

Johnson, C. L. (1983). Fairweather friends and rainy day kin: An anthropological analysis of old age friendships in the United States. *Urban Anthropology, 12,* 103–123.

Kaufman, G., & Raphael, L. (1996). *Coming out of shame: Transforming gay and lesbian lives.* New York: Doubleday.

Murray, S. (1996). *American gay*. Chicago: University of Chicago Press.

Quam, J. K., & Whitford, G. S. (1992). Adaptation and age-related expectations of older gay and lesbian adults. *The Gerontologist, 32,* 367–374.

Rawls, T. (2004). Disclosure and depression among older gay and homosexual men: Findings from the Urban Men's Health Study. In G. Herdt & B. de Vries (Eds.), *Gay and lesbian aging: Research and future directions* (pp. 117–142). New York: Springer.

Stone, R., Cafferata, G. L., & Sangl, J. (1987). Caregivers of the frail elderly: A national profile. *The Gerontologist, 27,* 616–626.

Weston, K. (1991). *Families we choose: Lesbians, gays, kinship*. New York: Columbia University Press.

# 15

# SAGE

## New York City's Pioneer Organization for LGBT Elders

### Elizabeth Kling and Douglas Kimmel

———————————— ⟨⟩ ————————————

*E*very year, New York City's Gay Pride Parade features a unique float that draws widespread attention: a motorized trolley transporting a troupe of elderly yet vibrant men and women. Members of SAGE (Services and Advocacy for GLBT Elders, changed from Senior Action in a Gay Environment in 2004), they wave enthusiastically from the vehicle, bearing celebratory banners and happily proclaiming their identities. The seniors invariably get loud cheers and applause as they chant to the group of onlookers, "Two, four, six, eight, how do you know your grandma's straight?" Marching alongside the bus is an intergenerational group of SAGE members.

On the other 364 days of the year, however, New York City's lesbian, gay, bisexual, and transgender (LGBT) seniors are much less visible, not to mention less appreciated. LGBT seniors face the dual challenges of homophobia in the mainstream elderly community and ageism in LGBT communities, which can be particularly virulent because LGBT culture tends to idolize youth even more than does mainstream society (Cahill, South, & Spade, 2000; Ehrenberg 1996). As a result, LGBT communities often ignore their elders, who may suffer an extreme form of isolation at a time when the physical problems that often accompany aging make it difficult to be active and involved (Brotman, Ryan, & Cormier, 2003).

LGBT seniors are among the most underserved and at-risk senior populations, in New York City and across the nation, especially in places that lack a visible LGBT community. Organizations such as SAGE—and other services for LGBT senior populations—are crucial. SAGE offers LGBT seniors in New York City's five boroughs access to much-needed clinical services and social activities in an LGBT-centered environment. Its innovative and effective programming has been reproduced in LGBT senior organizations across the country. In addition, its mounting public education and advocacy work is raising aware-ness about LGBT aging on a national level, helping to define and to meet the diverse and pressing needs of this growing population.

## SAGE: Striving to Meet the Needs of LGBT Seniors

### Clinical Services

A study conducted by the U.S. Department of Health and Human Services Ad-ministration on Aging (2001) found that LGBT seniors are only 20% as likely as heterosexual elders to access needed services such as senior centers, housing assistance, meal programs, food stamps, and other entitlements. This lack of access stems at least in part from a fear of mainstream institutions that derives from a legacy of harsh discrimination that branded LGBT persons in earlier de-cades as criminals, sinners, and physically or mentally ill. Making this situation even more serious, LGBT seniors tend to have a greater need for clinical and social services than their heterosexual counterparts because a larger number of LGBT elders have no children or partners to offer them daily assistance (Cahill, South, & Spade, 2000).

SAGE strives to bridge this gap by offering clinical services targeted to LGBT elders over age 60 (and to clients with HIV and AIDS over age 50) in New York City. SAGE has provided a variety of services since 1978, including friendly vis-iting to homebound elders. Professional social workers are available for crisis intervention and ongoing assistance in accessing medical and legal services, home care, and government benefits. Offering LGBT-friendly and supportive assistance, SAGE social workers ensure that a greater number of LGBT elders gain access to much-needed benefits for which many might otherwise resist ap-plying for fear of revealing personal information to government entities.

In addition, SAGE provides individual, homebound, family, and group coun-seling. Weekly and monthly groups offer help and support for the unique needs of LGBT elders, including coming out later in life and bereavement for same-sex partners. Support groups for Alzheimer's caregivers, veterans, and people with Parkinson's disease, among others, are conducted in an LGBT-centric environ-ment and address the particular challenges faced by LGBT elders.

In 1989, SAGE developed its AIDS and the Elderly Program, the first of its kind in the nation and a critical service for an expanding segment of the HIV and AIDS community: those 50 and over. Now called SAGE Positive, the program currently serves clients ranging in age from 50 to 80. Offering case management, mental health services, benefits counseling, friendly visitors, and support groups, SAGE Positive helps HIV-positive elders deal with the extreme isolation of living with HIV and growing old in the LGBT community, the conflicts between medications for AIDS and those prescribed to treat ailments common in old age, and the physical and emotional changes that often accompany aging.

Through collaboration between staff members and volunteers, SAGE offers other forms of basic assistance to LGBT elders. In 1999 SAGE created the Lend-a-Hand Program, which provides a corps of volunteers to give seniors various kinds of ad hoc assistance, including running errands or accompanying them to appointments or SAGE events. Since SAGE's founding, the organization has had a vibrant friendly visiting program supervised by SAGE staff and operated by volunteers who provide companionship to homebound elders. Volunteers are carefully screened and matched with homebound SAGE clients (called "friends-at-home"), whom they visit weekly. SAGE staff provides support to these volunteers in the form of ongoing training, regular meetings, periodic workshops, and community dinners where friendly visitors can share their experiences and work together to solve problems. Some friendly visitors have developed rich, meaningful relationships with their friends-at-home that have lasted for years.

## Social and Recreational Activities

With the goal of enriching the aging experience of LGBT elders, SAGE works to provide this community with high-quality, life-affirming social, cultural, intellectual, and recreational programming. This effort has been crucial to the organization since its founding in 1977. In that year, SAGE's first social—a gathering of people to share food, conversation, and dancing—was held as a potluck dinner at St. Luke's Church in Manhattan. This event grew and developed, becoming a monthly staple and drawing increasing numbers of attendees and members to SAGE. The socials, which continue to be held monthly today, attest to the need for LGBT elders to break out of their isolation and spend time with others who share their experiences of being old and LGBT.

In 1984, SAGE started offering another opportunity for LGBT elders to enjoy socializing and create community when it opened the nation's first lesbian and gay senior drop-in center at the Lesbian, Gay, Bisexual, and Transgender Community Services Center in New York. Like any mainstream senior drop-in center, SAGE's center provides an informal meeting place where attendees enjoy coffee, conversation, laughter, cards, and board games. Volunteer hosts prepare refreshments, welcome new members, and interact with the crowd, which can include up to 85 people.

In addition to hosting a drop-in center and monthly socials, SAGE currently offers more than 100 activities a month to address the cultural, intellectual, and social concerns of LGBT elders as well as legal, health, financial, political, and spiritual matters. Activities and programs include classes in various subject areas such as creative writing and painting; discussion groups on a wide range of topics, including age-specific rap groups; opera and classical music appreciation programming; dances and workshops targeted specifically to older lesbians; a theater desk that offers low-priced tickets; a legal clinic; brunches, dances, and day trips; and periodic seminars and workshops on subjects of interest. This programming gives LGBT seniors the chance to meet one another, build new friendships, explore new and old interests together, and discuss their thoughts and feelings on various topics in an LGBT-centric environment.

## Vibrancy in Old Age:
## A Different Kind of Social Service Agency

Rather than simply providing clinical services and offering programming to a diverse group of LGBT elders, SAGE is actively collaborating with its members and volunteers to create an agency—and an aging experience—that incorporates the ideas, talents, and contributions of LGBT elders. Since its early years, SAGE has benefited from the significant contributions of volunteers in nearly every arena of its work, including friendly visiting; facilitating workshops, classes, and discussion groups; serving as office assistants and receptionists; hosting socials and brunches; writing, editing, and photographing for SAGE's newsletter; and speaking at senior centers, schools, and nursing homes about LGBT aging concerns. In all areas, elders are involved in developing (and sometimes in providing) programs and services for themselves and for their communities.

SAGE Neighbors is an excellent example of programming created and implemented by LGBT elders. Instigated by a SAGE member, SAGE Neighbors provides a support team of volunteers available to offer assistance, in times of illness or injury, to one another and to other SAGE members in the same Upper West Side neighborhood of Manhattan. Members of this support team alternate between serving as providers and acting as clients, depending on their abilities and needs at any given time. This is a departure from the traditional relationship between client-in-need and professional service provider, which places power and authority largely in the hands of the "professional," often at the expense of participation and empowerment of the "client." With SAGE Neighbors, the "client" plays a more active role, making contributions and shaping the development of the programming.

SAGE Neighbors has a social, recreational, and cultural component, also created and run by volunteers. The group plans its own programming and meets for monthly gatherings, potluck dinners, talent nights, and facilitated discussions. Out of this social group, shared interest groups have developed informally, and several meet regularly. SAGE Neighbors also publishes its own monthly newsletter to keep members abreast of activities.

Central to SAGE's work is the push to use creative means to enrich the aging experience for LGBT elders. One of SAGE's recent initiatives is a curriculum, developed in collaboration with volunteers, that incorporates the concept of conscious creative aging, an approach that encourages self-reflection, awareness, and examination of the culture and society, with the purpose of creating a more meaningful aging experience. Through its conscious creative aging curriculum, SAGE is beginning to offer LGBT elders the opportunity to explore various aspects of aging, including fears, changing self-definitions and perceptions, the relationship of sexuality to aging, and the losses and gains that accompany aging. Other issues significant to the aging process, such as religion and spirituality, physical and mental health, and community building, are also addressed through this curriculum. The goal of SAGE's effort to promote conscious creative aging is to help LGBT seniors find value in aging; approach aging with awareness, thoughtfulness, and creativity; and play a role in building a community that validates their experiences.

## Advocacy and Education: Working to Change Society and Culture

SAGE's work to create a positive, enriching LGBT aging experience involves a growing effort to educate the local and national community about LGBT aging concerns and to advocate for the needs of LGBT elders in local and national government. Recognizing that systemic homophobia and invisibility have contributed to a lack of targeted services for LGBT elders and that ageism has separated elders from their LGBT communities, SAGE and its volunteers have embarked on a wide array of initiatives to address the ignorance and misconceptions that rob LGBTs of a viable aging experience.

## Educating Social Service Providers and Providing Technical Assistance

One of the most significant target populations for SAGE's educational efforts has been social service and health care providers from mainstream elderly agencies, most of which are not designed to meet the particular needs of LGBT residents and often fail even to recognize and acknowledge their existence. SAGE provides training for care professionals at conferences, senior centers, hospitals, nursing homes, and other venues, seeking both to increase individual professionals' sensitivity about LGBT aging and to provide information on how facilities can create policies and practices that include LGBT elders. Technical assistance is available to those who ask.

In addition to its local efforts in this area, SAGE has embarked on a national initiative to sensitize social service and health care providers about LGBT aging issues. Named SAGE Safe Havens, this project involves the development and national dissemination of a facility-wide training curriculum titled "No Need to Fear, No Need to Hide: A Training Program About Inclusion and Understanding of Lesbian, Gay, Bisexual, and Transgender Elders." Recently completed, the curriculum is designed for use in a variety of social service environments to educate and sensitize individual workers to their LGBT residents and to help facilities foster inclusive, accepting environments for all their residents and clients.

## National Needs Assessment: Developing an LGBT Aging Agenda

SAGE's work in the area of national advocacy has grown with its recent completion of a widespread initiative to assess existing services for LGBT elders in communities across the country. Called the National Needs Assessment and Technical Audit, this project involved a variety of assessment tools, including a national online survey, interviews with a diverse range of professionals and advocates knowledgeable in LGBT aging, town hall meetings across the country, and a teleconference with transgender elders and advocates.[1] Concluding that the majority of communities across the country lack services or programs for LGBT elders, the National Needs Assessment was the first leg in an initiative to build a national movement on LGBT aging to advocate for improved services, expanded knowledge, and greater recognition of LGBT aging concerns. It is hoped that the agenda that results from this effort will inform the delegates at the next White House Conference on Aging.

## National Education Efforts

SAGE has long been a national clearinghouse on LGBT aging, providing information and technical support for local grassroots efforts that provide services to LGBT elders and challenge ageism and anti-LGBT discrimination. Specifically, SAGE offers assistance to a group of LGBT elder organizations that have replicated some of its programming. Formalized into a network called SAGE-Net in 1992, these organizations treat SAGE as a model and a source for expanding and refining their programming. SAGE-Net currently includes 12 groups located in several states across the country, as well as in Canada and Germany.

To further expand opportunities for collaboration and information exchange on LGBT aging, in 1998 SAGE sponsored its first National Conference on Aging in the Gay and Lesbian Community. The conference brought together researchers, advocates, service providers, and elders to discuss a wide range of topics and to network both formally and informally. A follow-up conference was held 2 years later (Kimmel & Martin, 2001). A third conference was held in June 2004 that provided people working in the field of aging and other related areas the opportunity to keep informed on one another's work and to explore new avenues for further research and program implementation.

## Local Organizing and Advocacy

Locally, LGBT elders have been actively involved in SAGE's work to influence legislation and policy to successfully redress anti-LGBT discrimination and recognize and affirm LGBT identities and families. SAGE volunteers have joined SAGE staff in lobbying state legislators in Albany, New York, for much-needed changes in legislation. In summer 2003, more than 100 LGBT seniors met with members of local government to develop strategies for successful advocacy before New York's City Council. And in early 2002, SAGE volunteers protested a projected loss in city funding for SAGE as a result of the attacks on the World Trade Center. The successful restoration of a city grant to SAGE as a result of sustained protest was a significant victory for these LGBT elder activists.

One of the cornerstones of SAGE's advocacy and education work is the initiative to challenge ageism—the systemic fear, intolerance, and devaluation of elders and of the aging experience—and to confront the dual discrimination of ageism and homophobia. SAGE's Ageism Task Force, composed of volunteers and staff, has sponsored town hall meetings on ageism in the LGBT community and in the mainstream community, allowing elders and youth alike to share experiences and air ideas. An improvisational theater troupe called Old Queers Acting Up performs skits to raise awareness about the particular concerns that accompany LGBT aging. Using techniques founded on the concepts designed by Brazilian educator Paolo Friere and his contemporary Augusto Boal (1979), who developed Theatre of the Oppressed, the actors create a dialogue with audiences to explore these issues in depth, brainstorming possible responses to oppressive treatment.

All of SAGE's local and national advocacy and public education endeavors expand the significance of LGBT aging concerns beyond the elderly to include people of all ages. Advocating for changes in law, challenging ageism in public forums, strategizing to find effective ways to better serve LGBT aging communities—all have the effect of raising awareness about aging among young and old. LGBT youth increasingly realize the importance of older role models for them as they look to their own futures, and LGBT communities as a whole benefit from discussion and increased awareness of aging. Equally important, LGBT seniors gain much-needed allies among young and middle-aged people.

## SAGE: The Challenge to Build a Multicultural Community

SAGE strives to provide LGBT seniors with highly original programming and clinical services in an environment that values diversity in age, gender, race, religion, ethnicity, culture, and socioeconomic status. Toward this end, SAGE has embarked on a number of initiatives to create a diverse community of LGBT elders that welcomes all genders, races, ethnicities, ages, and socioeconomic groups. Meeting this goal has been among SAGE's biggest challenges.

Since 1993, SAGE's Older Lesbian Project has worked to attract more women to the organization, offering them support, advocacy, and opportunities for social activities. The volunteer-run Women's Task Force provides workshops and groups on topics of special interest to women, a drop-in center for women, and dances, dinners, and other social events for older lesbians. Despite this programming, however, the challenge to achieve gender parity in the organization has not been met. To address the issue, SAGE's Board of Directors, which has worked toward gender parity since its beginning, has created a special task force to investigate possible solutions. Meanwhile the volunteer-run Women's Task Force continues to develop creative, enriching programming for elder lesbians.

SAGE's effort to create a multicultural organization began with the establishment of an Anti-Discrimination Task Force. Under this task force, SAGE has been working to make fundamental internal changes by encouraging staff of all races to address their own experiences with racism and white privilege and by hiring more people of color. Under the umbrella of the Rainbow Aging Awareness Project, SAGE and several LGBT elder organizations have co-sponsored events, including a forum on Racism in the LGBT Community and Senior LGBT Pride Day, which strive to be inclusive in terms of race, gender, ethnicity, and culture.

Central to SAGE's work to expand its mission is the effort to reach out to communities of color. Toward this end, SAGE has developed the Harlem and Bronx Initiative, a community-building effort meant to help SAGE and the LGBT aging community address the needs and concerns of LGBT elders of color. Run by SAGE staff in collaboration with the Bronx Lesbian and Gay Health Resource Consortium and Gay Men of African Descent in Harlem, the program is based on the development of community groups in these neighborhoods. Furthermore, its success relies on the participation of these community members in creating programming to meet their needs.

A crucial part of this initiative has been the establishment and growth of discussion groups that meet monthly in members' homes in the Bronx and Harlem. These meetings serve multiple purposes, including relieving isolation and encouraging members to build connections. They also provide opportunities to develop a political agenda around LGBT aging in communities of color. At the meetings, members can discuss how to combat racism, poverty, homophobia, and isolation and how to encourage SAGE to support healthy, conscious aging in these communities. The group meetings also provide a forum for educational workshops on various issues, including health and economics. Finally, the Harlem and Bronx Initiative serves a social and cultural function. SAGE community organizers and community members are developing ways to celebrate the traditional cultural events of various groups, relating these events to LGBT concerns. Examples include a dance in honor of the Day of the Dead (*Día de los Muertos*, an annual Mexican holiday celebrated on November 2 when Mexicans honor their dead with food, flowers, and a decorative altar) and celebrations of Black History Month and Women's History Month.

In building a multicultural organization with gender parity, SAGE faces many challenges. In addition to attracting more women and people of color and developing programming that meets their diverse needs, the biggest challenge is finding ways to build connections between all the different groups that make up the organization. For this to happen, people of different genders, ethnicities, races, ages, and socioeconomic classes must be willing to examine their own relationships to racism, sexism, classism, ageism, ableism, and other "isms"; to acknowledge the ways these systems may benefit or hurt them; and to explore areas of common ground with one another so that they can interact rather than simply coexist within the same organization.

SAGE's ability to create a vibrant, diverse LGBT elder community also rests, paradoxically perhaps, on its capacity to function as an intergenerational organization, an area in which it has had much success. Its first board of directors in 1977 included people of all ages, its current staff varies widely in age, and its volunteer corps ranges in age from 25 to 90. Although certain clinical services are available only to people over age 60 (age 50 for those with HIV and AIDS), membership is open—and actively encouraged—for everyone, regardless of age. As a result, SAGE members, volunteers, and staff can enjoy intergenerational collaborations and social activities. SAGE spreads the message that LGBT elders are crucial to LGBT communities and should be recognized and included, that old age is a part of life to be celebrated by all, and that engagement with SAGE and with LGBT elders is an investment in the future for everyone. SAGE—and its efforts to build an enriching aging experience—benefits not only elders but all members of the community.

## Conclusion

As this chapter is being written, SAGE continues to serve a diverse and growing LGBT elder population. With federal funding channeled through the New York City Department for the Aging, SAGE has expanded its programming to support LGBT caregivers and caregivers of LGBT elders. The organization celebrated its twenty-fifth anniversary recently and is currently preparing for the Tenth Annual SAGE Awards, an event recognizing people who have made significant contributions to the LGBT elder community. For one of the co-founders (D.K.), seeing SAGE develop is very sweet, like being a grandparent watching the grandchildren develop—a process in which I take great pride, although I only watch from a distance.

When the first small group met in Jim Dorff's living room in the autumn of 1977, we were idealistic young people concerned about lonely homebound elders. We called on like-minded friends and set up a program of friendly visitors, with appropriate supervision and ethical standards, but no one called on us for services. We contacted a reporter from the *New York Times,* who wrote a fine feature article about this new organization, but the *Times* would not print positive articles about homosexuals in those days. Today it is hard to imagine the grassroots beginning of SAGE and our board meetings in various living rooms. At the time, we thought of the other major social service organizations in the city and wondered whether they began in a similar fashion. Eventually, Chris Almvig, a lesbian who was director of a program for seniors and a co-founder of SAGE, hit on the idea of holding socials, and the rest is history.

In those early days, we committed to gender parity on the board and did our best to maintain co-chairs or leadership that rotated between women and men. As several other organizations in New York City formed during the 1970s fell into disunity or decided to leave the city, perhaps it was SAGE's clear mission, its commitment to gender parity, and the dedication of many volunteer leaders that prevented its early demise. It was also fortuitous that SAGE was well established at the time the AIDS crisis emerged, as that crisis robbed the gay male community of many leaders and competed with SAGE for funding.

Other communities that are developing services for older LGBT neighbors can take heart from the modest beginnings, difficult struggles, and eventual success of SAGE. Its resources are now national in scope, and the organization can provide guidance and models for other groups with similar goals.

Additional information on SAGE, including new projects, SAGE-Net organizations, and a current calendar of events, is available on SAGE's Web site (www.sageusa.org). An archive of SAGE's early history is in the collection of Cornell University Library.

## NOTE

1. National Needs Assessment was funded by the Gill Foundation, the AARP Andrus Foundation, the Lily Auchincloss Foundation, Inc., and individual donors and members.

## REFERENCES

Boal, A. (1979). *Theater of the oppressed.* New York: Urizen Books.

Brotman, S., Ryan, B., & Cormier, R. (2003). The health and social service needs of gay and lesbian elders and their families in Canada. *The Gerontologist, 43,* 192–202.

Cahill, S., South, K., & Spade, J. (2000). *Outing age: Public policy issues affecting gay, lesbian, bisexual, and transgender elders.* Washington, DC: National Gay and Lesbian Task Force Policy Institute.

Ehrenberg, M. (1996). Aging and mental health: Issues in the gay and lesbian community. In C. J. Alexander (Ed.), *Gay and lesbian mental health: A sourcebook for practitioners* (pp. 189–209). New York: Harrington Park Press.

Kimmel, D. C., & Martin, D. L. 2001. *Midlife and aging in gay America: Proceedings of the* SAGE *Conference 2000.* Binghamton, NY: Harrington Park Press. [Published simultaneously as *Journal of Gay & Lesbian Social Services, 13*(4).]

U.S. Department of Health and Human Services, Administration on Aging. (2001). *Fact sheet: The many faces of aging.* Washington, DC: Author.

# 16

# Bibliography of Research and Clinical Perspectives on LGBT Aging

*Steven David*

*With updates by Tara Rose*

Adams, C. L. Jr., & Kimmel, D. C. (1997). Exploring the lives of older African American gay men. In B. Greene (Ed.), *Ethnic and cultural diversity among lesbians and gay men* (pp. 132–151). Thousand Oaks, CA: SAGE.

Adelman, M. (1986). *Long time passing: Lives of older lesbians.* Boston: Alyson.

Adelman, M. (1990). Stigma, gay lifestyles, and adjustment to aging: A study of later-life gay men and lesbians. *Journal of Homosexuality, 20*(3–4), 7–32.

Adelman, M. (2000). *Midlife lesbian relationships: Friends, lovers, children, and parents.* New York: Harrington Park Press/Haworth Press.

Allen, C. (1961). The aging homosexual. In I. Rubin (Ed.), *The third sex.* New York: New Book Co.

Almvig, C. (1982). *The invisible minority: Aging and lesbians.* Utica, NY: Institute of Gerontology, Utica College of Syracuse.

Anderson, G. (1996). The older gay man. In K. M. Nokes (Ed.), *HIV/AIDS and the older adult* (pp. 63–79). Philadelphia: Taylor & Francis.

Anetzberger, G. J., Ishler, K. J., Mostade, J., & Blair, M. (2004). Gray and gay: A community dialogue on the issues and concerns of older gays and lesbians. *Journal of Gay & Lesbian Social Services: Issues in Practice, Policy, and Research, 17*(1), 23–45.

Barker, J. C. (2004). Lesbian aging: An agenda for social research. In G. H. Herdt & B. De Vries (Eds.), *Gay and lesbian aging: Research and future directions,* pp. 29–72. New York: Springer.

Barnes, S. A. (2005). My life in a lesbian community: The joys and the pain. *Journal of Lesbian Studies, 9*(1–2), 45–54.

Baron, A., & Cramer, D. W. (2000). Potential counseling concerns of aging lesbian, gay, and bisexual clients. In R. M. Perez, K. A. DeBord. & K. J. Bieschke (Eds.), *Handbook of counseling and psychotherapy with lesbian, gay, and bisexual clients* (pp. 207–223). Washington, DC: American Psychological Association.

Beeler, J. A., Rawls, T. W., Herdt, G., & Cohler, B. J. (1999). The needs of older lesbians and gay men in Chicago. *Journal of Gay & Lesbian Social Services, 9*(1), 31–50.

Bennet, K. C. (1980). Social and psychological functioning of the ageing male homosexual. *British Journal of Psychiatry, 137,* 361–370.

Bennett, L., Gates, G. J., & Human Rights Campaign. (2004). *Cost of marriage inequality to gay, lesbian, and bisexual seniors: A Human Rights Campaign Foundation report.* Washington, DC: Human Rights Campaign Foundation. Retrieved December 25, 2005, from, www.hrc.org/Template.cfm?Section = About_HRC&Template = /ContentManagement/ContentDisplay.cfm& ContentID = 16569.

Berger, R. M. (1980). Psychological adaptation of the older homosexual male. *Journal of Homosexuality, 5*(3), 161–174.

Berger, R. M. (1982). The unseen minority: Older gays and lesbians. *Social Work, 29,* 236–242.

Berger, R. M. (1984). Realities of gay and lesbian aging. *Social Work, 29,* 57–62.

Berger, R. M. (1996). *Gay and gray: The older homosexual man* (2nd ed.). New York: Harrington Park Press/Haworth Press.

Berger, R. M., & Kelly, J. J. (1996). Gay men and lesbians grown older. In R. P. Cabaj & T. S. Stein (Eds.), *Textbook of homosexuality and mental health* (pp. 305–316). Washington, DC: American Psychiatric Press.

Berger, R. M., & Kelly, J. J. (2001a). The older gay man. In B. Berzon & B. Frank (Eds.), *Positively gay: New approaches to gay and lesbian life* (3rd ed.). Berkeley, CA: Celestial Arts.

Berger, R. M., & Kelly, J. J. (2001b). What are older gay men like? An impossible question? *Journal of Gay & Lesbian Social Services, 13*(4), 55–65.

Bergling, T. (2004). *Reeling in the years: Gay men's perspectives on age and ageism.* New York: Southern Tier Editions, Harrington Park Press.

Betschild, M., & Fortanier, A. (2003). Daring to take the risk. *Journal of Lesbian Studies, 8*(3–4), 57–72.

Blando, J. A. (2001). Twice hidden: Older gay and lesbian couples, friends, and intimacy. *Generations, 25*(2), 87–89.

Bond, L. A., Cutler, S. J., & Grams, A. (1995). *Promoting successful and productive aging.* Thousand Oaks, CA: SAGE.

Boston Lesbian Psychologies Collective (Ed.). (1987). *Lesbian psychologies: Explorations and challenges.* Urbana: University of Illinois Press.

\Bradford, J., & Ryan, C. (1991). Who we are: Health concerns of middle-aged lesbians. In B. Sang, J. Warshow, & A. Smith (Eds.), *Lesbians at midlife: The creative transition* (pp. 147–163). San Francisco: Spinsters.

Brotman, S., Ryan, B., & Cormier, R. (2003). The health and social service needs of gay and lesbian elders and their families in Canada. *Gerontologist, 43,* 192–202.

Brown, L. B., Alley, G. R., Sarosy, S., Quarto, G., & Cook, T. (2001). Gay men: Aging well! *Journal of Gay & Lesbian Social Services, 13*(4), 41–54.

Brown, L. B., Sarosy, S. G., Cook, T. C., & Quarto, J. G. (1997). *Gay men and aging.* New York: Garland.

Burda, J. M. (2004). *Estate planning for same-sex couples.* Chicago: American Bar Association.

Butler, S. (2002). Geriatric care management with sexual minorities. *Geriatric Care Management Journal, 12*(3), 2–3.

Butler, S. S. (2004). Gay, lesbian, bisexual, and transgender (GLBT) elders: The challenges and resilience of this marginalized group. *Journal of Human Behavior in the Social Environment, 9*(4), 25–44.

Butler, S. S., & Hope, B. (1998). Health and well-being for late middle-aged and old lesbians in a rural area. *Journal of Gay & Lesbian Social Services, 9*(4), 27–46.

Butt, A. A., Dascomb, K. K., DeSalvo, K. B., Bazzano, L., Kissinger, P. J., & Szerlip, H. M. (2001). Human immunodeficiency virus infection in elderly patients. *Southern Medical Journal, 94,* 397–400.

Cahill, S. (2002). Long term care issues affecting gay, lesbian, bisexual and transgender elders. *Geriatric Care Management Journal, 12*(3), 4–8.

Cahill, S., South, K., & Spade, J. (2000). *Outing age: Public policy issues affecting gay, lesbian, bisexual, and transgender elders.* Washington, DC: National Gay and Lesbian Task Force Policy Institute.

Cantor, M. H., Brennan, M., & Shippy, R. A. (2004). *Caregiving among older lesbian, gay, bisexual, and transgender New Yorkers.* New York: National Gay and Lesbian Task Force Policy Institute.

Charbonneau, C., & Lander, P. (1991). Redefining sexuality: Women becoming lesbian in midlife. In B. Sang, J. Warshow, & A. Smith (Eds.), *Lesbians at midlife: The creative transition* (pp. 35–43). San Francisco: Spinsters.

Chen, S. Y., Weide, D., & McFarland, W. (2003). Are the recent increases in sexual risk behavior among older or younger men who have sex with men? Answer: both. *AIDS, 17*(6), 942–943.

Chin Hong, P. V., Vittinghoff, E., Cranston, R. D., Browne, L., Buchbinder, S., Colfax, G., Da Costa, M., Darragh, T., Benet, D. J., Judson, F., Koblin, B., Mayer, K. H., & Palefsky, J. M. (2005). Age-related prevalence of anal cancer precursors in homosexual men: The EXPLORE study. *Journal of the National Cancer Institute, 97*(12), 896–905.

Christian, D. V., & Keefe, D. A. (1997). Maturing gay men: A framework for social service assessment and intervention. *Journal of Gay and Lesbian Social Services, 6*(1), 47–70.

Christiansen, V., & Johnson, A. B. (1973). Sexual patterns in a group of older never-married women. *Journal of Geriatric Psychiatry, 6,* 80–89.

Claassen, C. (2005). *Whistling women: A study of the lives of older lesbians.* Binghamton, NY: Haworth Press.

Claes, J. A., & Moore, W. (2000). Issues confronting lesbian and gay elders: The challenge for health and human services providers. *Journal of Health and Human Service Administration, 23,* 181–202.

Claes, J. A., & Moore, W. (2001). Caring for gay and lesbian elderly. In L. K. Olson (Ed.), *Age through ethnic lenses: Caring for the elderly in a multicultural society.* Lanham, MD: Rowman & Littlefield.

Clunis, D. M., Fredriksen-Goldsen, K. I., Freeman, P. A., & Nystrom, N. M. (2004; 2005 pbk.). *Lives of lesbian elders: Looking back, looking forward.* Binghamton, NY: Haworth Press.

Cohler, B. J. (2004). Saturday night at the tubs: Age cohort and social life at the urban gay bath. In G. H. Herdt & B. De Vries (Eds.), *Gay and lesbian aging: Research and future directions*, pp. 211–234. New York: Springer.

Cohler, B. J., & Galatzer-Levy, R. M. (2000). *The course of gay and lesbian lives: Social and psychoanalytic perspectives.* Chicago: University of Chicago Press.

Cohler, B. J., & Hostetler, A. J. (2002). Aging, intimate relationships, and life story among gay men. In R. S. Weiss & S. A. Bass (Eds.), *Challenges of the third age: Meaning and purpose in later life* (pp. 137–160). London: Oxford University Press.

Cohler, B. J., Hostetler, A. J., & Boxer, A. M. (1998). Generativity, social context, and lived experience: Narratives of gay men in middle adulthood. In D. P. McAdams & E. de St. Aubin (Eds.), *Generativity and adult development: How and why we care for the next generation* (pp. 265–309). Washington, DC: American Psychological Association.

Cole, E., & Rothblum, E. (1990). Commentary on "Sexuality and the midlife woman." *Psychology of Women Quarterly, 14,* 509–512.

Cole, E., & Rothblum, E. (1991). Lesbian sex after menopause: As good or better than ever. In B. Sang, J. Warshow, & A. Smith (Eds.), *Lesbians at midlife: The creative transition* (pp. 184–193). San Francisco: Spinsters.

Connolly, L. (1996). Long-term care and hospice: The special needs of older gay men and lesbians. *Journal of Gay & Lesbian Social Services, 5*(1), 77–92.

Cook-Daniels, L. (1997). Lesbian, gay male, bisexual and transgendered elders: Elder abuse and neglected issues. *Journal of Elder Abuse & Neglect, 9*(2), 35–49.

Cook-Daniels, L. (2002). *Transgender elders and SOFFAs: A primer.* Milwaukee, WI: Forge. Retrieved August 30, 2004, from www.forge-forward.org/handouts/Trans-EldersSOFFAs-web.pdf.

Cook-Daniels, L. (2004). Why gay marriage is an issue for abuse professionals. *Victimization of the Elderly and Disabled, 7*(2), 20, 27.

Cope, J. (2002). Age concern: Older lesbian & gay men's initiative. *Nurse 2 Nurse, 2*(8), 8–9.

Copper, B. (1980). On being an older lesbian. *Generations, 4*(4), 39–40.

Copper, B. (1988). *Over the hill: Reflections on ageism between women.* Freedom, CA: The Crossing Press.

Cornett, C. W., & Hudson, R. A. (1987). Middle adulthood and the theories of Erikson, Gould, and Vaillant: Where does the gay man fit? *Journal of Gerontological Social Work, 10*(3–4), 61–73.

Cruikshank, M. (1991). Lavender and gray: A brief survey of lesbian and gay aging studies. *Journal of Homosexuality, 20*(3–4), 77–88.

Cruz, J. M. (2003). *Sociological analysis of aging: The gay male perspective.* Binghamton, NY: Harrington Park Press/ Haworth Press.

Crystal, S., Akincigil, A., Sambamoorthi, U., Wenger, N., Fleishman, J. A., Zingmond, D. S., Hays, R. D., Bozzette, S. A., & Shapiro, M. F. (2003). The diverse older HIV-positive population: A national profile of economic circumstances, social support, and quality of life. *Journal of Acquired Immune Deficiency Syndromes: JAIDS, 33*(2), S76–S83.

Cummings, S. M., & Galambos, C. (2005). *Diversity and aging in the social environment*. Binghamton, NY: Haworth Press. [A monograph published simultaneously as the *Journal of Human Behavior in the Social Environment, 9*(4) and *10*(1).]

D'Augelli, A. R. (1994). Lesbian and gay male development: Steps toward an analysis of lesbians' and gay men's lives. In B. Greene & G. M. Herek (Eds.), *Lesbian and gay psychology: Theory, research, and clinical applications* (Vol. 1, pp. 118–132). Thousand Oaks, CA: SAGE.

D'Augelli, A. R., & Grossman, A. H. (2001). Disclosure of sexual orientation, victimization, and mental health among lesbian, gay, and bisexual older adults. *Journal of Interpersonal Violence, 16*, 1008–1027.

D'Augelli, A. R., Grossman, A. H., Hershberger, S. L., & O'Connell, T. S. (2001). Aspects of mental health among older lesbian, gay, and bisexual adults. *Aging & Mental Health, 5*, 149–158.

Davis, N. D., Cole, E., & Rothblum, E. D. (1993). *Faces of women and aging*. New York: Haworth Press.

Dawson, K. (1982). Serving the older gay community. *SEICUS Report, 11*(2), 5–6.

Deevey, S. (1990). Older lesbian women: An invisible minority. *Journal of Gerontological Nursing, 16*(5), 35–39.

DeMonnin, J., & Fun, J. (2005). Elder abuse manslaughter case between gay domestic partners. *Victimization of the Elderly and Disabled, 7*(5), 65–68.

Dening, T., & Barapatre, C. (2004). Mental health and the ageing population. *Journal of the British Menopause Society, 10*(2), 49–53.

De Vries, B., & Blando, J. A. (2004). The study of gay and lesbian aging: Lessons for social gerontology. In G. H. Herdt & B. De Vries (Eds.), *Gay and lesbian aging: Research and future directions*, pp. 3–28. New York: Springer.

Diamant, A. L., Schuster, M. A., & Lever, J. (2000). Receipt of preventive health care services by lesbians. *American Journal of Preventive Medicine, 19*(3), 141–148.

Dibble, S. L., & Roberts, S. A. (2003). Improving cancer screening among lesbians over 50: Results of a pilot study. *Oncology Nursing Forum, 30*(4), 71–79.

Dickie, J. R., Cook, A., Gazda, R., Martin, B., & Sturrus, E. (2005). The heirs of Aradia, daughters of Diana: Community in the second and third wave. *Journal of Lesbian Studies, 9*(1–2), 95–109.

Dolcini, M. M., Catania, J. A., Stall, R. D., & Pollack, L. (2003). The HIV epidemic among older men who have sex with men. *Journal of Acquired Immune Deficiency Syndromes, 33*(2), S115–121.

Donovan, T. (2001). Being transgender and older: A first person account. *Journal of Gay & Lesbian Social Services: Issues in Practice, Policy & Research, 13*, 19–22.

Dorfman, R., Walters, K., Burke, P., & Hardin, L. (1995). Old, sad and alone: The myth of the aging homosexual. *Journal of Gerontological Social Work, 24*(1–2), 29–44.

Dubois, M. (1999). Legal planning for gay, lesbian, and non-traditional elders. *Albany Law Review, 63*(1), 263–332.

Dubois, M. (2003). Elder law: Answers for gay and lesbian elders. *Maine Lawyers Review, 11*(1), 16–17.

Dubois, M. (2004). Elder law: Adding "domestic partner" in Maine's probate code. *Maine Lawyers Review, 12*(11), 21–23.

Dunker, B. (1987). Aging lesbians: Observations and speculations. In Boston Lesbian Psychologies Collective (Ed.), *Lesbian psychologies* (pp. 72–82). Urbana: University of Illinois Press.

Dwight, M. B. (2004). Searching for the sample: Researching demand for senior housing in the LGBT community. *OutWord, 11*(2), 2, 8.

Edwards, D. J. (2005). Designing for the gay seniors population. *Nursing Homes Long Term Care Management, 54*(10), 42–44.

Ehrenberg, M. (1996). Aging and mental health: Issues in the gay and lesbian community. In C. J. Alexander (Ed.), *Gay and lesbian mental health: A sourcebook for practitioners* (pp. 189–209). New York: Harrington Park Press/Haworth Press.

Ellis, A. (2001). *Gay men at midlife: Age before beauty.* New York: Harrington Park Press.

Fassinger, R. E. (1997). Issues in group work with older lesbians. *Group, 21*, 191–210.

Finnegan, D. G., & McNally, E. B. (2000). Making up for lost time: Chemically dependent lesbians in later midlife. *Journal of Gay & Lesbian Social Services, 11*, 105–118.

Fitzpatrick, T. R. (2000). Sexuality and aging: A timely addition to the gerontology curriculum. *Educational Gerontology, 26*, 427–446.

Francher, J. S., & Henkin, J. (1973). The menopausal queen: Adjustment to aging and the male homosexual. *American Journal of Orthopsychiatry, 43*, 670–674.

Fredriksen, K. I. (1999). Family caregiving responsibilities among lesbians and gay men. *Social Work, 44*, 142–155.

Friend, R. A. (1980). Graying: Adjustment and the older gay male. *Alternative Lifestyles, 3*, 231–284.

Friend, R. A. (1987). The individual and social psychology of aging: Clinical implications for lesbians and gay men. *Journal of Homosexuality, 14*(1–2), 307–331.

Friend, R. A. (1989). Older lesbian and gay people: Responding to homophobia. *Marriage & Family Review, 14*, 241–263.

Friend, R. A. (1990). Older lesbian and gay people: A theory of successful aging. *Journal of Homosexuality, 20*(3–4), 99–118.

Fritsch, T. (2005). HIV/AIDS and the older adult: An exploratory study of the age-related differences in access to medical and social services. *Journal of Applied Gerontology, 24*(1), 35–54.

Frost, J. C. (1997). Group psychotherapy with the aging gay male: Treatment of choice. *Group, 21*, 267–285.

Gabbay, S. G., & Wahler, J. J. (2002). Lesbian aging: Review of a growing literature. *Journal of Gay & Lesbian Social Services, 14*(3), 1–21.

Gallo, J. J. (2004). Unique estate planning opportunities for gay and lesbian couples. *Journal of Financial Planning, 17*(8), 28–30.

Garnets, L. D., & Kimmel, D. C. (2003). Adolescence, midlife, and aging. In L. D. Garnets & D. C. Kimmel (Eds.), *Psychological perspectives on lesbian, gay, and bisexual experiences* (2nd ed.), pp. 563–570. New York: Columbia University Press.

Genevay, B. (1978). Age kills us softly when we deny our sexual identity. In R. L. Solnick (Ed.), *Sexuality and aging.* Los Angeles: University of California Press.

Gershick, Z. Z. (1998). *Gay old girls.* Boston: Alyson.

Goldberg. S. (1986). GLOE: A model social service program for older lesbians. In M. Adelman (Ed.), *Longtime passing: Lives of older lesbians* (pp. 236–246). Boston: Alyson.

Goldberg, S., Sickler, J. J., & Dibbler, S. (2005). Lesbians over sixty: The consistency of findings from twenty years of survey data. *Journal of Lesbian Studies,* 9(1–2), 195–213.

Goldfried, M. R. (2001). Integrating gay, lesbian, and bisexual issues into mainstream psychology. *American Psychologist,* 56, 977–988.

Gorman, E. M., & Nelson, K. (2004). From a far place: Social and cultural considerations about HIV among midlife and older gay men. In G. H. Herdt & B. De Vries (Eds.), *Gay and lesbian aging: Research and future directions,* pp. 73–93. New York: Springer.

Gray, H., & Dressel, P. (1985). Alternative interpretations of aging among gay males. *The Gerontologist,* 25, 83–87.

Greene, B. (2002). Older lesbians' concerns and psychotherapy: Beyond a footnote to the footnote. In F. K. Trotman & C. M. Brody (Eds.), *Psychotherapy and counseling with older women: Cross-cultural, family, and end-of-life issues* (pp. 161–174). New York: Springer.

Grossman, A. H. (1995). At risk, infected, and invisible: Older gay men with HIV/AIDS. *Journal of Association of Nurses in AIDS Care,* 6, 13–19.

Grossman, A. H. (2000). Homophobia and its effects on the inequitable provisions of health and leisure services for older gay men and lesbians. In C. Brackenridge, D. Howe, & F. Jordan (Eds.), *JUST leisure: Equity, social exclusions and identity* (pp. 105–118). Eastbourne, UK: Leisure Studies Association.

Grossman, A. H., D'Augelli, A. R., & Hershberger, S. L. (2000). Social support networks of lesbian, gay, and bisexual adults 60 years of age and older. *Journals of Gerontology: Series B: Psychological Sciences & Social Sciences,* 55B, P171–P179.

Grossman, A. H., D'Augelli, A. R., & O'Connell, T. S. (2001). Being lesbian, gay, bisexual, and 60 or older in North America. *Journal of Gay & Lesbian Social Services,* 13(4), 23–40. [Reprinted in L. D. Garnets & D. C. Kimmel (Eds.), *Psychological perspectives on lesbian, gay, and bisexual experiences* (2nd ed., pp. 629–645). New York: Columbia University Press.]

Grossman, A. H., Hershberger, S. L., & O' Connell, T. S. (2001). Aspects of mental health among older lesbian, gay, and bisexual adults. *Aging & Mental Health,* 5, 149–158.

Grube, M. A. (1991). Natives and settlers: An ethnographic note on early interaction of older homosexual men with younger gay liberationists. *Journal of Homosexuality,* 20(3–4), 119–136.

Gutiérrez, F. J. (1992). Eros, the aging years: Counseling older gay men. In S. H. Dworkin & F. J. Gutiérrez (Eds.), *Counseling gay men and lesbians: Journey to the end of the rainbow.* Alexandria, VA: American Association for Counseling and Development.

Gwenwald, M. (1985). The SAGE model for serving older lesbians and gay men. In R. Schoenberg, R. S. Goldberg, & D. A. Shore (Eds.), *With compassion toward some: Homosexuality and social work in America* (pp. 53–64). New York: Harrington Park Press.

Hader, M. (1968). Homosexuality as part of our aging process. *Psychiatric Quarterly, 40,* 515–524.

Haile, B. (1998). The forgotten tenth: AIDS in the older generation. *Research Initiative, Treatment Action: RITA, 4*(3), 15–16.

Hajek, C., & Giles, H. (2002). The old man out: An intergroup analysis of intergenerational communication among gay men. *Journal of Communication, 52,* 698–714.

Hamburger, L. J. (1997). The wisdom of non–heterosexually based senior housing and related services. *Journal of Gay and Lesbian Social Services, 6*(1), 11–24.

Harrison, J. (1999). A lavender pink grey power: Gay and lesbian gerontology in Australia. *Australasian Journal on Ageing, 18*(1), 245–250.

Harry, J. (1982). Decision making and age differences among gay male couples. *Journal of Homosexuality, 8*(2), 9–21.

Harry, J., & DeVall, W. (1978). Age and sexual culture among homosexually oriented males. *Archives of Sexual Behavior, 7,* 199–209.

Hart, S., Gordon, N., & Ackerson, L. (2001). Patterns of cigarette smoking and alcohol use among lesbians and bisexual women enrolled in a large health maintenance organization. *American Journal of Public Health, 91,* 976–979.

Harwood, G. (1997). *The oldest gay couple in America: A 70 year journey through same-sex America.* Secaucus, NJ: Carol Publishing.

Hash, K. M. (2000). Preliminary study of caregiving and post-caregiving experiences of older gay men and lesbians. In D. C. Kimmel & D. L. Martin (Eds.), *Midlife and aging in gay America* (pp. 87–94). New York: Haworth Press.

Hash, K. M., & Cramer, E. P. (2003). Empowering gay and lesbian caregivers and uncovering their unique experiences through the use of qualitative methods. *Journal of Gay & Lesbian Social Services, 15*(1–2), 47–63.

Hawton, K., Gath, D., & Day, A. (1994). Sexual function in a community sample of middle-aged women with partners: Effects of age, marital, socioeconomic, psychiatric, gynecological, and menopausal factors. *Archives of Sexual Behavior, 23,* 375–395.

Hayden, G. (2003). Gray and gay: Helping elders stay out of the closet. *Long-Term Care Interface, 4*(10), 28–32.

Hayes, S. (1991). Financial planning for retirement. In B. Sang, J. Washow, & A. Smith (Eds.), *Lesbians at midlife: The creative transition* (pp. 245–257). San Francisco: Spinster.

Healey, S. (1994). Diversity with a difference: On being old and lesbian. *Journal of Gay & Lesbian Social Services, 1*(1), 109–117.

Heaphy, B., Yip, A. K. T., & Thompson, D. (2003). The social and policy implications of non-heterosexual ageing: Selective findings. *Quality in Ageing, 4*(3), 30–35.

Heaphy, B., Yip, A. K. T., & Thompson, D. (2004). Ageing in a non-heterosexual context. *Ageing and Society, 24*(6), 881–902.

Heath, H. (2002). Opening doors. *Nursing Older People, 14*(4), 10–13.

Herdt, G. (1997). Intergenerational relations and AIDS in the formation of gay culture in the United States. In M. P. Levine & P. M. Nardi (Eds.), *In changing times: Gay men and lesbians encounter HIV/AIDS* (pp. 245–281). Chicago: University of Chicago Press.

Herdt, G., & Beeler, J. (1998). Older gay men and lesbians in families. In C. J. Patterson & A. R. D'Augelli (Eds.), *Lesbian, gay, and bisexual identities in families: Psychological perspectives* (pp. 177–196). New York: Oxford University Press.

Herdt, G., Beeler, J., & Rawls, T. W. (1997). Life course diversity among older lesbians and gay men: A study in Chicago. *Journal of Gay, Lesbian, and Bisexual Identity, 2*, 231–246.

Herdt, G. H., & De Vries, B. (2004). *Gay and lesbian aging: Research and future directions.* New York: Springer.

Herdt, G., Hostetler, A. J., & Cohler, B. J. (Eds.). (1997). Coming of age: Gays, lesbians, and bisexuals in the second half of life. *Journal of Gay, Lesbian, and Bisexual Identity, 2* (whole numbers 3–4).

Hoctel, P. D. (2002). Community assessments show service gaps for LGBT elders. *Aging Today, 23*(1), 5–6.

Hoctel, P. D. (2003). Former NVL partner's program teaches about service needs of African American LGBT elders. *Diversity Currents, 4*(3), 3,6.

Hostetler, A. J. (2004). Old, gay, and alone? The ecology of wellbeing among middle-aged and older single gay men. In G. H. Herdt & B. De Vries (Eds.), *Gay and lesbian aging: Research and future directions.* pp. 143–176. New York: Springer.

Howell, L. C., & Beth, A. (2004). Pioneers in our own lives: Grounded theory of lesbians' midlife development. *Journal of Women and Aging, 16*(3–4), 133–147.

Humphreys, N., & Quam, J. (1998). Middle-aged and old gay, lesbian, and bisexual adults. In G. Appleby & J. W. Anastas (Eds.), *Not just a passing phase: Social work with gay, lesbian, and bisexual people* (pp. 245–267). New York: Columbia University Press.

Hunter, S. (2005). *Midlife and older LGBT adults: Knowledge and affirmative practice for the social services.* Binghamton, NY: Haworth Press.

Iasenza, S. (2004). Lesbian psychoanalytic foremothers making waves: Interviews with Joanne Spina, Lee Crespi, and Judy Levitz. *Journal of Lesbian Studies, 8*(1–2), 11–43.

Icard, L. D. (1996). Assessing the psychosocial well-being of African American gays: A multidimensional perspective. In J. F. Longres (Ed.), *Men of color: A context for service to homosexually active men* (pp. 25–49). New York: Harrington Park Press/Haworth Press.

Inelman, E. M., Gasparini, G., & Enzi, G. (2005). HIV/AIDS in older adults: A case report and literature review. *Geriatrics, 60*(9), 26–30.

Isaac, B., & Herringer, B. M. (1998). Lesbian passages: Invisible lives and issues of community. *Journal of Lesbian Studies, 2*(1), 49–59.

Jacobs, R. J., Rasmussen, L. A., & Hohman, M. M. (1999). The social support needs of older lesbians, gay men, and bisexuals. *Journal of Gay and Lesbian Social Services, 9*(1), 1–30.

Jacobson, S. (1995). Methodological issues in research on older lesbians. *Journal of Gay & Lesbian Social Services, 3*(1), 43.

Jacobson, S., & Grossman, A. H. (1996). Older lesbians and gay men: Old myths, new images, and future directions. In R. C. Savin-Williams & K. M. Cohen (Eds.), *The lives of lesbians, gays, and bisexuals: Children to adults* (pp. 345–373). Orlando, FL: Harcourt Brace.

Jacobson, S., & Samdahl, D. M. (1998). Leisure in the lives of old lesbians: Experiences with and responses to discrimination. *Journal of Leisure Research, 30*(2), 233–255.

Jensen, K. L. (1999). *Lesbian epiphanies: Women coming out in later life.* New York: Harrington Park Press.

Jimenez, A. D. (2003). Triple jeopardy: Targeting older men of color who have sex with men. *Journal of Acquired Immune Deficiency Syndromes: JAIDS, 33*(2), S222–S225.

Jo, B. (2005). Lesbian community: From sisterhood to segregation. *Journal of Lesbian Studies, 9*(1–2), 135–143.

Johnson, M. J., Jackson, N. C., Arnette, J. K., & Koffman, S. D. (2005). Gay and lesbian perceptions of discrimination in retirement care facilities. *Journal of Homosexuality, 49*(2), 83–102.

Johnson, M. T., & Kelly, J. J. (1970). Deviant sexual behavior in the aging. In D. J. Kaplan (Ed.), *Psychopathology and aging.* New York: Academic Press.

Jones, B. E. (2001). Is having the luck of growing old in the gay, lesbian, bisexual, transgender community good or bad luck? *Journal of Gay & Lesbian Social Services, 13*(4), 13–14.

Jones, T. C., & Nystrom, N. M. (2002). Looking back … looking forward: Addressing the lives of lesbians 55 and older. *Journal of Women & Aging, 14*(3–4), 59–76.

Joyce, G. F., Goldman, D. P., Leibowitz, A. A., Alpert, A., & Bao, Y. (2005). A socio-economic profile of older adults with HIV. *Journal of Health Care for the Poor and Underserved, 16*(1), 19–28.

Kehoe, M. (1986a). Lesbians over 65: A triply invisible minority. *Journal of Homosexuality, 12*(3–4), 139–152.

Kehoe, M. (1986b). A portrait of the older lesbian. *Journal of Homosexuality, 12*(3–4), 157–161.

Kehoe, M. (1988). Lesbians over 60 speak for themselves. *Journal of Homosexuality, 16*(3–4), 111.

Kehoe, M. (1989). *Lesbians over sixty speak for themselves.* New York: Haworth Press.

Kehoe, M. (1990). Loneliness and the aging homosexual: Is pet therapy an answer? *Journal of Homosexuality, 20*(3–4), 137–142.

Kehoe M. (1991). Caring for the aging homosexual. *Focus on Geriatric Care and Rehabilitation, 4*(9), 1–9.

Kelly, J. (1977). The aging male homosexual: Myth and reality. *Gerontologist, 17,* 328–332.

Keppel, B. (1991). Gray-haired and above suspicion. In L. H. Hutchins & L. Kaahumanu (Eds.), *Bi any other name: Bisexual people speak out* (pp. 154–158). Boston: Alyson.

Keppel, B. (2002) The challenges and rewards of life in an outspoken bisexual elder. *Outword, 8*(4), 1, 6.

Kertzner, R. M. (2001). The adult life course and homosexual identity in midlife gay men. *Annual Review of Sex Research, 12,* 75–92.

Kertzner, R. (1999). Self-appraisal of life experience and psychological adjustment in midlife gay men. *Journal of Psychology & Human Sexuality, 11*(2), 43–64.

Kertzner, R. M., Meyer, I., & Dolezal, C. (2004). Psychological well-being in midlife and older gay men. In G. H. Herdt & B. De Vries (Eds.), *Gay and lesbian aging: Research and future directions*, pp. 97–115. New York: Springer.

Kertzner, R. M., & Sved, M. (1996). Midlife gay men and lesbians: Adult development and mental health. In R. P. Cabaj & T. S. Stein (Eds.), *Textbook of homosexuality and mental health* (pp. 289–303). Washington, DC: American Psychiatric Press.

Kimmel, D. C. (1977). Psychotherapy and the older gay man. *Psychotherapy: Theory, Research & Practice, 14,* 386–393.

Kimmel, D. C. (1978/1993). Adult development and aging: A gay perspective. *Journal of Social Issues, 34*(3), 113–130. [Reprinted in L. D. Garnets & D. C. Kimmel (Eds.), *Psychological perspectives on lesbian and gay male experiences* (pp. 517–534). New York: Columbia University Press.]

Kimmel, D. C. (1979a). Adjustment to aging among gay men. In B. Berzon & R. Leighton (Eds.), *Positively gay* (pp. 146–158). Millbrae, CA: Celestial Arts.

Kimmel, D. C. (1979b). Life-history interviews of aging gay men. *International Journal of Aging & Human Development, 10,* 239–248.

Kimmel, D. C. (1992). The families of older gay men and lesbians. *Generations, 17*(3), 37–38.

Kimmel, D. C. (1995). Lesbians and gay men also grow old. In L. A. Bond, S. J. Cutler, & A. Grams (Eds.), *Promoting successful and productive aging* (pp. 289–303). Thousand Oaks, CA: SAGE.

Kimmel, D. C. (2000). Including sexual orientation in life span developmental psychology. In B. Greene & G. L. Croom (Eds.), *Education, research, and practice in lesbian, gay, bisexual, and transgendered psychology: A resource manual* (Vol. 5, pp. 59–73). Thousand Oaks, CA: SAGE.

Kimmel, D. C. (2002). Aging and sexual orientation. In B. E. Jones & M. J. Hill (Eds.), *Mental health issues in lesbian, gay, bisexual, and transgender communities* (pp. 17–36). Washington, DC: American Psychiatric Publishing.

Kimmel, D. C. (2004). Issues to consider in studies of midlife and older sexual minorities. In G. Herdt & B. de Vries (Eds.), *Gay and lesbian aging: Research and future directions* (pp. 265–283). New York: Springer.

Kimmel, D. C., & Martin, D. L. (Eds.). (2001). *Midlife and aging in gay America: Proceedings of the SAGE Conference 2000.* New York: Harrington Park Press/Haworth

Social Work Practice Press. [Published simultaneously as the *Journal of Gay and Lesbian Social Services* 13(4).]

Kimmel, D. C., & Sang, B. E. (1995). Lesbians and gay men in midlife. In A. R. D'Augelli & C. J. Patterson (Eds.), *Lesbian, gay, and bisexual identities over the lifespan: Psychological perspectives* (pp. 190–214). New York: Oxford University Press.

Kingston, T. (2002). "You have to speak up all the time": Bisexual elders address issues, concerns of aging. *Outword, 8*(4), 4–5.

Kling, E. (2004). SAGE New York: A pioneer in serving LGBT older adults. *OutWord, 10*(3), 3.

Kochman, A. (1997). Gay and lesbian elderly: Historical overview and implications for social work practice. *Journal of Gay and Lesbian Social Services, 6*(1), 1–9.

Kooden, H. (1997). Successful aging in the middle-aged gay man: A contribution to developmental theory. *Journal of Gay & Lesbian Social Services, 6*(3), 21–43.

Kooden, H., & Flowers, C. (2000). *Golden men: The power of gay midlife.* New York: Avon Books.

Kooperman, L. (1994). A survey of gay and bisexual men age 50 and older: AIDS-related knowledge, attitude, belief, and behavior. *AIDS Patient Care, 8*(3), 114–117.

Koskovich, G. (2004). ASA and LGAIN: A timeline of milestones in LGBT aging. *OutWord, 10*(3), 7–8.

Koskovich, G. (2004). Lesbian, gay, bisexual and transgender issues at ASA: Looking back, looking ahead. *OutWord, 10(3),* 4–7.

Koskovich, G. (2004). Partners in life and in community organizing: A gay Asian couple discusses issues of aging. *Diversity Currents, 5*(2), 4.

Kristiansen, H. W. (2004). Narrating past lives and present concerns: Older gay men in Norway. In G. H. Herdt & B. De Vries (Eds.), *Gay and lesbian aging: Research and future directions,* pp. 235–261. New York: Springer.

Laner, M. R. (1978). Growing older male: Heterosexual and homosexual. *Gerontologist, 18,* 496–501.

Laner, M. R. (1979). Growing older female: Heterosexual and homosexual. *Journal of Homosexuality, 4*(suppl), 267–275.

Lavick, J. (1994). Psychosocial considerations of HIV infection in the older adult. *AIDS Patient Care, 8*(3), 127–129.

Lee, A. (2004). Signposts of aging: The transitions to later life of a sample of older gay men. *Ageing International, 29*(4), 368–384.

Lee, J. A. (1987). What can homosexual aging studies contribute to theories of aging? *Journal of Homosexuality, 13*(4), 43–71.

Lee, J. A. (1989). Invisible men: Canada's aging homosexuals—Can they be assimilated into Canada's "liberated" gay communities? *Canadian Journal on Aging, 8,* 79–97.

Lee, J. A. (1990). Can we talk? Can we really talk? Communication as a key factor in the maturing homosexual couple. *Journal of Homosexuality, 20*(3–4), 143–168.

Lee, J. A. (1991). *Gay midlife and maturity.* New York: Haworth Press.

Lee, J. A. (1993). Special problems of older gay employees. In L. Diamant (Ed.), *Homosexual issues in the workplace. Series in clinical and community psychology* (pp. 217–223). Philadelphia: Taylor & Francis.

Leiblum, S. R. (1990). Sexuality and the midlife woman. *Psychology of Women Quarterly, 14,* 495–508.

Lekas, H. M., Schrimshaw, E.W., & Siegel K. (2005). Pathways to HIV testing among adults aged fifty and older with HIV/AIDS. *AIDS Care, 17*(6), 674–687.

Linsk, N. L. (1997). Experience of older gay and bisexual men living with HIV/AIDS. *Journal of Gay, Lesbian, and Bisexual Identity, 2,* 285–308.

Lipman, A. (1984). Homosexuals. In E. R. Palmore (Ed.), *Handbook on the aged in the United States* (pp. 323–337). Westport, CT: Greenwood Press.

Lipman, A. (1986). Homosexual relationships. *Generations, 10*(4), 51–54.

Lockhart, J. (2002). *The gay man's guide to growing older.* Los Angeles: Alyson.

Lucco, A. J. (1987). Planned retirement housing preferences of older homosexuals. *Journal of Homosexuality, 14*(3–4), 35–56.

Lundberg, P. (2004). Housing our elders: Snapshots of projects across North America. *OutWord, 11*(2), 1, 6–7.

Macdonald, B. (1984). A call for an end to ageism in lesbian and gay services. *Lesbian Ethics, 1*(1), 57–64. [In B. Macdonald & C. Rich. (2001). *Look me in the eye: Old women, aging and ageism* (pp. 129–138). Denver: Spinster Ink.]

Macdonald, B. (1991). A movement of old lesbians. In B. Macdonald & C. Rich (Eds.), *Look me in the eye: Old women, aging, and ageism* (pp. 147–153). San Francisco: Spinster Books. [Reissued 2001, Denver: Spinster Ink.]

Mackey, R. A., Diemer, M. A., & O'Brien, B. A. (2004). Relational factors in understanding satisfaction in the lasting relationships of same sex and heterosexual couples. *Journal of Homosexuality, 47*(1), 111–136.

Markovic, N., Danielson, M. E., Honnold, J. A., Janosky, J. E., & Schmidt, N. J. (2001). Behavioral risk factors for disease and preventive health practices among lesbians. *American Journal of Public Health, 91,* 972–975.

Martin, D., & Lyon, P. (1979). The older lesbian. In B. Berzon & R. Leighton (Eds.), *Positively gay.* Milbrae, CA: Celestial Arts.

Martinez, R. (2005). Prostate cancer and sex, *Journal of Gay & Lesbian Psychotherapy, 9*(1–2), 91–99.

McDevitt, R. J. (1974). The older homosexual. *Human Sexuality, 2,* 191–195.

McDougall, G. J. (1993). Therapeutic issues with gay and lesbian elders. *Clinical Gerontologist, 14,* 45–57.

McFarland, P. L., & Sanders, S. (2003). A pilot study about the needs of older gays and lesbians: What social workers need to know. *Journal of Gerontological Social Work, 40*(3), 67–80.

Mcleod, B. (1997). Yvonne and Helen: Finding a way to trust. *Journal of Gay and Lesbian Social Services, 6*(1), 105–107.

McMahon, E. (2003a). The older homosexual: Current concepts of lesbian, gay, bisexual, and transgender older Americans. In J. E. Morley (Ed.), *Geriatric sexuality.* Philadelphia: W.B. Saunders.

McMahon, E. (2003b). The older homosexual: Current concepts of lesbian, gay, bisexual, and transgender older Americans. *Clinics in Geriatric Medicine, 19,* 587–593.

Metz, P. (1997). Staff development for working with lesbian and gay elders. *Journal of Gay & Lesbian Social Services, 6*(1), 35.

Minnigerode, F. A. (1976). Age-status labeling in homosexual men. *Journal of Homosexuality, 1*(13), 273–276.

Minnigerode, F. A., & Adelman, M. R. (1978). Elderly homosexual women and men: Report on a pilot study. *Family Coordinator, 27,* 451–456.

Minter, S. (2001). *Transgender elders and marriage: The importance of legal planning.* Milwaukee, WI: Transgender Aging Network. Retrieved August 30, 2004, from www.forge-forward.org/handouts/TGElders-Marriage-ShannonMinter.pdf.

Mock, S. E. (2001). Retirement intentions of same-sex couples. *Journal of Gay and Lesbian Social Services, 13*(4), 81–86.

Moore, W. R. (2000). Adult protective services and older lesbians and gay men. *Clinical Gerontologist, 21,* 61–64.

Moore, W. R. (2002). Lesbian and gay elders: Connecting care providers through a telephone support group. *Journal of Gay & Lesbian Social Services, 14*(3), 23–41.

Morrow, D. F. (2001). Older gays and lesbians: Surviving a generation of hate and violence. *Journal of Gay & Lesbian Social Services, 13*(1–2), 151–169.

Murray, J., & Adam, B. D. (2001). Aging, sexuality, and HIV issues among older gay men. *Canadian Journal of Human Sexuality, 10*(3–4), 75–90.

Noyes, L. E. (1982). Gray and gay. *Journal of Gerontological Nursing, 8,* 636–639.

Nystrom, N. M., & Jones, T. C. (2003). Community building with aging and old lesbians. *American Journal of Community Psychology, 31,* 293–300.

Orel, N. A. (2004). Gay, lesbian, and bisexual elders: Expressed needs and concerns across focus groups. *Journal of Gerontological Social Work, 43*(2–3), 57–77.

Parks, C. A., & Hughes, T. L. (2005). Alcohol use and alcohol-related problems in self-identified lesbians: Age and racial/ethnic comparisons. *Journal of Lesbian Studies, 9*(3), 31–44.

Peacock, J. R. (2000). Gay male adult development: Some stage issues of an older cohort. *Journal of Homosexuality, 40*(2), 13–29.

Poor, M. (1982). Older lesbians. In M. Cruikshank (Ed.), *Lesbian studies: Present and future* (pp. 165–173). Old Westbury, NY: Feminist Press.

Pope, M. (1997). Sexual issues for older lesbians and gays. *Topics in Geriatric Rehabilitation, 12*(4), 53–60.

Pope, M., & Schulz, R. (1990). Sexual attitudes and behavior in midlife and aging homosexual males. *Journal of Homosexuality, 20*(3–4), 169–177.

Porter, M., Russell, C., & Sullivan, G. (2004). Gay, old, and poor: Service delivery to aging gay men in inner city Sydney, Australia. *Journal of Gay Lesbian Social Services, 16*(2), 43–57.

Price, E. (2005). All but invisible: Older gay men and lesbians. *Nursing Older People, 17*(4), 16–18.

Purcell, D. W., Wolitski, R. J., Hoff, C. C., Parsons, J. T., Woods, W. J, & Halkitis, P. N. (2005). Predictors of the use of viagra, testosterone, and antidepressants among HIV-seropositive gay and bisexual men. *AIDS, 19* (1), S57–66.

Quam, J. K. (1993). Gay and lesbian aging. *SIECUS Report, 21*(5), 10–12.

Quam, J. K. (1996). Old lesbians. In T. McNaron & B. Zimmerman (Eds.), *Lesbian studies*. New York: Feminist Press.

Quam, J. K. (1997a). *Social services for senior gay men and lesbians*. New York: Haworth Press.

Quam, J. K. (1997b). The story of Carrie and Anne: Long-term care crisis. *Journal of Gay and Lesbian Social Services, 6*(1), 97–99.

Quam, J. K., & Whitford, G. S. (1992). Adaptation and age-related expectations of older gay and lesbian adults. *Gerontologist, 32*, 367–374.

Rabin, J. S., & Slater, B. (2005). Lesbian communities across the United States: Pockets of resistance and resilience. *Journal of Lesbian Studies, 9*(1–2), 169–182.

Raphael, S. M., & Meyer (Robinson), M. R. (1984). The older lesbian: Love relationships and friendship patterns. In T. Darty & S. Potter (Eds.), *Women-identified women*. Palo Alto, CA: Mayfield Press.

Raphael, S. M., & Meyer, M. K. (2000). Family support patterns for midlife lesbians: Recollections of a lesbian couple 1971–1997. *Journal of Gay & Lesbian Social Services, 11*(2–3), 139–151.

Raphael, S., & Meyer, M. K. (2004). The first national association for professionals addressing the issues of lesbian and gay aging. *OutWord, 10*(3), 2–3, 8.

Raphael, S. M., & Robinson, M. K. (1980). The older lesbian. *Alternative Lifestyles, 3*, 207–229.

Raphael, S. M., & Robinson, M. K. (1981). Lesbians and gay men in later life. *Generations, 6*(1), 16–18.

Rathbone-McCuan, E. (2005). Couples dynamics for gay and lesbian older adults. *Dimensions, 12*(1), 3, 8.

Ratigan, B. (1996). Working with older gay men. In D. Davies & C. Neal (Eds.), *Pink therapy: A guide for counselors and therapists working with lesbian, gay and bisexual clients* (pp. 159–169). Buckingham, UK: Open University Press.

Rawls, T. W. (2004). Disclosure and depression among older gay and homosexual men: Findings from the Urban Men's Health Study. In G. H. Herdt & B. De Vries (Eds.), *Gay and lesbian aging: Research and future directions*. New York: Springer.

Rayner, C. (2002). Health care, older lesbians and gay men. *Working with Older People, 6*(4), 26–28.

Reid, J. D. (1995). Development in late life: Older lesbian and gay lives. In A. R. D'Augelli & C. J. Patterson (Eds.), *Lesbian, gay, and bisexual identities over the lifespan: Psychological perspectives* (pp. 215–240). New York: Oxford University Press.

Reyes, K. W., Thompson, M., & Adleman, J. (1993). *Lambda gray: A practical, emotional, and spiritual guide for gays and lesbians who are growing older.* Van Nuys, CA: Newcastle.

Rosenfeld, D. (1999). Identity work among lesbian and gay elderly. *Journal of Aging Studies, 13,* 121–144.

Rosenfeld, D. (2002). Identity careers of older gay men and lesbians. In J. F. Gubrium & J. Holstein (Eds.), *Ways of aging* (pp. 16–181). Oxford, UK: Blackwell.

Rosenfeld, D. (2003). *The changing of the guard: Lesbian and gay elders, identity, and social change.* Philadelphia: Temple University Press.

Ross, E., Scott, M., & Wexler, E. (2003). *Environmental scan on the health and housing needs of aging lesbians.* Toronto: OLIVE and Sherbourne Health Centre.

Rothblum, E. D. (1990). Depression among lesbians: An invisible and unresearched phenomenon. *Journal of Gay & Lesbian Psychotherapy, 1*(3), 67–87.

Sang, B. (1990). Reflections of midlife lesbians on their adolescence. In E. Rosenthal (Ed.), *Women, aging, and ageism* (pp. 111–117). New York: Harrington Park.

Sang, B. E. (1992). Counseling and psychotherapy with midlife and older lesbians. In S. H. Dworkin & F. J. Gutierrez (Eds.), *Counseling gay men and lesbians: Journey to the end of the rainbow.* Alexandria, VA: American Association for Counseling and Development.

Sang, B. E. (1993). Existential issues of midlife lesbians. In L. D. Garnets & D. C. Kimmel (Eds.), *Psychological perspectives on lesbian and gay male experiences* (pp. 500–516). New York: Columbia University Press.

Sang, B. E., Warshow, J., & Smith, A. J. (1991). *Lesbians at midlife: The creative transition.* San Francisco: Spinsters.

Schaffer, R. S. (1972). Will you still need me when I'm 64? In K. Jay & A. Young (Eds.), *Out of the closets: Voices of gay liberation.* New York: Douglas Books.

Schoonmaker, C. V. (1993). Aging lesbians: Bearing the burden of triple shame. *Women & Therapy, 14*(1–2), 21–31.

Schope, R. D. (2005). Who's afraid of growing old? Gay and lesbian perceptions of aging. *Journal of Gerontological Social Work, 45*(4), 23–38.

Shankle, M. D., Maxwell, C. A., Katzman, E. S., & Landers, S. (2003). An invisible population: Older lesbian, gay, bisexual, and transgender individuals. *Clinical Research and Regulatory Affairs, 20*(2), 159–182.

Shannon, J. W., & Woods, W. J. (1991). Affirmative psychotherapy for gay men. *Counseling Psychologist, 19,* 197–215.

Sharp, C. E. (1997). Lesbianism and later life in an Australian sample: How does development of one affect anticipation of the other? *Journal of Gay, Lesbian, and Bisexual Identity, 2*(3–4), 247–263.

Shenk, D., & Fullmer, E. (1996). Significant relationships among older women: Cultural and personal constructions of lesbianism. *Journal of Women and Aging,* 8(3–4), 75–88.

Shernoff, M. (Ed.). (1998). *Gay widowers: Life after the death of a partner.* Binghamton, NY: Harrington Park Press.

Siegel, K., Schrimshaw, E. W., & Karus, D. (2004). Racial disparities in sexual risk behaviors and drug use among older gay/bisexual and heterosexual men living with HIV/AIDS. *Journal of the National Medical Association,* 96(2), 215–223.

Sitter, K. (1997). Jim: Coming out at age sixty-two. *Journal of Gay and Lesbian Social Services,* 6(1), 101–104.

Slater, S. (1995). *The lesbian family life cycle.* New York: Free Press.

Slusher, M. P., Mayer, C. J., & Dunkle, R. E. (1996). Gay and Lesbians Older and Wiser (GLOW): A support group for older gay people. *Gerontologist,* 36, 118–123.

Smith, P. R. (2002). Bisexuality: Reviewing the basics, debunking the stereotypes for professionals in aging. *Outword,* 8(4), 2, 8.

Stanley, J. L. (2002). Young sexual minority women's perceptions of cross-generational friendships with older lesbians. *Journal of Lesbian Studies,* 6(1), 139–148.

Stein, G. L., & Bonuck, K. A. (2001). Attitudes on end-of-life care and advance care planning in the lesbian and gay community. *Journal of Palliative Medicine,* 4(2), 173–190.

Steinman, R. (1991). Social exchanges between older and younger gay male partners. *Journal of Homosexuality,* 20(3–4), 179–206.

Thomas, J. L. (1996). Expanding knowledge of older gay men and lesbians: Retrospect and prospect. In L. Sperry & H. Prosen (Eds.), *Aging in the twenty-first century: A developmental perspective.* New York: Garland.

Thompson, K. M., Brown, N., Cassidy, J., & Gentry, J. H. (1999). Lesbians discuss beauty and aging. *Journal of Lesbian Studies,* 3(4), 37–44.

Tirrito, T. (2003). *Aging in the new millennium: A global view.* Columbia: University of South Carolina Press. [Includes "Experiences of aging for women, gay men and lesbians, and ethnic and minority older adults," pp. 168–189.]

Truax, J. (2003). HIV infection and aging: A personal journey. *Journal of Acquired Immune Deficiency Syndromes: JAIDS,* 33(2), S169–S170.

Tully, C. T. (1989). Caregiving: What do midlife lesbians view as important? *Journal of Gay & Lesbian Psychotherapy,* 1(1), 87–103.

Tully, C. T. (1992). Research on older lesbian women: What is known, what is not known, and how to learn more. In N. J. Woodman (Ed.), *Lesbian and gay lifestyles: A guide for counseling and education* (pp. 235–264). New York: Irvington.

Turner, H. A., & Pearlin, L. I. (1989). Informal support of people with AIDS: Issues of age, stress, & caregiving. *Generations,* 13(4), 56–59.

Vacha, K. (1985). *Quiet fire: Memoirs of older gay men.* Trumansburg, NY: Crossing Press.

Van de Ven, P., Rodden, P., Crawford, J., & Kippax, S. (1997). A comparative demographic and sexual profile of older homosexually active men. *Journal of Sex Research, 34,* 349–360.

Vance, D. E., & Woodley, R. A. (2005). Strengths and distress in adults who are aging with HIV: A pilot study. *Psychological Reports, 96*(2), 383–386.

Wahler, J. J., & Gabbay, S. G. (1997). Gay male aging: A review of the literature. *Journal of Gay & Lesbian Social Services, 6*(3), 1–20.

Waite, H. (1995). Lesbians leaping out of the intergenerational contract: Issues of aging in Australia. In G. Sullivan & L. W.-T. Leong (Eds.), *Gays and lesbians in Asia and the Pacific: Social and human services* (pp. 109–127). New York: Harrington Park Press/Haworth Press.

Wallace, J. I., Paauw, D. S., & Spach, D. H. (1993). HIV infection in older patients: When to suspect the unexpected. *Geriatrics, 48*(6), 61–70.

Weinberg, M. S. (1969). The aging male homosexual. *Medical Aspects of Human Sexuality, 3*(12), 66–72.

Weinberg, M. S. (1970). The male homosexual: Age-related variations in social and psychological characteristics. *Social Problems, 17,* 527–537.

Weinberg, M. S., Williams, C. J., & Pryor, D. W. (2001). Bisexuals at midlife: Commitment, salience, and identity. *Journal of Contemporary Ethnography, 30,* 180–208.

Weinstock, J. S. (2004). Lesbian friendships at and beyond midlife: Patterns and possibilities for the 21st century. In G. H. Herdt & B. De Vries (Eds.), *Gay and lesbian aging: Research and future directions,* pp. 177–209. New York: Springer.

Whalen, D., Bigner, J., & Barber, C. (2000). The grandmother role as experienced by lesbian women. *Journal of Women and Aging, 12*(3–4), 39–57.

White, H. (1995). Lesbian leaping out of the intergenerational contract: Issues of aging in Australia. *Journal of Gay and Lesbian Social Services, 3*(3), 109–127.

Whitford, G. S. (1997). Realities and hopes for older gay males. *Journal of Gay & Lesbian Social Services, 6*(1), 79–96.

Whitford, G. S., & Quam, J. K. (1995). Old lesbians and old gay men. In M. Kimble, J. W. Ellor, S. H. McFadden, & J. J. Seeber (Eds.), *Aging, spirituality and religion: A handbook.* Minneapolis: Fortress Press.

Wiggins, P. (Ed.). (2003). *LGBT persons in Chicago: Growing older—A survey of needs and perceptions.* Chicago: Chicago Task Force on LGBT Aging.

Winterich, J. A. (2003). Sex, menopause, and culture: Sexual orientation and the meaning of menopause for women's sex lives. *Gender & Society, 17,* 627–642.

Witten, T. M. (1999). Transgender aging: Introduction to an emerging field. *Gerontologist, 39,* 79–80.

Witten, T. (2002). Geriatric care and management issues for the transgender and intersex populations. *Geriatric Care Management Journal, 12*(3), 20–24.

Witten, T. M. (2004). Life course analysis: The courage to search for something more—Middle adulthood issues in the transgender and intersex community. *Journal of Human Behavior in the Social Environment, 8*(2–3), 189–224.

Wynden, I. (2003). A gay Latino activist's story: "I'm a very happy, very content, very satisfied 51-year-old ..." *OutWord*, 9(4), 3, 8.

Yoakam, J. R. (1997). Playing BINGO with the best of them: Community initiated programs for older gay and lesbian adults. *Journal of Gay & Lesbian Social Services*, 6(1), 27–34.

Yoakam, J. R. (2001). Gods or monsters: A critique of representations in film and literature of relationships between older gay men and younger men. *Journal of Gay & Lesbian Social Services: Issues in Practice, Policy & Research*, 13(4), 65–80.[1]

## NOTE

1. This LGBT aging bibliography was compiled from multiple sources including databases, search engines, and a variety of individuals and organizations that offered references and revisions. This bibliography is intended to be a complete list of the LGBT aging literature; however, it is likely that references inadvertently have been left out. This bibliography will be updated and posted on the American Psychological Association Division 44 Web site through the Division 44 Task Force on Aging (www.apa.org/divisions/div44/). Feedback is welcome and should be directed to the Division 44 Task Force on Aging.

# INDEX